GW01033014

# FROM CAMP TO CITY

# FROM CAMP TO CITY

# Refugee Camps of the Western Sahara

Edited by Manuel Herz

ETH Studio Basel
Lars Müller Publishers

SPAIN
Algiers
Rabat
MOROCCO
ALGERIA
CANARY ISLANDS
Tindouf
Refugee Camps of the Western Sahara
El Aaiún
LIBYA
WESTERN
SAHARA
MAURITANIA
Nouakchott
NIGER
MALI

# THE REFUGEE CAMPS OF THE WESTERN SAHARA

In recent years, the notion of the refugee camp has gained prominence and even notoriety in the fields of spatial studies and the social sciences. References to camps occur in great numbers in various texts and discourses. They are featured in books on architectural theory or reports on the processes of urbanization and are often mentioned in the context of violence and conflicts, and also slums or natural catastrophes. We see them regularly in news reports and documentaries. Even though they have become something of a heterotopia, gaining wide currency, surprisingly little understanding and knowledge exists in the disciplines of planning and spatial practices, and also by the general public, about these spaces that are home to several million people in many parts of the world. What exactly are refugee camps? For whom are they constructed, and who invests interest in them? How are they planned? What kinds of spaces exist in them? How do the refugees use them? What is their relationship to the respective underlying conflict?

Different concepts abound of what a refugee camp is or is not. We come across descriptions of specific camps when reading about the hundreds of thousands of refugees that have fled from Darfur into eastern Chad. In reports on the conflicts in war-torn Somalia, we see images from the camps of Dadaab in Kenya, close to the Somalian border, described to be the largest in the world. Refugee camps are referenced when reporting on natural catastrophes and the attempts of the victims to establish new livelihoods. They are often compared to slums and the vast shanty towns that are located on the fringes of many African or South American cities. The image of refugee camps is also evoked when describing authoritarian spaces of control such as prison camps, Guantanamo Bay, foreign worker camps, and sometimes even gated communities. While all these different typologies of spaces share certain characteristics that could be summarized under the notions of control and exception, the difference between them remains unclear.

Many authors even play with the seeming openness of the term "camp." The Italian philosopher Giorgio Agamben, writes in his book *Homo Sacer:* "Today it is not the city but rather the camp that is the fundamental biopolitical paradigm of the West."[1] A little bit further on, he continues: "The camp is the space that is opened, when the state of exception begins to become the rule. In the camp, the state of exception, which was essentially a temporary suspension of the rule of law … is now given a permanent spatial arrangement …" With this, he means to say that the camp is the spatial manifestation, and the central mechanism, of the state of exception,

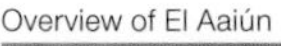
Overview of El Aaiún

which has come to define the political structure of our Western world. He goes on to write, "The camp as dislocating localization is the hidden matrix of the politics in which we are still living, and it is this structure of the camp which we must learn to recognize in all its metamorphoses into the *zones d'attentes* of our airports and certain outskirts of our cities."[2] The same rules and logics of the camp can therefore be identified within holding areas of our airports or the *banlieues* of our cities. Here, Agamben comes dangerously close to generalization. Even if it is true that the biopolitical operations of our society are active in refugee camps as well as in slums or detention centers, the individual problems that are triggered by each of those cases remain unrecognized, and the specific nature of a refugee camp seems more opaque than ever. It appears that refugee camps are rarely considered to be an independent category. Instead, although central, they seem to be conditioned by, and referenced through, other seemingly similar spacial categories.

Nevertheless, if we try to look at how refugee camps themselves are understood, we can identify three different predominant notions in contemporary discourse and in today's media landscape. Refugee camps are seen as humanitarian spaces where lives are saved. They are also conceived of as spaces of control where all aspects of the refugees' lives are supervised by other institutions. Lastly, they are depicted as spaces of destitution and misery. These three ways of representing and describing refugee camps do not exclude one another, but often coexist or complement each other.

## A Humanitarian Space

The most obvious and maybe the most "classical" reading of a refugee camp is that of a humanitarian space. Refugee camps are constructed to protect and save lives.

On March 17, 2003, the then incumbent president of the Central African Republic, Ange-Félix Patassé, was overthrown by his former army chief of staff, François Bozizé. The timing for this coup d'état could not have been more unfortunate for the affected population, as on the following day the United States declared war on Iraq. It was destined to be one of the many coups in Africa that almost no one in the Western world took notice of, with any news reports relegated to the last pages of the papers, if published at all. The general violence that it triggered led to tens of thousands of Central Africans fleeing over the border into its northern neighbor of Chad. Nevertheless, within a few days UNHCR, the UN body that is responsible for refugees, was able to move into the densely forested area of southern Chad, locate the refugees where they had gathered after crossing the border, and identify two potential locations for erecting refugee camps. After negotiating with the local and national Chadian authorities, together with a few nongovernmental organizations such as MSF and Oxfam, it cleared the area, laid out the perimeter and camp sectors, distributed tents, installed a well, and set up medical facilities. Being just one of countless examples, it shows how, with unquestionable efficiency and swiftness, UNHCR and its implementing partners are able to operate in remote locations. They can provide accommodation, water, food, health care, and basic education to a refugee population. It is this efficiency that establishes refugee camps as humanitarian spaces, able to protect refugees and save lives.

## Camps and the State of Exception

The care of others more often than not transforms into a governing of others, however. Care is often a Janus-faced notion. Refugees are given water, food, and health care, but they are also kept in one place, without the

MSF Hospital in southern Chad

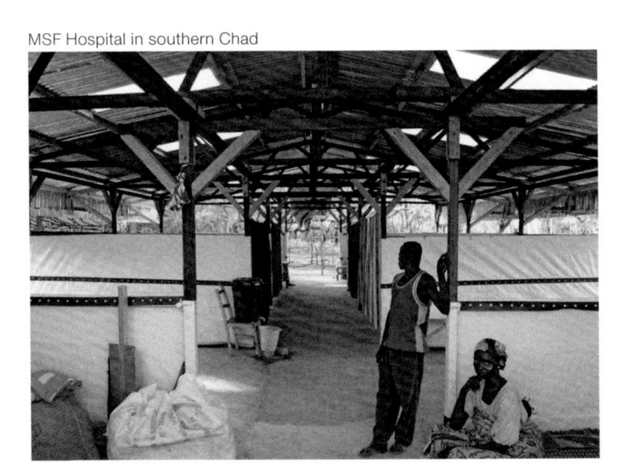

Refugees in the eastern Congo

freedom to move or settle elsewhere. Not allowed to express themselves politically, and without the right to take on work or employment outside of the camps, refugees are reduced to being recipients of welfare, condemned to a life of waiting, dependent on the actions of others. Refugees sometimes spend decades living in the same camps, often located in remote places, removed from most economic, cultural, or social exchange. These conditions of exile, or humanitarian enclaves—where the refugees are reduced to liters of water and calories per day and are seen purely in their biological or physical state—is understood to have become the norm, serving the specific interests of a globalized world order. The refugee camp is seen as the spatial manifestation of the state of exception, which has become the central aspect of our era. The work of Giorgio Agamben, already mentioned above, gives testimony to this authoritarian and dystopian view of the camp.

## Camps as Places of Desperation

The third reading of refugee camps emerges especially when we look at the images dominating the media. We see people in the blazing sun, queuing for water or sitting motionless in the heat with their emaciated and naked bodies covered in flies. Tents are mere rags that hardly provide shade from the merciless sun. Neither seen as humanitarian spaces nor spaces of control, these images represent the camp as a place of desperation. Sebastião Salgado is a prominent voice among those photographers representing the refugee as a suffering being. His photos combine a cunning, maybe uncanny, sense of aesthetic in the genre of misery. The refugee is always the victim. The victim is always unnamed. He neither has a history, nor are we to believe that he has a future. He has no biography and simply represents pure suffering. The photos do not give us any information beyond this fact of suffering. They do not aid understanding and they do not elucidate the underlying disaster or conflict. Refugee camps are seen as places of misery where refugees are reduced to beings of wretchedness, with no claim for identity or individuality in its social dimension.

All three readings are problematic. They might elucidate certain vital aspects of a refugee camp. Nevertheless, they are all formulated from an outsider's perspective. They are not about how the refugees understand their own physical environment, but how (mostly Western) researchers, aid workers, artists, etc., understand the camps. So what remains beyond the readings of refugee camps as either humanitarian spaces, spaces of control, or spaces of desperation? Can we not understand camps in any different way? Are we caught up in an endless circle of technocratic naivete, totalitarian authority or endless suffering?

## Counter Model: the Camps of the Western Sahara

In reaction to the aforementioned lack of clarity about categories, and the level of generalization that we have observed in the context of refugee camps, this book will focus on a very specific case study: the refugee camps of the Western Sahara, located in a remote corner of southwest Algeria. By looking at such a precise case, we can reveal some of the particularities of what we call a camp. We can see whether it is elements of control, humanitarianism, or misery that shape the camp, or if other forces are at play. We can show how aspects of resources, politics, geography, and economy influence camps in a very specific way. Looking at a specific case also allows us to compare it with others, as well as identifying the differences between camps and the settlements they are often categorized with, such as slums or prisons. The starting point is thus not to approach the camps with a given theory of control, as the state of exception, humanitarianism, or the "responsibility to protect." We do not look at the widest range of conditions, but at specifics, and from this we

Historical map of the Spanish Sahara, 1958

Sebastiao Salgado: Rwandan refugee camp of Benako, Tanzania

try to understand the larger context. Instead of going from the general to the specific, this study will attempt to go from the very specific to the general. The case study of the Western Saharan camps is carefully and consciously chosen because it allows for an alternative reading within the dominant discourse on camps. Instead of forcing us into narratives of domination, authority, misery, or technocratic formulas, it brings up notions of political agency and social emancipation.

## History of the Western Sahara

The Western Sahara is one of the very few remaining non-self-governing countries in the world. It has previously been described as the world's last remaining colony, as most of its territory is occupied by Morocco. The disputed territory is located at the western edge of the African continent, where the Sahara meets the Atlantic Ocean. Its terrain consists almost exclusively of very dry and relatively flat desert landscape, with no permanent river. Traditionally an area populated by the Sahrawis, a group of nomadic tribes related to Berber culture, the area was colonized by Spain in the nineteenth and twentieth centuries. Initially it was not of much economic benefit to colonial Spain, whose presence was limited to a few trading posts and bases of a mostly military nature. This changed when large deposits of phosphate were discovered during the middle of the twentieth century. Exploitation began in the 1960s, resulting in considerable economic growth as well as tendencies of urbanization. This coincided with increasing pressure on Spain by the international community, especially by the United Nations, to release the Spanish Sahara into independence.

The Sahrawi population organized itself into a liberation movement and added further pressure on Spain. Towards the end of 1975, on the eve of Franco's rule, Spain started to pull out of its colony, having previously negotiated with neighboring Morocco and Mauritania for them to fill its place. Morocco invaded the Western Sahara, first with a civilian occupation and then by a military campaign. The Sahrawi population was forced to flee to temporary camps in the eastern parts of the territory, from which they were again quickly displaced by Moroccan attacks. From late 1975, and over the whole period of spring and summer 1976, Sahrawis fled over the border into southwest Algeria and settled in camps near the Algerian town of Tindouf. It was mostly women, children, and the elderly that fled to the camps. The Sahrawi men were fighting in the ensuing guerilla war against Morocco and Mauritania. Due to highly successful attacks by the Sahrawis, its own weak army, and political turmoil at home, Mauritania was quickly forced to withdraw from the territory. These areas were eventually occupied by Morocco, which embarked on one of the most extreme and absurd construction endeavors in history: building a 2,500-km-long sand wall (the berm) through the desert and thereby separating its occupied territories (amounting to almost three-quarters of the whole Western Sahara) from the Sahrawiheld liberated territories.[3]

## History of the Camps

The camps started as a collection of tents pitched on the dry and rocky desert sand, organized in rows and clusters. As most of the men were fighting the Moroccans, the women took a leading role in the establishment of the camps and in the organization of daily life. With little help from the international community and the virtual noninvolvement of the United Nations, schools, medical stations, and hospitals were set up by the refugee community. Later, the tents were supplemented or replaced by small clay huts, eventually growing in number and developing into the little residential compounds that the refugees occupy today. Initially settling in a single

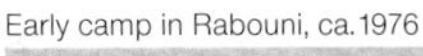

Early camp in Rabouni, ca.1976

Residential compound with a tent and clay huts in El Aaiún

camp, Rabouni, the Sahrawi refugees soon established two new camps, Smara and El Aaiún. They eventually spread to five camps, with Dakhla and Awserd being founded later and the women's school, 27 February, growing into a settlement. Meanwhile, Rabouni was transformed into an administrative center. During the Spanish colonial era, Polisario, the Sahrawi independence movement, had already sketched out a vision for a social order that departed from many of the historical and traditional features of Sahrawi society. Originally intended to be implemented in an independent Western Sahara, the refugee camps became the testing ground for this new vision of a community. Fleeing from their homeland into the camps forced a social revolution upon the society over a very short period of time. The tribal system, which had dominated and structured life as well as Sahrawi identity over centuries, was rejected in favor of a national identity. Emancipation of women took place almost automatically because of their central role in the camps, and much of the nomadic culture was discarded, as life in the camps did not lend itself to the keeping of large camel herds. Over time, within the exceptional situation of being a nation of refugees, an everyday normality started to emerge. This research study hence focuses on these spaces of everyday life and their urban dimension in the refugee camps.

## Urban Activities

In order to escape the predominant ways of seeing camps as spaces of humanitarianism or a state of exception, we did not want to focus on the technicalities of the camps—such as the provision of how many liters of water or the amount of calories—nor by analyzing the camps using abstract theory. Rather, we are trying to understand the camps in the way they are used by the population and how spaces are created and shaped by the different uses. We describe the camp by looking at some of its main activities, including living; working; moving; trading and shopping; learning; and recreation, among others. These are the activities that one would find in any other settlement throughout the world. They are some of the fundamental activities that organize urban life. Using these activities, we formulate seemingly innocent questions. How do people live in the camps? What residential typologies have developed? Where do refugees work and what kind of work is pursued? How do people move through the camps, or from camp to camp? What kinds of recreational activities exist in the camps, and what type of spaces are they carried out in?

These questions initially seem naive to pose in the context of refugee camps. Why should we be interested in the ways of moving through a camp, in the residential spaces of the refugees, or in some of their recreational activities, when questions of human rights, global politics, and potential human suffering are at stake? Do we not thereby normalize an exceptional situation and extreme living conditions? Yes and no. First of all, as these camps are often inhabited by tens of thousands of people, and there are hundreds of them all over the world, they deserve to be taken seriously as settlements. And even if only intended to exist temporarily (but often ending up becoming semi-permanent), questions about how people live in these camps, what spaces they work in, or where they go for leisure are important. Beyond this level, we believe that it is by asking seemingly innocent questions that the political dimension of the camp is exposed more precisely. Politics is never an abstract notion. In the camps it manifests itself in the very materiality of the tents and huts, the cars and the roads refugees drive on, or the solar panels that collect energy and the mobile phones that use them. When approaching a camp with a theory of the state of exception or of authority and control, there is a risk of remaining blind to the physical manifestation of politics in the camps. In the end, we hope to see that the seemingly innocent questions turn out not to be naive at all, but make us aware of how strategic every spatial decision, every architectural move, and every act of planning in the camp is.

Scenes of everyday life in El Aaiún: goats and football among residential spaces

Urban activities such as living, working, and moving create spaces in the camps that were studied and analyzed. Obviously the separation between some of these categories is hard to draw. Doesn't living always also incorporate an element of leisure and recreation, especially when considering the tea-drinking ceremony that is pervasive in the camp? How can we distinguish administration from working? And where is the line that separates moving from working, when the movement involves people driving to work? Indeed, the organization into discrete categories might be one of the weaknesses of this study. Nevertheless, we believe that it is important to create a certain clarity in the structure of the work. One of the questions in deciding upon the categories and distinguishing between the different activities was whether they produce a different or a distinct set of spaces. Whenever a space turned out to be important to two or more activities, a common-sense approach was chosen, and it is covered in the relevant chapters.

After describing how the refugee camps were planned, we look at activities of living; administration; moving and communication; commerce and working; and health and education, ending up with recreation and leisure. Whether these activities encompass all aspects of life in the camps remains to be seen. We have included spaces for cultural production in the chapter on leisure. This might not seem to do them justice. Nevertheless, we would like to think of leisure and recreation beyond the narrow, lighthearted sense of the word, which often carries connotations of triviality. On the contrary, activities of leisure can be said to stand most clearly in opposition to the view of the camp as a space of exception, or as a space where refugees are reduced to mere recipients of aid, and hence can be said to include cultural production. The order of the activities in this book carries little significance. In a pragmatic way and for reasons of practicality, after having outlined the organization of the camps and how they were set up, we start with the activity of living, as this covers the largest areas of the camps. Residential spaces represent the majority of construction in each refugee camp. We then take a trajectory via moving, commerce, and the other activities, ending up with leisure. As mentioned above, we think this is an activity of high significance, if only for the reason that it is often ignored when considering refugee camps. It seems to stand at odds with the common notion of camps as a spatial reaction to violence, conflict, and suffering.

## Spaces of Everyday Life

## Living

Today, Sahrawi families usually occupy more than one structure, often splitting their time between a tent and one or more clay huts. Besides its link to the nomadic tradition, the tent offers certain climatic benefits. Beyond these reasons, though, the tent signifies the intended temporary nature of the refugees' stay in the camps in Algeria. It marks the will to return to the homeland and is meant to give evidence that the camps are not permanent settlements. The tent has become a political signifier. This notion of temporariness is important and touches upon many aspects of architectural production in the camp, which tend to the mobile and spartan. Nevertheless, the refugees have started to decorate their huts and tents. Usually taking the shape of movable carpets or curtains (i.e. staying within the logic of the temporary), the decorations often now enter the sphere of the stable or permanent. The walls of the clay huts are plastered and painted, the ceilings are decorated with wallpaper or colored textiles. Windows are decorated by pronounced reveals or elaborate frames. Most recently, huts have become more like houses, with architectural elements like columns, arches, and parapets being introduced, sometimes reminiscent of postmodernism of the 1980s and 1990s. Inscribed into many of these elements are expressions of national identity, first and foremost the Sahrawi flag. Thus, the population

Residential complex in El Aaiún

Ministry of Building in Rabouni

finds itself in a tension between the desire for individual expression and a certain level of comfort and beauty on the one hand and the demonstration of the temporal nature of their presence in the camp and the determination to return. Residential architecture in the camps finds itself the central medium where this struggle is carried out.

## Administration

When accessing a refugee camp—whether in Kenya, Chad, Pakistan, or almost any other place—one usually has to pass through checkpoints where UNHCR, or more often the local host country's police force, controls access. In the case of the Sahrawi camps there are checkpoints, but with a major difference. The checkpoints leading to the camps are not manned by Algerian policemen or military personnel, but by the Sahrawis themselves. The Sahrawi camps are located 20–30 km from the Algerian city of Tindouf (with the exception of Dakhla, which is farther away), setting up a matrix of settlements in the Algerian Sahara and being home to altogether approximately 160,000 refugees. On first glance this arrangement seems similar to other refugee settlements in Africa. For example, the 260,000 refugees from Darfur living in twelve camps in eastern Chad, or the 300,000 Somalis living in three camps near Dadaab in eastern Kenya. In contrast to these camps, which are governed by the hosting nations of Chad and Kenya, the Sahrawis live in a territory where Algeria has ceded most of its control, allowing refugees to establish a semi-autonomy. This autonomy gives refugees the right to control access to their camps themselves.

The partial autonomy has led to an extensive administrative structure and its respective spaces, most of them being located in Rabouni, the administration center for the camps. When walking through Rabouni, one passes the Ministry of International Affairs, the Ministries of Health, of Defense, of Planning, and various others. Rabouni also houses the main national hospital, the national museum, and the national archive. A large central market is located at the main transport hub, where every day hundreds, if not thousands, of Sahrawis arrive to work at the ministries. What emerges is unique for refugee settlements: a seat of government for a refugee nation where refugees govern themselves instead of being governed by a host nation or the international humanitarian regime. What also emerges is a certain kind of normality: people arriving in the morning, going to work, having lunch in the canteen of their ministry or in a sandwich shop, and returning home in the evening. It is the normality of participating in a self-governed life and being able to shape it.

## Moving and Communication

Maybe it comes as no surprise that activities of moving, transport, and communication occupy a central place in the life of the camps. To a certain extent this can be traced back to the nomadic tradition and participation in the trans-Saharan trading networks, of which movement is an integral part. Hence trading and the transport of goods to and from the camps seems inscribed in a customary practice. But, more than that, aspects of moving in all variations are ever-present in the spaces of the camps. Whether it be the constant flow of cars—mostly aging Land Rovers or Mercedes 190s—either in the shape of carcasses of once-functioning vehicles left to rot in the desert sand or reused as fences and demarcation devices; in the shape of endless rows of car-repair shops, used-parts dealerships, or petrol stations; or in the shape of the probably one-and-only car wash of the Sahara Desert, cars, trucks, and the paraphernalia of mobility are ubiquitous.

Traffic in Smara

Market street in Smara

Being located in such a remote place, in the middle of the biggest desert in the world, mobility becomes a larger issue than just a matter of utility. It is a way (and a promise) to connect with one's surroundings, with the regional and national territory, and with the world at large. It is also why communication plays a strong role, though still on a basic level. Most refugee families are equipped with at least one mobile phone and radio, as well as with a television. Despite the extraordinary effort to bring a telecommunications infrastructure serving 160,000 people without a centralized electricity supply into the middle of the desert, the phone becomes a tool to connect to friends and relatives abroad, to conduct business, and to receive vital news and information. It becomes the extension of the car or the truck: mobile, and seemingly fitting perfectly with the national agenda of a population in waiting, only settled temporarily, always ready to get up and move again.

## Commerce and Working

The refugee camps were founded with a vision of an economy not based on money, but on an exchange in kind. The basic food for survival was donated by the Algerian state or the World Food Programme (WFP), and extra goods and services were bartered among the refugees. Working in the administration or in any of the institutions such as the schools or hospitals was done without payment, but for the service of the general public, and sometimes rewarded by extra portions of vegetables or other goods. Social and economic difference was minute among the refugees, money hardly circulated, and hence almost no shops or markets existed until the late 1980s or early 1990s.

This changed with the signing of the cease-fire agreement between Polisario and Morocco in 1991, after which a referendum over the future of the Western Sahara was to take place (though endlessly delayed by Morocco). A Polisario congress in June 1991 called for a free-market economy. At the same time, the men returned back from the war zone. The resident population within the camps grew substantially, and no longer being engaged in active battle, they had more time in their hands. At the same time, though unrelated, Spain started paying out pensions to former Sahrawi employees who had formerly worked in the colonial administration or in the phosphate mines of Bou Craa. This led to an inflow of money into the camps and for the first time established noticeable economic differences within the camp population. Thus, slowly, the economy changed from one based on exchange in kind to one based on money. In addition to the pensions, a considerable number of Sahrawis started working in Algeria or Spain, regularly sending back money to their families in the camps. This led to an investment into shops and other businesses, such as the before-mentioned cars and car-repair shops, and into a small service economy such as barber shops, photography labs, or video-game stalls. A certain level of "luxury" or consumer culture entered the camps. Today, these stores and markets are quite prevalent.

What is interesting to see is how different structures emerge in the different camp markets. Whereas in the camp El Aaiún every daïra (the major subdivision within every camp) has a market with twenty or thirty shops, and a single central market exists on its western perimeter, the camp Smara features just two central markets, west and east of its central administration zone, with basically no additional shops located in the individual daïras. This has to do with the higher density of Smara, the location of its daïras, and the presence of a higher number of international visitors, which tends towards a centralization of service functions. What is most interesting to observe is how in an environment that could not be more homogenous—with the same ethnic group, no cultural or religious differences, almost no economic differences, and no geographical or climatic differences—difference still emerges.

Newly built hospital, El Aaiún

Independent language school, El Aaiún

## Health and Education

Beyond securing bare survival by providing accommodation, water, and food, it is education and medical services that are usually the main activities (and spaces) set up by humanitarian organizations in refugee camps. Similarly, the construction of the Sahrawi camps went hand in hand with the establishment of schools and hospitals from the very start. Again, the main difference was that these schools and hospitals were not developed by an international organization such as Médecins Sans Frontières or Oxfam, but by the Sahrawis themselves. Starting with a few central schools, such as the women's boarding school 27 February (commemorating the date of the inauguration of the Sahrawi Republic in 1976), soon every camp and every daïra within each camp established its own school. In a similar fashion, clinics, hospitals, and dispensaries for medications were set up, serving the refugee population. Teachers were educated, a national curriculum was formulated, and doctors and nurses were trained, mostly abroad, bringing back valuable knowledge to run these new institutions.

What emerges when looking at health and education is a central dilemma of the Sahrawi refugees. When living under Spanish occupation in colonial Spanish Sahara, and leading a much more traditional lifestyle, the level of education and health services was very basic. To set up a decent education and health system for a relatively small population over such a vast territory was daunting to say the least. Especially with the then available resources and technologies, the country seemed just too big and too thinly inhabited to set up systems serving the whole Sahrawi population. But it was precisely the loss of their homeland and the transformation into a refugee nation that enabled the Sahrawis to set up a national system of schools and medical institutions in the first place. The relative density of life in the camps, the accessibility of these new institutions, and the mobility and communication services that the camps facilitate allow for the creation of an extensive system of schools and clinics. The flight from the Western Sahara was, in fact, something like an overnight urbanization, with the "proto-urban" environment of the camps offering the benefits that this more centralized way of living can provide.

Today, Sahrawis have reached a level of education (measured in literacy and schooling rate) and level of health (measured in life expectancy) that surpasses that of most countries of the Maghreb. The central dilemma: the tragedy of losing one's homeland leads to a system bringing emancipation to a refugee nation. Thus, the camps act also as a training phase, during which the Sahrawi society can develop ideas and concepts of what system of education they want to establish, and learn about public health and medical service provision. The camps become a space where nation-building can be learned and performed, to be later transferred to their original homeland, if it becomes available in the future. What remains interesting to see, but also challenging, is how the Sahrawis will be able to project the benefits of centralized quasi-urban life enacted in the camps onto the vast territory of the Western Sahara.

## Recreation and Leisure

While health and education are at the core of humanitarian action, recreation and leisure are hardly ever dealt with in the context of refugee camps. Spaces of emergency just seem too extreme to deal with something as mundane as recreation. When human life is reduced to bare life, and hence to its pure biological and physical existence and to the provision of food and medications, activities of enjoyment are disregarded, if not even shunned for being disrespectful in a situation of conflict. The "official" planning strategy of refugee camps, as set up out the UNHCR *Handbook for Emergencies*[4], for example, does not mention aspects of recreation or leisure

Kids playing football, El Aaiún

Vegetable garden, El Aaiún

anywhere. What we see when looking at the Sahrawi camps is a wide range of spaces where these activities take place. From the private spaces of the tea ceremony, via activities of a celebratory nature like weddings in tents, to the distribution centers in every daïra that become spaces for lingering, talking, meeting, and playing. Sporting activities, especially football, take place almost everywhere, from the empty spaces between the houses to the official football fields in the center of each camp. Also, cultural activities such as youth theater or painting are pursued. Most of these activities are not neutral or "innocent" but are imbued with a political message. The theater play is about the (supposedly) lush landscape of the lost homeland in contrast to the barren desert of the refugee camp. Every painting is a call to action, to redeem the homeland or to commemorate the crushed independence movement and the martyrs of the guerilla war against Morocco. The football teams are organized into a national football organization and a national team, albeit one that has never played an international tournament. Thus, on the one hand, these activities of recreation establish a level of normality and everyday quality within a space of extreme conditions. On the other hand, they serve to construct an image and common memory of a homeland. They act as a national unifier and are imbued by a strategic and political dimension.

It comes as no surprise that green spaces, such as gardens and trees, are extremely rare in the camps. Being located in one of the most inhospitable zones on the planet means that extracting produce or greenery from the dry, salty desert sand is an arduous and often frustrating undertaking. Nevertheless, some vegetable gardens have been planted in El Aaiún (which is blessed with a large underground water source beneath the camp), and some inhabitants have started growing their own tomatoes, onions, or lettuce. Even in Smara, a large agricultural garden exists. El Aaiún once had something like a central park when an area located in the center of the camp was planted with palm trees and greenery. Due to the salty ground conditions, however, the plants and most of the trees dried up and died. The green spaces are almost exclusively treated as utilitarian market gardens. They are kept for their produce rather than for their pleasure. Only very rarely can one see people lingering beneath the shadows of a tree, and hardly ever can one observe a family preparing tea or having a picnic in one of the gardens. This is astonishing, as our Western perspective would assume that the shade of some trees and the smell of plants and flowers would be taken advantage of more often.

## Between the Temporary and the Permanent

What these observations show is that activities of everyday life shape the spaces of the Sahrawi camps. In contrast to the prevailing idea of a camp as a space of exception, where aspects of misery, control, and destitution dominate, it is rather this notion of "normality" within an abnormal situation that is present everywhere, shaping the physical space.

Maybe more so than any other refugee situation existing today, the Sahrawi camps expose the dilemmas and tensions between the "orthodox" notion of the camp as only being a temporary, interim solution, and the reality on the ground that often develops into a quasi-permanent condition. Suspended in a life that is neither here nor there, inhabiting one of the most inhospitable places on this planet after thirty-five years still living in tents, the Sahrawi refugees are proof of the contradictions of the refugee camp concept. But permanence cannot merely be seen as an unfortunate outcome of a development gone awry. Permanence seems to be inscribed into the whole process of refugee camps. We have observed how refugee camps are creating a normality within the abnormal situation of "refugee-ness." The Sahrawis have set up an elaborate infrastructure to manage and organize their daily lives. They have enough food and water, and their levels of education and life expectancy are above average.

27 February: from a school to a camp with electricity

The mayor of El Aaiún

With the help of the camps, emergency has been averted. People are not suffering anymore. But just as the battles have ended and nobody is dying anymore, just as the Sahrawis are in the safe shelter of the camps, the political pressure to resolve the underlying conflict has faded. Instead of solving the Western Sahara conflict politically, camps are being built. Architecture and planning becomes a replacement for a political solution.

Just as permanence is not merely an unfortunate or unintended consequence, temporality is not simply a technical dimension. In view of the stalemate in this conflict, the call for the provisional gains a strategic and political dimension. And, again, architecture is the field in which this temporality is played out. Tents are not merely used for their utilitarian purposes, but to visibly proclaim a demand to return to the homeland. Very little infrastructure, such as roads, electricity, or water supply, is installed permanently, but a more mobile system is used. Instead of paved roads, four-wheel-drive vehicles on desert sand are omnipresent; instead of an electricity grid, solar cells and car batteries supply power to each residential unit; instead of water pipes, trucks bring potable water to every house. Of course, this also has to do with the lack of resources and money, but at the same time a temporary and "cellular" solution to services and infrastructure is preferred, as it signifies the wish to return to the homeland.

## The Camp as a Catalyst: the Camp as a Project

Whereas refugee camps are most often seen as places of desperation, as spaces of total control, or as territories of a humanitarian regime, the Sahrawi refugee camps unfold an environment of self-administered daily life. The camps are used by the Sahrawis to develop institutions that can be transferred to their own country once a solution (of independence) is found to the as-of-yet-unresolved Western Sahara conflict. The camps can be seen as a period of practice in which the Sahrawi state is "pre-figured."[5] The time in the camps is used by the refugees for a major cultural and social shift from their tribal-based tradition, developing a quasi-urban, emancipated society.

## The Camp as a City?

When asking the mayor of the camp El Aaiún if he would use the term "city" when describing the camp, he vehemently rejected this word. "Nothing," he continued, "would justify calling the camp a city. The houses are not permanent, the streets not paved, and no water lines are installed." Understandably for the mayor, the use of the word "city" for the camp is virtually outlawed, as this implies a permanent settlement. Instead, he falls into a slightly clichéd comprehension of paved streets and stone houses being the main ingredients of a city. Nevertheless, if we look at the camps through the lenses of its inhabitants, how they make use of the environment, how daily lives are acted out in them, how they become a medium to play out their desires and aspirations, and how local culture develops within these spaces, we can certainly perceive the existence of urban qualities. We can observe how difference emerges, how the development of neighborhoods diverges over time, and we can see how certain fashions and urban cultures manifest themselves in the environment and influence it. Moreover, we can observe how the camps become a space where political aspirations are not only allowed to take place, but how the physical fabric of the camps becomes the very medium with which these political aspirations are expressed. In that sense, and with a reference to the urban geographer David Harvey[6], the camps can be seen as expressing an essence of urbanity. But, and this is the remarkable strategy, they are always ready to be abandoned should the opportunity arise to return to the Western Sahara. The camps are indeed urban environments, to be discarded at any time if the underlying conflict is resolved. In that sense, they offer an impressive model for refugee camps on a global scale.

Residential compounds of El Aaiún

Looking over El Aaiún

## Urban Research on Refugee Camps

Is it legitimate, one could ask, to conduct an urban research project on refugee camps? Certain questions come to mind. Does this not preempt a conclusion that the camps are akin to urban environments? Is it not almost irreverent—or at least irrelevant—to look at urban qualities when, in fact, everything should be about protecting and saving lives? And even if it were relevant to refugee camps, does it have any implications on the wider field of urbanism? Is it not so extreme a case that there is no feedback into the profession at large?

The starting assumption for the research was that it is important to look at refugee camps through the eyes of an urbanist in order to see if these camps contain qualities of the urban and, if so, to what extent and of what kind. It is precisely the use of tools of urbanism that allow us to assess the ways in which these settlements differ from cities, and how they are alike. If, to take an extreme example, the tools of urbanism are used to describe a prison camp, the outcome would quickly make clear that these prison camps are very different from the refugee camps we have observed, and very far away from anything resembling urbanity. But it is exactly that predominant focus on the bare necessities of survival in the context of refugee camps that prevents some of the qualities of urbanity to develop in the camps (or to become apparent to us), and hence also preventing the use of the camps as places of emancipation and responsibility. One aim of this research is to shift the vocabulary used in the framework of refugee camps from one which revolves around technicalities towards one that understands these settlements as environments having some, or many, urban qualities.

Of the approximately thirty-five million refugees and displaced people in the world today, maybe half live in refugee camps or in camp-like conditions. The research is therefore concerned not with a fringe condition, but one in which millions of people spend often tens of years. And, for millions of people, these refugee camps are their first contact with something akin to an urban environment. Especially in Africa, with its still relatively large rural population, these camps act as an "urban transformer," changing the lifestyles of the refugees from a rural background to an urban one. Refugee camps can be seen as motors of urbanization, as many refugees do not go back to their rural villages when returning to their home countries after conflict has abated, but resettle in the major cities. The camps prepare the refugees for an urban life after the camps, and in that sense it is very important to analyze and be aware of their urban dimensions, their possible lack of that, and in which ways they prepare a population for a life after the camps.

Last but not least, we can observe the origination of city conditions when looking at refugee camps: how from a collection of tents on a sandy patch of the Sahara, to the development of clay huts, to the development of neighborhoods, markets, local styles, and expressions of culture, a proto-city slowly emerges. We can also observe the materialization of difference. Despite starting from identical geographic, demographic, cultural, ethnic, and economic conditions, Smara and El Aaiún have developed differently and today exhibit different kinds of urban cultures, atmospheres, and range of habitats. In the blazing sun of the Sahara Desert we can observe the birth of the urban condition with a clarity and crispness almost unlike anywhere else in the world.

1 Giorgio Agamben, *Homo Sacer: Sovereign Power and Bare Life*, Stanford University Press, 1998
2 Ibid.
3 See Mundy, Jacob, and Stephen Zunes, *Western Sahara: War, Nationalism & Conflict Irresolution* for a thorough history of the conflict
4 See UNHCR *Handbook for Emergencies*, 2007, Geneva: especially section 3/12, site selection, planning, shelter
5 Mundy, Jacob, "Performing the Nation, Pre-figuring the State; the Western Saharan Refugees, Thirty Years Later," *The Journal of Modern African Studies*, 2007, p. 45: 275–297
6 Harvey, David, "The Right to the City," *New Left Review*, 2008, p. 53

Market and residential quarters in El Aaiún

Overlooking daïra Daura in El Aaiún

Overlooking daïra El Guelta in El Aaiún

Distribution of vegetable oil in Smara

Shop in a market of El Aaiún

Containers for drinking water outside a residential compound

FIFA
2008
SAHA
RA

Goat barns in El Aaiún

Residential tent in the daïra Amgala of El Aaiún

# A BRIEF HISTORY OF REFUGEES AND REFUGEE CAMPS

UNHCR tents in camp Gaga in eastern Chad

In 2011 there were 35.5 million displaced people registered by UNHCR, with 10.5 million of them being refugees, 15.5 million internally displaced (i.e. fleeing within their own country), and the remaining 9.5 million consisting of stateless people and asylum seekers. This number does not include the five million Palestinian refugees that are registered with UNRWA, a different UN organization dealing with Palestinians who were displaced by the establishment of Israel in 1948. All these displaced people live in approximately 1,000 different camps located in many parts of the world, though predominantly in Central and Eastern Africa, the Middle East, and Central Asia. UNHCR, being the central organization responsible for most of the refugees, has developed an elaborate system of conventions, protocols, guidelines, and handbooks for defining refugees as well as other categories of displaced people; registering them; setting up refugee camps; and providing them with water, food, medical aid, and other aspects of protection.

Before going into the principles of spatial planning and the layouts of refugee camps, this chapter traces a history of the notion of the refugee, the different categories and definitions, and the implications on the ground.

# Refugees

## A Brief History of Refugees

People have been fleeing from conflict, natural disasters, droughts, or other causes and migrating across territories to more favorable regions ever since the dawn of time. The migration period of late antiquity, with major movements of whole peoples and tribes across Eastern Europe, as well as the continent at large, is just one of many examples. Over the course of time, though, a number of migration movements stand out. The Huguenots fleeing France during the late seventeenth century (with estimates ranging between 200,000 and one million) and later settling in England, Switzerland, or the Netherlands, among others, were one of the first groups of displaced people consciously referred to as refugees. Persecuted for reasons of religion, their original homeland not willing to afford them protection, and fleeing across a national border into foreign countries, they retrospectively fulfill many of the aspects that were later to define the refugee in an international legal system.

The revolutions that swept across Europe in 1848 sparked another period when people left their traditional home and moved to other countries. Often a painful process, with misery during the time of flight and tension in the new host territories, it can still be said that overall, refugees were relatively well received during early modernity. The right to asylum was commonly recognized, and movement from country to country did not require passports or visas. Immigration was frequently even seen as economically beneficial to the new host country. The Huguenots found a new home in Switzerland, often working in the silk-dyeing industry, or were welcomed in England, where they settled in Canterbury, among other places. The liberal climate of the mid-nineteenth century was favorable in the wake of the failed revolutions of that time, and exiles were well received in European capitals such as London, which sometimes even celebrated their arrival.

This changed, however, when the romantic nationalism that had characterized much of the nineteenth century transformed into a more authoritarian nationalism towards the end of that century. Loyalty and obedience to the state, as well as differentiation and disassociation from others, gave rise to a rudimentary mistrust in foreigners. The late nineteenth and early twentieth century was also a time when the sheer number of refugees in Europe grew substantially. With approximately two million Jews fleeing the pogroms of Russia around the turn of the century, several hundred thousand refugees fleeing the Balkan Wars of 1912–1913, and more than a million refugees migrating across Europe in the wake of World War I, the continent was seen to be swarming with displaced people. In a climate of economic insecurity, having experienced years of horrendous suffering during World War I and with growing xenophobia, refugees were no longer welcome. They were now seen as a problem.

The League of Nations—founded at the Paris Peace Conference of 1919 and representing one of the first supranational bodies, with the mission of promoting and maintaining world peace—took the initiative to deal with the refugee problem. What followed was the foundation of an institution tasked with the responsibility to protect and resettle displaced populations, as well as with defining who is to be considered a refugee in the first place.

View over camp Farchana in eastern Chad

Fridtjof Nansen

Nansen passport

FRANCE

PASSEPORT *NANSEN*

CERTIFICAT D'IDENTITÉ ET DE VOYAGE

GRATUIT

N° AS44233

TITULAIRE :

*Nom :* SPECIMEN

*Prénoms :* SPECIMEN

Ce certificat d'identité et de voyage comprend 18 pages non compris la couverture

**Precursors to UNHCR**

The devastation, suffering, and cynicism of World War I led to a global anti-war sentiment. Learning the lesson, it was to have been "the war to end all wars." The foundation of the League of Nations was one of the measures taken to prevent future war by open diplomacy, international cooperation, and general disarmament. Its Commission for Refugees was established on June 27, 1921, and was led by Fridtjof Nansen, a Norwegian scientist, explorer, diplomat, and later Nobel laureate.

The commission was tasked with dealing with the refugees of World War I as well as with the millions of prisoners of war that were dispersed throughout Russia. It was successful in bringing a significant number home or resettling them permanently in a new country. Nansen's proposal for a refugee identification certificate that all nations would accept as a passport was approved at an international meeting in Geneva in 1922. These so-called Nansen Passports were later recognized by fifty-two governments. Nansen died in 1930, but during the same year the League of Nations decided to establish the Nansen International Office for Refugees, thereby elevating its status within the organization, making it permanent, and acknowledging the achievement of its name bearer. In 1938, just on the eve of World War II, which was also to be the collapse of the League of Nations, the Nansen Office was awarded the Nobel Peace Prize.

After World War II the United Nations was established in 1945 to replace the flawed League of Nations. With masses of refugees in Europe and Asia as a result of the war, the United Nations Relief and Rehabilitation Administration was set up in the same year. It was responsible for bringing relief to victims of war, providing food, shelter, and medical services, as well as aiding the return of the displaced people. In 1947 it ceded operations, and in its stead the International Refugee Organization (IRO) was founded, which took over the responsibility of dealing with refugees and displaced people.

As a separate entity, and dealing only with a specific geographical region and related events, the United Nations Relief and Works Agency for Palestine Refugees in the Near East (UNRWA) was established, following the 1948 Arab-Israeli War. Still operating today, UNRWA is a relief and human development agency, providing education, health care, social services, and emergency aid to more than five million Palestinian refugees.

UNHCR is awarded the Nobel Peace Prize in 1954 (shown) and in 1981

**UNHCR**

The United Nations High Commissioner for Refugees was founded in late 1950 as a successor to the International Refugee Organization, which had fallen out of favor with the UN and the major donor countries. UNHCR is headquartered in Geneva, Switzerland. It is mandated to protect and support refugees. Apart from providing or organizing aid such as food, water, shelter, and medical aid through implementation partners, it strives to solve refugee situations by assisting in their voluntary repatriation to the original home country, supporting local integration in their current country of asylum, or attempting resettlement in a new country.

The founding document of UNHCR is the 1951 Convention Relating to the Status of Refugees. This convention defines who is eligible to be granted refugee status and what rights a refugee enjoys. Originally, UNHCR focused its activities on (mostly European) refugees displaced in the wake of World War II. This was reflected in the convention, limiting the organization's responsibility for events occurring before 1951. With the decolonization struggles in Asia and Africa starting in the late 1950s, UNHCR understood that it had to expand its mandate and operate globally. The 1967 Protocol Relating to the Status of Refugees reflects this transformation by omitting the condition and reference to World War II, enabling UNHCR to react worldwide to new refugee emergencies.

**UNHCR**

Coordination, Registration, Planning

**Implementation partners**

| **IGOs Intergovernmental organizations** | **NGOs Nongovernmental organizations** |
| --- | --- |
| WFP, ECHO ... | MSF, OXFAM ... |

CHAPTER I: General Provisions

*Article 1*

DEFINITION OF THE TERM "REFUGEE"

A. For the purposes of the present Convention, the term "refugee" shall apply to any person who:

(1) Has been considered a refugee under the Arrangements of 12 May 1926 and 30 June 1928 or under the Conventions of 28 October 1933 and 10 February 1938, the Protocol of 14 September 1939 or the Constitution of the International Refugee Organization;

Decisions of non-eligibility taken by the International Refugee Organization during the period of its activities shall not prevent the status of refugee being accorded to persons who fulfil the conditions of paragraph 2 of this section;

(2) As a result of events occurring before 1 January 1951 and owing to well-founded fear of being persecuted for reasons of race, religion, nationality, membership of a particular social group or political opinion, is outside the country of his nationality and is unable or, owing to such fear, is unwilling to avail himself of the protection of that country; or who, not having a nationality and being outside the country of his former habitual residence as a result of such events, is unable or, owing to such fear, is unwilling to return to it.

In the case of a person who has more than one nationality, the term "the country of his nationality" shall mean each of the countries of which he is a national, and a person shall not be deemed to be lacking the protection of the country of his nationality if, without any valid reason based on well-founded fear, he has not availed himself of the protection of one of the countries of which he is a national.

B. (1) For the purposes of this Convention, the words "events occurring

— 16 —

This paragraph refers to the previous refugee organizations of the League of Nations and the International Refugee Organization.

Implies refugees from World War II. This clause was later dropped in the 1967 protocol to give UNHCR a global mandate.

The central condition for claiming status as a refugee is that one must have crossed a national boundary. Otherwise, one can only be considered internally displaced.

Reasons for persecution. War or general violence is not mentioned. The Organisation of African Unity (OAU) expanded this list of reasons in its own declaration to also include occupation, foreign domination, and aggression.

Stateless persons

The protection of refugees is the core task of UNHCR

## Definition of a Refugee

Under the UNHCR Convention of 1951, a refugee is a person who, "owing to a well-founded fear of being persecuted for reasons of race, religion, nationality, membership of a particular social group, or political opinion, is outside the country of his nationality..." Two aspects of this definition stand out. The first one is regarding the physical location of refugees. Only after having crossed a national border and entered a foreign country can someone apply for refugee status. People fleeing within their own country are not considered refugees, but internally displaced people, for which UNHCR was not originally responsible.

The second aspect of note are the reasons upon which a claim as a refugee is assessed. Even though seemingly spanning a wide range, most obviously missing is a general condition of war or violence as a reason for flight. Surprising as it might sound, people fleeing from war are not officially considered refugees. Only if the war is based on ethnic or religious conflict is it possible to claim the status of a refugee. This gap in the definition of refugees has been repeatedly criticized over time. As a reaction, the Organisation of African Unity (OAU) formulated an extended definition of refugees that includes "aggression, occupation, foreign domination, or events seriously disturbing public order," better reflecting the conditions of the African continent. A similar definition was formulated by a group of Latin American countries.

Convention and Protocol Relating to the Status of Refugees of the UNHCR

*Convention and Protocol*

RELATING TO THE STATUS OF REFUGEES

UNHCR

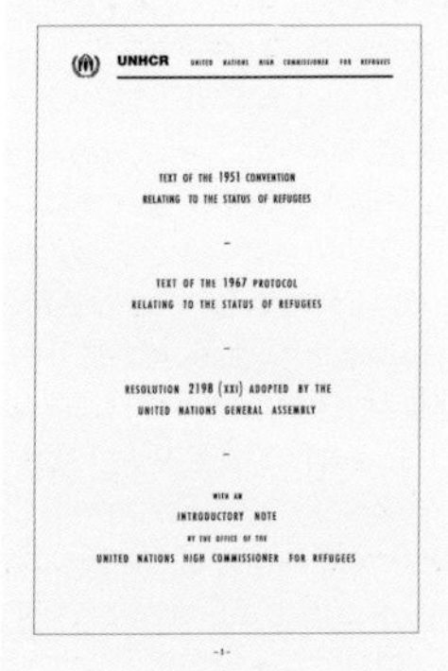

UNHCR

TEXT OF THE 1951 CONVENTION
RELATING TO THE STATUS OF REFUGEES

TEXT OF THE 1967 PROTOCOL
RELATING TO THE STATUS OF REFUGEES

RESOLUTION 2198 (XXI) ADOPTED BY THE
UNITED NATIONS GENERAL ASSEMBLY

WITH AN
INTRODUCTORY NOTE
BY THE OFFICE OF THE
UNITED NATIONS HIGH COMMISSIONER FOR REFUGEES

-1-

CHAPTER I: General Provisions

*Article 1*

DEFINITION OF THE TERM "REFUGEE"

A. For the purposes of the present Convention, the term "refugee" shall apply to any person who:

(1) Has been considered a refugee under the Arrangements of 12 May 1926 and 30 June 1928 or under the Conventions of 28 October 1933 and 10 February 1938, the Protocol of 14 September 1939 or the Constitution of the International Refugee Organization;

Decisions of non-eligibility taken by the International Refugee Organization during the period of its activities shall not prevent the status of refugee being accorded to persons who fulfil the conditions of paragraph 2 of this section;

(2) As a result of events occurring before 1 January 1951 and owing to well-founded fear of being persecuted for reasons of race, religion, nationality, membership of a particular social group or political opinion, is outside the country of his nationality and is unable or, owing to such fear, is unwilling to avail himself of the protection of that country; or who, not having a nationality and being outside the country of his former habitual residence as a result of such events, is unable or, owing to such fear, is unwilling to return to it.

In the case of a person who has more than one nationality, the term "the country of his nationality" shall mean each of the countries of which he is a national, and a person shall not be deemed to be lacking the protection of the country of his nationality if, without any valid reason based on well-founded fear, he has not availed himself of the protection of one of the countries of which he is a national.

B. (1) For the purposes of this Convention, the words "events occurring

CHAPTER IV: Welfare

*Article 20*

RATIONING

Where a rationing system exists, which applies to the population at large and regulates the general distribution of products in short supply, refugees shall be accorded the same treatment as nationals.

*Article 21*

HOUSING

As regards housing, the Contracting States, in so far as the matter is regulated by laws or regulations or is subject to the control of public authorities, shall accord to refugees lawfully staying in their territory treatment as favourable as possible and, in any event, not less favourable than that accorded to aliens generally in the same circumstances.

*Article 22*

PUBLIC EDUCATION

1. The Contracting States shall accord to refugees the same treatment as is accorded to nationals with respect to elementary education.

2. The Contracting States shall accord to refugees treatment as favourable as possible, and, in any event, not less favourable than that accorded to aliens generally in the same circumstances, with respect to education other than elementary education and, in particular, as regards access to studies, the recognition of foreign school certificates, diplomas and degrees, the remission of fees and charges and the award of scholarships.

*Article 23*

PUBLIC RELIEF

The Contracting States shall accord to refugees lawfully staying in their territory the same treatment with respect to public relief and assistance as is accorded to their nationals.

| Refugees | People in refugee-like situations | Asylum seekers | Internally displaced persons (IDPs) | Stateless people | Palestine refugees |
|---|---|---|---|---|---|
| Individuals recognized under the 1951 Convention and the 1967 Protocol relating to the Status of Refugees. | People who are outside their country and facing risks similar to those of refugees, but for whom refugee status has not been ascertained. | Asylum seekers are persons who have applied for asylum or refugee status, but who have not yet received a final decision on their application. | IDPs are people or groups of individuals who have been forced to leave their homes, but who have not crossed an international border. | Stateless people are individuals not considered as nationals by any state under relevant national laws. | Under the mandate of UNRWA, people whose normal place of residence was Palestine before May 1948 and who lost homes and livelihood as a result of the 1948 Arab-Israeli conflict. |
| 9.8 million | 0.6 million | 0.9 million | 15.6 million | 3.5 million | 5.0 million |

**Different Categories of Displaced People**

Depending on their location and status, forced migrants are grouped into different categories. What might seem (and often actually is) a pedantic exercise in the idiosyncrasies of bureaucracy has crucial implications on the ground. One pivotal difference exists between refugees and IDPs. Whereas the former enjoy (at least officially) certain rights, such as the right of movement, and will be supported and protected by UNHCR, people fleeing within their own country are not afforded these rights. This is based on the assumption that a person's home country is ultimately responsible for guaranteeing the protection of its citizens. An international body–such as UNHCR or another country–is not allowed to interfere in the internal affairs of a sovereign country. IDPs therefore cannot count on the protection of UNHCR, even though, in many cases, they have been allowed to assist them.

Similarly crucial, and usually not revealed by the prevalent statistics, is the difference between regular and "prima facie" refugees. Normally, refugee status is only afforded on a case-by-case basis and applies to people based on their individual experiences and histories. But if, for example, in the case of civil war, tens of thousands of people flee across a border, an individual assessment of every person becomes logistically impossible. People fleeing en masse are therefore declared by the fact that they belong to that group, as prima facie refugees. In most countries these refugees do not enjoy the same rights as "proper" refugees. Kenya, to name just one example, does not allow the Somali refugees, who are all classified as prima facie refugees, to leave the refugee camps of Dadaab nor to take on work–both of which are rights a regular refugee would normally be entitled to.

Palestinian refugees are protected under the mandate of UNRWA. These are people who have lost their homes and livelihoods in the context of the 1948 Arab-Israeli war and the establishment of the state of Israel. In this case, the rule of having crossed a national boundary does not apply any more because many of those refugees still live in the territory of former Palestine, though the nation itself has changed. The descendents of Palestinian refugees are also eligible for refugee status. Today, UNRWA is responsible for more than five million refugees. One-third of registered Palestinian refugees, more than 1.4 million people, live in fifty-eight recognized refugee camps in Jordan, Lebanon, the Syrian Arab Republic, the Gaza Strip, and the West Bank, including East Jerusalem.

World map population of concern

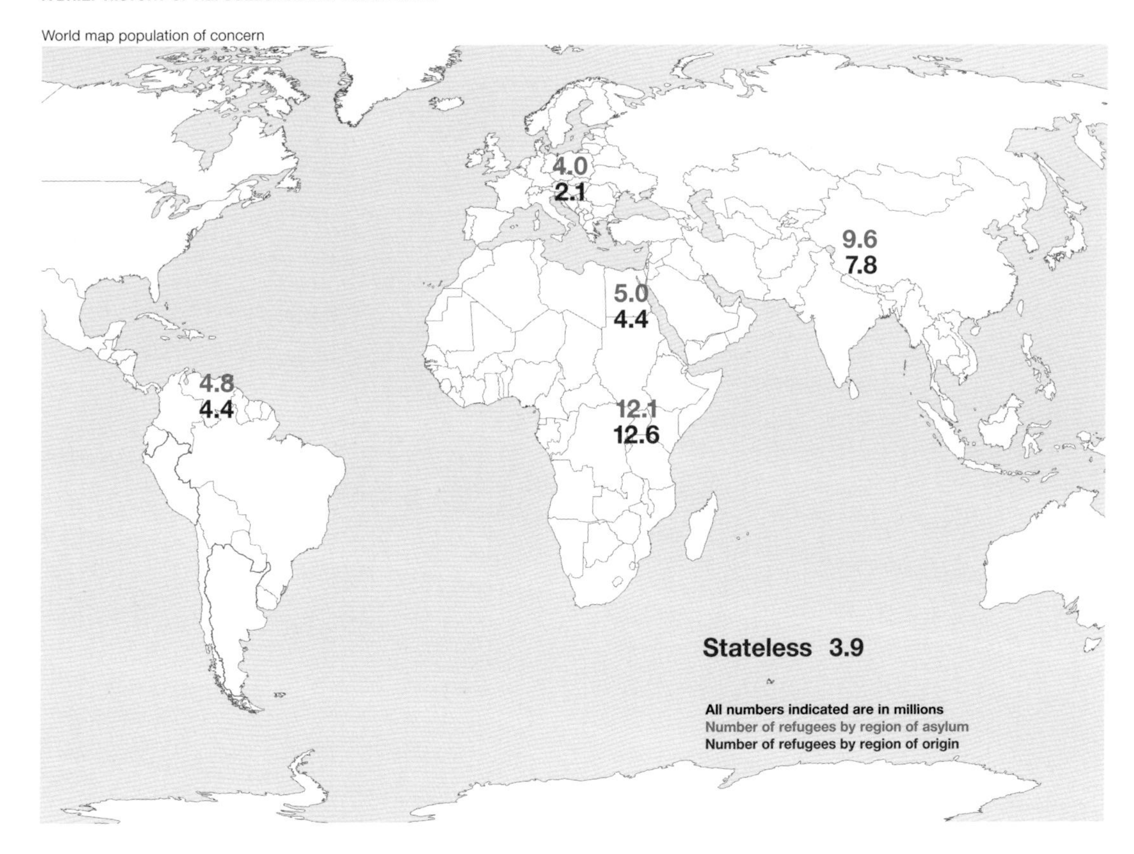


**Refugee Statistics**

Nothing seems more prominent when dealing with refugees than statistics. Refugees are constantly counted, so statistics play a fundamental part in almost all aspects of people in flight. There is probably not a single text, news report, or other document focusing on refugees where statistics are not mentioned or used to support an argument and underline a specific issue. Even though statistics hold such a central place in the discourse on refugees, a critical questioning on their validity and sources rarely takes place. This is even more surprising in view of the fact that the main sources for most statistics, UNHCR and the US Committee for Refugees and Immigrants (USCRI), quote figures that are sometimes drastically different. Refugees are usually counted by their host countries, UNHCR, and sometimes by the larger humanitarian organizations. Reasons for incorrect numbers can be attributed to logistical and political reasons, as well as to aspects of definition.

But why count at all? Doesn't the counting and quantification of refugees simply underline their position as passive objects of welfare and ascribe them to the regime of control? The act of counting can be connected to a regime of power and society of control. He or she becomes the infamous "faceless statistic," which can go hand in hand with the warehousing of refugees and a dismissal of their personal identities. The whole idea of classifying people in flight as refugees, asylum seekers, or internally displaced people can also feed into a system of bureaucracies and the organization of unwanted people. And additional practical reasons for not counting refugees can come in to play too. Sometimes, it is exactly the process of counting that exposes refugees to additional risks, as they can often profit from invisibility. The conflict in eastern Congo is infamous for militias trailing refugee organizations and thus being led directly to the refugees who have just fled from them.

On the other hand, counting refugees is the basis for most support activities. Only when one has assessed how many refugees exist in a certain situation can UNHCR send tents, WFP send food, and others provide sufficient resources for medical care, education, water, and protection. But apart from these quite obvious benefits in knowing quantities, the act of counting can also provide refugees with rights and possibilities. Separated families can only be brought back together when refugees have been registered, and they can more effectively voice demands for provisions, better equipment, and decent livelihoods when their number is known. The knowledge of quantity can give a group of refugees the power of influence and a political weight that they would not have had if their number was unknown.

Refugee movement in Central Africa

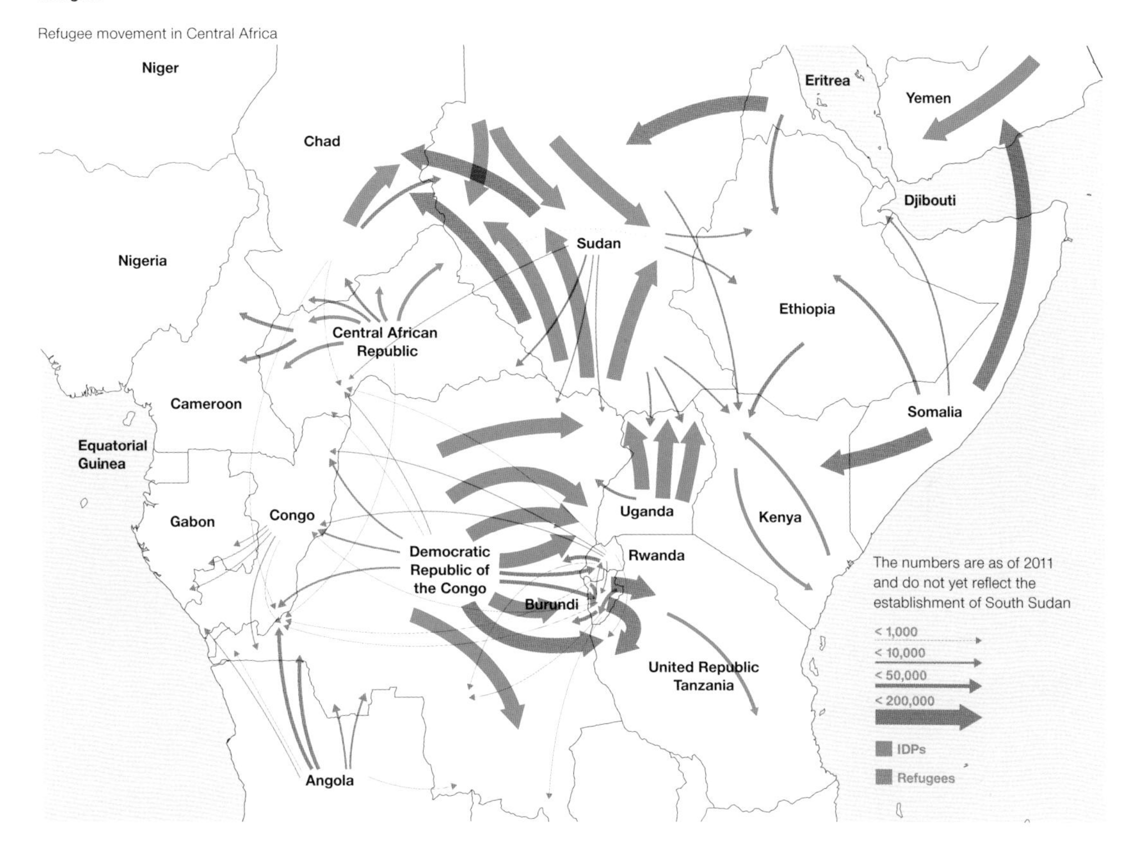


**Total population of concern by UNHCR and UNRWA end-2011**

| | by country/territory of asylum | by orgin |
|---|---|---|
| Africa | 12.1 million | 12.6 million |
| Middle East and North Africa | 5.0 million | 4.4 million |
| Europe | 4.0 million | 2.1 million |
| Asia and Pacific | 9.6 million | 7.8 million |
| Americas | 4.8 million | 4.4 million |
| Various/Stateless | – | 3.9 million |
| Total | 35.4 million | 35.4 million |

**Top countries/territories of asylum end-2011**

| Refugees: | | Total population of concern: | |
|---|---|---|---|
| Pakistan | 1.7 million | Colombia | 3.9 million |
| Iran | 0.9 million | Sudan | 2.9 million |
| Syria | 0.8 million | Pakistan | 2.8 million |
| Germany | 0.6 million | Dem. Rep. of the Congo | 2.7 million |
| Kenya | 0.6 million | Iraq | 1.8 million |
| Jordan | 0.5 million | Afghanistan | 1.5 million |

**Top orgins of population concerned by UNHCR and UNWRA end-2011**

| Refugees: | | Total population of concern: | |
|---|---|---|---|
| Afghanistan | 2.7 million | Colombia | 4.3 million |
| Iraq | 1.4 million | Afghanistan | 4.2 million |
| Somalia | 1.1 million | Stateless | 3.5 million |
| Dem. Rep. of the Congo | 0.5 million | Sudan | 3.3 million |
| Sudan | 0.5 million | Dem. Rep. of the Congo | 3.1 million |
| Vietnam | 0.3 million | Iraq | 3.1 million |

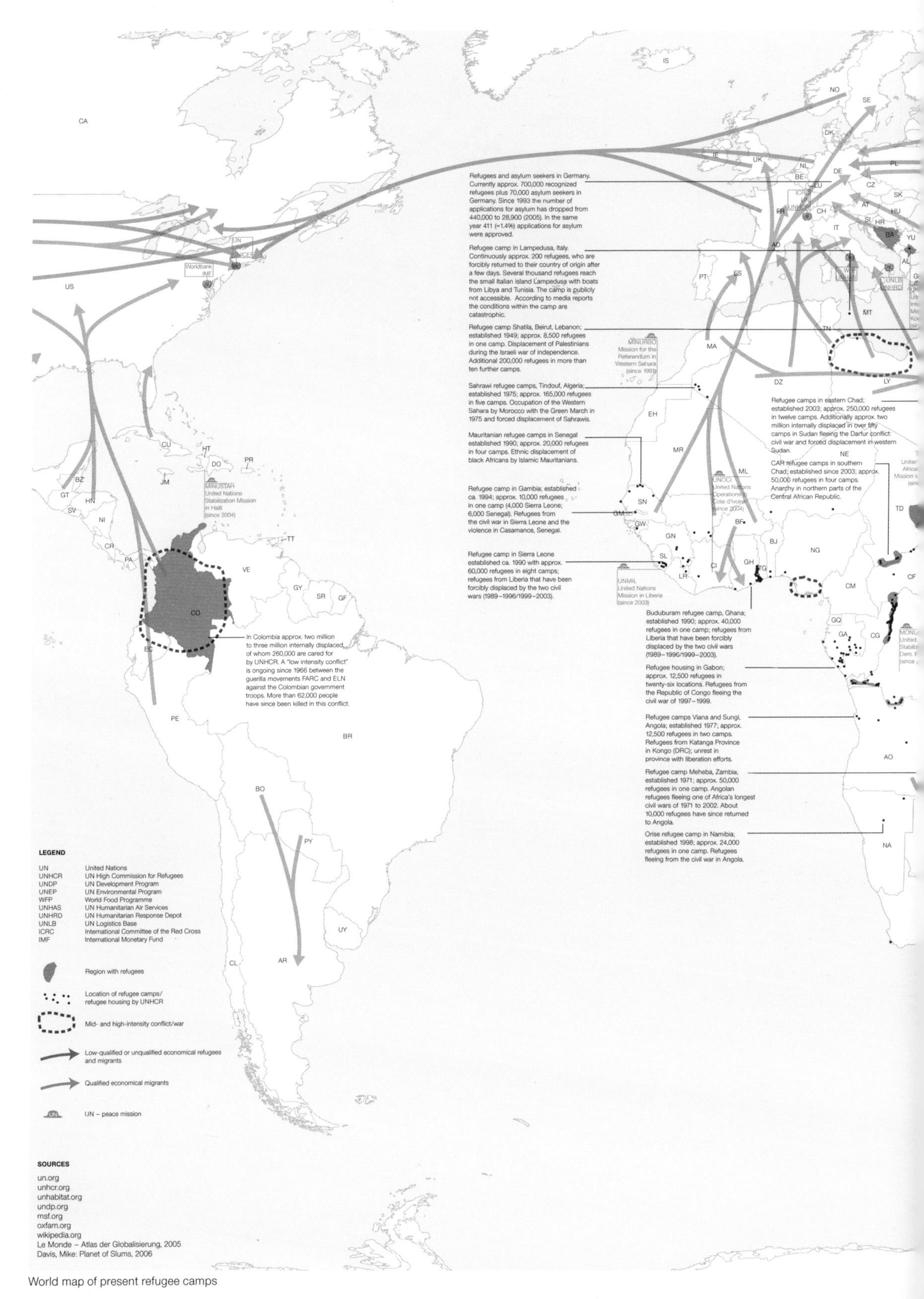


World map of present refugee camps

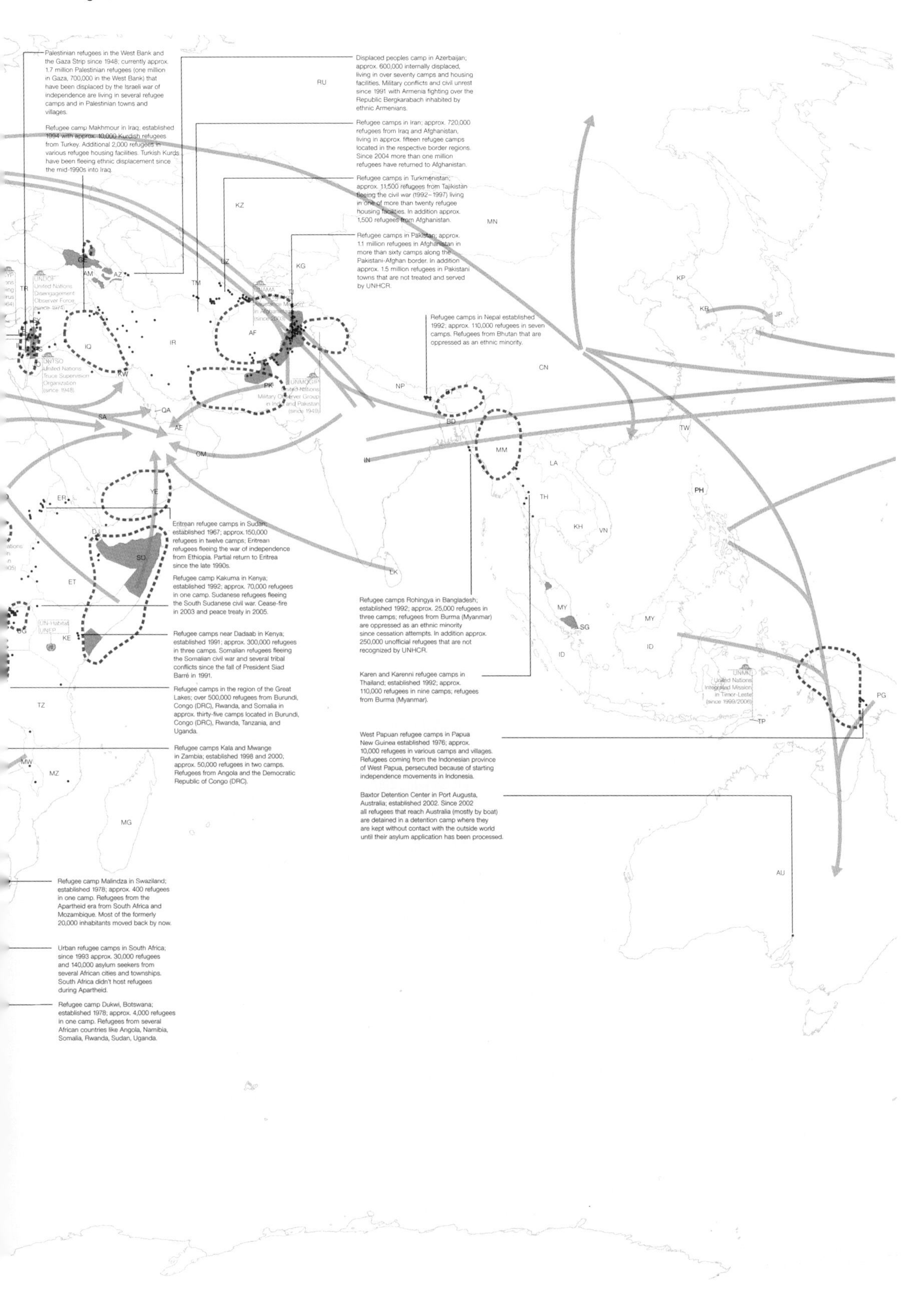
Palestinian refugees in the West Bank and the Gaza Strip since 1948; currently approx. 1.7 million Palestinian refugees (one million in Gaza, 700,000 in the West Bank) that have been displaced by the Israeli war of independence are living in several refugee camps and in Palestinian towns and villages.
Refugee camp Makhmour in Iraq; established 1994 with approx. 10,000 Kurdish refugees from Turkey. Additional 2,000 refugees in various refugee housing facilities. Turkish Kurds have been fleeing ethnic displacement since the mid-1990s into Iraq.
Displaced peoples camp in Azerbaijan; approx. 600,000 internally displaced, living in over seventy camps and housing facilities. Military conflicts and civil unrest since 1991 with Armenia fighting over the Republic Bergkarabach inhabited by ethnic Armenians.
Refugee camps in Iran; approx. 720,000 refugees from Iraq and Afghanistan, living in approx. fifteen refugee camps located in the respective border regions. Since 2004 more than one million refugees have returned to Afghanistan.
Refugee camps in Turkmenistan; approx. 11,500 refugees from Tajikistan fleeing the civil war (1992–1997) living in one of more than twenty refugee housing facilities. In addition approx. 1,500 refugees from Afghanistan.
Refugee camps in Pakistan; approx. 1.1 million refugees in Afghanistan in more than sixty camps along the Pakistani-Afghan border. In addition approx. 1.5 million refugees in Pakistani towns that are not treated and served by UNHCR.
Refugee camps in Nepal established 1992; approx. 110,000 refugees in seven camps. Refugees from Bhutan that are oppressed as an ethnic minority.
UNDOF United Nations Disengagement Observer Force (since 1974)
UNTSO United Nations Truce Supervision Organization (since 1948)
UNMOGIP United Nations Military Observer Group in India and Pakistan (since 1949)
RU
KZ
MN
KG
UZ
TM
TJ
AF
IR
IQ
TR
AM
AZ
KW
SA
QA
AE
OM
YE
PK
NP
BD
IN
LK
CN
KP
KR
JP
TW
MM
LA
TH
KH
VN
PH
MY
SG
ID
PG
TP
AU
ER
DJ
SO
ET
KE
TZ
MW
MZ
MG
UN-Habitat UNEP
Eritrean refugee camps in Sudan; established 1967; approx. 150,000 refugees in twelve camps; Eritrean refugees fleeing the war of independence from Ethiopia. Partial return to Eritrea since the late 1990s.
Refugee camp Kakuma in Kenya; established 1992; approx. 70,000 refugees in one camp. Sudanese refugees fleeing the South Sudanese civil war. Cease-fire in 2003 and peace treaty in 2005.
Refugee camps near Dadaab in Kenya; established 1991; approx. 300,000 refugees in three camps. Somalian refugees fleeing the Somalian civil war and several tribal conflicts since the fall of President Siad Barré in 1991.
Refugee camps in the region of the Great Lakes; over 500,000 refugees from Burundi, Congo (DRC), Rwanda, and Somalia in approx. thirty-five camps located in Burundi, Congo (DRC), Rwanda, Tanzania, and Uganda.
Refugee camps Kala and Mwange in Zambia; established 1998 and 2000; approx. 50,000 refugees in two camps. Refugees from Angola and the Democratic Republic of Congo (DRC).
Refugee camps Rohingya in Bangladesh; established 1992; approx. 25,000 refugees in three camps; refugees from Burma (Myanmar) are oppressed as an ethnic minority since cessation attempts. In addition approx. 250,000 unofficial refugees that are not recognized by UNHCR.
Karen and Karenni refugee camps in Thailand; established 1992; approx. 110,000 refugees in nine camps; refugees from Burma (Myanmar).
UNMIT United Nations Integrated Mission in Timor-Leste (since 1999/2006)
West Papuan refugee camps in Papua New Guinea established 1976; approx. 10,000 refugees in various camps and villages. Refugees coming from the Indonesian province of West Papua, persecuted because of starting independence movements in Indonesia.
Baxtor Detention Center in Port Augusta, Australia; established 2002. Since 2002 all refugees that reach Australia (mostly by boat) are detained in a detention camp where they are kept without contact with the outside world until their asylum application has been processed.
Refugee camp Malindza in Swaziland; established 1978; approx. 400 refugees in one camp. Refugees from the Apartheid era from South Africa and Mozambique. Most of the formerly 20,000 inhabitants moved back by now.
Urban refugee camps in South Africa; since 1993 approx. 30,000 refugees and 140,000 asylum seekers from several African cities and townships. South Africa didn't host refugees during Apartheid.
Refugee camp Dukwi, Botswana; established 1978; approx. 4,000 refugees in one camp. Refugees from several African countries like Angola, Namibia, Somalia, Rwanda, Sudan, Uganda.

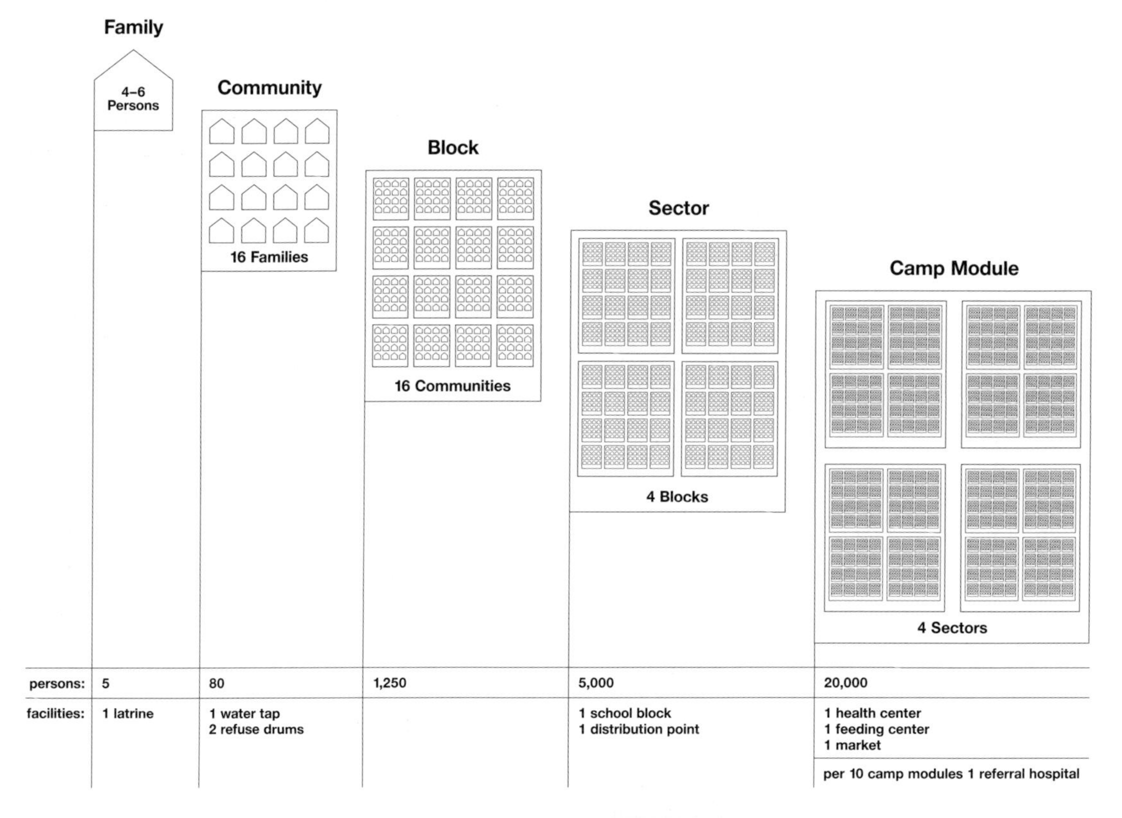


| | Family | Community | Block | Sector | Camp Module |
|---|---|---|---|---|---|
| persons: | 5 | 80 | 1,250 | 5,000 | 20,000 |
| facilities: | 1 latrine | 1 water tap<br>2 refuse drums | | 1 school block<br>1 distribution point | 1 health center<br>1 feeding center<br>1 market |
| | | | | | per 10 camp modules 1 referral hospital |

## UNHCR Handbook for Emergencies

The *UNHCR Handbook for Emergencies* is the main guideline for responding to refugee situations. It deals with questions of organization, resource management, and registration, among others. One chapter within the 600-page book, called Site Selection, Planning and Shelter, deals with the planning and construction of refugee camps. Most of the several hundred UNHCR-run refugee camps that currently exist in the world, whether in the central African savanna, the Pakistani highlands, or the thick forests of northern Thailand, can be traced back to these twenty pages.

The main principle of these planning guidelines is its modularity. Starting from the smallest unit of the refugee family, with an average of four to six members, the guidelines structure the camp into a community, a camp block, a sector, and the complete camp, which "ideally" houses 20,000 refugees. Each scale is related to certain service installations, such as latrines, water taps, schools, markets, or health centers. Another key element of planning is the concept of hygiene. Camp blocks are separated from each other to prevent fire or diseases from spreading. The location of wells and water fountains, slaughtering places, and graveyards is of strategic importance. In this way a highly modular, hierarchical and almost modernistic planning principle emerges.

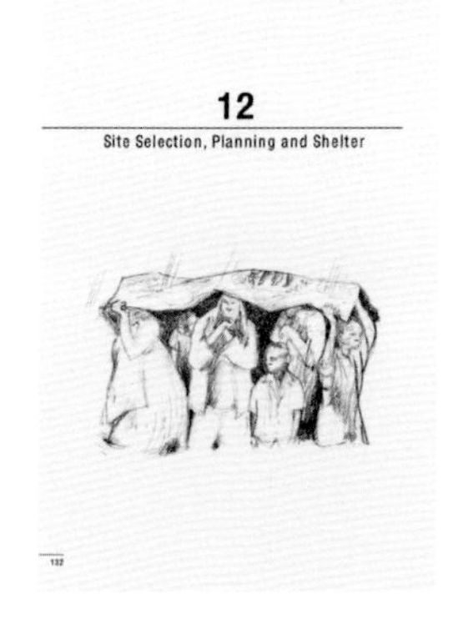

■ CONTENTS

| | Paragraph | Page |
|---|---|---|
| Overview | | |
| Introduction | 1-14 | 135-136 |
| Dispersed Settlement<br>Mass Shelter<br>Camps | | |
| Organization of Response | 15-21 | 136-137 |
| Introduction<br>Contingency Planning<br>Information for Site Selection and Planning<br>Expertise and Personnel | | |
| Criteria for Site Selection | 22-37 | 137-139 |
| Introduction<br>Water Supply<br>Size of Camp Sites<br>Land Use and Land Rights<br>Security and Protection<br>Topography, Drainage and Soil Conditions<br>Accessibility<br>Climatic Conditions and Local Health and Other Risks<br>Vegetation<br>Site Selection Methodology | | |
| Site Planning: General Considerations | 38-59 | 139-142 |
| Introduction<br>Master Plan<br>Services and Infrastructure<br>Modular Planning<br>Environmental Considerations<br>Gender Considerations | | |
| Site Planning: Specific Infrastructure | 60-70 | 142-144 |
| Sanitation<br>Water Supply<br>Roads<br>Fire Prevention<br>Administrative and Communal Services | | |
| Shelter | 71-87 | 144-146 |
| Introduction<br>Type of Shelter<br>Standards<br>Plastic Sheeting<br>Tents<br>Prefabricated Shelters<br>Shelter for Cold Conditions | | |
| Reception and Transit Camps | 88-93 | 146 |
| Public Buildings and Communal Facilities | 94-98 | 147 |

12 Site Selection, Planning and Shelter

133

Plan for camp Amboko in southern Chad. The original plan for the camp of 2003 was altered for an extension in 2006

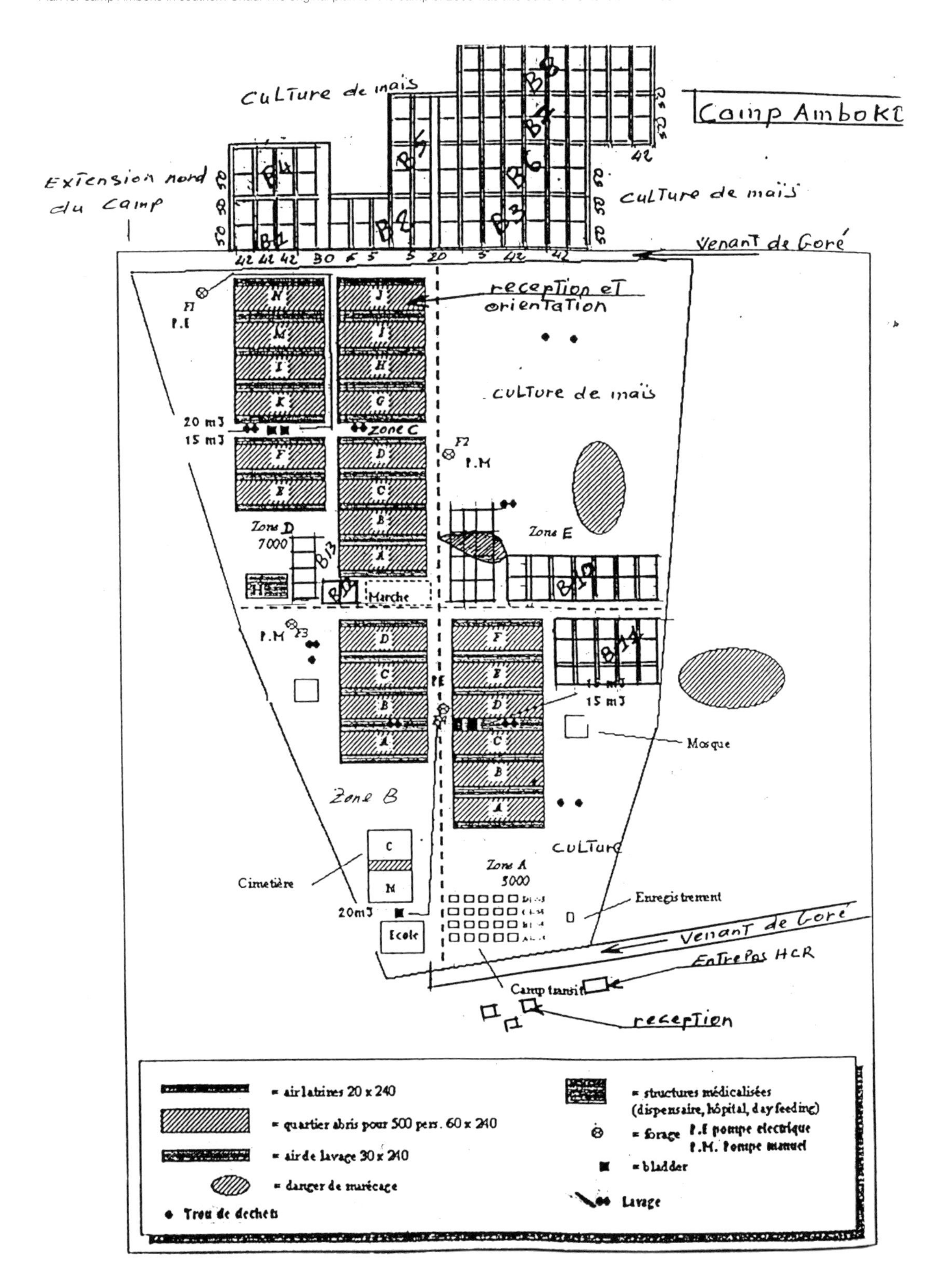

# Case Studies of Refugee Camps

While most of the several hundred UNHCR-run refugee camps can be traced back to the planning regulations laid out in the *Handbook for Emergencies,* a relatively large range of conditions emerges when looking at case studies of refugee camps in history and in the contemporary world. The gridded layout seems to be the constant among virtually all refugee camps, however. It expresses the balance, and sometimes the thin line, between the specific local condition arising from climate, topography, terrain, culture, and tradition, as well as the availability of resources on the one hand, and the need for efficiency and rapid response on the other hand. Beyond that, the grid can also be seen as a psychological expression of the desire for order and stability at a time of turmoil and insecurity.

The historical examples on the following pages show how the typology of the refugee camp has changed very little over time. Similar grids and modules seem to have been the main elements of the planning principles at the beginning of the twentieth century, as they are a hundred years later. Also, at that time, ideas of improving the well-being of refugees, providing better health conditions or personal security were actively and consciously debated. What the examples also show is how a refugee camp can be the seed for future urbanization. A site, sometimes chosen just by chance and settled by refugees with the intention of soon returning to their home country, often becomes permanent over time, developing into the neighborhoods of an adjacent city, or into a town in its own right. Bourj Hammoud and Anjar in Lebanon, and Mitterndorf in Austria are impressive examples of this phenomenon, where the original layout of the refugee camp is still clearly visible in today's street layout. They also give testimony to the fact that, once established, roads and paths—even if only for organizing tents on the ground—are one of the most stable elements in any process of urbanization.

The contemporary examples document a range of different geographical and climatic conditions. While Beldangi camp lies in a heavily forested area in a low-lying valley of Nepal, Ifo camp near Dadaab in eastern Kenya is characterized by its dry savanna environment. The camp Gihembe, which houses Ugandan refugees, is located at an altitude of 2,200 m in the highlands of Rwanda, its layout clearly shaped by the mountainous topography, while the camp Ouré Cassoni represents an almost ideal manifestation of the gridded layout in the desert landscape of eastern Chad. Most of these camps house refugees from conflicts that have not abated, with the refugees unwilling to return home or be resettled. All of these camps might be in the early stages of a city yet to come.

New extension to Ifo camp near Dadaab, Kenya in 2011

**Norval's Point, South Africa (1901)**

The "concentration camp" at Norval's Point was established towards the end of the Second Boer War (1899–1902), when the British empire was fighting the Afrikaans-speaking Dutch settlers. The war was won by the British, who then incorporated the Boer republics into their Union of South Africa, a dominion of the British Empire.

The camp was established in early 1901, housing prisoners of war as well as refugees trying to escape the general violence of the conflict. During mid-1901 it was inhabited by in excess of 3,000 refugees and prisoners. The conditions within the camp were problematic, with more than fifteen percent of the population dying of a measles epidemic and typhoid fever.

The camp is located in the Eastern Cape province. The region has since become a tourist destination famed for its natural beauty and historical setting.

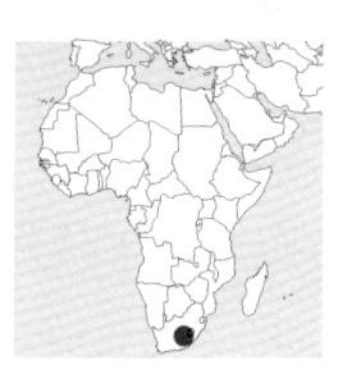

**Mitterndorf, Austria (1915)**

The Kaiserlich-Königliche Barackenlager (Imperial and Royal Baracks-Camp) of Mitterndorf, approximately 20 km south of Vienna, was built in the year 1915 as a temporary home for refugees from Italy during World War I. It consisted of over 440 wooden barracks on a site of approximately 0.6 km$^2$. The camp was home to around 17,000 refugees. In addition to residential barracks housing between thirty-five to a hundred people, the camp consisted of further barracks for schools, hospitals, and administrative buildings. Other functions provided included a church, a pharmacy, an open swimming pool, a post office, and a cinema.

In spite of these facilities, the living conditions were problematic, with approximately twenty percent of the camp population dying in the three years of its existence. At the end of the war the refugees were sent home. Nevertheless, some had settled permanently in the camp, so thirty barracks were left standing. Today the main street running through Mitterndorf still carries the name Lagerstrasse (Camp Street) and is a remnant of the original layout of the camp.

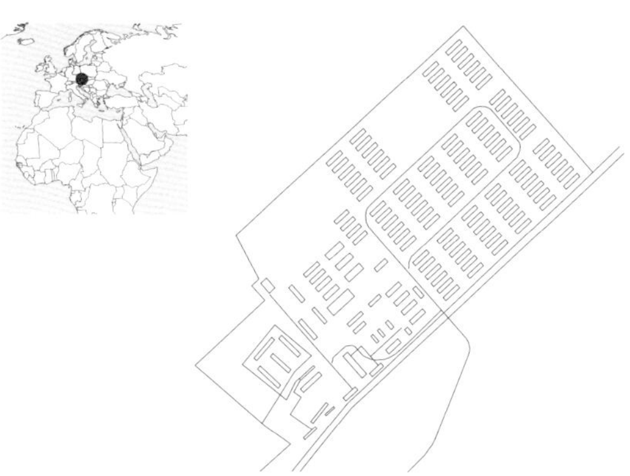

**Bourj Hammoud, Lebanon (1929)**
Escaping the Armenian genocide (1915–1923), Armenians started to arrive in Lebanon and Syria in the late 1910s. They settled in the coastal cities of Tripoli, Saida, and Beirut, as well as establishing camps in the interior of the country. The newly arrived refugees lived in miserable conditions for almost ten years in two major camps in northern Beirut. In the late 1920s, a major effort was started by the French Mandate government of Lebanon, the League of Nations, and the Armenians themselves to find a permanent solution for settling in Beirut. Bourj Hammoud, the area chosen in 1929, is located just east of the Beirut River, an area that at that time consisted of swamps and marshy lands.

Initially, Bourj Hammoud was made up of individual camps–Nor Marach, Camp Sandjak, Nor Sis, and Gulabachène–each featuring a grid layout, though each with a slightly different orientation. Over time, the individual camps grew and merged together. In the early stages the Armenian refugees lived in wooden huts, but the buildings were eventually replaced by single-story brick buildings, with additional floors being added later. Today Bourj Hammoud is part of the greater Beirut municipality. The tightly gridded street network has remained, and the original camps can still be discerned by the different orientations of the grids. It is inhabited predominantly by Armenians, with an intense street life playing out in between the buildings.

## Westerbork, Netherlands (1939)

Westerbork was built in 1939 to house Jewish refugees fleeing from Nazi Germany. The Dutch government had planned to build an exemplary refugee camp, providing all the necessary features for giving comfort to the refugees. The planners had previously traveled to England to gain experience in the modern standards of camp planning. Westerbork, located at a distance from the nearest town, in an isolated part of the country, was modeled on a small village, featuring a library, a school, a hospital, sport facilities, and even a synagogue. The refugees were to feel as comfortable as possible. Westerbork was a testament to the Dutch government's humanist leanings.

The camp only operated a single year as a refugee camp for Jewish refugees. In 1940 the Germans invaded the Netherlands, and by 1942 the camp was operated by the SS. What had started off being an ideal camp, giving refuge and protection to fleeing Jews, was turned into a prison camp from which the same Jews were sent to the concentration camps of Bergen-Belsen and the gas chambers of Auschwitz. In 1970 the camp was partially destroyed and a radio telescope was built on the site.

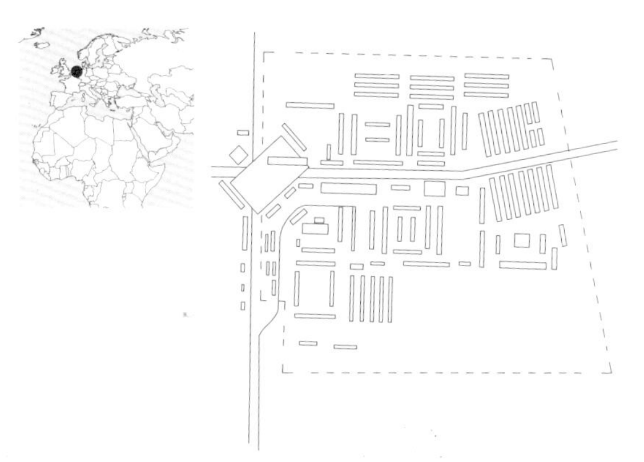

**Anjar, Lebanon (1939)**

Anjar was founded in 1939 to resettle Armenian refugees who had fled the Armenian genocide. Having previously lived in problematic conditions dispersed throughout the Beqaa Valley of Lebanon, the city was founded as a permanent settlement. It was understood that a return to Armenia was no longer possible.

The settlement was designed by an Armenian engineer and features the shape of a bird, with its six quarters named after the six villages of Musa Dagh, a famous and celebrated site of Armenian resistance during the genocide.

Overlapping one of the neighborhoods is the Umayyad stronghold Gerrha, which was built during the eighth century. The early medieval military camp features a perfectly square shape with a gridded internal layout. Thus, by historical coincidence, two different manifestations of the camp, built more than a thousand years apart, coincide at the same geographical location.

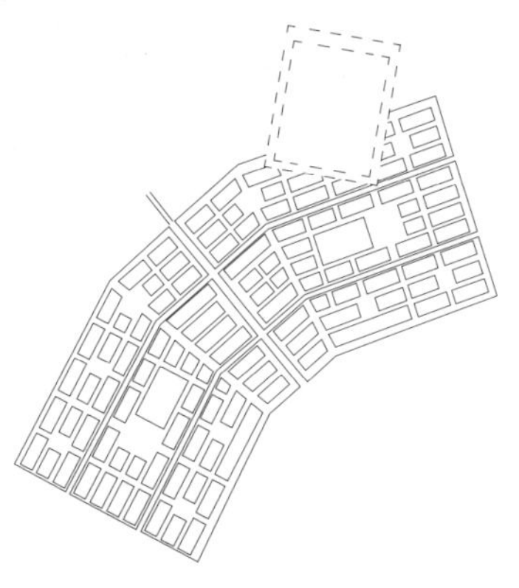

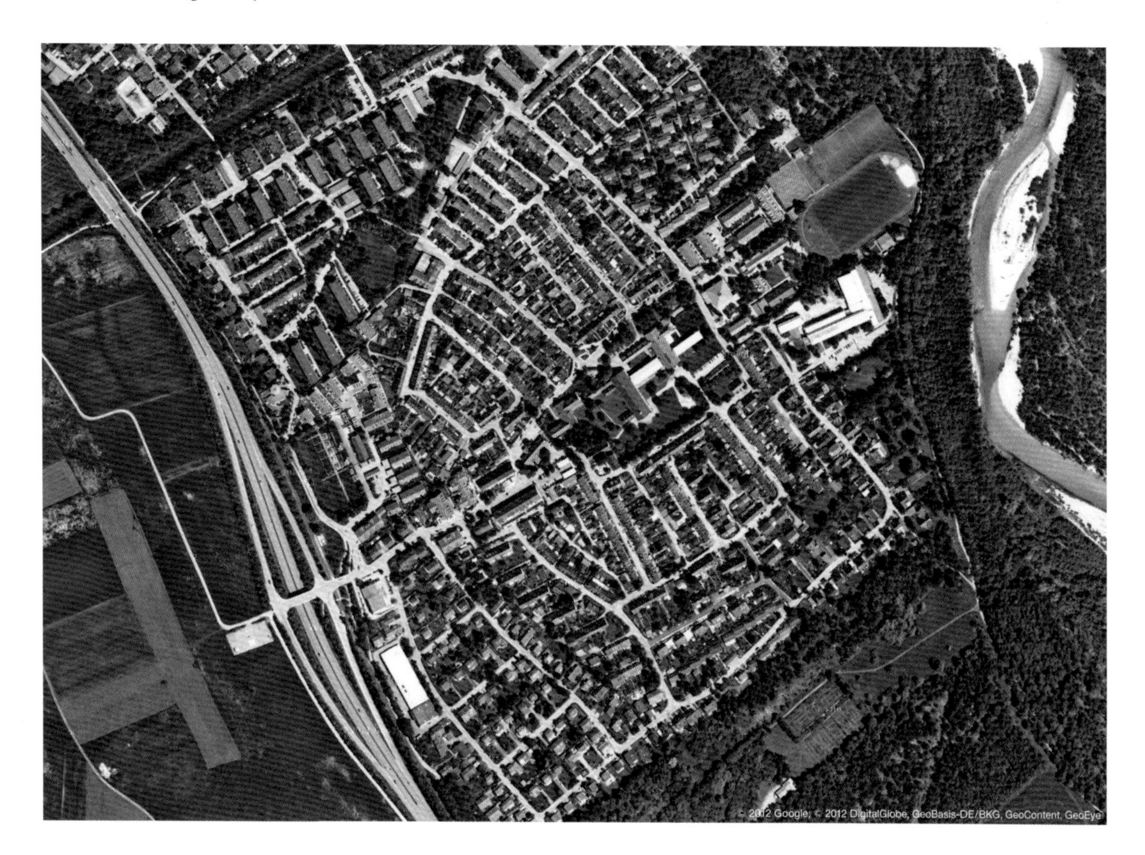


## Föhrenwald, Germany (1945)

Camp Föhrenwald operated as a displaced persons (DP) camp at the end of World War II. It became a temporary home, mostly to Jews waiting for resettlement in other countries. These Jews were not willing to live in Germany any longer, having experienced the Holocaust. The camp consisted mainly of solid houses that had belonged to Germans before the war. Having been abandoned, the US Army used the infrastructure to establish the DP camp. The living conditions were said to be better than other DP camps.

After the foundation of the State of Israel, many of the Jewish residents of the camp immigrated there in the late 1940s and early 1950s. The camp was supposed to close, but some of the families and older people decided to stay. In 1951 the camp was handed over to German administration by the US Army. It continued operating as a camp until 1957. Today the camp has become a part of the town of Wolfratshausen.

© 2012 Google; © 2012 DigitalGlobe, GeoEye

### Coopers Camp, India (1947)

Coopers Camp was established in 1947 to house refugees that were fleeing East Bengal (today's Bangladesh) during the partition war in the wake of India's independence. Intended to be only a temporary shelter for refugees waiting to be resettled permanently in the newly established sovereign India, the camp has remained in operation ever since. At sixty-five years old it is one of the longest-established refugee camps in the world. Some of the refugees–Hindus who fled from Muslim East Bengal with the hope for a new life–have remained stateless and in a bureaucratic limbo ever since.

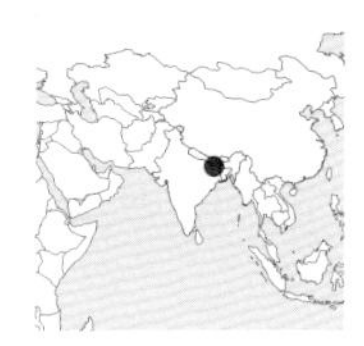

## Djebabra, Algeria (1954)

Camp Djebabra in the northern Algerian province of Chelif was founded by the French colonial power in the wake of the Algerian independence war. It was meant to house Algerians in an attempt to relocate and resettle large parts of the civilian population. Camp Djebabra was just one of several hundred camps built by the French. The underlying intention of building these militarily surveilled *centres de regroupement* was to break the population's resistance and isolate guerrilla fighters.

The camps were analyzed and described by the French sociologist Pierre Bourdieu in the late 1950s and early 1960s. Looking at the morphological and cultural transformations effected by displacement in the camps in Ain-Aghbel, Kerkera, and Djebabra, Bourdieu states that the overall movement of more than two million people is among the most brutal in history and has to be seen as "a pathological answer on the deadly crisis of the colonial system."

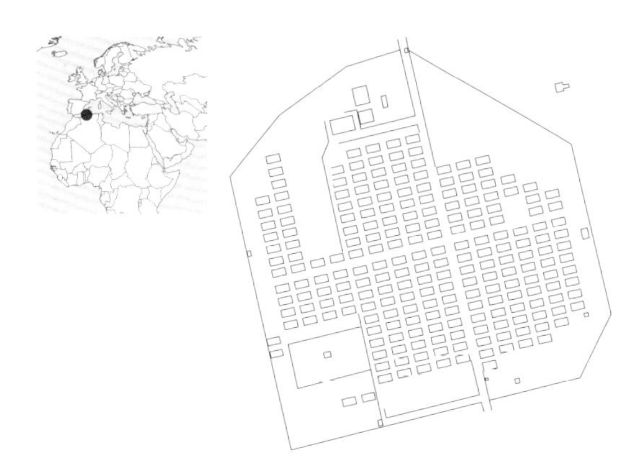

Refugee camp Farchana in Chad

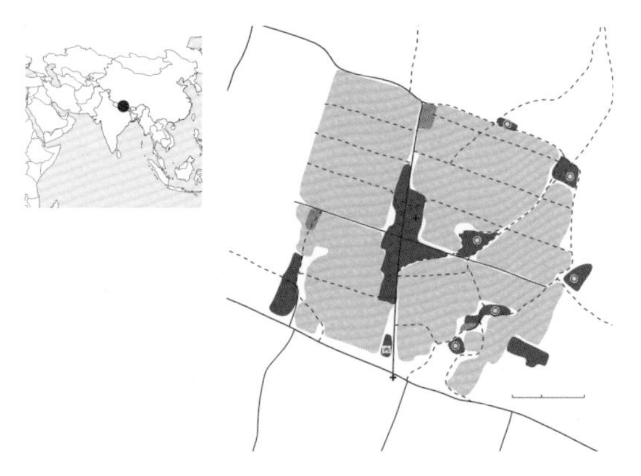

**Beldangi II Camp, Nepal (1991)**
After the revolution in 1989, the Bhutanese government evicted thousands of settlers with Nepali ethnicity, forcing them to move out of their country of residence to Nepal, where they were given refuge.

The camp's nine sectors are divided into four units each. The refugees live in thatched huts built in rows. In total, 3,604 huts were counted in the year 2006. The camp offers two secondary-level schools.

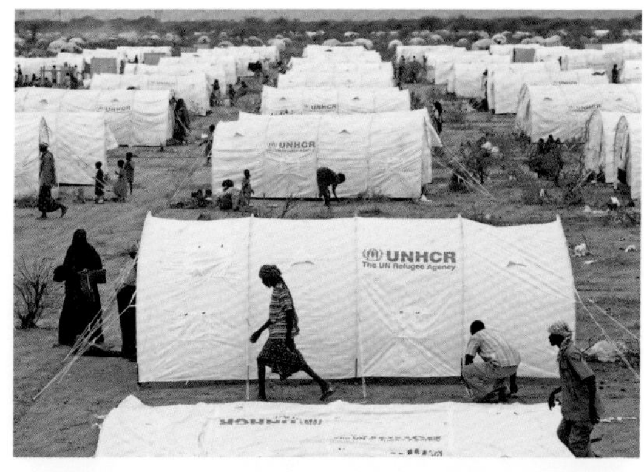

**Ifo Camp, Dadaab, Kenya (1991)**
The three camps around Dadaab (Ifo, Dagahaley, and Hagadera) in eastern Kenya are home to approximately 300,000 refugees. Most of them are fleeing from the ongoing civil war in Somalia, although there are also refugees from Uganda, Sudan, and the Democratic Republic of Congo. The camps were initially planned for 90,000 inhabitants, but have been expanded numerous times. There is a constant influx of people seeking refuge in Kenya.

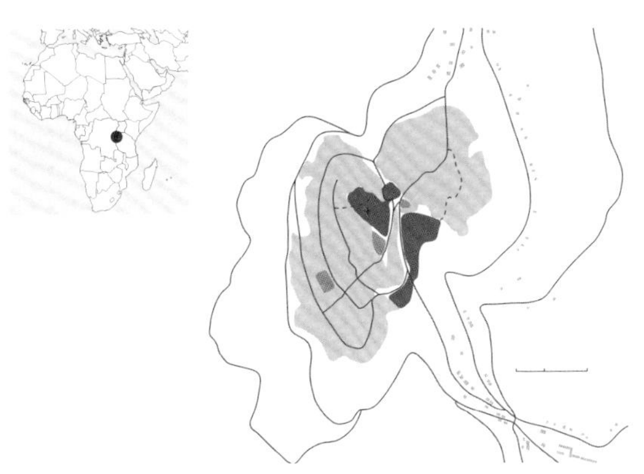

**Gihembe Camp, Rwanda (1997)**

Gihembe refugee camp is home to more than 20,000 refugees from the Democratic Republic of Congo, who have been fleeing the regional wars of eastern Congo. The camp, which is run and administered by UNHCR, consists of twelve villages housing mostly women and children. Due to the ongoing violence in eastern Congo, the refugees have not been able to return home.

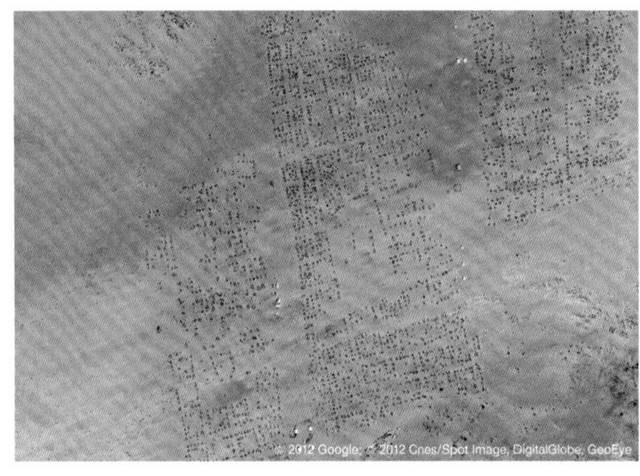


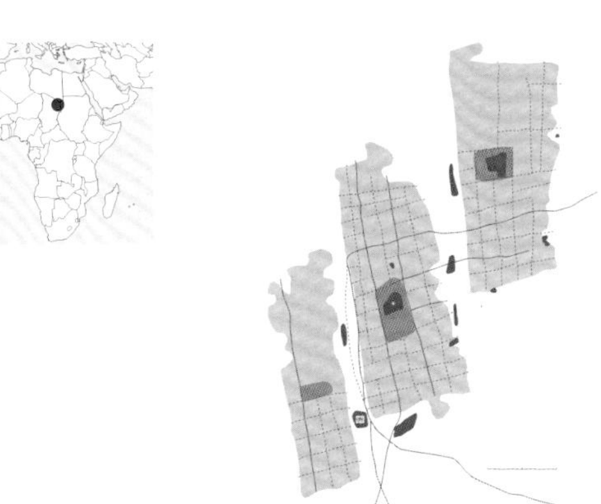

**Ouré Cassoni Camp, Chad (2004)**

Ouré Cassoni is one of twelve refugee camps altogether housing approximately 250,000 Sudanese refugees from Darfur in the eastern region of Chad. Located in the desert landscape only 5 km from the Sudanese border, it consists of three sectors all arranged in a nearly perfect grid layout, home to 30,000 refugees. Established by UNHCR in 2004, the refugees are provided with water, food, shelter, schooling, and medical aid by Médecins Sans Frontières (MSF), International Rescue Committee (IRC), and Oxfam, among others.

Refugee camp El Aaiún

# A BRIEF HISTORY OF THE WESTERN SAHARA

Wall painting in the Nacional de la Resistencia museum in camp Rabouni

The Sahrawi people can be traced back to the Berbers, who migrated to the territory of today's Western Sahara during the first millennium. Subsequent waves of migration led to Arabization of the area during the seventh and eighth centuries, as well as the introduction of Islam. Spain had held an intermittent presence along the coastline of the territory since the sixteenth century, but with the Berlin Conference of 1884, it formalized its claim over the land and established the Spanish Sahara. Contact with the local Sahrawi population was limited and mostly characterized by mutual fear and animosity. Financially, the Spanish Sahara only proved viable to the colonizer during the last few years of the occupation, when Spain started excavating the phosphate mines of Bou Craa. By that time, a strong independence movement had already formed, aiming to liberate the territory from colonial power. Muhammad Bassiri, El-Ouali Mustapha Sayed, and Mohamed Abdelaziz (right to left) were the first leaders—with the first two also some of the first martyrs—of this independence movement that went on to shape a national consciousness. As depicted by a wall mural by Sahrawi artist Fadili Yeslem in the refugee camps' museum, the Spanish withdrawal on the eve of Franco's rule led only to the occupation of the territory by Mauritania and Morocco, the establishment of the refugee camps in southern Algeria, and an ensuing guerilla war that only ended in 1990 with the signing of an armistice.

# The World's Last Colony

*The World in 1945* map was published by the cartography section of the United Nations Department of Peace-keeping Operations and shows the status of the world's countries just after World War II with a wide array of colors. Independent and self-governing nations are colored in yellow and blue, with the latter representing the founding countries of the United Nations. Red, purple, and different shades of green are used to denote different relationships of dependency to the sovereign nations. Thus, the colorful and confetti-like map depicts the colonial world order that governed global politics during the mid-twentieth century. *The World Today,* a map representing the same kind of relationships for today's times, has turned almost entirely blue: virtually every country is sovereign and a member state of the United Nations. Only one single red spot, indicating a non-sovereign nation, remains in the very center of the map. With the exception of a few islands in the Atlantic and Pacific Ocean, the Western Sahara is the only non-self-governing country in the world. It is the world's last remaining colony.

The following pages give a brief account of the history of the territory that makes up today's Western Sahara. Moving from the precolonial era to the colonial period, it depicts the transformation process and the relationship with its region as well as with Europe, finally examining the events of the conflict with Morocco and Mauritania that led to the establishment of the refugee camps and ended with the cease-fire agreement and political stalemate between the warring factions.

*The World in 1945* and *The World Today*, by the UN Cartography Department

# THE WORLD IN 1945

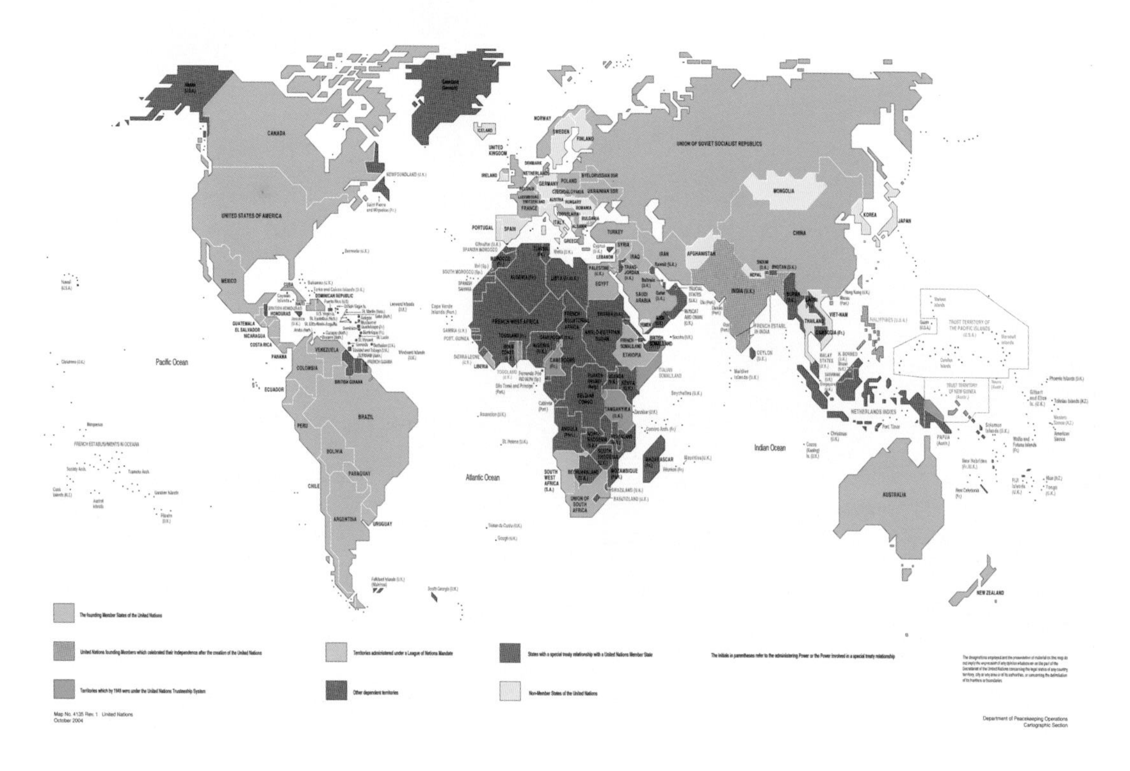


# THE WORLD TODAY

# The Precolonial Period

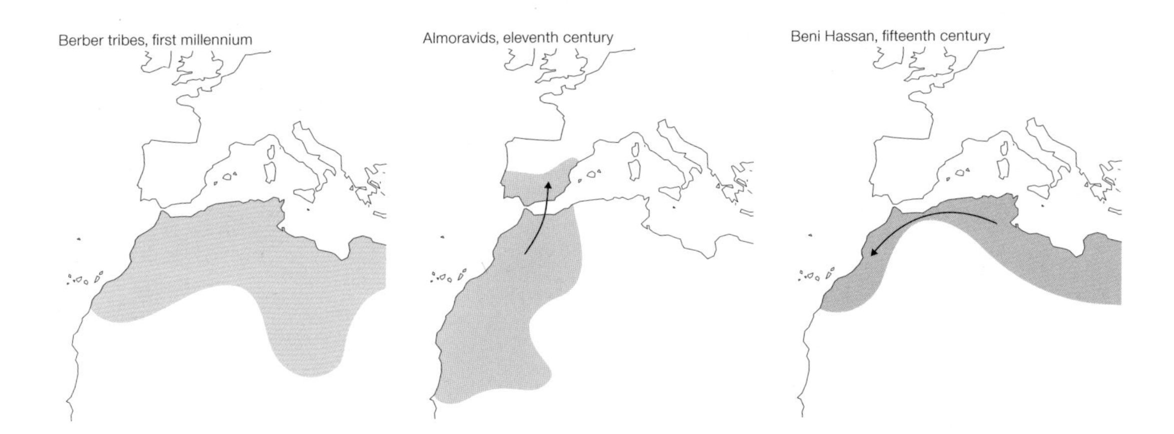


**Berber Tribes and Arabization**
The first settlement by Berbers in the geographical region of the contemporary Western Sahara was around 1000 BC. With the introduction of the camel, the territory obtained economic importance. From 50 to 700 AD, the Sanhaja Berbers, one of the largest Berber tribal confederations of the Maghreb, were able to control the trans-Saharan trade routes in the area.

The first Arab expeditions reached the Maghreb in the seventh and eighth centuries, and introduced Islam. Between 1040 and 1147, the Almoravids, a Muslim Berber dynasty, conquered large parts of North Africa. Their empire stretched from today's Mauritania to Spain, and during the early twelfth century they were one of the most important powers in North Africa and the Mediterranean.

In the fourteenth century, the Muslim Bedouin tribes of Beni Hassan arrived in the northwest of Africa. These tribes originally came from Yemen to Egypt and moved farther along the northern coast to West Africa. In the following centuries they dominated the Sanhaja Berber tribes and achieved the complete Arabization of the Maghreb.

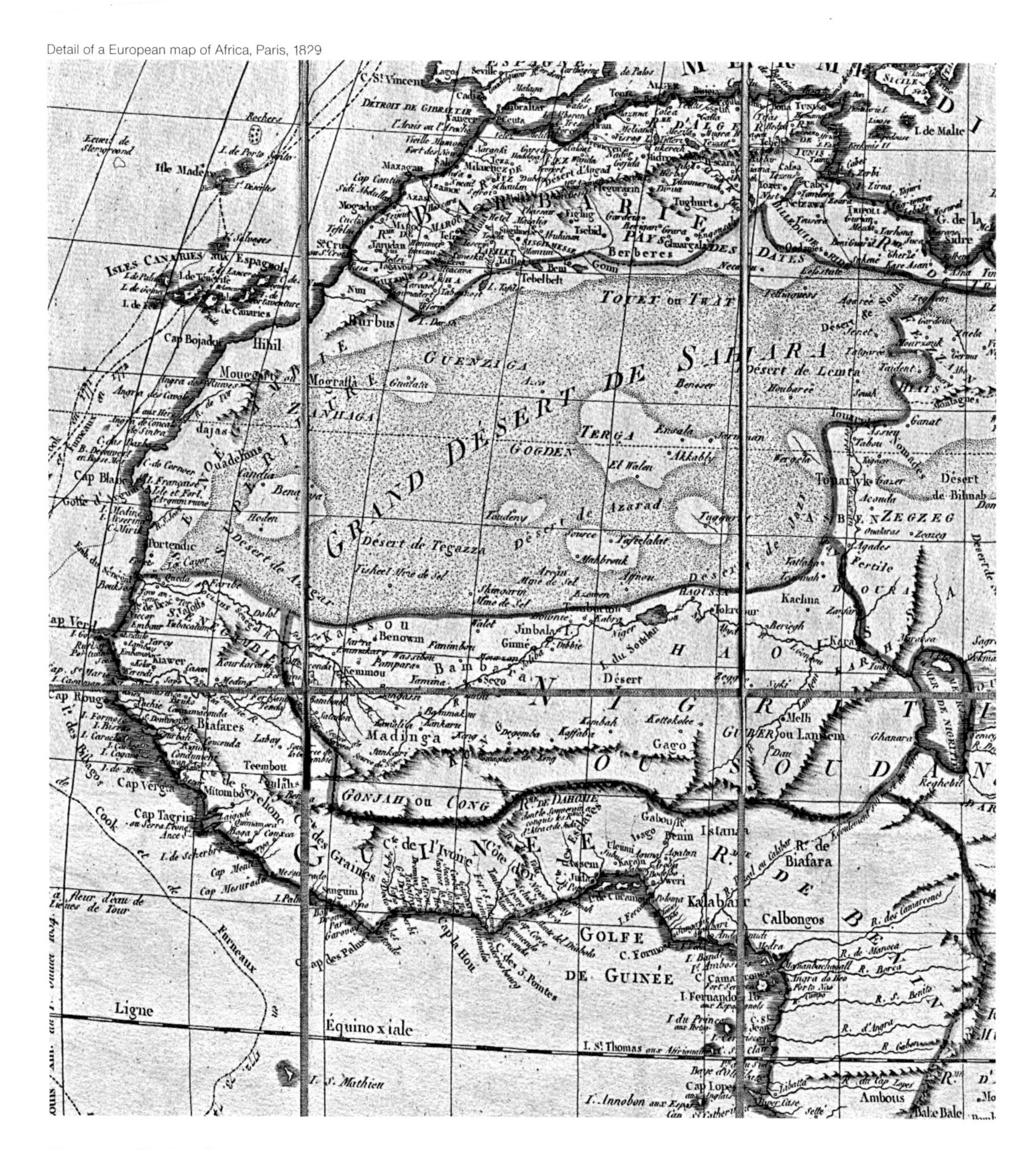


Detail of a European map of Africa, Paris, 1829

### European Exploration

During the fifteenth century, with enhanced navigation techniques, European explorers opened trading routes along the coast of West Africa to the Canary Islands. At the end of the fifteenth century, Spanish fishermen based on the Canary Islands began to fish in the waters off the coast of West Africa.

In 1502, Spanish settlers founded Villa Cisneros, today's Dakhla, as a means of expanding the Spanish empire and establishing the first colonial outposts. Apart from a few small bases along the coast, the mainland was not the focus of European interests until the nineteenth century.

In the middle of the nineteenth century, the Europeans conquered farther areas of the Maghreb. At the same time, Ma al-'Aynayn, an esteemed Islamic scholar, attempted to develop a resistance movement against the European claims. In 1869 he founded Smara as a sacred center of learning, the only major precolonial city in the territory of today's Western Sahara. Ma al-'Aynayn was highly respected in much of the western Maghreb. Today he is still revered by the Moroccans and Sahrawi alike. Both take his name for their own interests.

# The Colonial Period

The Berlin Conference in 1884–1885

Spanish and French territories, 1885

Spanish expedition, 1886

Trading post Villa Cisneros, 1893

**Foundation of Spanish Sahara**

In 1884, Spain proclaimed a protectorate along the coast and set up Villa Cisneros (Dakhla) as a trading post. At the Berlin Conference in 1884–1885, the European powers agreed upon a virtually complete colonization of the African continent. One main principle of this colonization was the concept of a potential exercise of power. For the foundation of colonies, the physical on-site presence of the colonizer was required. With its trading post in Dakhla, Spain met these conditions and was recognized as the official colonial power of the territory, which was hence called Sáhara Español. The colony of the Spanish Sahara was soon surrounded by French colonies. In three secret meetings between 1900 and 1912, the borders of the Spanish Sahara, still valid today, were established.

Spain was partially motivated by the loss of its South American colonies during the first half of the nineteenth century, and the defeat it suffered in the Spanish-American wars (1898–1899) leading to the loss of Cuba, Puerto Rico, and today's Philippines. Spanish interest concentrated on the coastal regions, and trading links with the inner areas of the territory were weak. Organized resistance against Spain was limited to the movement around Ma al-'Aynayn and subsided when he died in 1910. Nevertheless, with the help of French military forces, Spain finally succeeded in controlling the complete territory by 1934.

Unsuccessful search for oil

Trading port and fish industry in Villa Cisneros, 1969

A view of the Bou Craa phosphate mine today

**Economic Interests**

Originally, the economic emphasis for Spain was on the fishing industry. Its attention was therefore focused on the coastal region of the Spanish Sahara. In the early and mid-twentieth century, a search for oil began in parts of the country, as well as in the territorial waters, which has so far proven unsuccessful.

In 1945, Spanish geologist Manuel Alia Medina discovered one of the biggest high-grade phosphate deposits in the world. Spain began to exploit these deposits in the 1950s and 1960s, though on a relatively small scale. In 1972 it started operating the largest open-pit mining facility in Bou Craa, with a 92-km-long conveyor belt connecting the mines to the harbor of El Aaiún. Today Bou Craa is still one of the world's largest phosphate mines, though the conveyor belt proved to be its Achilles heel during the early years of the independence movement against Spanish and later Moroccan occupation.

Sahrawi Berbers

Sahrawis in Villa Cisneros (Dakhla) in the 1950s

Spanish civilians

Tropas Nómadas del Sahara

**Civic Life in Spanish Sahara**

In 1919, just 500 Spaniards lived around the trading post of Villa Cisneros in the Spanish Sahara. Until then, the impact on local people was minimal. The Sahrawis lived in strictly separated areas, and their tribes moved as nomads trough the desert. In 1928, the Spanish founded the city of El Aaiún. The city grew slowly, and in 1963 approximately 8,500 people lived there, two-thirds of whom were Sahrawis. By 1974, the population of El Aaiún had swelled to 38,500.

El Aaiún was by far the largest settlement in the Spanish Sahara. Due to the infrastructure, increasing numbers of Sahrawis settled with their tents around the city and began a partially sedentary life. Many Sahrawis worked for colonial Spain in its administration or in the mines of Bou Craa. From the 1930s onwards, Sahrawis even served as troops in the colonial army, having previously been trained by the Spanish military. During the final years of Spanish occupation, almost 1,400 Sahrawis were enrolled in the Spanish army, most of them in the Tropas Nómadas del Sahara, which, as they were on camelback, were best equipped for security tasks in the desert.

1956 **Morocco** became **independent** of France
1956 First **Sahrawi** tribes called **for independence**
1958 The **Sahrawi** wing of the Liberation Army was **defeated** by military force of Spain
1960 **Mauritania** became **independent** of France
1961 Special Committee on Decolonization was created by General Assembly of the UN
1962 Algeria became independent of France
1963 UN Special Committee on Decolonization declared the Spanish Sahara as a "non-self-governing territory to be decolonized"
1966 The OAU and the UN General Assembly adopted resolutions on the Spanish Sahara calling for independence
1967 New anti-colonial movement against Spain with the **founding** of the **Harakat Tahrir movement for liberation**
1970 Collapse of the **Harakat Tahrir movement** after a **defeated** civil demonstration
1972 Inauguration of the aboveground mining of Bou Craa and the conveyor belt to the coast
1973 **Founding of Polisario Front** by Sahrawi **and first attacks** on Spanish targets
October 17, 1975 Francisco Franco fell into a coma and died on November 20, 1975
November 14, 1975 Spain transferred the administration control to Morocco and Mauritania
December 1975 **Invasion by Morocco** in the north **and Mauritania** in the south
1976 Spain claimed economic interests in fishing rights and in phosphate production
February 26, 1976 **Spain's** official **withdrawal**

Spanish army

Sahrawi demonstration for independence, 1975

## First Independence Movements

The first movements towards independence started in the 1950s and 1960s, when the Movimiento Para la Liberación del Sahara was motivated and supported by the independence movements in neighboring countries. Initially, it was largely based on the actions of individuals rather than a unified and centrally organized resistance movement. Furthermore, a concept of national identity and an independent statehood had not yet been shaped as the movement's final aim.

While the decolonization of Africa started with the independence of Tunisia and Morocco in 1956 and picked up speed during the early 1960s, the Spanish regime in the Western Sahara initially seemed to be unaffected by these movements. General Franco, Spain's dictator ruler, subsequently came under pressure from the UN Assembly and the Special Committee on Decolonization.

As the main Sahrawi independence movement, Polisario was founded in 1972 and started attacks on Spanish civilian and military infrastructures. In addition, pressure from the UN, and Franco's age and failing health eventually led to the decision to withdraw Spanish troops from the territory.

# The Conflict Period

1956 **Morocco** became **independent** of France
1956 Sovereignty **claim by Mauritania**'s Istiqlal Party of the territory and launch of the ideology of Greater Morocco
1957 Sovereignty **claim by Mauritania**'s Moktar Ould Daddah of the territory of the Spanish Sahara
1960 **Mauritania** became **independent** of France
1960 Moktar Ould Daddah became president of Mauritania
1961 Hassan II of Morocco became king
1962 Algeria became independent of France
1963 Moroccan–Algerian border war
1970 Morocco and Mauritania signed a friendship treaty
1972 Inauguration of the aboveground mining of Bou Craa and the conveyor belt to the coast
1973 **Founding of Polisario Front** by Sahrawi **and first attacks** on Spanish targets
November 6, 1975 Launch of the Green March
November 14, 1975 Spain transferred the administration control to Morocco and Mauritania
December 1975 **Invasion by Morocco** in the north **and Mauritania** in the south
February 27, 1976 **Self-proclamation** of the Sahrawi Arab Democratic Republic, or **SADR**
May 1976 The first refugee camps were established near Tindouf, Algeria
1976 Polisario destroyed the conveyor belt of Bou Craa and stopped the exploration of phosphate
1979 The OUA launched a **mediation** initiative for a peaceful solution and truce **with Mauritania**
1979 **Withdrawal** of **Mauritania**
July 16, 1980 The SADR formally applied for membership in the OAU
1980 **Morocco began** the construction of the **sand berms** to protect its conquered territory
1980–1981 First wall
1982 Reinauguration of the Bou Craa conveyor belt, restart of the aboveground mining
1982 SADR was admitted to membership in the OAU, Morocco withdrew from OAU
1982–1984 Second and third Dakhla wall
1985 UN and OAU began to work on the **"Settlement Plan"** for a solution
1985–1986 Fourth and fifth wall
1987–1988 Sixth wall
April 9, 1991 The Security Council established **MINOURSO**
September 6, 1991 **Truce** between **Polisario** and **Morocco**

1955 1960 1965 1970 1975 1980 1985 1990

## Spanish Withdrawal and Invasion

Back in the 1950s and 1960s, Morocco and Mauritania had already expressed their claims over the territory of the Spanish Sahara. Initially they supported the efforts of Sahrawi independence, as ridding the territory from Spanish occupation seemed to be in their own interests.

In November 1975, Spain agreed to withdraw from the territory while at the same time ceding control to Morocco and Mauritania, in clear violation of UN demands. The parties agreed on a division of the territory with a partition line, bisecting the country into a southern part under the control of Mauritania and a larger northern part controlled by Morocco. This agreement guaranteed Spain's continued economic involvement in phosphate production and the fishing industries. During this time the Sahrawi independence movement reached critical momentum and Morocco organized the Green March, with 100,000 Moroccans moving into the territory. This Green March of Moroccan civilians was a symbolic act declaring their claim over the Spanish Sahara.

With the last Spanish soldiers withdrawing from the territory at the end of 1975, the Spanish Sahara was then invaded by Moroccan troops in the north and Mauritanian troops in the south. A large portion of the Sahrawi population (mostly women and children) fled into Algeria, settling in refugee camps, while the men fought a guerilla war. In spite of the ongoing occupation,

Moroccan Green March in November 1975

Polisario declared independence and the foundation of the Sahrawi Arab Democratic Republic (SADR) on February 27, 1976.

Sahrawi troops with heavy artillery

Sahrawi guerrilla

Events during Spanish withdrawal, 1975–1976

Development of the berms, 1980–1988

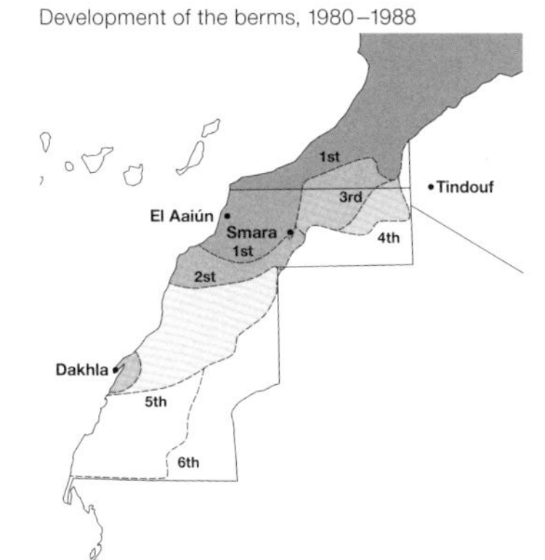


Current situation

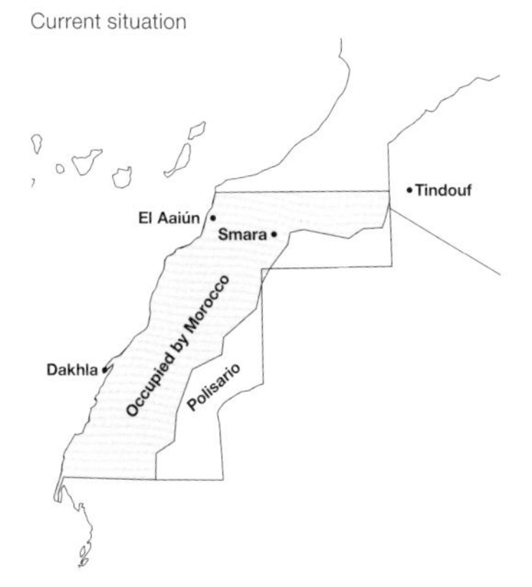


## The Sixteen-Year War

Polisario, having first fought against the Spanish colonial power, now took up the fight against the invading forces of Morocco and Mauritania. With guerrilla tactics they managed to destroy important infrastructures, such as the conveyor belt of the Bou Craa mine in 1976. Continuous attacks against the weak Mauritanian army and a coup in that country led to the withdrawal of Mauritania from the territory of the Western Sahara in 1978–1979.

With the logistical support of Algeria, the Sahrawi were able to achieve countless victories against the numerically superior Moroccan army, even partially invading Moroccan territory. In 1980, Morocco started building a wall through the desert, allowing for better defense of the land they had occupied. First only partitioning off the northwestern part of the country with a succession of berms, the constructions carved ever deeper into the territory of the Western Sahara, allowing civilian occupation of the Moroccan-held areas.

Since 1986, the parties have negotiated on a Settlement Plan, under mediation of the UN and the Organization of African Unity (OAU), aiming for a resolution of the conflict. A truce was established in 1991, calling for a referendum for the future and potential independence of the country.

## Truce and Referendum

The Settlement Plan proposed a referendum for the Sahrawis and inhabitants of the Spanish Sahara to decide whether they choose independence or annexation to Morocco. Ever since agreeing to the referendum in principle, Morocco has continuously delayed its implementation for various reasons. The main point of disagreement is the eligibility of participation, i.e. who is allowed to vote in the referendum. While theoretically still pending, it seems uncertain as to whether the referendum will ever actually be carried out. Since the cease-fire agreement in 1991, no shot has been fired between Polisario and Morocco. The berm is heavily guarded and is accompanied by a 200-km-long mine belt. Besides the refugee camps, Sahrawis also live in the occupied territories as "Moroccans," where their freedom of expression is severely restricted.

## Stalemate

With the signing of the cease-fire agreement, a UN peacekeeping mission, MINURSO, was established and tasked to oversee the armistice and carry out the referendum. Nevertheless, no political developments have been achieved in the past 20 years. The refugees are living in relatively safe circumstances in the camps of southwest Algeria. The fact that the refugees are not suffering and are living in a stable condition means that international pressure to solve the underlying conflict has decreased.

Morocco's berm in March 2011

# PLANNING

The refugee camps of the Western Sahara are a global rarity, in that they were set up without the involvement of UNHCR. Although the Sahrawis had little experience in urban planning or a notion of urbanity in general, the original camps nevertheless followed a standardized layout of rows of tents organized in a grid with services centrally located. Soon after their establishment, the refugees faced questions about how the camps were to be adapted over time to react to the continuous influx of inhabitants. The refugees also had to plan the camps' stabilization and transformation into more permanent structures, even though they were originally only intended to exist temporarily.

This chapter looks at the cities of the Western Sahara before the conflict as case studies of a local urbanization process. It then documents the establishment of the camps, their constituting elements, and modules, as well as their gradual evolution, before finally giving an overview of their current status, size, and location. It concludes with a comparison of other refugee camps, as well as contemporary cities in Algeria and the occupied Western Sahara itself, placing the Sahrawi camps into a regional context.

# Urban Life in the Colonial Era

The flight from the Western Sahara and the subsequent establishment of the Sahrawi refugee camps near Tindouf was an almost overnight transformation in the living conditions of a previously mostly nomadic or semi-nomadic society. The density and proximity that the Sahrawis found themselves in when living in the camps was a dramatic change from the kinds of spaces in which they had resided before and the extent of the territory that was previously accessible to them.

The Sahrawis are often described as a nomadic culture. Nevertheless, a number of cities had been well established in the Spanish Sahara, and the Sahrawis were certainly accustomed to urban life. In fact, according to various accounts, at the time of the Spanish withdrawal, around half of the local population was living in or near cities, or moving between the desert and the outskirts of towns, so thereby exposed to urban conditions. Many Sahrawis had developed a truly urban culture, with Western film, literature, and pop music having a larger impact on their lives than traditional Sahrawi culture. As one Sahrawi growing up in El Aaiún in his twenties remembers: "Young people went to bars and discos; we bought good clothes and smoked Marlboro. We got Ray-Ban glasses. In El Aaiún there was a group of hippies and they were really into Jimi Hendrix."[1]

But for other parts of Sahrawi society, life was still traditional. The importance and influence of the tribal structure was very strong, with few people marrying outside their tribes or clans. The tribe was considered family, which gave rise to a feeling of belonging. It also created a hierarchy of castes that the independence movement worked hard to overcome. The move to the city was one step towards the transformation of a society based on tribes and clans into a society based on the nuclear family. Changing from a nomadic to a semi-sedentary or urban way of life gave increased importance to the smaller family unit, as this was the social and physical context that life hence proceeded.

It was in the cities of the Spanish Sahara in which the struggle against Spanish occupation first arose. Muhammad Bassiri, one of the primary figures in the independence movement, moved to Smara to assemble a group of Sahrawi sympathizers in the first coordinated protest movement against the Spanish. Other major events, such as the Zemla Uprising—where ten Sahrawis were killed by Spanish troops—also took place in cities, in this case in El Aaiún. Even though nomadic culture figures strongly in the imagination and common memory of the Sahrawis, it is in fact the urban dimension, its easy access to information and people, the spread of media, and the possibility of assembling a large number of people that played an important role in the formation of the independence movement and the construction of a new concept of Sahrawi national identity.

1 Quoted in: San Martin, Pablo, *Western Sahara,* p. 55

Settlement El Aaiún, 1974/1975

El Aaiún, 1962

Smara: a corner of the Great Kasbah

Smara from the southwest

## Smara

Smara was founded by the Sahrawi Shaykh Ma al-'Aynayn in 1898.[1] It is the only major urban settlement without a colonial foundation, being established by the Sahrawis themselves. It developed into a trading hub and religious center for the local Sahrawi tribes. Due to the difficulty of its access and its being of Sahrawi foundation, it obtained an almost mythical image. More or less deserted at the beginning of the twentieth century, the local population nevertheless declared it off limits to any Western traveler. The French adventurer Michel Vieuchange describes his painful expedition to Smara in the book *The Forbidden City,* published after he died from an illness contracted during his journey.

Smara was one of the early centers of resistance against colonial infiltration. In 1904, Shaykh Ma al-'Aynayn started a holy war against the French, who were extending their influence into the Sahrawi territories. During the 1920s and early 1930s the city was a base for attacks by Sahrawis on Spanish colonial troops. In a highly symbolic move, the city was taken by Spanish troops in 1934, who subsequently used it to establish the Spanish Sahara's first interior military post.

Similar to Dahkla and El Aaiún, the city became one of the centers for the independence movement against the Spanish colonial power in the late 1960s and early 1970s. It was abandoned by the Spanish in late November 1975,

Mosque of Smara, 1967

Old postcard from Smara, early 1970s

and shortly after by the Sahrawis, who had to flee when Moroccans took the town.

1 1869, according to other sources

Villa Cisneros, 1970

Villa Cisneros

**Villa Cisneros–Colonial Dakhla**

Dakhla, or Villa Cisneros as it was initially called, was the first settlement to be founded by Spain. First established in 1502 by Spanish settlers, it was the base for fishermen and traders taking advantage of the coastal waters, which were rich in fish and seal colonies. After being abandoned for more than 300 years, it was refounded in 1884 when the Spanish claimed rule over the territory of "Spanish Sahara" at the Berlin Conference of the same year, formalizing the colonization of Africa by European nations.

Well into the twentieth century, Villa Cisneros was not much more than a small factory and a few wooden houses. Threatened with constant attack by the local population, Spanish soldiers lived in a permanent state of fear and hardly ever ventured out. Only in the 1930s and 1940s did the colonial army try to take control of the hinterland, leading to an expansion of the settlement.

It wasn't until the 1960s, when Spain transformed its colonial possession into a tax-free zone, acting as a bridge between the Canaries and Western Africa, that development gained momentum. Dakhla became a destination not only for a Spanish civilian population, but also for local Sahrawis giving up their nomadic culture in favor of economic potential in the "city."

El Aaiún

Settlement El Aaiún, 1974/1975

## Colonial El Aaiún

El Aaiún was founded in 1938, and in 1958 it became the capital of the Spanish Sahara. With its increasing importance, more and more people moved to the city, resulting in its rapid expansion. Local Sahrawis mostly lived on the outskirts of the city in barracks or tents, where they also kept livestock. This lifestyle allowed them to take advantage of the city's potential without having to give up their traditional way of living. Life was often semi-nomadic, and the Sahrawis would go back to their relatives and tribes for a several months at a time.

In 1963, the population of El Aaiún was approximately 8,500, of which 5,000 were Sahrawis. In 1974, the population had grown to 38,000, with approximately 10,000 Spanish and 28,000 Sahrawis.

In 1970, the suburb of Zemla was the site of the "Zemla Uprising," when the Spanish killed several Sahrawis at a public demonstration for independence. It is seen as one of the most important events in the formation of the Sahrawi independence movement.

# The Refugee Camps

In October 1975, the Spanish started to withdraw troops and civilians from the Spanish Sahara, while at the same time Moroccan soldiers infiltrated deeper into the country, resulting in clashes and fighting with Polisario units. The Sahrawi population started to flee from the larger cities, along the coast to Guelta Zemmur and Oum Dreyga in the eastern part of the country. After being attacked with napalm bombs by the Moroccan air force, they fled farther, to Al Mahbes in the far northeast, just 40 km from the border of Algeria, and afterwards towards the area around Tindouf. It was only here, approximately 60 km into Algeria, that the Sahrawis felt safe enough to set up camps. According to some sources, the number of refugees arriving in Tindouf rose quickly from 9,000 at the end of 1975 to 60,000 by mid-1976 and more than 100,000 by the end of that same year.[1] It was mostly children, women, and the elderly that settled in the camps, as able-bodied men were fighting the Moroccans.

On one hand, the region of Tindouf was an advantageous choice for the Sahrawi refugees. It was close to the short strip of border that Algeria—by then an ally of Polisario—shared with the Western Sahara. The region has also traditionally been inhabited by Berber tribes who are closely related to the Sahrawis, and by Sahrawis themselves, so therefore by people in support of the independence movement and the war against Morocco. On the other hand, the region's harsh climate presented a tough challenge for the refugees after their long flight through the desert. With temperatures in excess of 50°C but dropping to zero in the cold winter nights, and with virtually no rain at all, the climate of Tindouf is tougher than in the Sahrawi homeland.

Initially, the refugees assembled in a single camp called Rabouni, approximately 20 km south of Tindouf. They lived in tents donated by Algeria, with several families often within one space. During the first year the situation was extremely problematic: with many refugees injured from the war or the flight through the desert, a constant lack of food and clean water, and little protection from the cold of the winter nights and the heat of the summer days. Gradually the situation improved, though at the same time the refugees realized that their stay in Algeria, originally anticipated to last only days or weeks, was not likely to end soon. This went hand in hand with two important transformations. Tents were slowly replaced by clay huts—they were still covered with fabric, but nevertheless represented a first step towards permanence.

As the number of refugees grew, more camps were established, both for reasons of size and also for safety. Fear of attack by Moroccan planes meant that occupying several camps was strategically advantageous to being concentrated in a single location. Over time, the camps of Smara, Dakhla, El Aaiún and Awserd, as well as the school camp of 27 February, were established. Today they are home to approximately 165,000 refugees.

The "residential" camps are named after the largest cities in the Sahrawis' homeland. This constructs a link to the original territory and also helps create a national identity by inscribing the names into a common memory. Whether intentional or not, carrying the names of cities lends the camps an urban dimension.

1 San Martin, *Western Sahara*

The camps in 1975/1976, probably Rabouni

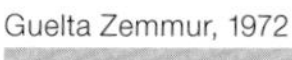
Guelta Zemmur, 1972

**Refuge in Western Sahara**
While the Spanish withdrew from their colony during the fall of 1975, Moroccan units started incursions, bringing them farther and farther into the territory. Following battles with Sahrawi troops, most of the civilian Sahrawi population started to flee towards the east of the country to Guelta Zemmur or Oum Dreyga, setting up camps there. After being attacked by the Moroccan air force in these locations, they then sought refuge in Al Mahbes, located in the northeast of the Western Sahara. From there they continued farther east, crossing the border into Algeria and settling in the region of Tindouf.

Being in Algeria gave the Sahrawis a certain security from air attacks, as Moroccan forces would not dare to attack in Algerian territory without risking a serious international outcry and retaliation by their disliked neighbor. Little did the Sahrawis suspect that this place would become their home, not for days or weeks as initially hoped, but for more than thirty years.

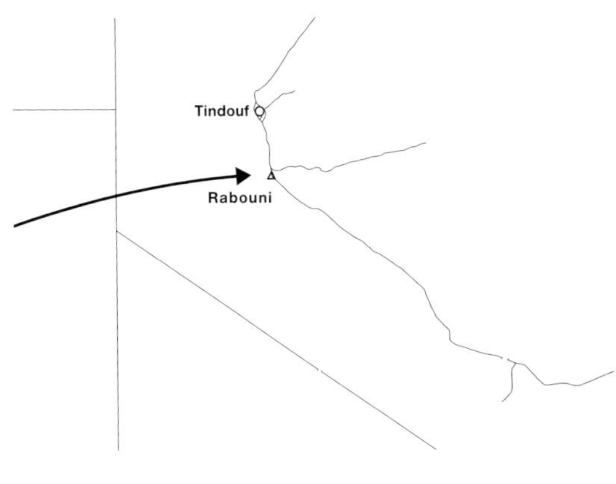


### Rabouni: the First Refugee Camp

Sahrawis initially settled in Rabouni, approximately 20 km south of Tindouf. The location featured a well and water pump that the Algerians had previously installed. As well as the proximity of water, Rabouni was a favorable location, as Algeria had become an ally of the Polisario, and because it was located approximately 50 km from the border, the refugees were relatively safe from Moroccan attacks but still close enough to their homeland.

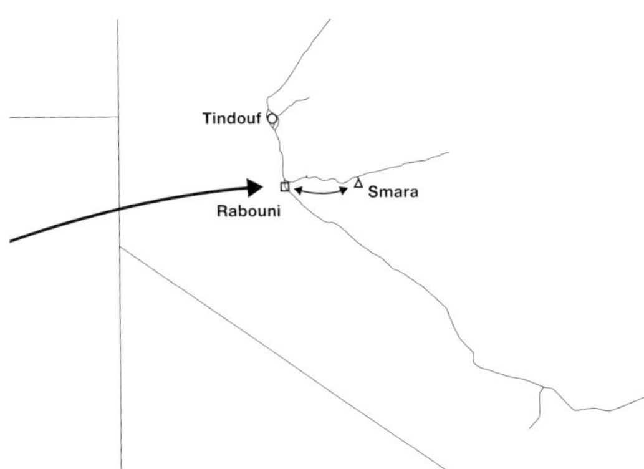


### Smara

Shortly after erecting Rabouni, and with the number of refugees rising rapidly, Polisario established Smara, approximately 30 km to the east. Smara itself has no water source, and water needs to be transported daily from Rabouni by trucks. Initially, Smara was organizationally treated as an extension of Rabouni and not as an independent camp.

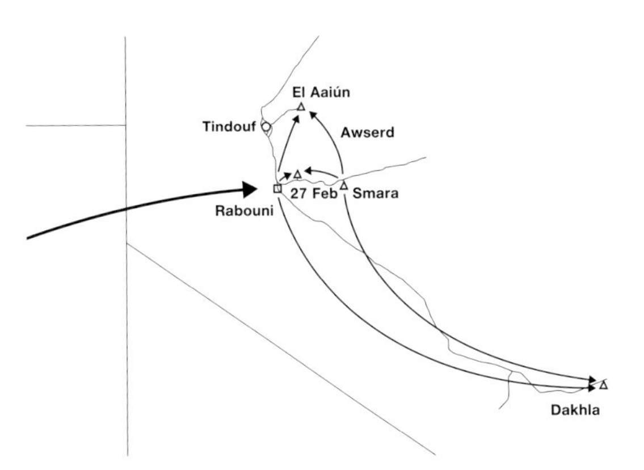


### El Aaiún, Dakhla, and 27 February

With the continuously rising number of refugees, Polisario founded two new camps, El Aaiún and Dakhla, as well as the boarding school of 27 February. The locations of El Aaiún and Dakhla were chosen because of the availability of groundwater close to the surface. Rabouni was transformed into an administration center and lost its residential function. 27 February was founded as a school for women and was initially only inhabited by teachers and families of the women who attended.

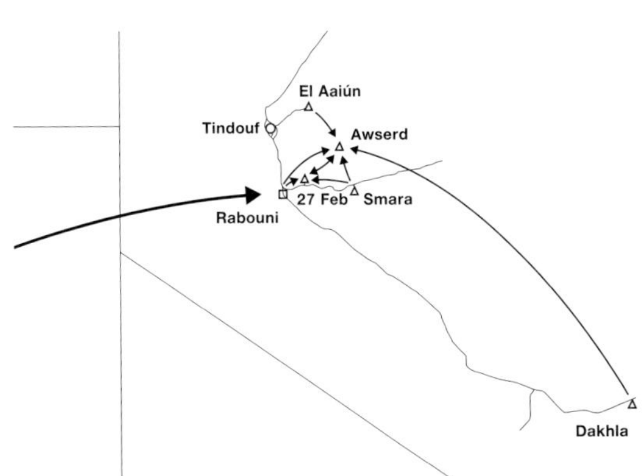


### Awserd

Awserd was established in 1986 after large numbers of additional refugees arrived throughout the 1980s, mostly from the occupied territories. At the same time, the boarding school of 27 February gained a growing, stable population and became a de facto camp in itself, administered by Smara. Today the total number of refugees in all camps is estimated to be 165,000.

# Organization

When the first Sahrawi refugees arrived near Tindouf in late 1975, they were given supplies by the Algerian government and established the first camp. Unlike almost all other refugee cases worldwide, the UNHCR—the main international organization that usually assumes responsibility for the protection of refugees—was not involved in setting up the camps. The main consequence of the UNHCR's absence is that the administration of the camps, usually carried out by the international refugee organization in conjunction with the host nation, in this case Algeria, is in fact implemented and enforced by the refugees themselves, specifically by Polisario.

Despite this, the spatial organization of the refugee camps does not differ significantly from the standard model UNHCR applies to camps worldwide. Depending on their size, refugee camps ("ideally" destined to be home to 20,000 refugees) are usually organized into four sectors, each of which is further subdivided into four blocks, and sixteen communities, with every community consisting of sixteen families. In the case of the Sahrawi camps, the terminology of the camps and their sub-units references the typical organization of a Maghreb nation-state. For example, in Algeria, the organizational unit of a camp is a "wilayah," the Arabic term for province. Each camp, or wilayah, is subdivided into several "daïras," or districts, which are further subdivided into "barrios," the Spanish term for neighborhood.

The layout of the camps originally mirrored this organization in a straightforward way. When Rabouni was established, all refugees lived in tents that were arranged in straight rows and organized into blocks or barrios. Four barrios formed a daïra, and together with the other daïras, a perfect grid layout emerged in the desert sand. When families moved into separate accommodation and tents were increasingly replaced by huts made of clay bricks, the camps rearranged themselves spatially. Nevertheless, even today the organizational structure is still often visible in the layout of the camps. Daïras are separated from each other by wide open spaces, and barrios by roads and sand paths, sometimes still with a orthogonal layout.

## Structure of a Camp

### Wilayah

A single camp is called a wilayah, meaning province. The refugee camps consist of the four wilayahs of Smara, El Aaiún, Awserd, and Dakhla. (Rabouni has the status of an administrative center, and 27 February belongs to the wilayah of Smara.)

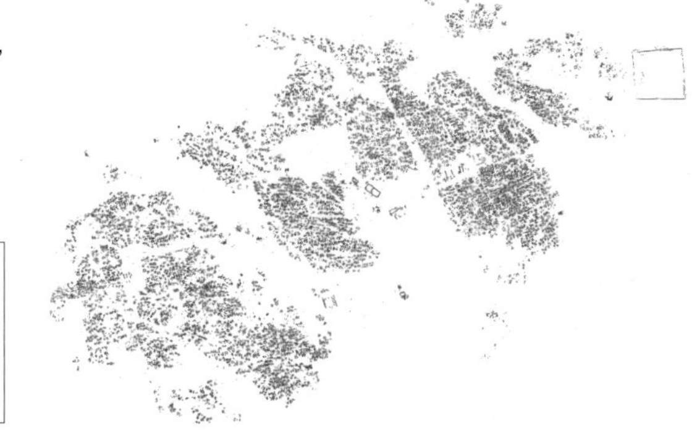

### Daïra

Each camp or wilayah is subdivided into daïras, meaning districts. El Aaiún, Awserd, and Dakhla have six daïras each. Smara has recently grown and gained a seventh. The camp of 27 February is considered a single daïra.

### Barrio

The daïras are further subdivided into barrios (meaning neighborhood), four of which make a daïra. Some daïras still show the spatial organization into barrios, with two wide orthogonal paths crossing each other at the daïra center. The sub-unit of a barrio is the khaliyah, which consists of twelve to fifteen families.

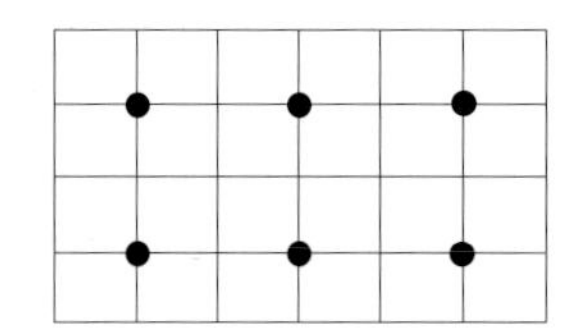

Smara in 1984

120 m

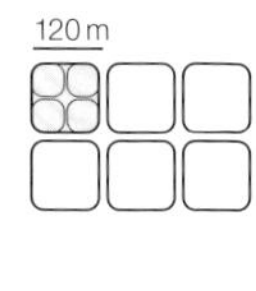

800 m

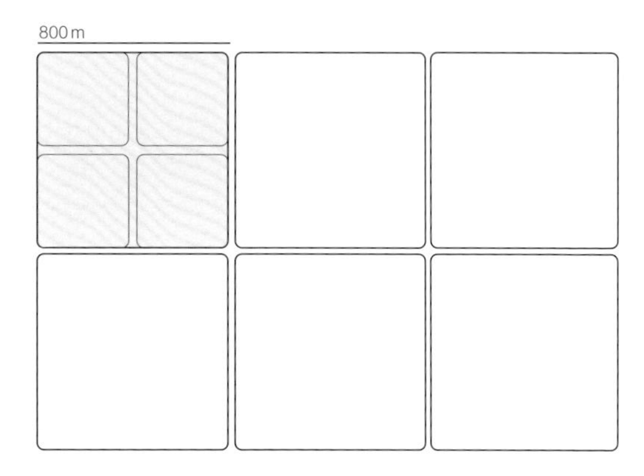

### High Density

The physical size and density of the camps has changed significantly since their establishment in late 1975 and early 1976. Judging from the few existing photographs, the first camp occupied a territory of approximately 90,000 m² with roughly 4,000 to 5,000 refugees. This would represent an area of 20 m² for each refugee on average, well below the UNHCR recommendation of 45 m² per refugee.

### El Aaiún

Today the average size of a typical El Aaiún daïra is approximately 800 × 800 m or 640,000 m². With an estimated average population of 8,000 inhabitants, this translates to 80 m² per inhabitant, exceeding UNHCR's recommendation. On a basis of one square kilometer, it translates to a population of more than 12,500, which is still relatively high when compared to "real" cities. It is similar to the population densities of New York City or Moscow (both 11,000/km²), but exclusively in one-story buildings.

## Transformation of the Camps

1975

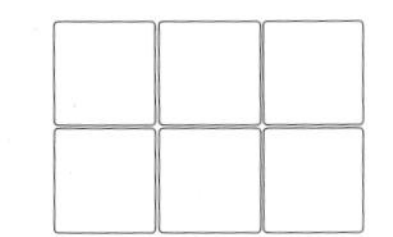

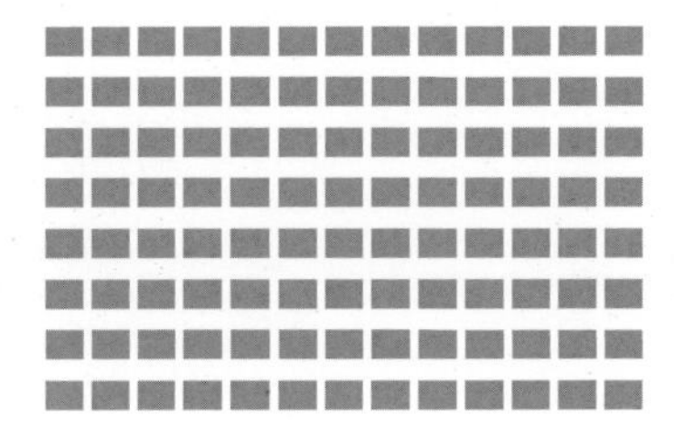

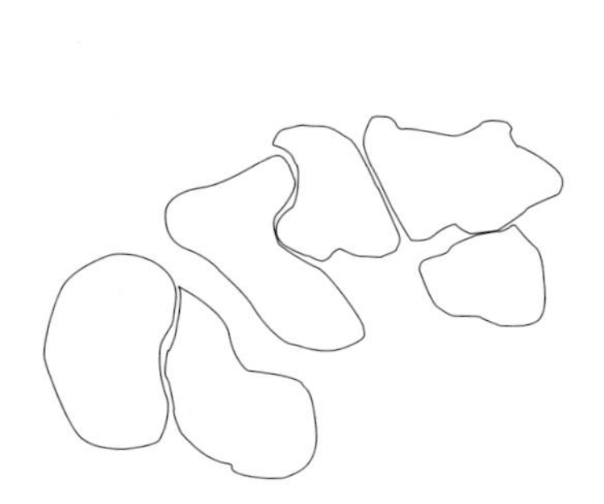

2011

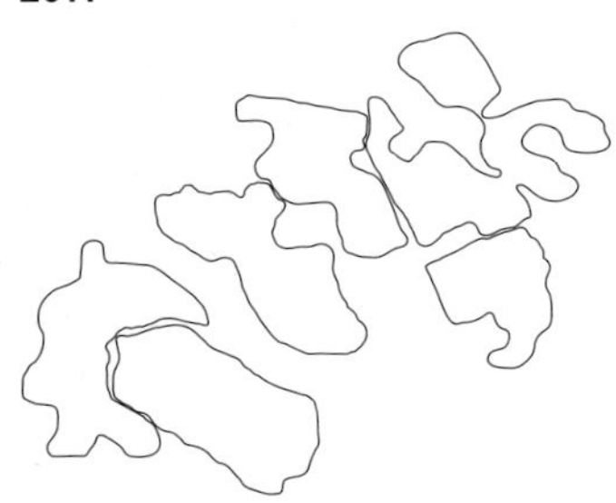

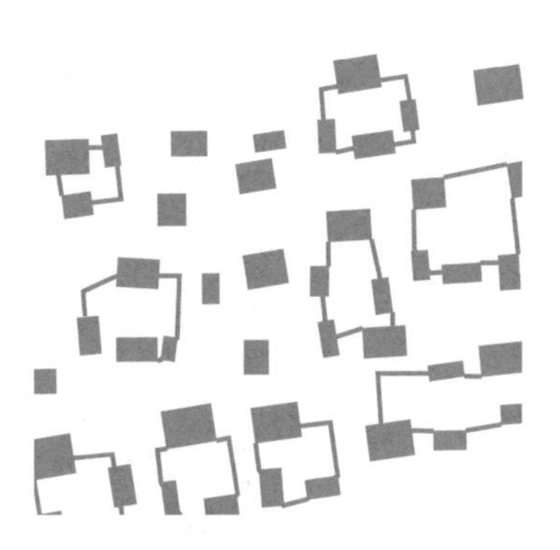

### Camps

The camp grows in size over time as more refugees arrive and the tents are replaced or supplemented by huts. The originally rigid structure changes to a more fluid or informal layout. Some families, preferring additional space, move to the periphery of the camp, resulting in a blurring of the camp's limits.

### Urban Fabric

The uniform rows of tents are dissolved and a more "organic" fabric starts to emerge. Families try to stay close to each other when children marry and move out. Initially in just single huts, over time families start to build additional structures. More recently, these structures are surrounded by walls to create enclosed compounds, separating private and public space.

### Housing Typologies

When camps are established, the refugees live in tents donated by the Algerian government. Over time these tents are replaced by those donated by UNHCR, later by clay huts, and more recently by huts constructed out of cement bricks. Today all typologies are still present in the camps.

## Growth of El Aaiún

Since its foundation, El Aaiún has changed its layout considerably. The growth of the camp is obviously based on an expanding population. Besides that, growth occurs when families have gained a modest income and start to build additional huts or erect more tents. Additionally, families try to stay together when their children marry, leading either to a densification of structures, or to a relocation to the periphery of the camp where space is more freely available.

The heavy rains of 1994 had a formative impact on El Aaiún, as it led to a major spatial reorganization of the camp. Large parts of the daïra El Guelta, lying slightly lower than the other daïras, were destroyed when the unplastered clay huts simply dissolved in the rain and streams of water that had formed in the downpour.

In the aftermath of the rains, it was decided to reconstruct the daïra on the western edge of the camp. As a result, El Aaiún now features a large empty space where El Guelta once stood. In its new location, the daïra has become an entry to the camp as a whole.

El Aaiún before the flood of 1994

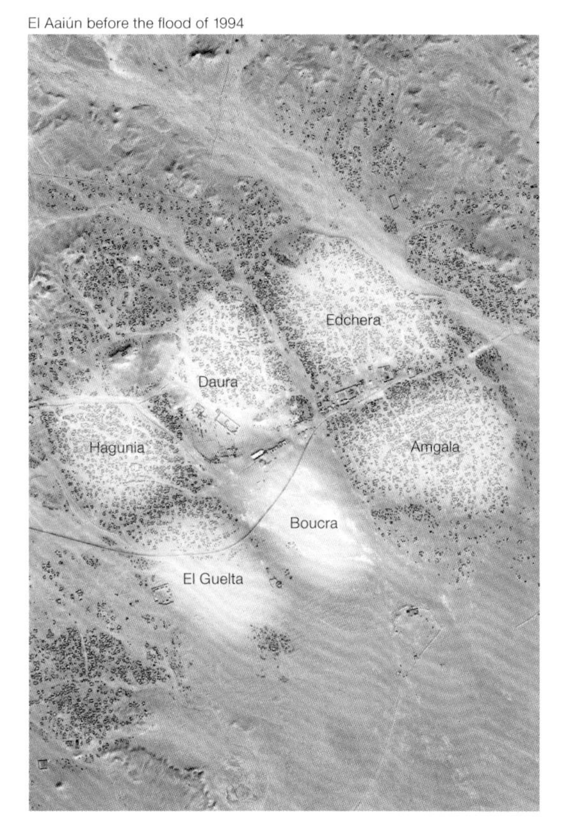


El Aaiún today

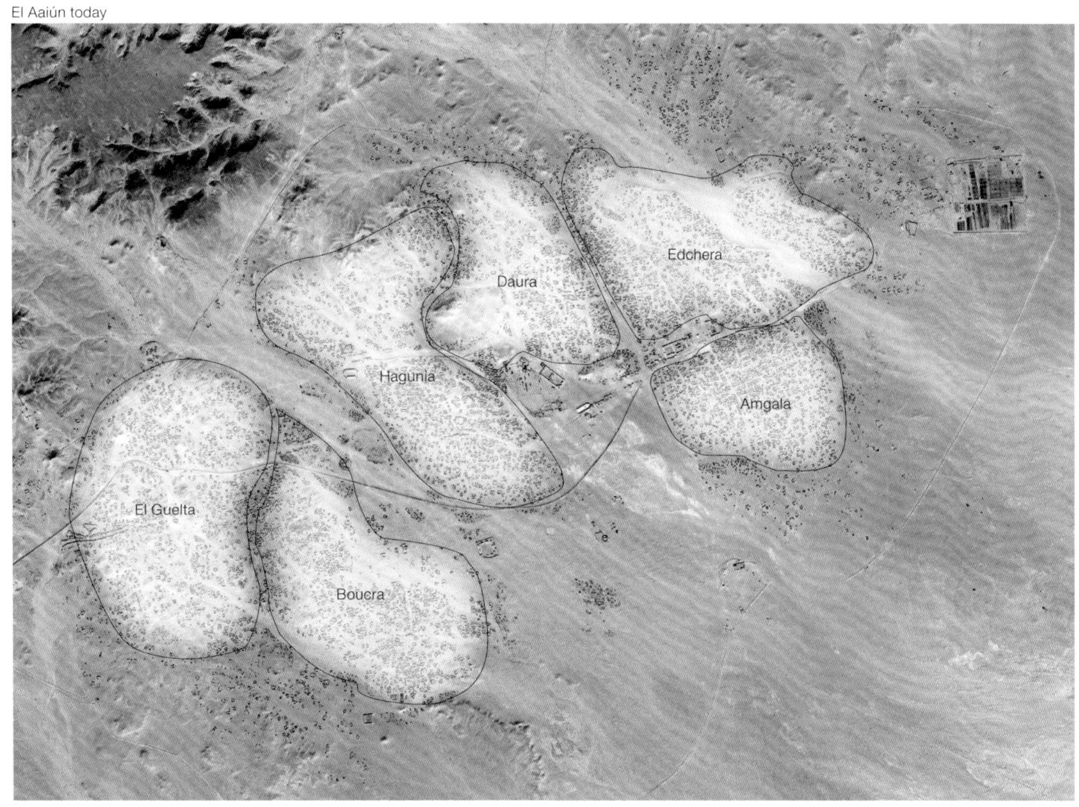

## Physical Grain

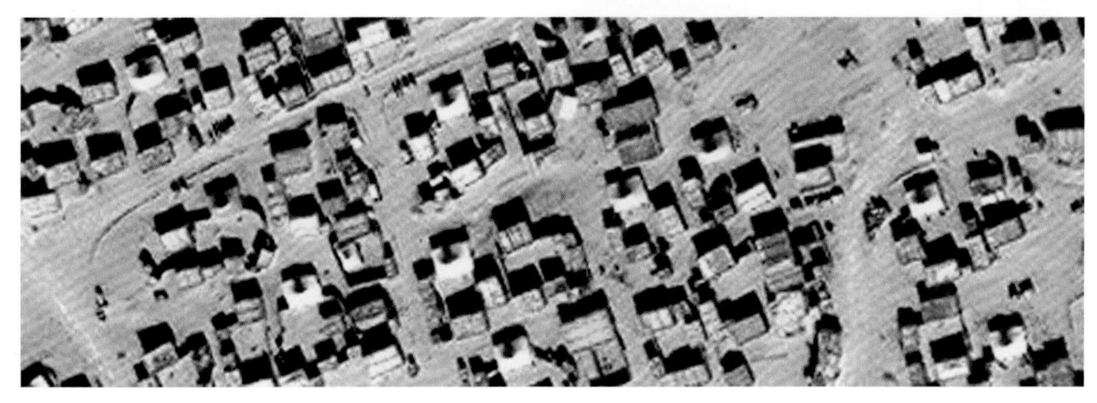

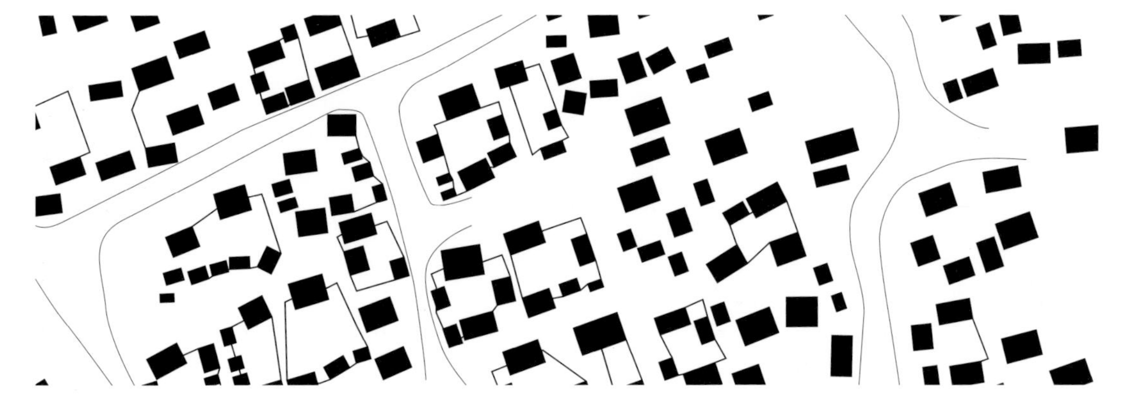

### Daïra Amgala

Over time, the daïras have developed their individual characters, and one can observe marked differences between them. This is already discernible on the level of the physical grain. When moving from the center to the edge of a daïra, one can usually perceive a difference in density. The central locations, often close to a small commercial area, are more densely occupied.

The daïra Amgala was not affected as badly as El Guelta and Boucra by the heavy rainfalls in 1994. It has a higher density than other daïras, and many huts form residential compounds, with walls connecting the individual buildings. This residential typology creates a clear distinction between private and public space, which is otherwise not present in the camp. The alleys that are formed by the compounds create a sense of urbanity that is sometimes reminiscent of a traditional Berber village.

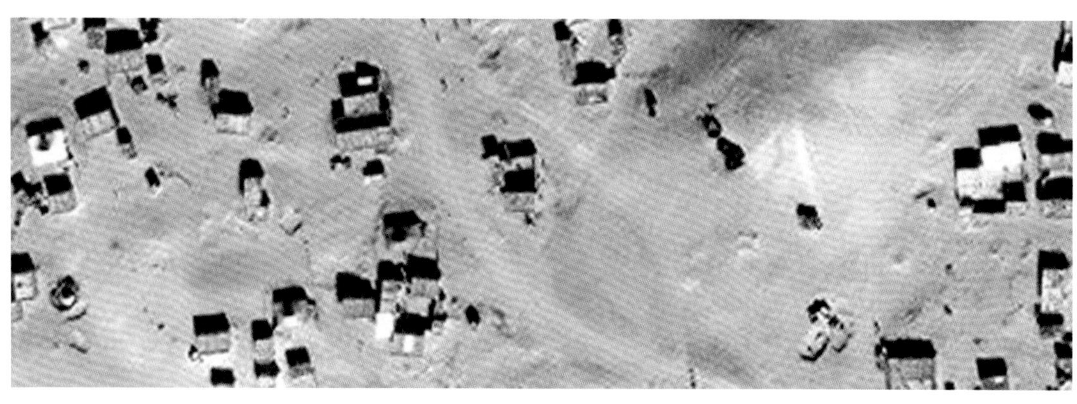

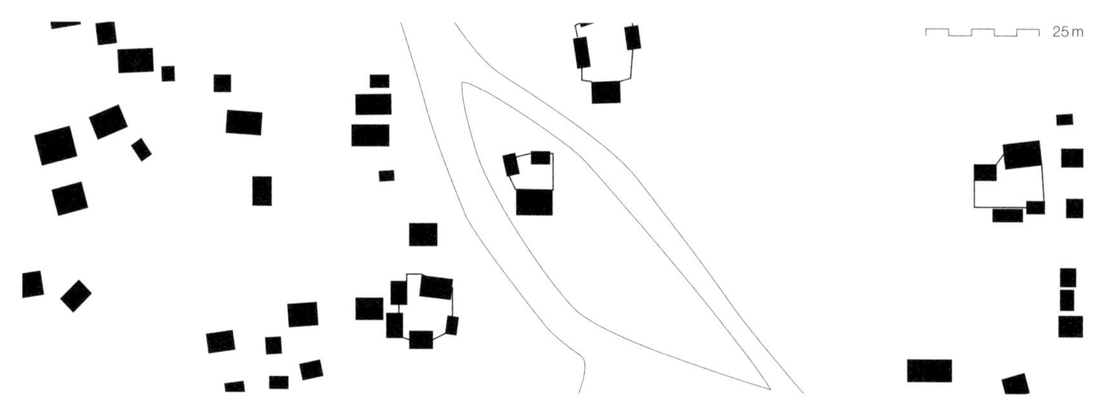


## Daïra El Guelta

The daïra El Guelta was relocated and completely reconstructed after the flood of 1994. It is now situated on the western edge of the camp, close to the entrance when arriving from Tindouf. Although the camp's main commercial market has developed in El Guelta, it does not seem to have made the daïra's physical grain particularly compact. Directly behind the shops the density of buildings drops sharply. The huts are constructed far apart from each other, and only a few compounds have perimeter walls.

The fact that this daïra was established only relatively recently is one of the reasons for the lower density.

The relocation of the daïra to its new location was taken as an opportunity to spread out over a larger territory, as its inhabitants prefer to be surrounded by more open space.

# The Camps Today

## An Overview

The camps of Smara, El Aaiún, Awserd, the school camp of 27 February, and the administrative center of Rabouni are located close to the Algerian city of Tindouf. Dakhla is located in a small oasis approximately 150 km away from the other camps. The city of Tindouf, having a major Algerian military base, features markets where the refugees can buy supplies and food, and an airport with frequent flights to Algiers and sometimes even direct international connections.

Asphalt roads lead from Tindouf to all camps (except Awserd, which is connected by a dirt road). Rabouni acts as a gateway from which the liberated territories and Mauritania can be accessed. There are no roads leading to Morocco, which is just 50 km west of Tindouf, as the Moroccan-Algerian land border has been closed for years.

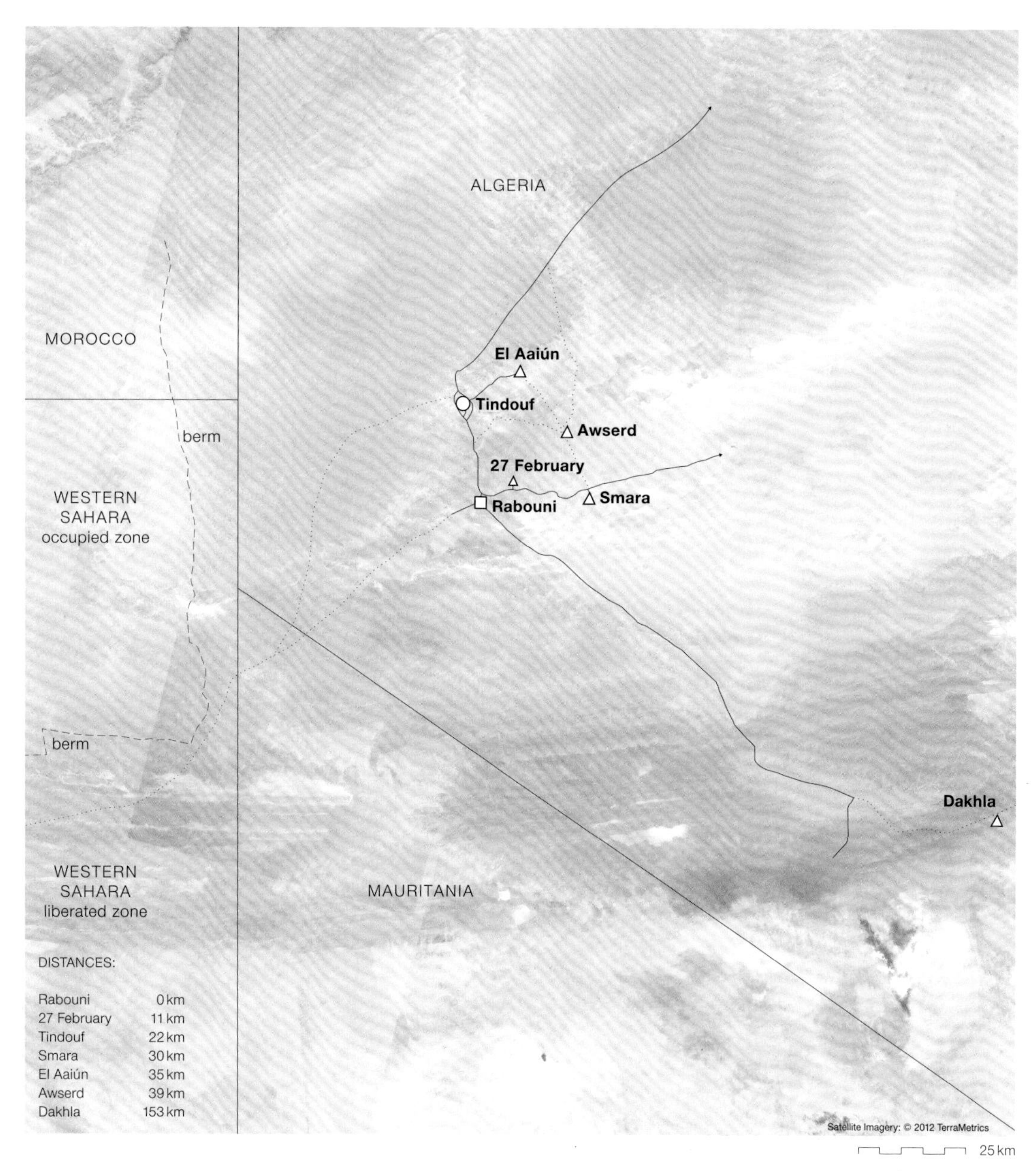
ALGERIA
MOROCCO
El Aaiún
Tindouf
Awserd
berm
27 February
Smara
Rabouni
WESTERN
SAHARA
occupied zone
berm
Dakhla
WESTERN
SAHARA
liberated zone
MAURITANIA
DISTANCES:
Rabouni 0 km
27 February 11 km
Tindouf 22 km
Smara 30 km
El Aaiún 35 km
Awserd 39 km
Dakhla 153 km
Satellite Imagery: © 2012 TerraMetrics
25 km

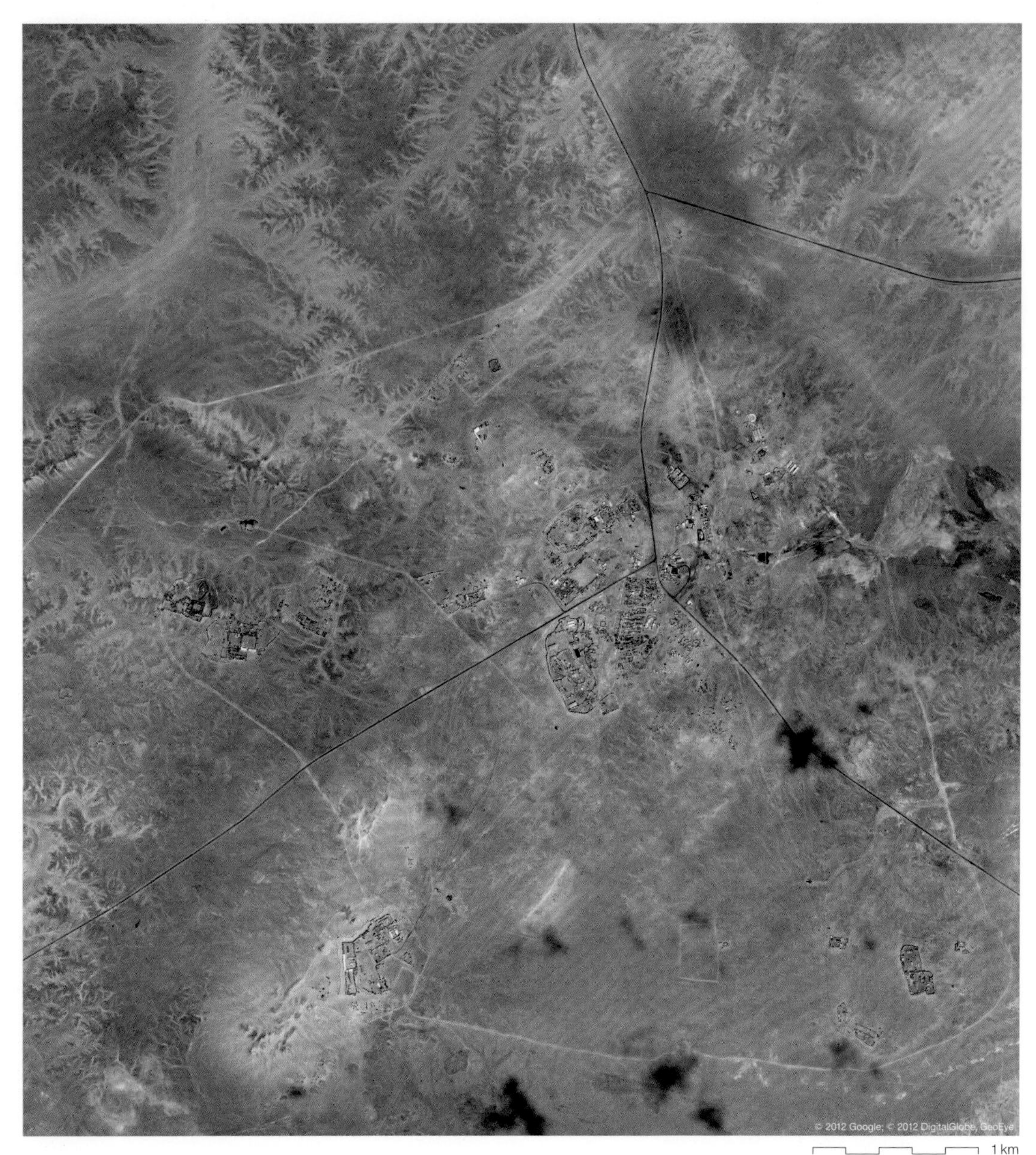

© 2012 Google; © 2012 DigitalGlobe, GeoEye

1 km

## Rabouni

Rabouni is the administrative center of the Sahrawi refugees. It was the first refugee camp to be established at the end of 1975, but was later transformed into the seat of the Sahrawi government. There are no permanent inhabitants, and all officials and workers commute daily (or sometimes weekly) between their houses in the other camps and Rabouni.

Because of its lack of residential buildings and the dominance of large administrative compounds, Rabouni has a very different appearance to the other camps. It features many ministry buildings, the national hospital, and a large depot for food and aid.

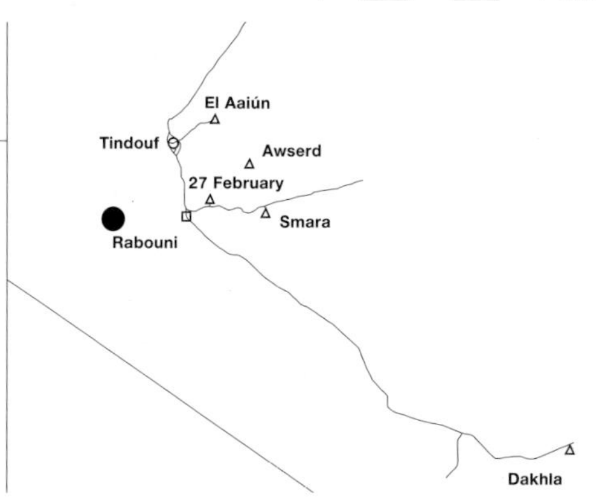

## Smara

Smara is the largest camp, with an estimated population of up to 60,000 inhabitants. Established in 1976, it is the second oldest camp. Originally, Smara consisted of four daïras, but was later enlarged to six daïras and more recently, seven. The original structure of the daïras and their respective barrios can be identified relatively clearly in the satellite image. Smara receives more international visitors (for example, NGO workers and partner families from Spain) than the other camps, which has resulted in the development of an infrastructure serving these outsiders. Smara was the first camp to have a mobile-phone antenna installed and has "souvenir" shops selling craft work and T-shirts.

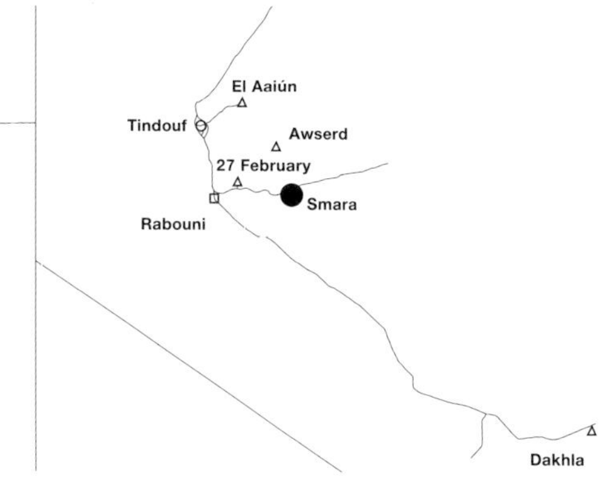

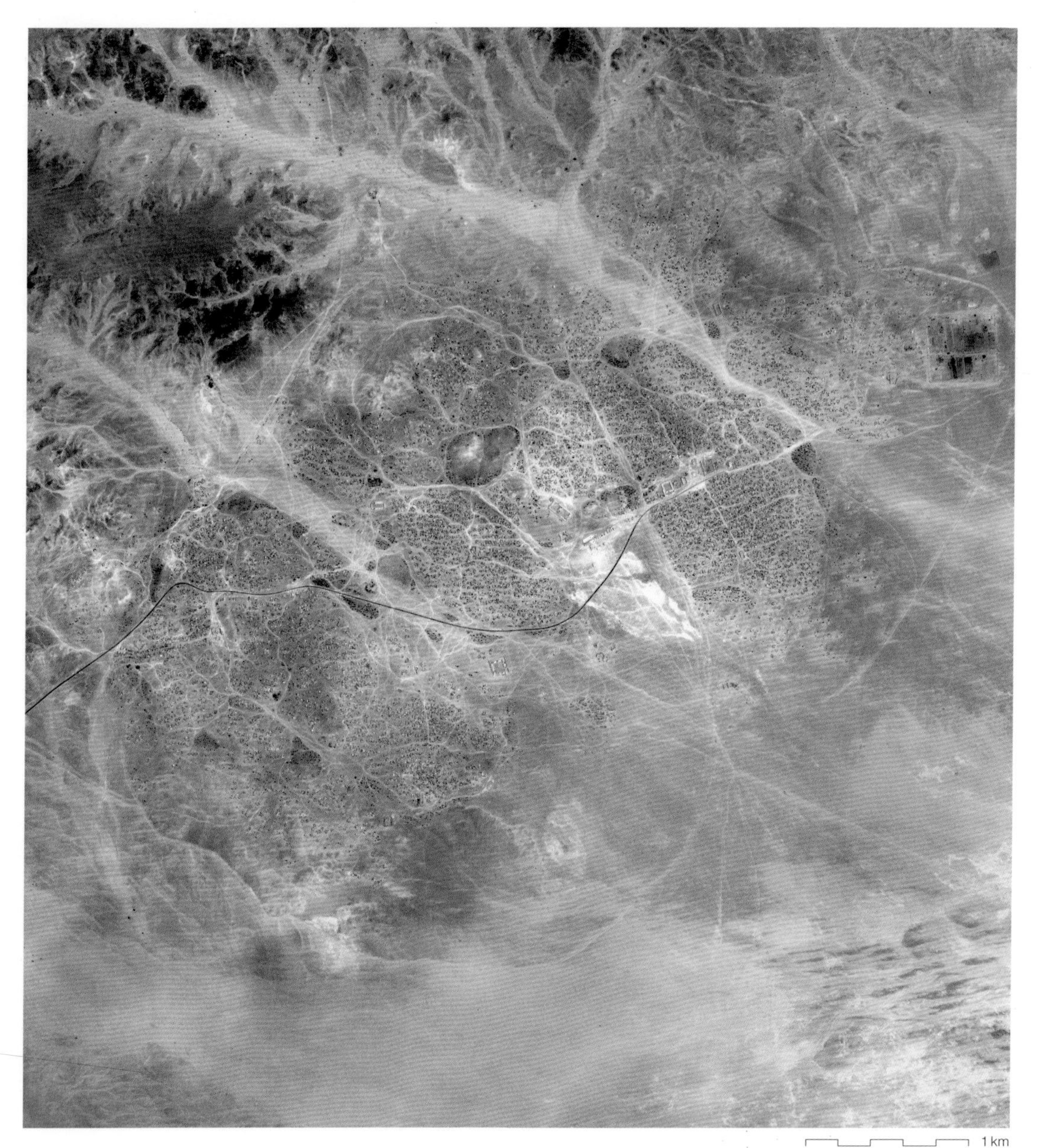


## El Aaiún

El Aaiún is the second largest camp, with an estimated population of 50,000 inhabitants. It is located closest to Tindouf, which is only 15 km to the west. El Aaiún has easy access to groundwater, which sits just a few meters below the surface. This reservoir supplies the water for Awserd, allowing for some gardening, greenery, and trees which are not present in the other camps, except Dakhla.

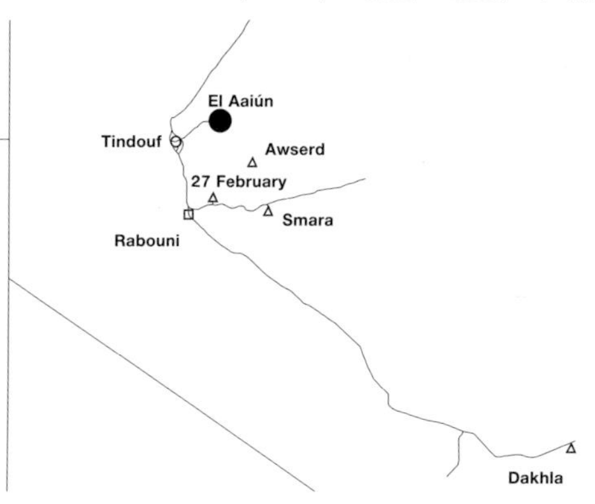

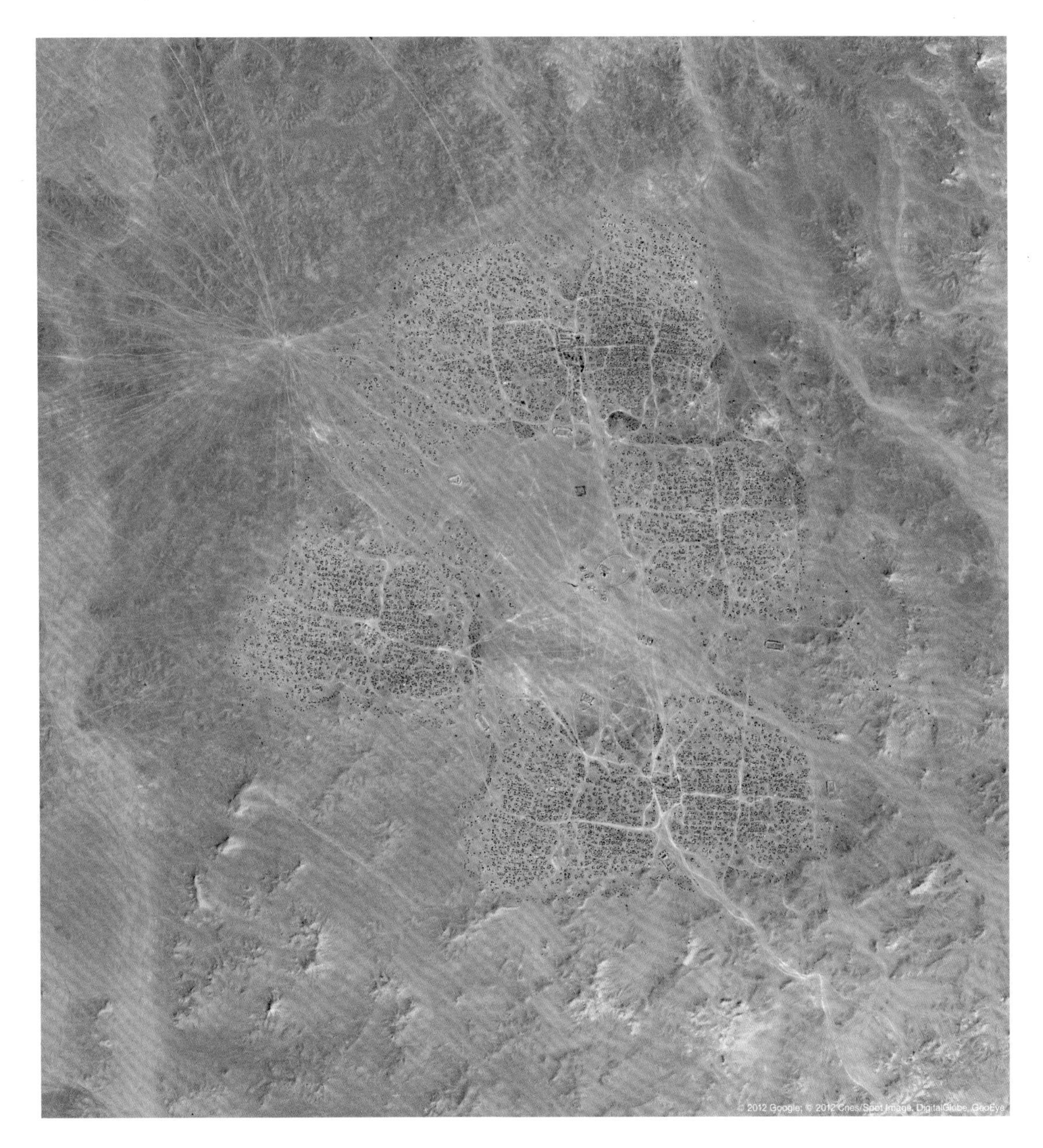


## Awserd

Established in 1986, Awserd is the most recent camp. It sits approximately midway between El Aaiún and Smara and is accessible by dirt, rather than asphalt, roads. Awserd consists of six daïras, whose sub-organization into barrios is clearly discernible. The individual daïras are located on slightly elevated areas, while a large empty zone in the center turns into a temporary river ("wadi") if it rains. Approximately 30,000 to 35,000 inhabitants live in Awserd.

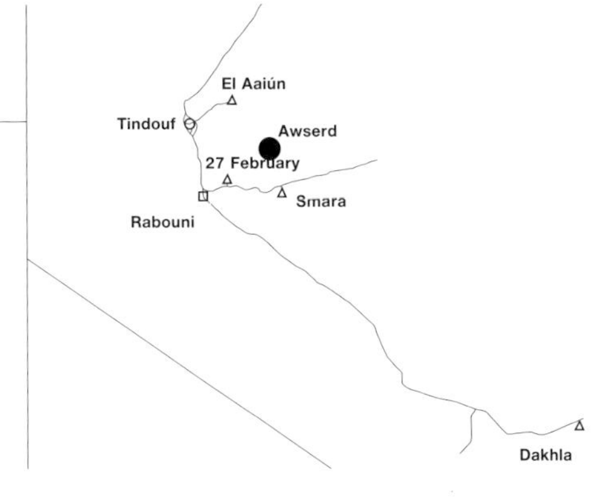

1 km

## Dakhla

Dakhla is the most remote camp, located approximately 150 km southeast of Rabouni. Before the construction of the asphalt road, the drive through the desert took more than five hours. Now it can be reached in two. Similar to El Aaiún, Dakhla sits on top of a groundwater reservoir and is therefore marked by trees and a few small gardens. Dakhla suffers from its remoteness, however, and families have started to move to Smara or 27 February in the hope of better economic potential. One initiative to support Dakhla is the international film festival that takes place every year. Dakhla has approximately 15,000 to 20,000 inhabitants.

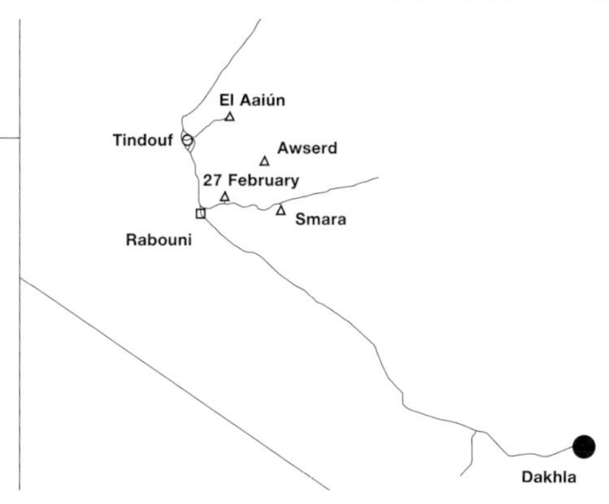

## 27 February

27 February was originally founded as a boarding school for women. In the beginning only the families of the women attending the school and teachers were allowed to settle in the camp. Over time 27 February transformed into a regular camp, even though it belongs to Smara for organizational purposes. The camp is popular because of its good location relatively near Tindouf and its small size. It is the first camp to receive electricity (donated by Algeria) via a power line. This has given rise to air-conditioning being installed in some of the private homes. It consists of a single daïra and has approximately 15,000 inhabitants, but is growing steadily.

## Comparison to Other Settlements

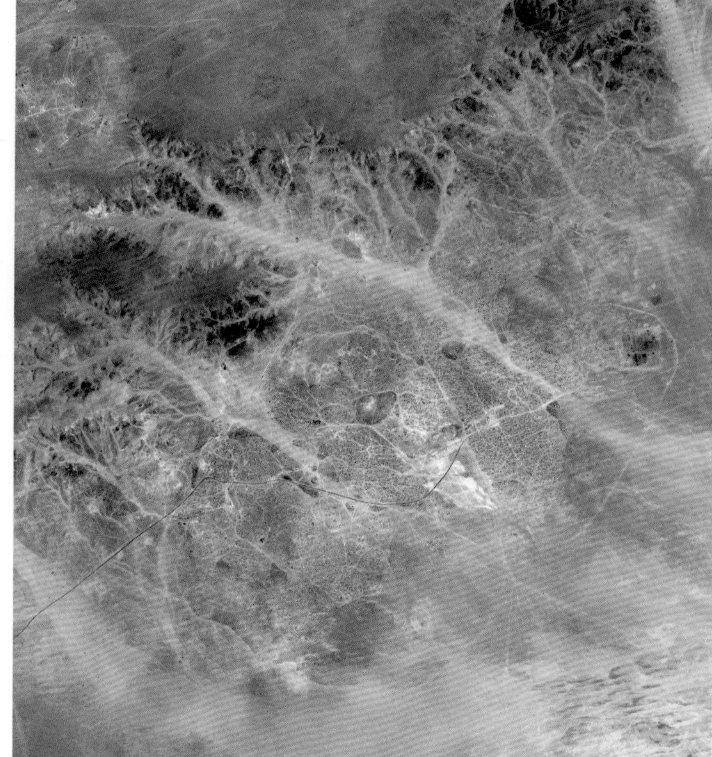

**El Aaiún, Algeria, refugee camp**

Inhabitants: ca. 50,000
Area: ca. 8 km²
Density: ca. 6,250 km²

**El Aaiún, Western Sahara**

Inhabitants: 196,000
Area: ca. 17 km²
Density: ca. 11,500 km²

**Treguine, Chad, refugee camp**
Inhabitants: ca. 13,000
Area: ca. 1.5 km²
Density: ca. 8,500 km²

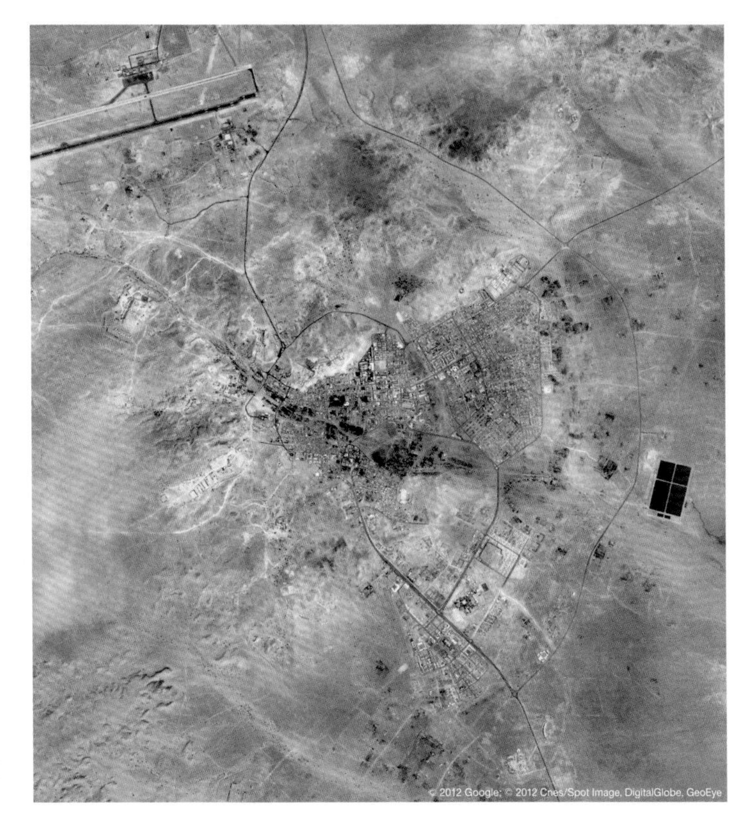


**Tindouf, Algeria**
Inhabitants: ca. 50,000
Area: ca. 8 km²
Density: ca. 6,250 km²

# Urbanization of a Nation in Exile

Fleeing to the refugee camps in 1976 represented a process of overnight urbanization for a whole nation. Even though approximately half of the Sahrawis had started to live in cities during the final years of Spanish colonial rule, many of these families still led lives that were marked by nomadic or semi-sedentary traditions. Often moving back to their camel herds throughout the year, the Sahrawi people held a strong connection to the territory's rural areas and deserts. The leaders of the Sahrawi decolonization movement and the founders of Polisario had a predominantly urban background. Nevertheless, Sahrawis that led an urbanized lifestyle were a minority and in a certain way represented an (urban) elite within Sahrawi society. Therefore the experience of setting up large settlements was limited.

Although not supported by UNHCR, the Sahrawi refugees adopted a standardized model for the refugee camps, with tents arranged in the form of a grid, packed relatively densely in the desert terrain. The camps were organized hierarchically, consisting of khaliyas, barrios, daïras, and the camps themselves. Soon the refugees were faced with two fundamental questions: how to absorb the growing number of refugees arriving in the camps and how to respond to the fact that the camps would remain much longer than originally intended or hoped for. The camps grew not only in size but also in number. Having initially settled only in Rabouni, other camps like Smara, El Aaiún, and Dakhla were established over time. The choice of location was motivated by logistical and environmental factors, predominantly—and not surprisingly—the availability of water. Additional infrastructure and institutions, such as schools and administration buildings, were constructed over time.

The biggest impact on the fabric of the camps, however, was the change in residential typologies, with families moving to private tents, constructing clay huts and other buildings, as well as settling over larger areas of the desert landscape. Over time, the formerly rigid and dense structure of tents transformed into the looser arrangement we can observe today. Today, with between 10,000 and 50,000 inhabitants, the camps have reached the size and density of cities such as Tindouf itself and are among the largest settlements in the Sahara Desert. Even without the official status of "cities," and even if they are only intended to exist for a transition period until a return to the homeland of the Western Sahara becomes possible, the camps are clearly marked by urban qualities and deserve to be analyzed, viewed, and assessed just as other cities are. This is not just based upon technical parameters and measures of survival, but on dimensions of the urban, i.e. aspects that touch upon social interaction, economic activity, cultural production, recreation, and quality of life, among other factors. The camps have become the places where Sahrawi society as a whole is going through the practices of urban life for the first time.

Smara, unknown date, probably 1980s

# LIVING

More than thirty-five years have passed since the first refugees fled to Algeria and set up camps near Tindouf. Ever since, about half of the Western Sahara's native population has been living in these refugee camps. The camps were set up with the belief that return to the homeland was imminent. The temporary nature of the camps was, and still is, visible in its construction, tents, and organization. As has happened with many other refugee situations, the return did not materialize, and the homeland has remained mostly inaccessible. Temporariness has transformed into a quasi-permanent condition. Life in the camps is a struggle between the hope for return and the transitory nature of the refugees' presence in the camps on the one hand, and the attempt to create a stable space with some, or most, of the qualities and features of everyday life on the other. The private huts, tents, houses, and their residential spaces are the spheres in which the individual dimension of this struggle becomes most clearly visible.

# Residential Typologies

When the camps were established, all refugees lived in tents supplied by the Algerian state. They were made of beige canvas, almost the color of the desert sand, and sometimes housed more than one family. When it became clear to the refugees that their flight to the camps near Tindouf would not last days or weeks as originally hoped, but much longer, the families started to improve their living conditions. They constructed their own tents in the traditional styles of their homeland using canvas later provided by UNHCR, or started constructing huts made of clay bricks that they formed from the desert sand.

Slowly, the uniformity of the original camp gave way to a diversity of living conditions, based on preference and taste, economic potential, opportunity of labor, and also on strategic decisions. More so than other buildings, the residential typologies exhibit the dilemma between the temporary status the refugee camp is meant to represent (and that is the hope of most, if not all, refugees) and the (quasi-) permanent condition that the camps often slip into, with the ensuing desire for increased comfort and better living conditions. Beyond their purpose of giving shelter, safety, and comfort to the refugees, we can use the residential spaces as indicators of different strategies to cope with the refugee condition. They become evidence of the strategic and political struggle of life as a refugee.

**Berber Khayma**
As nomads, the Sahrawis lived mostly in tents called khaymas. The tents were handmade by the women and were the preferred mode of living.

**Adobe Residential Compounds**
After the cease-fire, more adobe houses were built, often covered with zinc panels. To protect against sandstorms and theft they are combined with adobe brick walls.

**Algerian Tent**
The first tents received by the refugees were from Algeria. They consist of canvas with a metallic frame. The style has changed over time, but Algeria still provides similar tents to refugees.

**Cement-Brick House**
As clay bricks dissolve quickly in rain, more affluent families have recently started building huts with cement bricks. They are more expensive than clay bricks but provide less insulation.

**UNHCR Tent**
UNHCR started to distribute tents in the 1990s. Women are given wooden frames and sheets of fabric from which the covering is sown. New tent shapes have been developed over time.

**Sheet-Metal House**
Constructed with sheet metal taken from barrels, sheet-metal houses are water-resistant and cheaper than cement-brick houses. Due to their heat, however, it is impossible to use them during the summer.

**Adobe House Covered with Fabric**
In order to improve climatic conditions in the early years of the camp, refugees constructed huts with roofs made of canvas, as other roofing material was too expensive.

**Cement-Plastered Adobe House**
These buildings combine the benefit of improved insulation and the lower price of clay bricks with the water-resistance of cement plaster. Such houses have recently become popular.

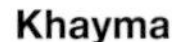

**Khayma**

Different types of khayma (Arabic for tent) are used in the camps. Traditionally, the Sahrawi tent canvas was made from goats' wool and had a natural black color. Today the canvas sheets are produced mostly by machine and are either white, beige, or green. The Sahrawi women receive the textile sheets and stitch them together to make the final tent covering.

The UNHCR tent with two inner poles is the tent most often used in the refugee camps today. The two poles and the relatively high side walls produce a large habitable space inside. The tent is often used for social functions, both within the family, such as drinking tea or eating, and for festivities such as weddings or other celebrations. During the summer, many families prefer to stay in tents, as the constant breeze produces a more comfortable climate than the clay huts. Apart from these functional reasons, the tent also signifies temporariness, which carries important connotations for the refugees.

**Adobe House**

Besides the tent, the adobe house made of clay bricks is the most common building typology in the camp. The bricks are made by simply mixing desert sand with water and leaving them to dry in the sun. The clay bricks have the benefit of being relatively good heat insulators. On cold winter nights the adobe houses don't cool down as much as the tents, but because of the lack of ventilation, adobe houses are less favorable on hot summer days.

The biggest threat to the adobe house is rain. The clay bricks very quickly dissolve into sand when exposed to water. During the rare thunderstorms, many huts are simply washed away, often even posing danger to their inhabitants. One can observe many abandoned huts in the camps that have fallen into ruin in this way. Nevertheless, most huts are built like this and are covered by zinc metal roofs, weighed down by heavy stones.

**Cement House**

In recent years, the Sahrawi refugees have started to construct houses with cement bricks. These bricks need to be bought in Tindouf and transported by truck to the camps. They are much more expensive than clay bricks and only affordable to more affluent families. The benefit of cement bricks is that they can withstand heavy rains. But their solidity also means that they are also one step further towards protraction or "permanentization" of the refugee condition–or at least an acknowledgement of that. This symbolic aspect, combined with their expense and the fact that the heat-insulation capacity is not as good as a clay-brick house, means that few cement houses are built.

Since 2006, refugees have started to use cement plaster as a finish on clay bricks, thus combining the benefits of both types. This gives the houses durability, while preserving the climatic advantage. These houses also often feature decorations and other design elements such as columns and detailed window frames.

**Sheet-Metal Huts**
Huts constructed from the sheet metal of barrels are the least common residential typology in the refugee camps. Even though they are cheap, sturdy, and can withstand heavy winds and rains, they can only be used in the colder months. During the summer, the space inside heats up so much that it becomes almost unbearable to stay inside. Sheet-metal huts are therefore used as additional rooms, supplementing other living spaces. Nevertheless, families that have constructed huts of sheet metal often decorate the inside very abundantly.

Sheet-metal huts are often used as storage spaces or workshops, and also in the few Sahrawi settlements of the liberated territories where people remain for shorter periods and the climate is slightly cooler than in the camps near Tindouf.

# Construction Process

As the adobe brick house is the most common construction method, people have started to produce and sell the bricks as a business. Several men therefore work on the periphery of the camps to produce them. Apart from sand, the only other necessary ingredient is water and a wooden mold to form the bricks. In fact, bricks are one of the few products actually produced and sold in the camps. Previously, bricks were produced on-site, using sand from or near the area where a new house was to be built. The production of bricks within the camps was recently forbidden, however, because of the danger of falling into the resulting deep holes. Nevertheless, people still produce bricks within the camp as it is cheaper than buying them ready-made and no transport is necessary.

There is a "high season" of construction lasting from February to May. During this time the temperature is most comfortable for working outside. Also, brick production works best during this period because water doesn't evaporate too quickly in the summer heat, leading to cracked bricks. Despite this, houses are built in the camp all year round.

Some of the new houses are designed and built by men who are specifically employed as construction workers. Wealthy families wanting to construct a larger hut are especially likely to pay workers to put up these buildings. Even though this is still a relatively rare occurrence, it represents the emergence of a new profession within the camp economy.

Brick construction worker, El Aaiún, 2011

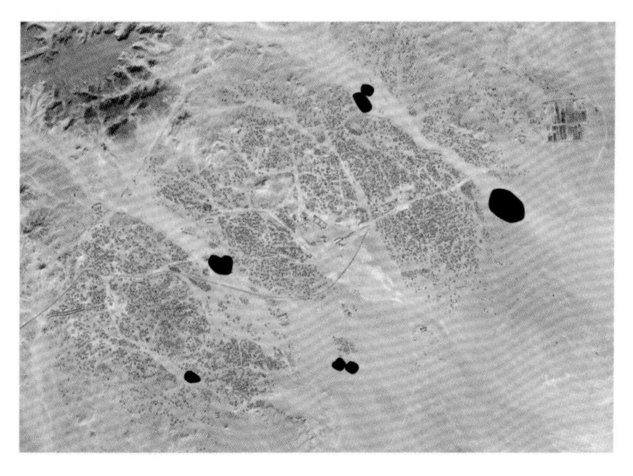

**Commercial Brick Production**
Bricks are made of sand and water. The sand from the lower layers is said to be better. A hole is dug and the sand is mixed with water. The muddy mixture is poured into a wooden mold to form the bricks. Removing the mold, the bricks are then left to dry in the sun. During winter it takes about five days and in summer only two days for the bricks to dry. A worker can produce fifty to sixty bricks a day. If there is a higher demand, a tractor is called to help dig the hole, allowing the production of one hundred bricks a day.

Price of bricks:
100 bricks ~ 1,000 dinar ~ €11

**Transportation**
Customers either transport the bricks themselves by car or donkey cart, or the brick worker arranges transport by donkey cart. If many bricks need to be transported, a truck is hired for additional costs.

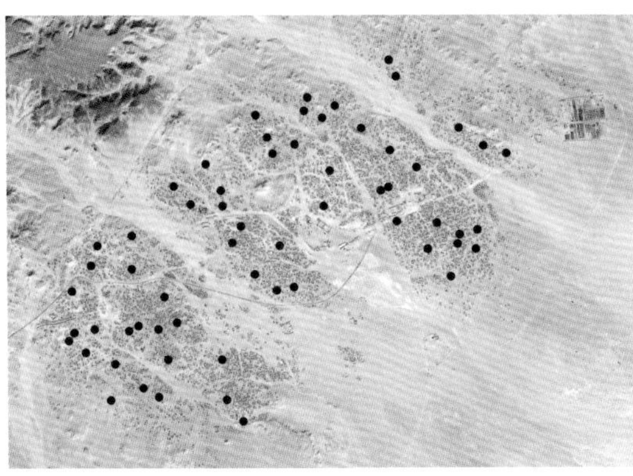

**Self-Made Brick Production**
The basic method for producing bricks is identical to the commercial method. Men who intend to construct a hut simply dig a hole next to the construction site in order to produce their own. As this requires considerable work they are usually helped by relatives and friends. The obvious advantage is the money saved, but the holes in the ground are often just left open, which poses the danger of accidents.

**Drying**
When producing one's own bricks, it is necessary to consider the time needed for drying them. Producing bricks on the construction site also requires enough space to lay them out to dry.

**Additional construction materials**
Most of the additional materials can be bought in one of the several building shops in the camps. The most important elements are the entrance door, shutters and windows (usually without glass), plaster, and roofing material. For the past ten to fifteen years the use of corrugated steel as roofing material has become popular. The roof is the most expensive part of a hut. After the heavy rains of 2006 people have also started to use cement plaster on the exterior walls.

Price of roofing material:
Corrugated metal for a standard house ~ €675

**Marking a Site**
Before construction of a house commences, people mark the plot that they intend to use, thereby claiming it for their own purposes. This is most often done with bricks to indicate the outline of the house, and additional bricks to demarcate the whole site. In the camp, one frequently sees marked plots that have remained untouched for a long period of time–the family has often either changed its plans or still saving enough money to build the house.

**Construction**
There are few rules that regulate the construction of houses in the camps. They are constructed throughout the year, even though people prefer to build from March to May because of the more comfortable temperature. All houses are exclusively single-story, because of the abundance of land, and because adding a second level would be too costly. The size of the buildings has increased over the years.

The construction process usually involves all members of a family and sometimes additional friends. When this help is not available, families are forced to buy the bricks and sometimes even hire construction workers. Two construction workers cost approximately €500 for one month, plus food. This is the average time it takes to build a single house. More recently, wealthier families have started building "designed" houses that are larger and more expensive. These take approximately three months to construct.

**Completed House**
The total amount of money needed to build a single house ranges from €1,500 to in excess of €4,000. This represents a major investment for a refugee family. The money is usually saved over many years and comes from relatives working abroad, donations from Spain, or money earned by the small commercial activities in the camps (see chapter on Working).

Price for a single house:
Regular house ~ €1,500
"Designed" house ~ up to €4,000

**Construction of a Khayma**
The fabric is sewn together from separate sheets provided by UNHCR or Algeria. It has to be attached firmly to the ground with ropes and stakes to withstand the regular strong sandstorms.

Every khayma has an inner frame made of steel or wooden poles. The frame holds the fabric and creates the inner space.

Once erected, a fence is often built around the tent to keep goats away and prevent them from eating the fabric.

The tent can be dismantled and stowed away in a box, ready to be moved to another place. Some refugees move into the desert or liberated territories periodically to pursue a nomadic lifestyle or to tend to camels that are grazing there.

### Construction of an Adobe House

Construction of a brick house starts by first building a base. The ground does not usually require flattening as it is already quite level. The first layer of bricks is double width, forming a foundation of sorts. The floor remains untreated and is later covered with mats and carpets.

The construction of the walls always starts from the corners of the house, giving them stability. Strings and levels are used to achieve straight lines and horizontal layers of bricks. Window openings are constructed either with wooden frames or slabs of cement.

After completing the walls, the roof is constructed. Wooden beams span from wall to wall. The corrugated sheets of metal are placed on top of the beams and are weighed down by rocks. The ceiling is often decorated with fabrics, which also creates a buffer for the heat.

The building is finished with the installation of the main door, which is usually made of metal. Windows are not made of glass but have metal shutters. If the family has enough money they will apply plaster to the internal surfaces of the walls.

# Residential Compounds

Due to the continual obstruction by Morocco, the referendum for the future and potential independence of the Western Sahara was officially put on hold in the year 2000. As a consequence, refugee families were less hopeful of being able to return to their original homeland in the foreseeable future, so they started to invest in more permanent constructions within the camps. This period coincided with the increased financial capacity of many of the refugee families. With a slow but steadily growing economy and more money flowing into the camps through donations and remittances, families had more economic potential to build additional huts or invest in furnishings and equipment for their living quarters.

Over time, families thus started to upgrade their residential spaces. The most fundamental change was that instead of using just a single tent or hut, families started to construct additional units. While previously a single tent or hut was used to house all family members and for all domestic activities, from now on purpose-built huts intended for a limited range of functions became the norm. This of course depended, and still depends, on the specific economical potential of each refugee family. While families with little disposable income might still live in a single hut, some families have started to reside in compounds consisting of six to eight individual units, each serving a specific purpose or housing just one or two family members. While mostly consisting of clay huts or huts constructed of cement bricks, almost all compounds still include the traditional tent as part of the residential arrangement. The differences in size and type of compound have thus become an indicator for the economic differences existing in the camps. Upgrading residential spaces is not limited to the construction of additional units, however. A substantial part of the investment is spent on interior furnishing, decoration, and equipment such as TVs, refrigerators, ovens, washing machines, or washroom facilities such as sinks, toilets, and showers.

More recently, families have started building walls to enclose their compounds. This serves to protect compounds from sandstorms and also from robbery, despite the fact that this is a relatively rare occurrence in the camps. These walls introduce a notion of privacy in a place where the ground cannot be privately owned. Unmistakably separating the spaces of the compound from the overall fabric of the camp, giving access only to the family and its guests, makes explicit the claim of land by the respective family and establishes a sense of ownership.

The following pages examine a series of residential compounds, giving evidence to the range of sizes and standards that can be found in the camps. The compounds vary from one that consists of just two or three units to one consisting of eight huts and tents for an extended family. Also shown is one of the newer "designer houses" that has introduced the notion of architectural design to the Sahrawi refugee camps for the first time, in a most explicit way.

Residential compound of a comparatively wealthy family, El Aaiún, 2011

Lala, age twenty-one years

**Lala's Family**

Lala's father left the family in the early 1990s to live in the Canary Islands. Her mother stayed behind to raise Lala, her two elder brothers, and her three sisters. Lala's aunts and cousins live next to them and provide some help.

Lala's mother is still used to a nomadic life from the colonial era. Today she still prefers living in the khayma, which represents the most important space in the compound. She almost never enters the brick houses and the whole family sleeps together in the khayma. Lala's brothers work and earn money to support the family. In addition, they receive support from a Spanish family. Recently, they were able to buy a refrigerator, for which they built an extra hut. The houses are simple and made of adobe brick. The toilet is in a separate small hut outside the compound.

Building area: ~ 130 $m^2$
Court area: ~ 90 $m^2$
Residential compound surface: ~ 220 $m^2$
Adobe brick construction with a khayma

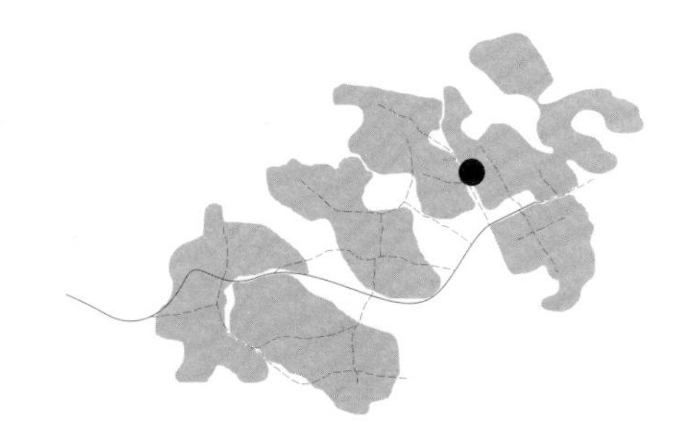

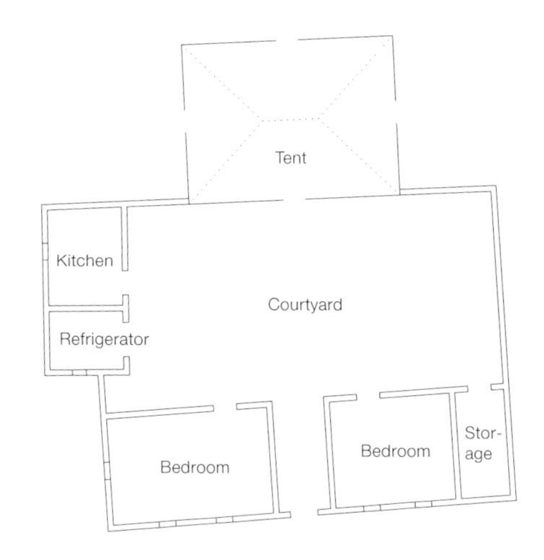

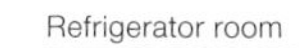

Women having tea inside the khayma

No plastered walls inside the kitchen

Refrigerator room

Overview of the compound: Jamila's grandmother's house is next to the teahouse

## Jamila's Family

Jamila lives with four generations of her family in a large residential compound. The housing compound includes the house of her grandmother, her family, and the family of her older sister. Unlike many others, the compound does not have a perimeter wall. The family sometimes receives money from international visitors, who at times stay in their home.

All internal walls are plastered, and the windows are framed and decorated. The new buildings are plastered on the outside with cement. They do not have a washing machine, nor furniture. A khayma is also integrated into the compound and is used as a bedroom by Jamila, her father and mother, and the daughter of her sister. The kitchen has a shaded area in front of it, which is used for social activities or to prepare food. International visitors sleep in the tearoom, which is well decorated with carpets.

Building area: ~ 200 m²
External area: ~ 350 m² (not precisely demarcated)
Residential compound surface: ~ 550 m²
Adobe brick construction and cement plaster
Compound does not have a perimeter wall

Jamila's mother

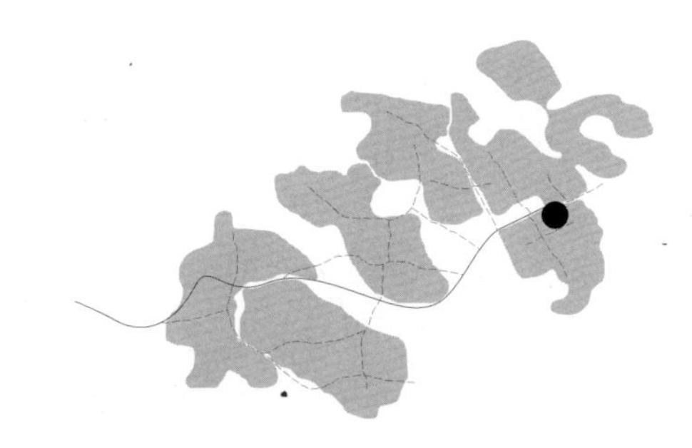

Shaded area in front of the kitchen

Interior of the large kitchen

Fatima with her children (and her children's friends)

**Fatima's Family**

Fatima is the mother of three small children. Her residential compound is located next to her mother's in the daïra of Edchera. The compound was constructed in 2006. Compared with others in the camp it is relatively small, but equipped with furniture, which is not standard. The compound includes a sheet-metal house, which is also rare in the camps. This sheet-metal house has the benefit of being resistant against rain and water, was relatively cheap to construct, and functions as a teahouse. The inside of the sheet-metal house is surprisingly cozy. Walls and ceilings are covered with colored fabrics and the floor with mats and carpets. The room is not used during the summer as the metal heats up the space excessively. During those summer months the bedroom also functions as the tearoom.

Building area: ~ 80 m²
Court area: ~ 50 m²
Residential compound surface: ~ 130 m²
Adobe brick construction
Teahouse is made from sheet metal

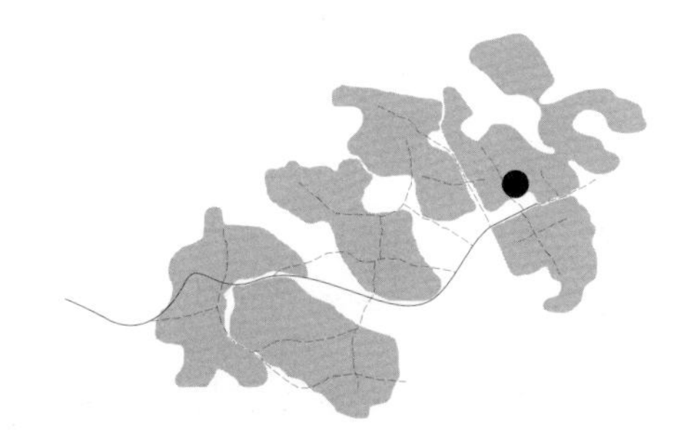

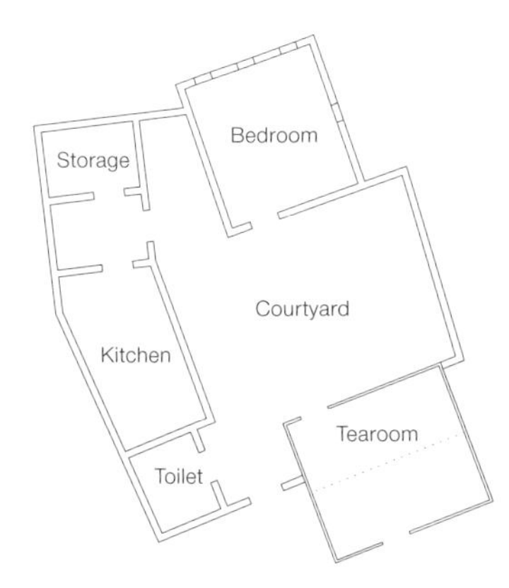


Court area

Bedroom

South façade

## Hamaa's Family

After studying in Algiers, Hamaa returned to the camp El Aaiún and got married. Her husband is from the camp Awserd, where he owns a shop and has gained some wealth. It is traditional that a daughter live close to her parents. Hamaa and her husband therefore built the house in El Aaiún next to her mother's house. It cost more than €4,000, and they invested all their money into its construction. The adobe house plastered with cement was designed by an "architect" and built by construction workers over three months in 2008.

Hamaa

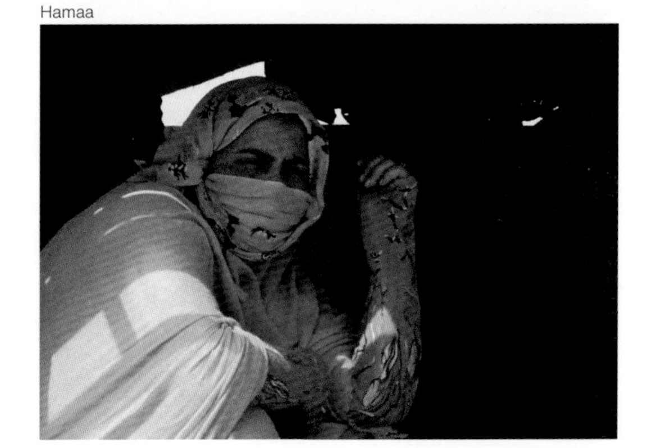

The family wanted a nice home and they keep it very clean, but don't use it often as Hamaa's husband spends only one day a week on the camp. So as not to be alone when her husband is in Awserd, Hamaa spends those days at her mother's house.

Building area: ~ 100 m$^2$
Court area: ~ 90 m$^2$
Residential compound surface: ~ 190 m$^2$
Adobe brick construction with cement plaster
"Design" house

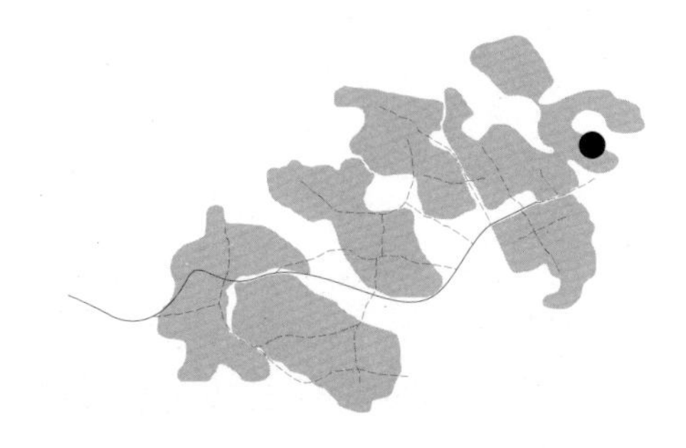

Inner courtyard with ornamentation

Tiled and plastered toilet

Well-equipped kitchen

Ornament detail

Inside the tearoom

# Land Planning

Land in the refugee camps cannot be bought. It has no monetary value and cannot be privately owned. This creates a unique situation where, in a quasi-urban context, the use of land is not determined through money and ownership, but through negotiation and convention. The reasons land cannot be owned can be traced back to the refugee condition. Living in Algeria on "borrowed" land, with a clear declaration that this is not the Sahrawis' homeland and their stay is only intended to be temporary makes the concept of land ownership contradictory. In addition, the nomadic character of Sahrawi society is traditionally at odds with the concept of land ownership (even though the zones and territories of influence were fiercely fought over by different Sahrawi tribes throughout history). The Sahrawis' stay in refugee camps went hand in hand with the idea of reducing the differences and hierarchies within Sahrawi society. As an additional benefit, the fact that land cannot be owned and carries no monetary value removes one of the main factors for social and economic difference from the refugee community.

The consequences on an urbanistic level are profound. If money as the typical means of acquiring land ownership drops out of the equation, other means need to be sought if two families are interested in the same site. This is often the case, especially in the center of the older daïras, where population density is relatively high and few open spaces remain between residential compounds. If a family wants to extend its compound or build additional huts (for example, for a daughter who has recently married), they need to consult with the neighbors if they also have interest in claiming the site. In the case of conflict of interest, and two parties claim the same site, a negotiation process starts with the aim of establishing whether the site can be used by both families, or if one of the families has more urgent needs for the site. If the difference of interest cannot be resolved, it is taken to the head of the barrio or daïra, who then tries to mediate the process. In the end, a solution is sought where either both parties use the same site partially, or one family has to build in a new location. The Sahrawi camp probably represents a unique case in which money as a means of deciding ownership and usage of land is replaced by a process of negotiation.

The lack of monetary value also leads to a relatively low density of construction and to something that, to borrow a term from a different context, could be called "junkspace."[1] If a family decides to move to a different location in the camp, or to a different camp altogether, their former house is often left deserted, slowly disintegrating into ruins. Walking through the camps, one can often see abandoned houses that have turned to rubble. Even relatively close to the central areas of the daïras, plots are sometimes deserted and create an uncanny sense of decay and abandonment. Along the same lines, the periphery of daïras is often marked by relatively large compounds, leaving significant open space between them and their neighbors. The ample amount of space available in the desert and the lack of monetary value of land results in a low density and, at least in the eyes of a Western visitor, something more akin to suburbia than bustling city life.

1 Koolhaas, Rem, "Junkspace," *October,* Vol. 100, 2002, pp. 175–190

Ruins, Smara, 2011

Marking a plot: the adobe bricks seem to have been placed a long time ago

Large residential compound with a gate

Widespread settlement on the outskirts of a daïra

Remaining ruins of a large residential compound

# The Politics of Housing

"There are two groups of people in the camps: the ones who don't want to establish anything that could even look permanent and the others who want to make their stay in the camps as comfortable as possible."
Taleb Brahim, engineer of agriculture, Smara, 2011

Walking through the Sahrawi refugee camps, one is initially struck by the abundance of tents. After existing for 35 years in one of the most inhospitable places on Earth, there is a certain disbelief that so many of these tents can still be found among the adobe huts, and that the refugees have not by now dismissed them in favour of more solid or stable building typologies. The adobe huts offer safety from animals and theft (even though this is an uncommon occurrence in the camps). They offer increased privacy, give protection against wind, and prevent sand from continuously seeping into every object and any crevice. But still, the tent persists as one of the residential typologies.

Obviously there are a number of pragmatic and rational reasons for keeping tents. First and foremost, they are much cheaper than either adobe huts or houses built of cement bricks. They have certain climatic benefits, especially in the relentlessly hot summer, when temperatures reach at least 55 °C, and stuffy huts are not able to cool down as quickly in the night. The tents also have a certain quality of space, with light being filtered through the canvas and a small but steady breeze blowing through the space, that the huts cannot match.

Nevertheless, beyond all these pragmatic reasons, tents also serve an important symbolic function. They reference the tradition of a nomadic society and are signifiers of the temporary nature of the refugee camp. The abundance of tents in the camps signal the intention of the Sahrawi refugees to return to their homeland, as the tent can easily be dismantled and moved to a new location. Having lived in the desert for 35 years, it is important to the Sahrawi refugees to proclaim that they do not intend to stay in the camps, but are full of conviction to return to the Western Sahara. The tents are a medium to symbolize and express this proclamation through architecture. In a world where images and photographs are so easily distributed around the globe, the importance of the tent cannot be understated. Even a person who knows nothing of the Sahrawi situation will understand that the situation of the refugees is not a permanent one, upon seeing a photograph of a refugee camp.

When we visited the camp 27 February, a restaurant owner proudly showed us the interior of his home. The interior walls were plastered with fine gypsum, and each room was decorated in a different style. One room had flower-like stucco applications along the upper part of the walls, while another room—in a style reminiscent of the once popular ceiling-high wallpapers—was decorated with the texture of fake rock, colored in a reddish brown, with a painting of a serene beach scene, some palm trees, and a few houses as its centerpiece. The corridor featured fake tree trunks applied in a semi-realistic stucco relief on the walls, framing the doorways and the cabinet. In between the trunks, plants made their way towards the ceiling. The next room featured a similar design with the Sahrawi flag framed by tree trunks.

Even if seemingly innocent and kitsch to the Western eye, the scenes are exemplary and indicative of the dilemmas and contradictions residential architecture finds itself in within the Sahrawi refugee camps. The decorations are an expression of the innate human desire to make one's surroundings comfortable and appealing. The search for beauty is one of the driving forces of architectural production, and hence one can genuinely say that the restaurant owner endeavored in an architectural project. After living for years in the desert, with limited resources, few natural colors or plants, and a ruthless climate, the strive for a more bucolic and idyllic setting seems only too natural.

But the very existence of this architectural endeavour is also its problem. The refugees are only meant to live in the camps temporarily, hoping to go back to their homeland whenever it becomes possible. The return to the Western Sahara is the main aim and is central to all of their actions. It is of vital importance that they express publicly to the whole world that the camps are not "home" and never will be. Their stay in the camps is not a natural one, and certainly not desired. The world should never get the sense that the refugees have resigned themselves to their fate of a life here. Therefore, any move towards stability—and architecture is the prime medium to express such a stability—works against this expression of temporariness. The interior decorations of the restaurant owner's house, as innocent as they might seem, are not only an expression of a drive for beauty and comfort, but also a tiny step towards giving in to one's destiny of life in the camps.

On another related level, as kitschy as they seem, the trees, plants, flags, and serene coastal scenes carry a message and political undertone. They are obviously a call for the liberation of the homeland and a reference to the lusher nature of the Western Sahara. The coastal scene is a memory of a time gone by, and can also be read as an assertion or entitlement to those lands alluded to in the painting. Unlike the ceiling-high wallpapers showing scenes from exotic places, the decoration is not just alluding to romantic desire, but proclaiming a political program. It is not naive—on the contrary, it speaks out a clear agenda. It is the attempt of the restaurant owner to reconcile the potential slippage into permanence with a political message expressing a clear demand for return.

The carpets and textiles found in many other refugee homes represent an alternative method of decorating private spaces and carry a different significance. Whereas stucco and painted plaster accepts and plays with the architecture of the building, the textiles construct an alternative reality. Within an adobe house, or even a hut constructed out of sheet metal, a landscape of traditional textiles and embroidery is unfolded that is meant to replace or overcome the nontraditional building structure. The appliance of the textiles is sometimes so complete that not even a single glimpse of the supporting structure remains visible, creating the almost perfect illusion of sitting in a tent—were it not for the lack of wind and the slightly different shape of the space. Apart from referencing tradition and craft, the textiles have the property of being easily dismantled and moved, supporting the notion of temporariness versus permanence. In this sense they represent the more proper, established, and accepted means of decorating one's private spaces.

27 February, inside the house of a restaurant owner, 2011

More recently, a few specifically designed residential houses have been constructed in the camps. These "design" houses feature elements such as columns and stepped parapets. They have bay windows or small recesses with ornamental elements. One house in the daïra of Edchera in the camp El Aaiún combines traditional "oriental" elements with a style almost reminiscent of Swiss minimalist architecture. The layout of these "design" houses differs substantially from the typical arrangement dominant in the camps. Instead of multiple volumes, each with a single room arranged around a central court, the new typology features multiple rooms within a single unit, often lacking the open court. In their design and layout, the design houses are similar to residential typologies that can be found in southern Europe.

In some cases, design houses are influenced by what family members experience when working or studying in Spain or the Canary Islands. After working in these countries, sometimes for several years, the refugees return not only with money but also cultural influences, and henceforth practice alternative ways of designing, constructing, and arranging their domestic spaces. In other cases, however, the specially designed house cannot just be traced back to the personal experience of a specific Sahrawi family, but also to the emergence of the "designer" within the camps. In the case of the design house in Edchera (camp El Aaiún), the Sahrawi family consciously hired an architect cum construction manager to design and construct their house. He has designed other houses in the same camp, as well as in the camp Awserd, and in some cases families have been influenced by the style and have employed similar elements when constructing their own houses. Not only can we therefore see the emergence of a new profession within the camp, but we can also perceive the manifestation of a local (urban) culture. The camps become the site where hybrid forms are invented, incorporating traditional Berber lifestyles, Western modes of living, resource-efficient construction methods, and the "culture" of humanitarianism.

Obviously, the design houses venture a step further into the dilemma of temporary versus permanent. The financial investment of the families into these houses is considerable. They fiercely object, however, when asked if the decision to construct these houses implies they have resigned themselves to a protracted life in the camps. They see their investment as being independent of the issue of permanence, rather focusing on the question of quality of life. And this, in the end, is maybe the most appropriate way of dealing with one's life as a refugee. The refugees continuously claim for their return to the homeland, are politically active, and construct a national identity with an awareness that their stay in the camps is not natural and is only temporary. Nevertheless, they are willing to invest in the structure of their camp, if only for the sake of achieving slightly increased comfort and as an expression of an individual and a collective culture, but (and this is an important but) not seeing them as elements of stability or permanence. The Sahrawis are willing to surrender their investment when the first opportunity arises of returning to the Western Sahara.

Seen together, the tent, hut, design house, interior decoration, and many other aspects of the built-up fabric form a quasi-urban landscape, where housing typologies, construction details, and ornamentation show a multitude of ways to deal with the refugee condition and the 35-year-long displacement. The different forms and elements of residential architecture give evidence of the different approaches to this displacement. Residential architecture becomes a testimony to political aspiration.

ALG
CK

# ADMINISTRATION

Refugee camps usually consist of residential areas where the refugees live; markets and distribution centers where foodstuff is distributed; and a zone of offices used by NGOs and international organizations such as UNHCR or WFP, from which the camp is administered. Although representatives of the refugees are often involved pro forma in committees for the administration of the camp in general, the formulation of policies on distributing resources or providing education or health care lie with the organization providing such resources, or with UNHCR as a controlling body. Administration of a camp usually therefore means the control of resources and services for refugees by others.

Refugee camps of the Western Sahara are some of the few instances worldwide where the refugee population is not only involved, but fully in charge of administering itself. Although largely dependent on foreign aid, the responsibility for the distribution of this aid and for the establishment of basic services such as health and education lies exclusively in the hands of the refugees. As a consequence, an administrative center has developed that represents a unique case in the context of refugee conditions: a camp as a proxy capital for a refugee nation in exile.

# A Unique Phenomenon

When approaching the camp El Aaiún from the Algerian city of Tindouf, one passes a checkpoint manned by Algerian soldiers. A few hundred meters later there is an additional checkpoint, this time manned by Sahrawi soldiers. It is this second checkpoint that sets the Sahrawi camps apart from almost all other refugee camps in the world. In most cases it is the hosting nation that controls access to and from camps. In the case of the Darfur refugees in Chad, to name one example, the Chadian police force and the Chadian Commission Nationale d'Accueil et de Réinsertion des Refugiés (Chadian National Commission for the Reception and Reintegration of Refugees, CNAR) man the checkpoints and access roads to the numerous refugee camps in the east of the country. The refugees cannot control who is allowed to enter the camps. In contrast to this, in the case of the Sahrawi camps, it is the Sahrawis themselves who ultimately have control over who enters their settlement.

The Sahrawi checkpoints and, by extension, the level of control that they provide, become an indicator of a larger question at stake—the issue of self-determination. When the Sahrawis arrived in the area of Tindouf in the mid-1970s, Algeria granted extensive autonomy to the refugees. The Sahrawis are allowed to set up their own organizations, formulate their own rules and laws, act or organize themselves politically and even militarily, and set up institutions of a civil society. This has given rise to the development of an extensive administrative system. It has also resulted in the establishment of Rabouni as the Sahrawis' administrative center, or acting capital for an exiled refugee nation. This is a unique phenomenon in the case of refugee populations worldwide.

Even though they are living as a group of approximately 160,000 refugees in the camps in Algeria, the Sahrawis have established their own country, the Sahrawi Arab Democratic Republic (SADR). The territory of this country corresponds to the Western Sahara. Due to the Moroccan occupation, the Sahrawis are not able to exercise control over, nor have access to, the territory of their country. The government of the SADR can therefore be described as a government in exile. While not being able to rule over the territory of its own country, the government of the SADR is in charge of governing and administering the Sahrawi refugee camps in Algeria.

SADR is hierarchically organized and led by a president who appoints a prime minister to be in charge of daily political affairs. Ministers deal with their specific portfolios of responsibilities, in fields such as education, economy, justice, health, and even defense. Politically, it is a one-party system. With the establishment of the refugee camps and the foundation of the SADR in 1976, Polisario transformed from an independence movement and military organization into a political party. Elections take place on a local and national level, but concern individual persons and movements within Polisario. The one-party system is argued to be a necessity arising from the refugee condition. Once the national homeland is resettled, a multi-party system will be installed. Perhaps surprising, especially to an outside visitor, is the fact that in spite of the one-party system, the range of opinions and political standpoints expressed in political debate is wide and does not necessarily follow a preset canon.

Sahrawi checkpoint when approaching El Aaiún

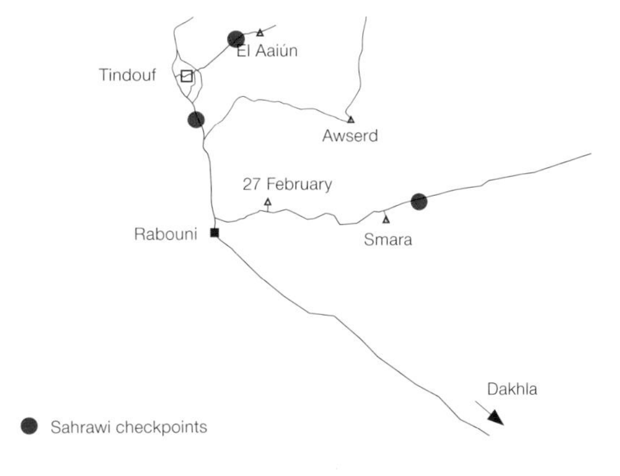

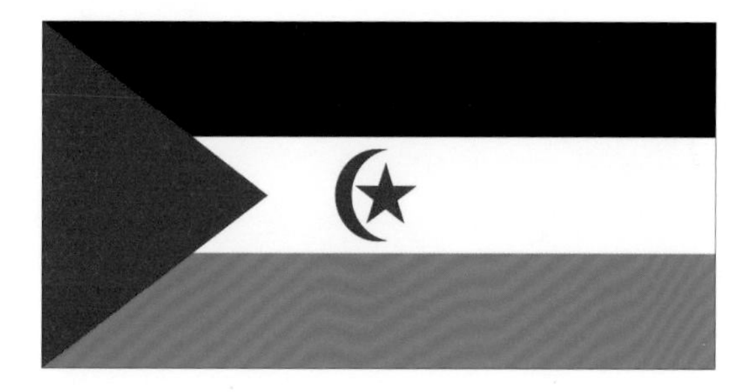

The national flag was created by Polisario and adopted as the flag representing the nation on February 27, 1976, the day the Sahrawi Arab Democratic Republic was declared. Black stands for death, while green symbolizes life, and white represents peace. The red star and crescent are major symbols of Islam.

It is almost identical to the Palestinian flag, and both are based on the flag of the Arab revolt against Ottoman rule in 1916–1918. The four colors are known as Pan-Arab colors and are used in many flags of Arab nations.

**Sahrawi Arab Democratic Republic**

| | |
|---|---|
| Name: | SADR (Spanish: República Árabe Saharaui Democrática, RASD) |
| Foundation: | February 27, 1976 |
| Territory: | Western Sahara |
| Status: | Occupied by Morocco |
| President: | Mohamed Abdelaziz |
| Prime minister: | Abdelkader Taleb Omar |
| Location: | Refugee camps near Tindouf and the liberated territories |
| Administrative headquarters: | Rabouni (refugee camp) |

"The Sahrawi republic sees itself as an independent state under illegal occupation, not as a government in exile. Polisario officials emphasize that the refugees are in Algeria for security and humanitarian reasons only.[1]"

**Development**

Polisario proclaimed the Sahrawi Arab Democratic Republic on February 27, 1976.

SADR has received recognition from a total of eighty-four countries, including Algeria, Libya, Syria, Kenya, Tanzania, Cuba, Peru, Vietnam, and, most recently, South Sudan. Of those eighty-four countries, several have, over time, withdrawn their recognition, such as Serbia, India, and Zambia, usually because of Moroccan initiatives. Since 1984, the SADR has been a member of the African Union–as a consequence of which, Morocco left the organization in protest.

**Organization**

SADR is hierarchically organized, with President Mohamed Abdelaziz at its head. The president appoints the prime minister, currently Abdelkader Taleb Omar.

The SADR constitution consists of a judicial branch that defines a law using a mixture of Western and Islamic principles. It further consists of legislature with the parliament of the Sahrawi National Council (SNC) and the executive with the Council of Ministries and the president.

Since the 1980s, SADR took steps towards a division of power similar to a republican structure.

**Key Points**

The SADR aims for the re-establishment of full control over the entire Western Sahara territory. The constitution foresees the establishment of a multi-party democracy with a market economy, the protection of human rights, and integration of the country into the region of the greater Maghreb as some of the central goals for the return to its homeland.

1 Mundy and Zunes, 2010, p. 123

**SADR**
Office of the president

Mohamed Abdelaziz
Current president

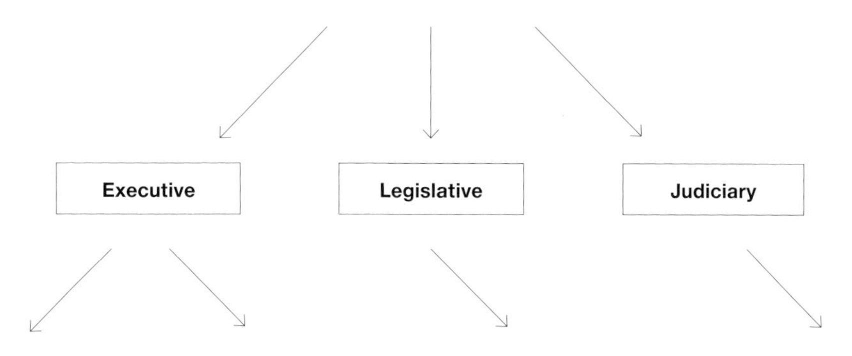

**Prime minister of the SADR**
Abdelkader Taleb Omar

**Council of Ministries**

Ministries:
- Economy and Employment
- Construction
- Commerce and Cooperation
- Environment and Transportation
- Rehabilitation of the Liberated Zones
- Interior
- Justice and Religious Affairs
- Health
- Culture
- Education
- Youth and Sport
- Defense
- Information
- International Affairs

**Parliament**
101 members
100 % Polisario Front

**Current speaker of Parliament**
Mahfoud Ali Beiba

**Law**
Mixture of Western and Islamic law

The national emblem of the SADR was designed by Polisario. The symbol presents two crossed rifles, each embellished with an SADR flag. In the top center is a red crescent and a star as a symbol of Islam. Two olive branches surround the guns, flags, and Islamic symbol. Written at the bottom is the Polisario motto, "Liberty, democracy, unity."

Until June 1991, when it was modified, the flag also depicted a hammer between the rifles.

**Frente Polisario**

| | |
|---|---|
| Name: | Polisario<br>Frente Popular de Liberación de Saguía el-Hamra y Río de Oro<br>(English: Popular Front for the Liberation of Saguia el-Hamra and Río de Oro) |
| Foundation: | 1973 |
| Status: | Political party |

**History**

| | |
|---|---|
| 1973 | Political and military organization fighting for liberation from colonial Spain and against the occupation by Morocco and Mauritania. |
| 1991 | Transformation into a political movement and party, with the adoption of a new constitution for the SADR and acceptance of the UN-brokered peace plan for a referendum on the status of the Western Sahara. |
| Today | Liberation movement, political party, and internationally accepted representative of the Sahrawi people. |

**Key Idea**

For most Sahrawis, Polisario is a coalition of Sahrawi nationalist political tendencies, spanning and going beyond Western notions of a left-right, progressive conservative spectrum.

**Organization of the Camps**

Polisario organizes the camps internally, developing political, educational, health, and social structures, and services to attend to the needs of its "refugee-citizens." Polisario officially emphasizes that refugees are in Algeria for security and humanitarian reasons only. Polisario's regional administration and military center is in Rabouni.

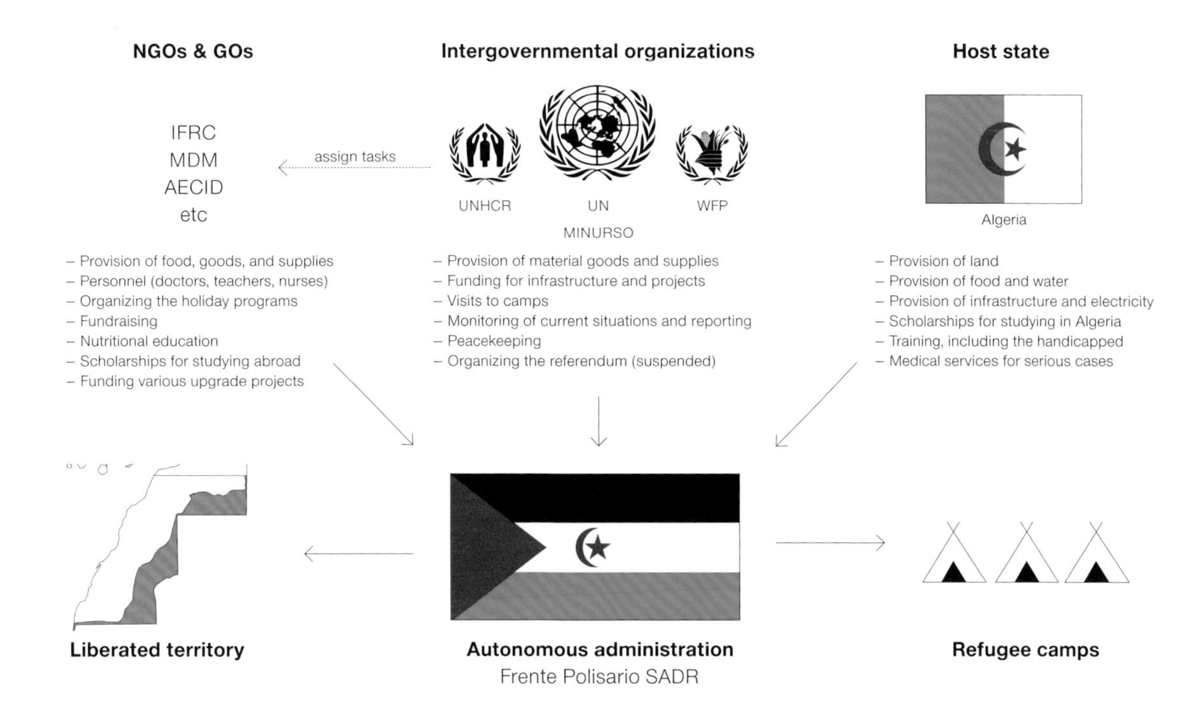


**SADR and the International Community**
Due to the extensive level of self-administration and organizational autonomy, NGOs, intergovernmental organizations, and friendly states don't play a direct role in the camp's management. They supply goods and personnel, and help develop strategies in Polisario's administration center, Rabouni, in corporation with SADR and the Sahrawi Red Crescent. Polisario/SADR chooses the NGOs it wants to work with and supervises every step of the organization.

**International Governmental Organizations**
(e.g. ECHO/UN; UNHCR, MINURSO, WFP)
These organizations visit the camps frequently for reports. They survey the current situation and fund infrastructure and various projects. MINURSO is responsible for peacekeeping operations, while WFP provides food.

**NGOs**
National and international NGOs, solidarity groups, and researchers provide material goods and supplies, as well as personnel, and support projects such as education centers or child-care projects.

**Algeria as Host State**
Algeria supports the Sahrawis in various ways:
- Until the 1980s it provided training to the Sahrawi People's Liberation Army (ELPS). This was terminated after the cease-fire was established.
- Provision of financial assistance to run the refugee camps for the supply of food, water, education, scholarships, medical services, etc.
- Construction and provision of services and infrastructure, such as asphalt roads and electricity.
- Permission for Sahrawis to enter formal employment for a period of up to three years. Refugees have no additional rights than other "foreigner" in Algeria.

**Friendly States**
Friendly states such as Algeria, Mauritania, and Cuba offer scholarships for higher education. Also, European countries such as Spain and Germany offer some grants and stipends for studying abroad.

## Milestones of SADR and the Frente Polisario

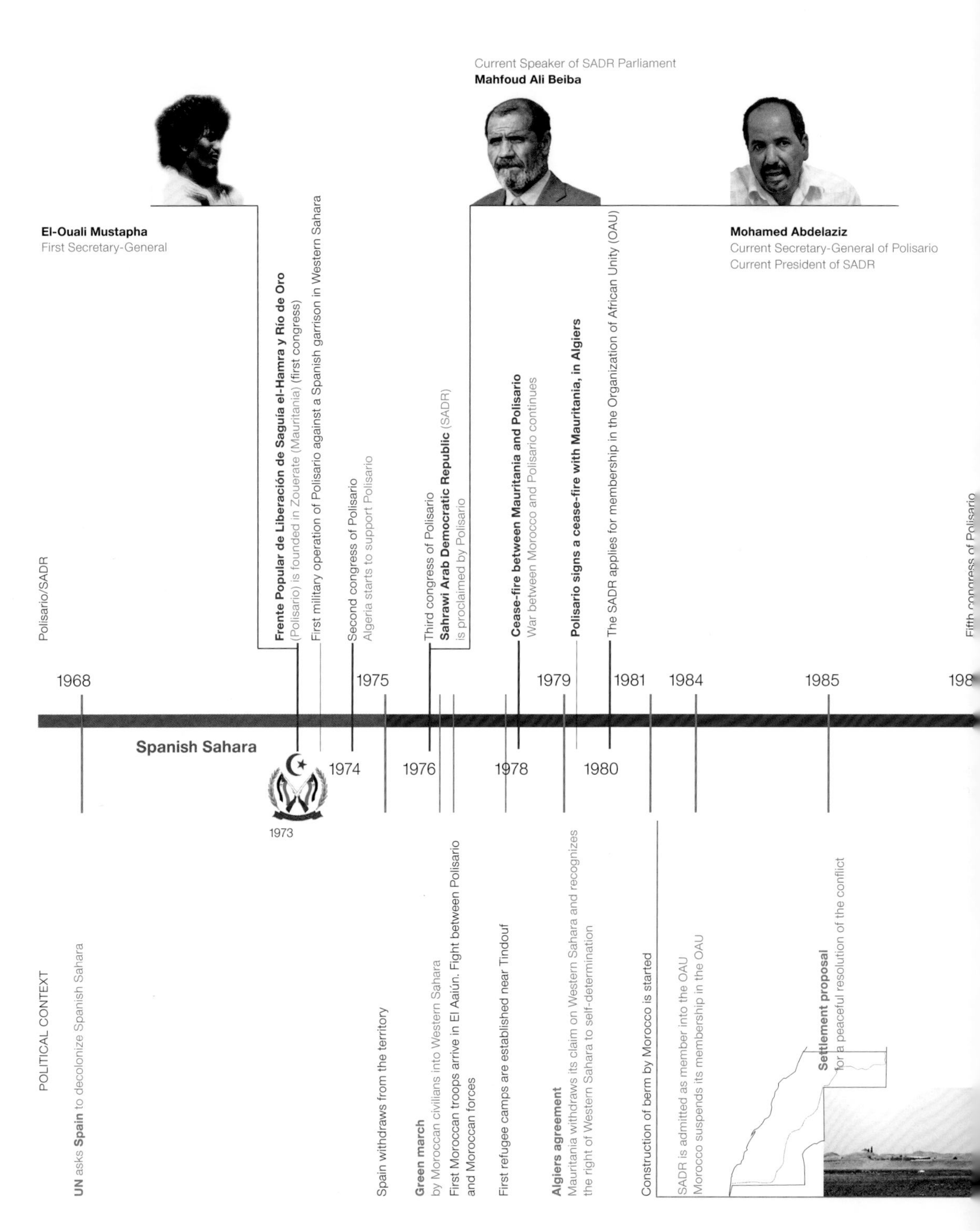

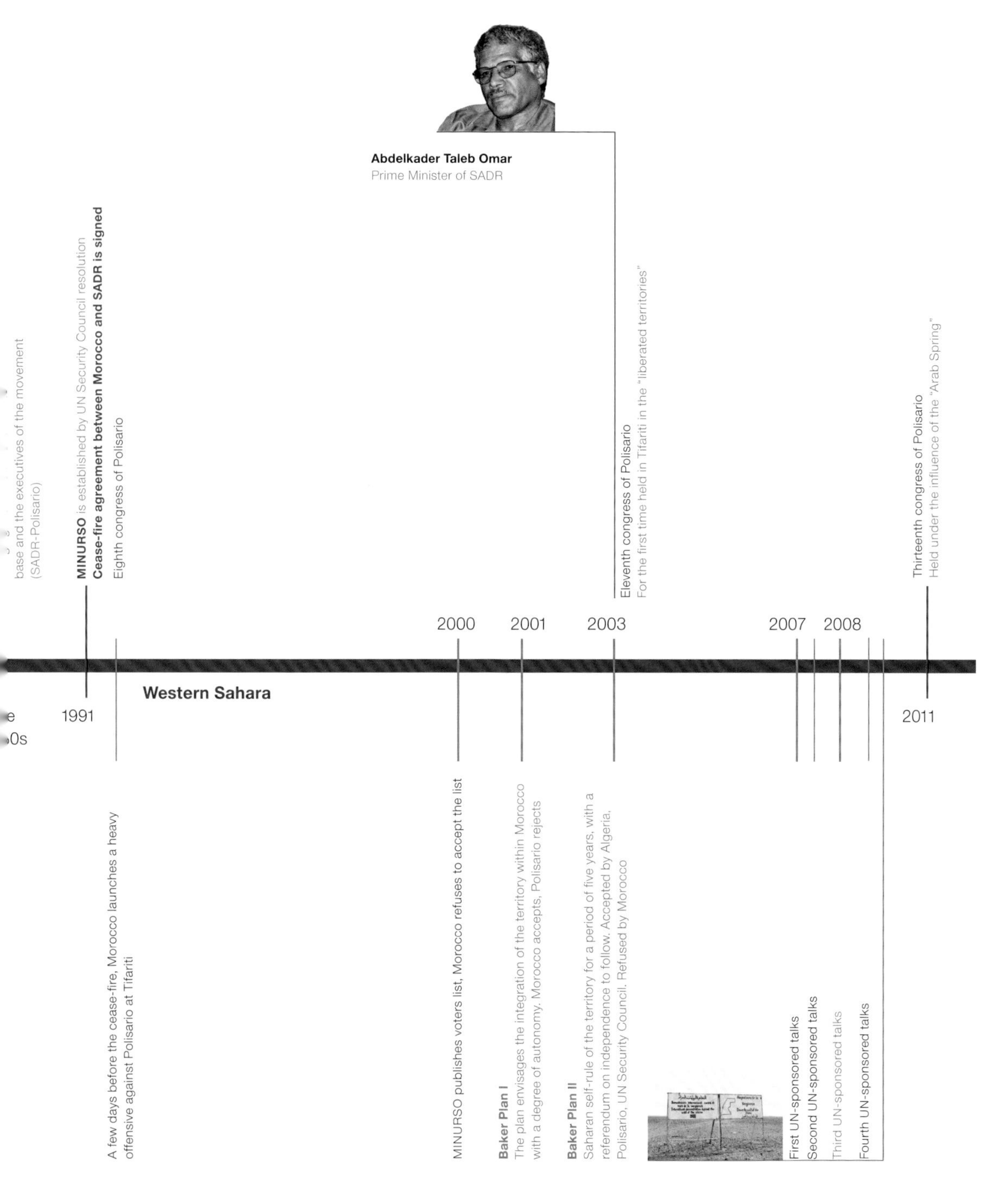
Abdelkader Taleb Omar
Prime Minister of SADR
base and the executives of the movement
(SADR-Polisario)
MINURSO is established by UN Security Council resolution
Cease-fire agreement between Morocco and SADR is signed
Eighth congress of Polisario
Eleventh congress of Polisario
For the first time held in Tifariti in the "liberated territories"
Thirteenth congress of Polisario
Held under the influence of the "Arab Spring"
2000
2001
2003
2007
2008
Western Sahara
1991
2011
A few days before the cease-fire, Morocco launches a heavy
offensive against Polisario at Tifariti
MINURSO publishes voters list, Morocco refuses to accept the list
Baker Plan I
The plan envisages the integration of the territory within Morocco
with a degree of autonomy. Morocco accepts, Polisario rejects
Baker Plan II
Saharan self-rule of the territory for a period of five years, with a
referendum on independence to follow. Accepted by Algeria,
Polisario, UN Security Council. Refused by Morocco
First UN-sponsored talks
Second UN-sponsored talks
Third UN-sponsored talks
Fourth UN-sponsored talks

## Organization of Frente Polisario and SADR[1]

Mundy and Zunes, 2010

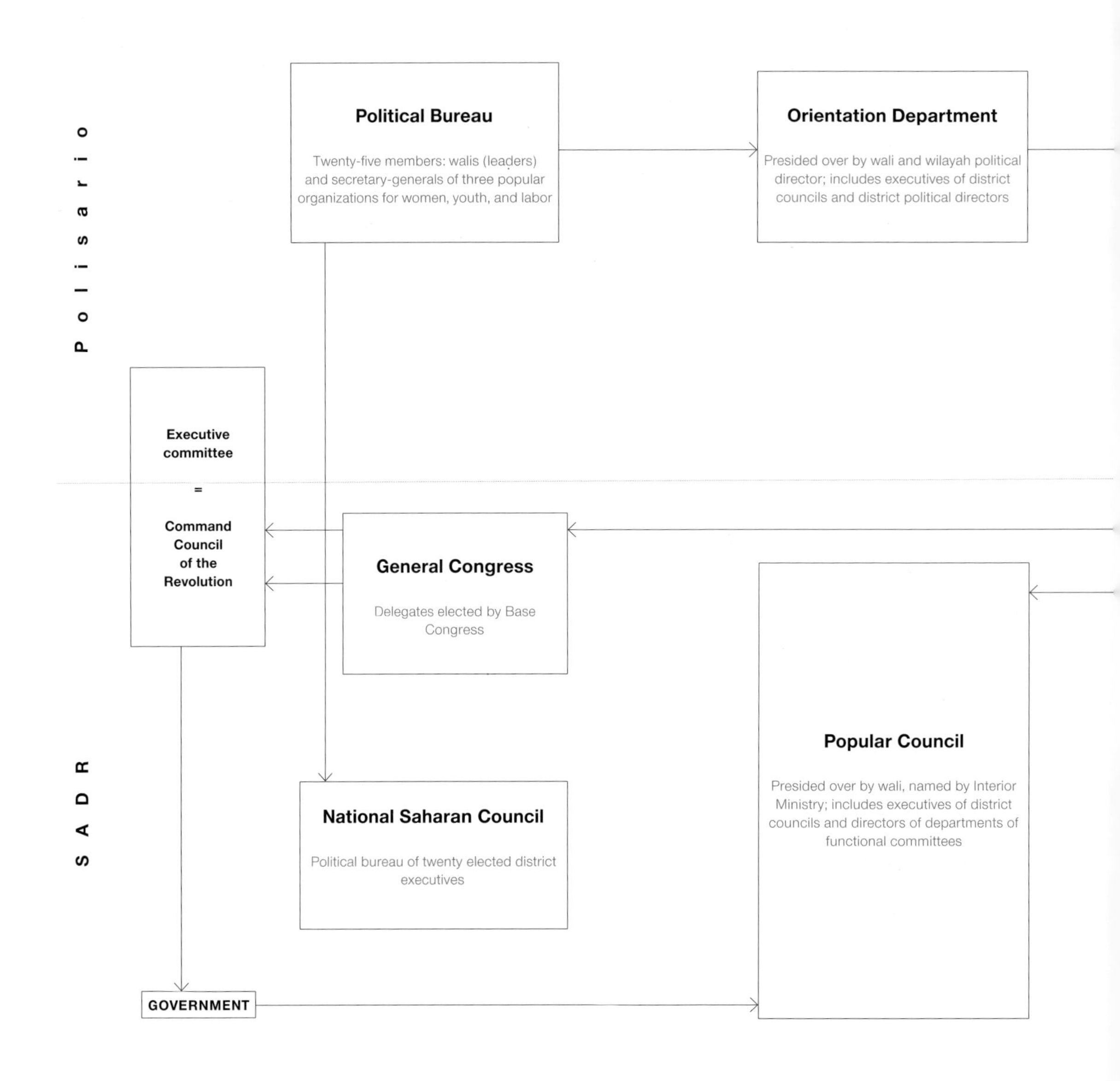


NATIONAL LEVEL

**Camps and liberated territories**

WILAYAH LEVEL

**Provincial level**
Each wilayah:
six primary schools,
one hospital

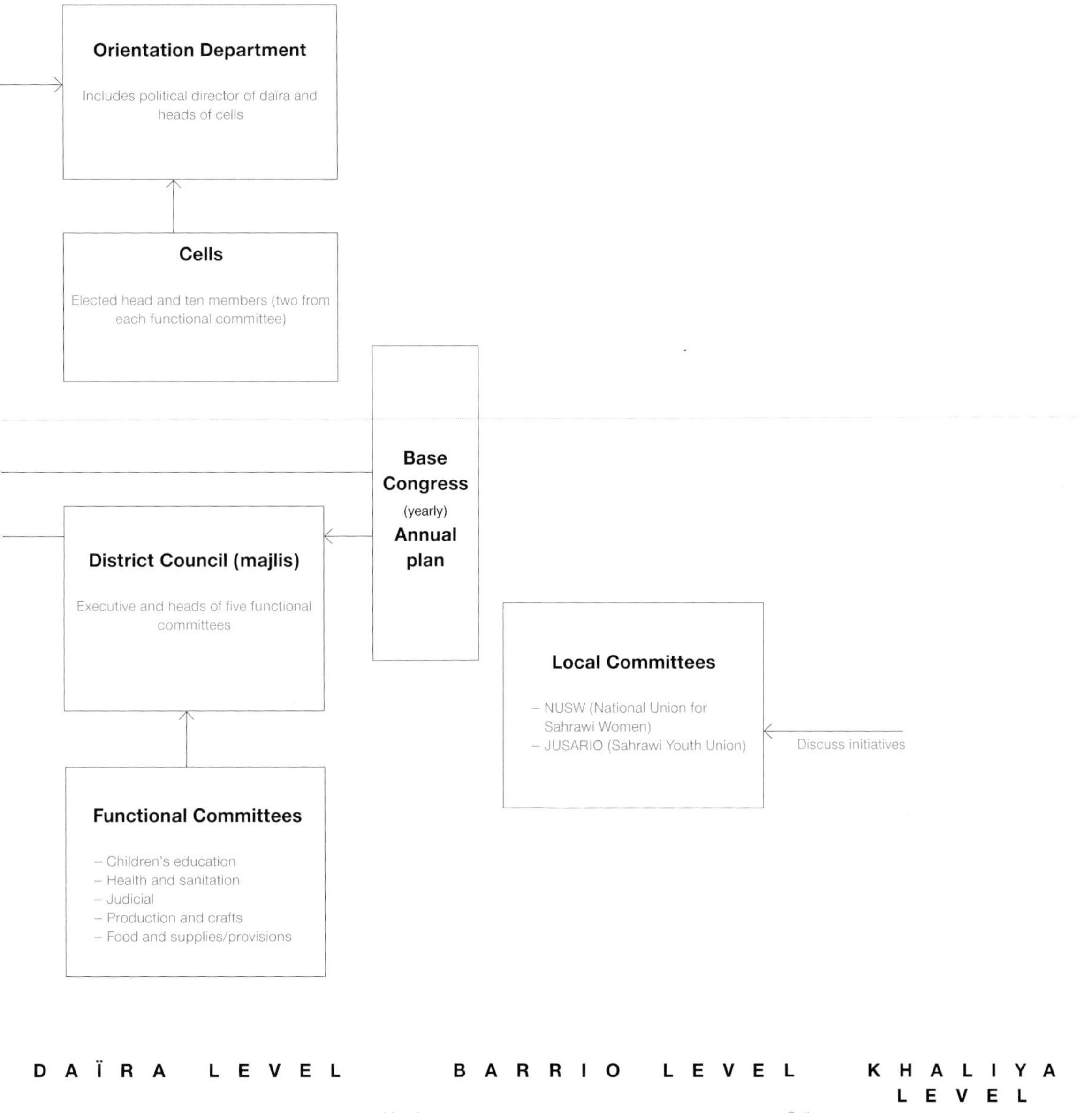
Orientation Department
Includes political director of daïra and heads of cells
Cells
Elected head and ten members (two from each functional committee)
Base Congress
(yearly)
Annual plan
District Council (majlis)
Executive and heads of five functional committees
Local Committees
– NUSW (National Union for Sahrawi Women)
– JUSARIO (Sahrawi Youth Union)
Discuss initiatives
Functional Committees
– Children's education
– Health and sanitation
– Judicial
– Production and crafts
– Food and supplies/provisions

DAÏRA LEVEL
BARRIO LEVEL
KHALIYA LEVEL
daïras
District level
Each daïra:
one medical clinic/dispensary,
one council (majlis)
4 barrios
Neighborhood level
Each barrio:
+200 residential compounds
Grassroots level of decision-making and management
Cells
Twelve-to-fifteen-person cell
Each refugee is officially a member of a local cell, which:
– organizes the sub-neighborhoods for specific activities (e.g. cleanups)
– reacts to emergencies (e.g. the floods in 2006)
– discusses political or social initiatives for functional committee

Museo Nacional de la Resistencia, Rabouni

Soldiers of the Saharan Liberation Army near Tifariti in the Liberated Territories

The ELPS has no navy nor air force, but the images seem to be attractive…

### ELPS

| | |
|---|---|
| Name: | ELPS<br>Ejército de Liberación Popular Saharaui<br>(Saharan Popular Liberation Army) |
| Foundation: | February 27, 1976 |
| Headquarters: | Rabouni |
| Commander: | Secretary-general of Polisario,<br>Chief Mohamed Abdelaziz |

### Polisario's Military

The army or military wing of Polisario (ELPS) is integrated into the SADR system through the institution of the Ministry of Defense. The precise size of the Polisario forces is unknown by outsiders. It is generally estimated to consist of between 3,000 and 6,000 soldiers.[1]

Both male and female refugees in the Tindouf camps undergo military training at the age of 18. During the war women formed auxiliary units to protect the camps.

### ELPS Regions

The ELPS area is divided into six military regions. Each region has five to six battalions, each of which is composed of approximately four to five military units, plus a specialized support unit (signals and communication, tactical analysis, medical, water location and drilling, and vehicle and weaponry repair).

### Tactics and Equipment

In the beginning of the guerrilla war against Morocco, with a knowledge and mastery of the terrain, ELPS developed a rapid hit-and-run-style tactic.

In this so-called *ghazzi* tactic they used numerous remodeled civilian Land Rovers, mounted with anti-aircraft machine guns, in which they tried to overwhelm garrisoned outposts in rapid surprise strikes.

Initially, during the anti-Spanish rebellion, Polisario moved only on foot or camelback. The guerrilla war against the Moroccans showed the importance of light vehicles, however. After the construction of the Moroccan sand berm, ELPS changed its tactics, focusing more on artillery, snipers, and other long-range attacks.

Algeria and Libya supported the ELPS with weapons until the armistice in 1991. Additionally, the ELPS received army training from Algeria.

The modern ELPS is now equipped with Soviet-manufactured weaponry, mainly donated by Algeria.

1 Bhatia, Michael, "Western Sahara under Polisario Control: Summary Report of Field Mission to the Sahrawi Refugee Camps," 2001

# Rabouni

On first sight, Rabouni seems like a slightly disorganized logistical center. It is a myriad of all-terrain vehicles, pickup trucks, taxis, and buses standing close to petrol stations, garages, distribution points, or improvised bus stands. Walls of stacked containers are located in proximity to warehouse-style structures and partition walls made of clay bricks. The streets are strewn with unidentifiable machines and spare parts of all descriptions.

Rabouni was the first camp of the Sahrawis. It was founded in 1976, just after the war with Morocco had begun. Initially, Rabouni was the camp that housed most of the Sahrawi refugees. It was divided into three daïras, with a small administration hub. Over the years, the new camps of Smara, El Aaiún, Awserd, and Dakhla were founded, becoming major centers of settlement.

By 1987 Rabouni was transformed from a residential camp into a center of administration for the Sahrawi government in exile. Moving out of Rabouni to the other settlements, the removal of tents and residential huts left many gaps and voids in the fabric of the camp. Rabouni's texture today is diverse and heterogeneous. The large compounds of various organizations and ministries occupy wide areas and shape Rabouni's map. Markets and ensembles of garages fill some of the areas in between the compounds, but the settlement as a whole remains ruptured and inconsistent.

What is unique about Rabouni is the fact that it exists in the first place. The settlement is a direct result of the semi-sovereignty that was granted to the refugees by Algeria when it donated the territory. The Sahrawi refugees are in charge of their own lives and are not governed by other authorities. Rabouni reflects this autonomy. Virtually all other refugee camps are administered by UNHCR from offices usually located outside the camp's perimeter, and by individual NGOs in their respective compounds. The fact that refugee camps are administered by others has the effect that the spaces of administration, and hence the spaces of control, are mostly hidden and remain at a distance, out of reach of the refugees.

Garage and workshop in the market area

Grocery store in the market area

Snack stand near the central bus stop

Petrol station at the central market

Central bus and taxi station

**Impressions of Rabouni**

Moving through Rabouni, one notices a substantial difference from the other camps. The lack of residential buildings, no children playing in the sand nor roaming goats gives the place a more pragmatic quality. On the other hand, the far-stretching, fortress-like construction of stacked containers, the funky, giraffe-patterned walls of the Ministry of Defense, and a junkyard full of derelict buses add a certain uncanny, maybe outlandish, and sometimes otherworldly character to the settlement.

This, though, is overlaid by the humdrum of everyday life. The settlement is filled with commuters coming to work each day in buses, taxis, or cars. They hurry to their offices, have lunch in a cantina or from a takeaway food stand. They move between the different buildings of the ministries and other institutions, then leave Rabouni again in the evening, going back to their own camps.

**Rabouni**

WFP food-storage compound with walls made of containers

Soldiers outside the Ministry of Defense

Junkyard of derelict buses

Bus stop

Commuters on their way back to the camps, passing the main water towers

**Government Facilities**

1 SADR Management/*Protocolo*
2 Ministry of Development and Construction
3 Ministry of Health
4 Ministry of Justice and Religious Affairs
5 Ministry of Culture
6 Ministry of Youth and Sport
7 Ministry of Defense
8 Ministry of Information
9 Ministry of International Affairs
10 Ministry of Education
11 Parliament
12 National Archive

**SADR Management/*Protocolo***

The *Protocolo* contains government offices and logistical facilities for the camps. It is also used as a guesthouse.

**Ministry of Development and Construction**

**Ministry of Public Health**

**Ministry of Justice and Religious Affairs**

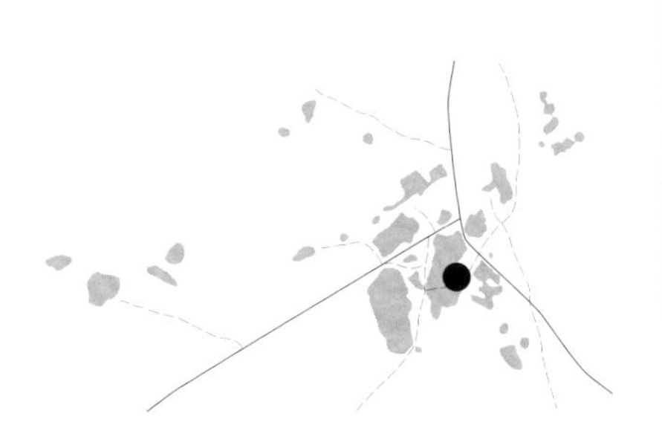

**Ministry of Public Culture**

**Ministry of Youth and Sport**

**Ministry of Defense**

**Ministry of Information**

The Ministry of Information runs a TV station, several radio stations in the camps, and maintains a website that publishes information on the conflict.

## Ministry of International Affairs

## Ministry of Education

## Parliament

The assembly building is the seat of the president and the prime minister's office.

## National Archive

The national archive holds documents, newspapers, photos, recordings, and videos, chronicling the history of the Sahrawi nation.

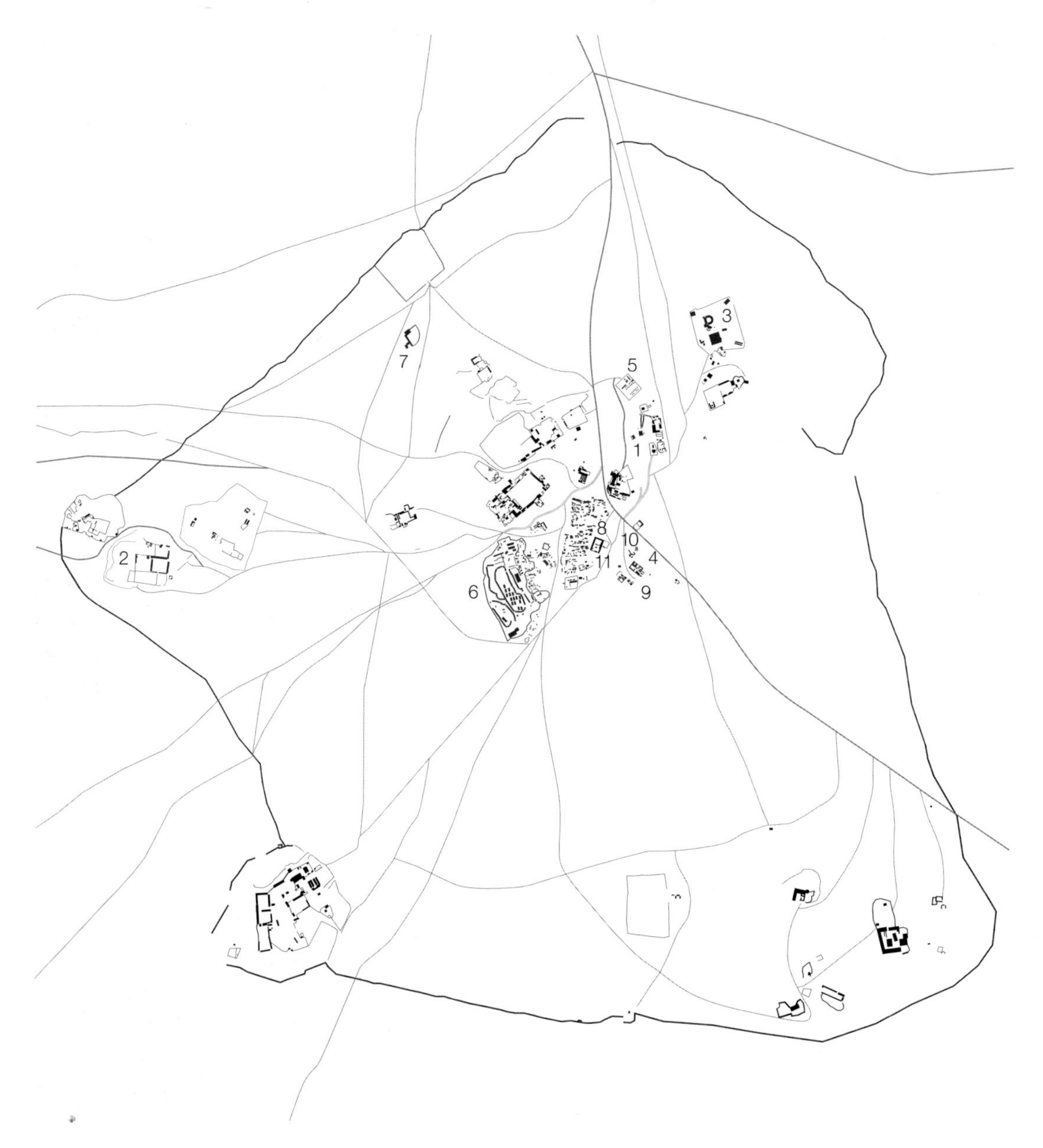


**Public Facilities**

1 TV/Radio RASD
2 Museo Nacional de la Resistencia
3 Hospital
4 UJSARIO
5 UNHCR
6 MLRS/WFP
7 AECID
8 Market
9 Accommodation
10 Garages
11 Mosque

**TV/Radio RASD**

Radio RASD and TV belong to the Ministry of Information. Radio RASD was founded on December 28, 1975, while TV RASD was founded in 1999.

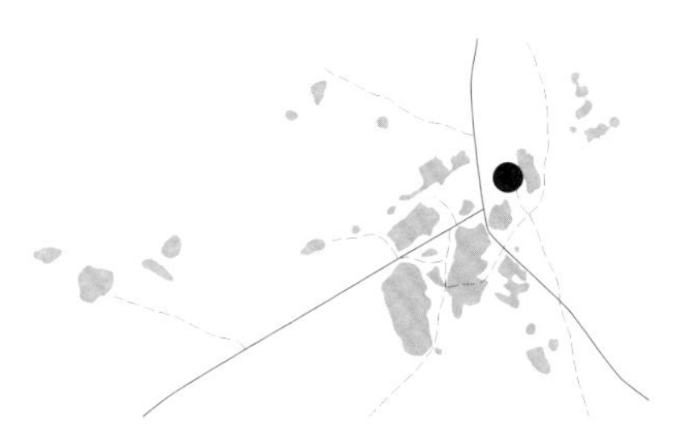

**Museo Nacional de la Resistencia**

The museum opened in 1976. Its aim is to commemorate the Sahrawi people and their resistance fight. It exhibits historical documents, photos, and military equipment.

**Hospital**

The national hospital is located in Rabouni and is equipped with operating theaters. It offers the highest level of medical care among all camps.

**UJSARIO**

The youth organization of Polisario, Unión de la Juventud de Saguia el-Hamra y Rio de Oro. It has a political influence and plays a role in parliamentary elections.

**UNHCR**

United Nations High Commissioner for Refugees. UNHCR is involved in refugee registration, food distribution, capacity building, and family programs.

**MLRS**
**WFP**

Media Luna Roja Sahrawi (Sahrawi Red Crescent) and the World Food Programme organize food aid and run the large storage facility made of containers.

**AECID**

Agencia Española de Cooperación Internacional para el Desarrollo (Spanish Agency for International Development).

**Market**

The central market of Rabouni supplies mainly food and automotive parts. It also has a few snack stores.

## Garages

The proportion of garages in Rabouni is higher than in the camps due to the high number of transport facilities and vehicles.

## Mosque

A few years ago a mosque was constructed near the central bus and taxi station.

## Residential Buildings

Very few residential buildings exist in Rabouni. They are mostly used by employees staying there during the week.

# Administration in the Camps

On a national level, SADR has twelve ministries and a parliament of 101 members at its Rabouni headquarters. It is in Rabouni where major strategical decisions affecting the nation in exile at large are taken. The implementation of these decisions takes place in the camps themselves, however, through the administrative center of each camp and the smaller-scale daïra centers. At a grassroots level, the camp becomes the space of a lived nationalism, where a political agenda is enacted by the Sahrawi refugees in their daily lives. The camps are self-managed with locally elected functionaries. These functionaries can be seen as representatives and mediators between the general population of the camps and Rabouni. The administrative infrastructure in the individual camps thus acts as a relay, with the opinions, interests, and demands of the population influencing national politics in Rabouni.

Administration in the camps takes place on two levels. The central administration building in the camp is the seat of the mayor, who is in charge of developing policies for the camp as a whole, overseeing activities and decision-making in the individual daïras. It is usually located in a central part of each camp and holds additional functions as a space for public, social, or cultural gatherings, and political assembly. Closer to the residents, and consequently playing a more important role in the day-to-day relationship between the population and its political representation, are the daïra centers. In the camp El Aaiún they follow a standardized layout, with a circular footprint and a partially radial, partially ring-like organization of their individual spaces. The daïra centers house administration spaces, a small facility for medication and health services, and storage areas. They also act as distribution points for food and other resources for the inhabitants of the daïra, and offer spaces for public assembly and the discussion of political issues among the local population. Being embedded in the routine of everyday life, daïra centers have often become places of informal gathering and social exchange.

Daïra center of Amgala, El Aaiún

**Daïra Centers**

Camps (wilayahs) are, in most cases, divided into six daïras (districts), which are further subdivided into four barrios (neighborhoods). The daïra centers are the administrative hubs of each daïra. They are multi-functional buildings and act as distribution points and public assembly spaces, offering medical services and serving as office space. The daïra centers in the camp El Aaiún have a circular footprint and an iconic architectural quality. The images show the daïra center of El Guelta in El Aaiún.

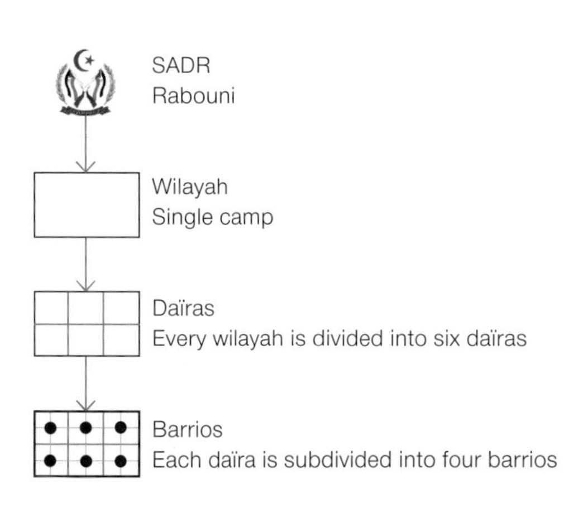


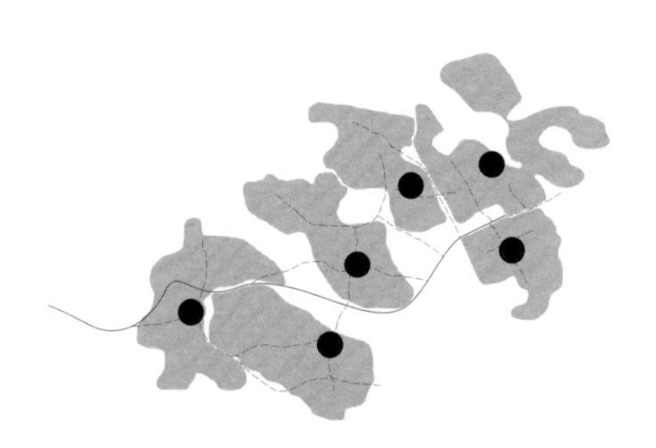

Mohamed Lamine, mayor of El Aaiún

**"The definition of 'city' cannot be used for the camps. We have many tents in our settlement. We can't live without them ..."**
**Mohamed Lamine, mayor of El Aaiún**

Wilayah administration, El Aaiún

### A Camp Is Not a City...

Mohamed Lamine has been the mayor of El Aaiún since his appointment in 2008. Previously, he was the minister of interior.

Every four years, the mayor of a wilayah is appointed by the national secretary of the SADR, the district councils and the directors of the functional committees.

### Administration of Wilayahs

The national secretary is the highest institution and acts over all wilayahs. Each wilayah has six to seven daïras, which are managed by a district council and various functional committees (including children's education, health and sanitation, judicial, production/crafts, food, and supplies/provisions). The functional committees try to organize parties and sporting activities and are responsible for the distribution of food, water, gas, and other supplies that arrive via Rabouni.

The very limited budgets and unpredictability of the economical situation makes it difficult to develop any reasonable budget plans. Governing the camps becomes a demanding task, based mostly on contingencies and day-to-day decisions. Mohamed Lamine shows a sign of resignation when he says that "It's hard to be the mayor of El Aaiún. I count the days until the end of my period..." (Conversation with the mayor, March 2011.)

### Shaping Camps

When asked about the transformation camps have seen over the years, Mohamed Lamine points to the densification that has taken place.

In the early years, the organization into wilayahs, daïras, and barrios was clearly visible and readable. Today the camps have became more dense, and the clear structure has disappeared. This process has partially developed without regulation, and partially with a certain control by the camp authorities. If someone intends to enlarge his home, he has to get permission from the responsible daïra council. In between daïras or outside the camp, the popular council of the wilayah has to decide.

Another significant factor is the markets. In the beginning, the construction of markets was spontaneous. Initially there was only one shop per daïra. After the cease-fire, men came back and set up businesses, so markets developed in several places and have since grown quickly. The administration of the daïra tries to control this growth by requiring the registration of all market shops and other businesses.

### Camps as a City?

In the words of Mohamed Lamine, the term "city" cannot be applied to the camps. "We have many tents in our settlement. We can't live without them."

Furthermore, the camps have no infrastructure and no permanent installation of electricity or water–something you would find in a city. Land ownership also plays a role in how the settlements are perceived. The land is not owned by the refugees. "This is Algeria. Not the Western Sahara."

# Spaces of Autonomy

In 1976, when Algeria provided Sahrawi refugees fleeing the guerilla war with Morocco with a territory to set up camps near Tindouf, it also gave approval to the refugees' semi-autonomy. Such autonomy is probably unique in the case of the refugee condition. Everywhere else (with the exception of Palestinian refugees in the West Bank and Gaza Strip, who are mostly in effective control of the spaces of their camps), refugees are governed by others. This means that all organizational, economical, administrative, and political decisions regulating the daily lives of refugees are made by either the respective host nation, or by one of the international and intergovernmental humanitarian organizations such as UNHCR, WFP, or ECHO. While the refugees might be represented in the decision-making committees, they are not in charge of their own lives. The semi-autonomy granted by Algeria to the Sahrawi refugees includes the right to establish their own civil institutions such as schools, libraries, or hospitals; the right to establish political institutions and a political system of representation; the right to set up a legal system with its own set of laws and law enforcement; and even the right to defend themselves by operating a police force and an army.

Rabouni is where this semi-autonomy manifests itself in the most explicit way and is spatially evident through the ministries, the parliament, a national archive, and other governmental institutions. Rabouni, as a self-run administrative capital for a refugee nation in exile, is probably a unique case in the global landscape of refugee camps. Having a rather pragmatic and utilitarian charm, it is nevertheless the place where a national consciousness is shaped and communicated, and where a certain level of sovereignty is exercised. Every day, people from other camps travel in to work and then return home in the evening. By going to work, the refugees not only busy themselves with organizational tasks, but also practice running a nation. In the absence of their own homeland, refugees learn the administration of a state in exile: what curriculum to develop for the educational system; what measures to take in response to food shortages or the threat of disease; what kind of foreign policy to develop; and how to deal with limited resources.

If Rabouni is one of the main focal points for developing a national consciousness for and by the refugees, it allows us to reflect upon the nature of this consciousness. If the traditional notion of national identity ties a collective of people with shared citizenship, culture, history, and language to a common territory, we can say that Sahrawi national consciousness is developing in the absence of this territory, and maybe also (at least partially) because of this absence. Practicing the state in exile, living on "borrowed" land, with most of the population never having experienced the homeland, but instead having established life in exile (in Rabouni), with a blueprint for a new society and social organization that is radically different from the past, Rabouni stands metonymically for a national consciousness. This consciousness is based on a common political project rather than territoriality and tradition.

Ministry of Defense (above); main road passing the square in front of the Ministry of International Affairs (below)

# MOVING AND COMMUNICATION

Moving and communication are strategies to link two or more geographically distant points with each other. Infrastructure of movement and the availability of communication resources bridge the gap between spaces and people. At the same time, they are catalysts for interaction and exchange, which are crucial factors for cultural and economic development.

Given the extremely remote and harsh location of the Sahrawi camps near Tindouf, the distance separating them from the rest of the world is arguably a multiple of the actual distance measured in miles or kilometers. Geographically, the camps are isolated. This fact alone calls for an elaborate network of linkage, embedding the camps in a chain of cultural, political, and economic connections on a regional and global scale. This chapter focuses on these networks, which permit and facilitate the connection of people and spaces, both within the camps and between the camps and the rest of the world.

# Global Spheres of Exchange

When first arriving at El Aaiún or any of the other Sahrawi camps, the prominent role that mobility plays is easily noticeable. What is not seen at first is the multitude and complexity of exchanges and what effect the influx of people, goods, and information has had on the camps. Often, the aspect of humanitarian aid and the unilateral relation or dependency it creates become the main issues of interest. Meanwhile, the paths of exchange and how they take place are much more intricate.

The question invariably arises as to why this society emphasizes mobility and interaction as much as it does. A nomadic background can be understood as an underlying and important cause, but only explains the present condition to a certain extent. Political intention is also a key factor, as it dictates most debates on permanence versus the ephemeral.

Communication and mobility take place within different domains and territorial spheres. On the smallest scale there is the issue of mobility within and between the camps. The inhabitants travel daily in their camps and from camp to camp for work, pleasure, to buy goods, or meet people. As the closest Algerian city, Tindouf is an important destination for the refugees and is somewhere they can, for example, buy products not available in the camps.

Slightly farther away are the "Liberated Territories" of the Western Sahara, with the small settlements of Tifariti and Bir Lahlou, and grazing grounds for camel herds. Mauritania is the destination for trade and the purchase of merchandise to be resold in the camp shops. The Algerian cities of Algiers and Oran are used as bases to travel to other countries and as destinations for higher education. Spain and the Canary Islands are places where a substantial number of Sahrawis work, either seasonally or more permanently, sending back goods and money (remittance) to the camps. Finally, the Sahrawi refugees go to Cuba or Lebanon, Libya, and other Middle Eastern countries for higher education, studying to become doctors, engineers, and teachers, among other things. All these destinations occupy a different position in the mental, organizational, and physical map of the Sahrawi population in the camps, and are accessed through different means and methods. Put together, they result in a surprisingly connected society located in the middle of the Sahara Desert.

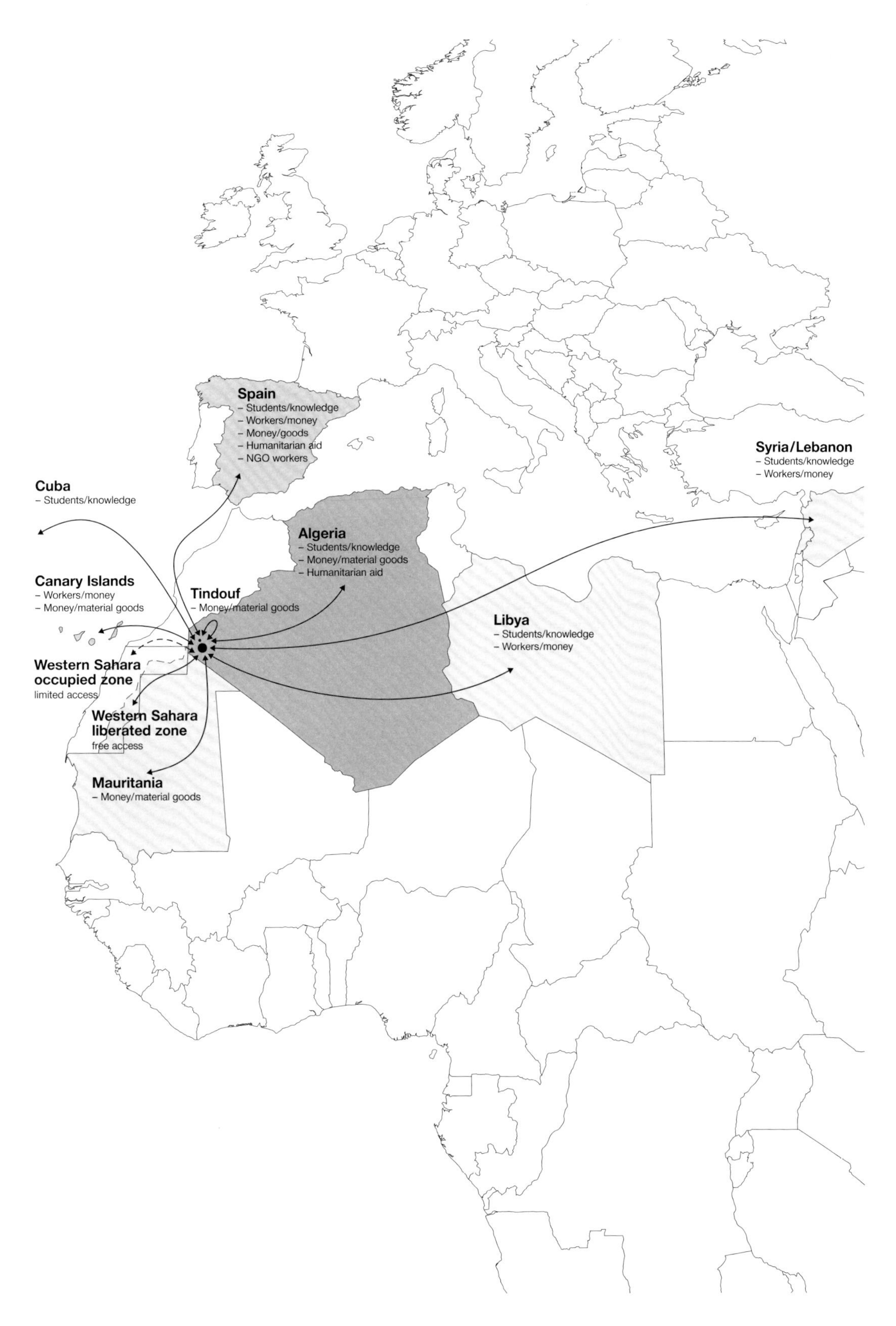
Spain
– Students/knowledge
– Workers/money
– Money/goods
– Humanitarian aid
– NGO workers
Syria/Lebanon
– Students/knowledge
– Workers/money
Cuba
– Students/knowledge
Algeria
– Students/knowledge
– Money/material goods
– Humanitarian aid
Canary Islands
– Workers/money
– Money/material goods
Tindouf
– Money/material goods
Libya
– Students/knowledge
– Workers/money
Western Sahara
occupied zone
limited access
Western Sahara
liberated zone
free access
Mauritania
– Money/material goods

# Connecting by Moving

Moving is the most obvious and direct way to establish a connection between two locations. Different factors like speed, frequency, and availability further define the performance of such movement, giving it a characteristic value and purpose. An efficient, quick and easily accessible infrastructure for moving therefore makes spaces seem closer together, especially due to the shortening of time necessary for transit.

This chapter first analyzes the topic of moving within a single camp and between different camps, then on subsequently larger scales, in which refugees establish relationships with places like Tindouf or Mauritania and countries including Spain and Cuba.

The ease and accessibility of transportation within the camps is quite astonishing, and it is not uncommon to be asked to get into a car when walking around the camp. The drivers are eager to help and find it unusual to see pedestrians walking when they could be driving. The Sahrawi refugees show no kind of aversion to vehicles. Family cars are often parked within the walls of the residential compound, shaded and protected from the sun. Cars are used for everything from visiting family members in a different camp and buying food in Tindouf to going to work in a shop at the main market.

This chapter discusses not just the vehicles themselves, but also the interrelated infrastructure and necessary spaces that evolve around them. Although there are several different means of transportation, the prevalent mode is by car, while the others, e.g. bus or donkey cart, are only used for specific tasks and thus applied selectively.

Main bus and taxi station in Rabouni

Truck driver outside Smara

# The Omnipresence and Importance of Mobility

Mobility is an aspect that is so omnipresent in everyday life, it inevitably leaves considerable traces on the landscape. Apart from the continuous activity of moving itself, all other aspects pertaining to mobility and its by-products are also very apparent. All types of vehicles are visible in the desert landscape in and around the camps, from eccentric-looking trucks, via the ubiquitous aging Land Rover, to the slightly shabby Mercedes or a pristine VW Golf. Car-repair shops, garages, and petrol pumps are among the most successful and frequent business activities in the camps. Besides that, there is an abundance of car parts and car wrecks—skeletons, so to speak—that are so pervasive, they are inseparable from the image of the landscape itself. The remains of cars are scattered throughout the camps, sometimes seemingly left behind, placed rather haphazardly; sometimes used to demarcate the boundaries of a plot or a playing field; and sometimes carefully staged and pieced together as a decorative, sculptural ensemble of objets trouvés.

The most radical and extreme collection of car parts is the scrapyard outside Rabouni where countless derelict buses and trucks have been dumped next to, and on top of each other to resemble the largest mass pileup in the history of motorized traffic.

SEVILLA CAPITAL

MICHELIN

NISSAN
LAND ROVER
TOYOTA

قطع غيار

LAND ROVER
قطع غيار السيارات
TOYOTA

Shuttle from Rabouni arriving at the bus stop

Repair shop and fuel pump

Repair shop

Old tires

Shop selling spare parts

Scrap vehicles

## Signs of Mobility

In any given neighborhood of El Aaiún one finds traces of mobility and the infrastructure that is needed to maintain the vehicles as well as the spaces created by these elements. Cars and trucks are not only a reliable source of income, they are an integral part of everyday life for most refugees and also a dominant part of the townscape.

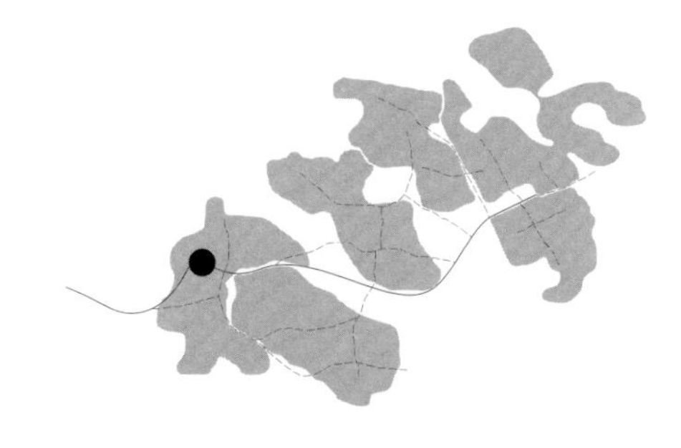

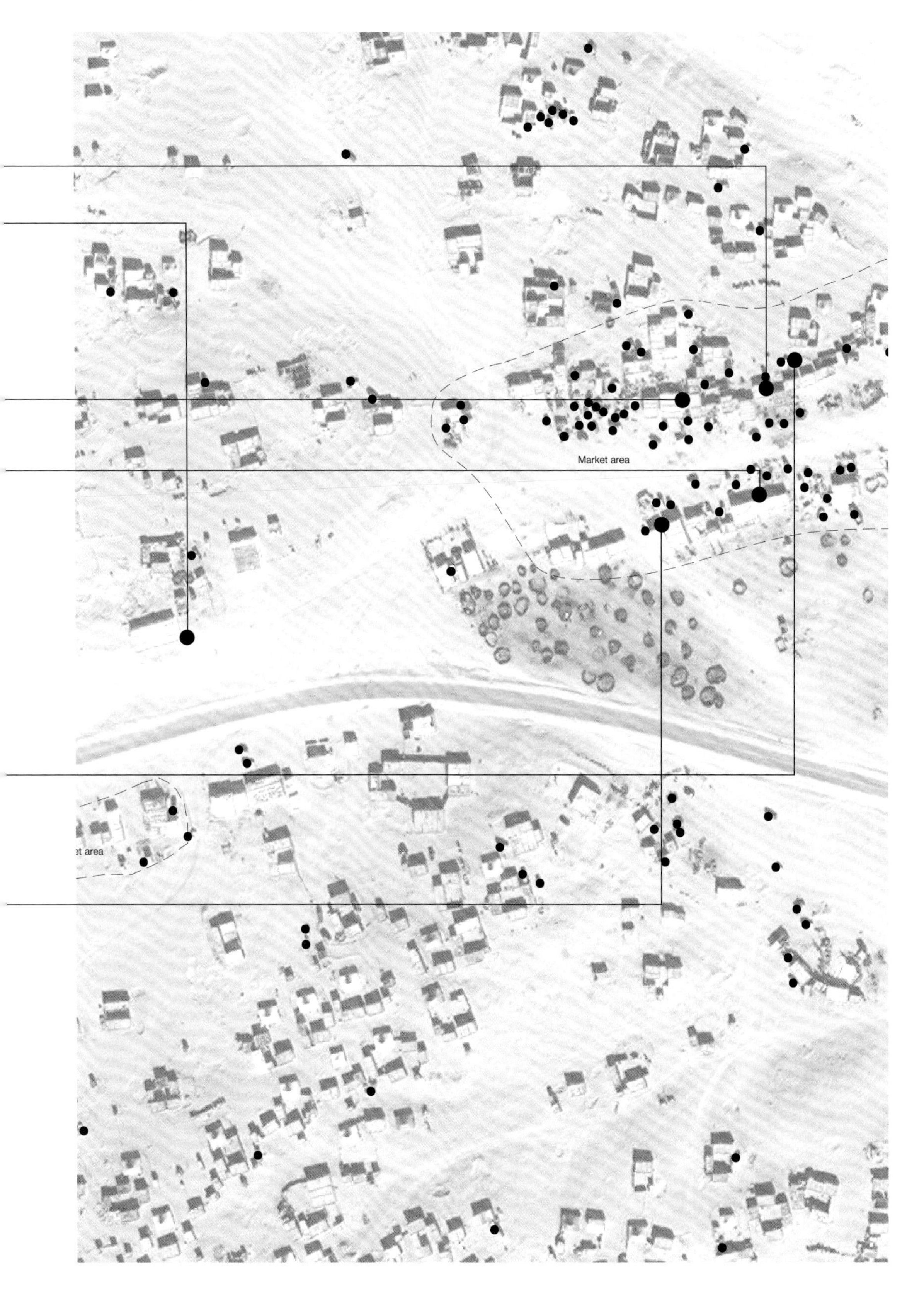
Market area
et area

### A Figure-Ground Plan of Cars

The number of cars and trucks in the Sahrawi camps is impressive, though traffic jams never occur. The black dots show the mass of cars present in El Aaiún. The cars are dispersed throughout the whole camp, but some higher densities can be spotted around the repair shops, market streets and other public centers.

The density around the markets, the main market in El Guelta, and the animal market in particular, are evidence of the importance of the relationship between movement and trade.

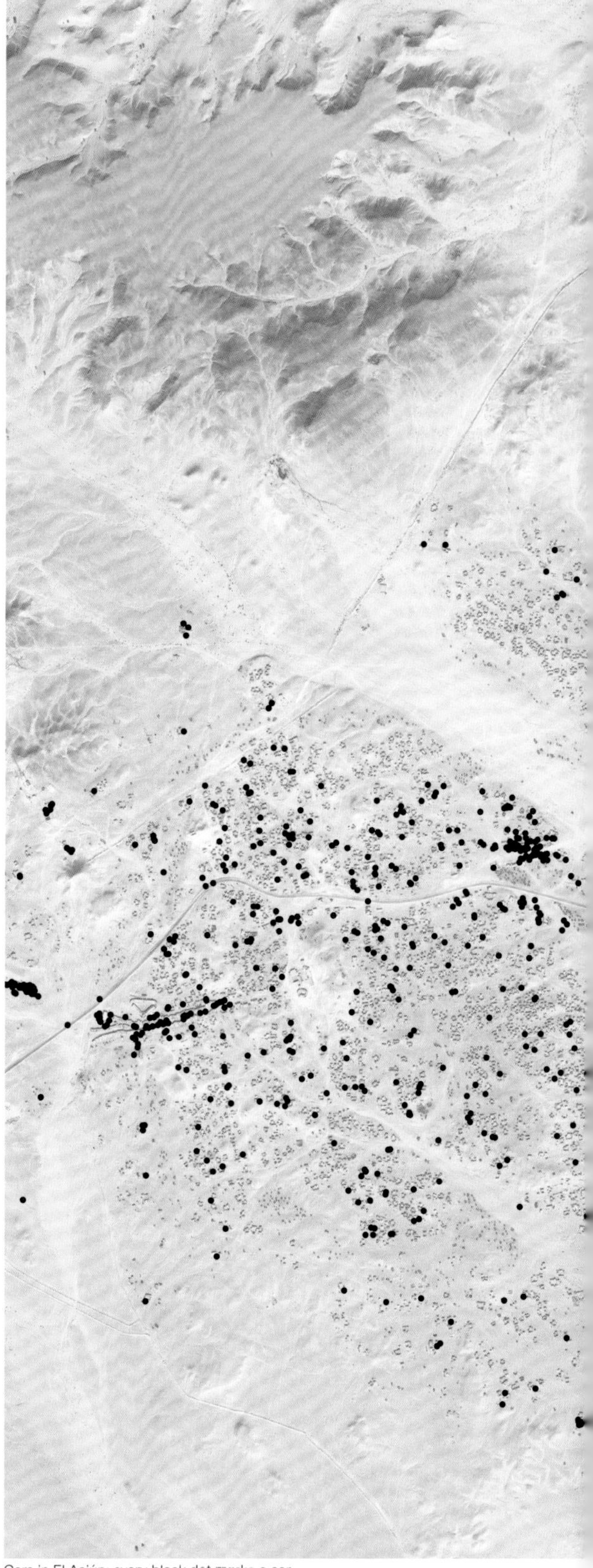

Cars in El Aaiún; every black dot marks a car

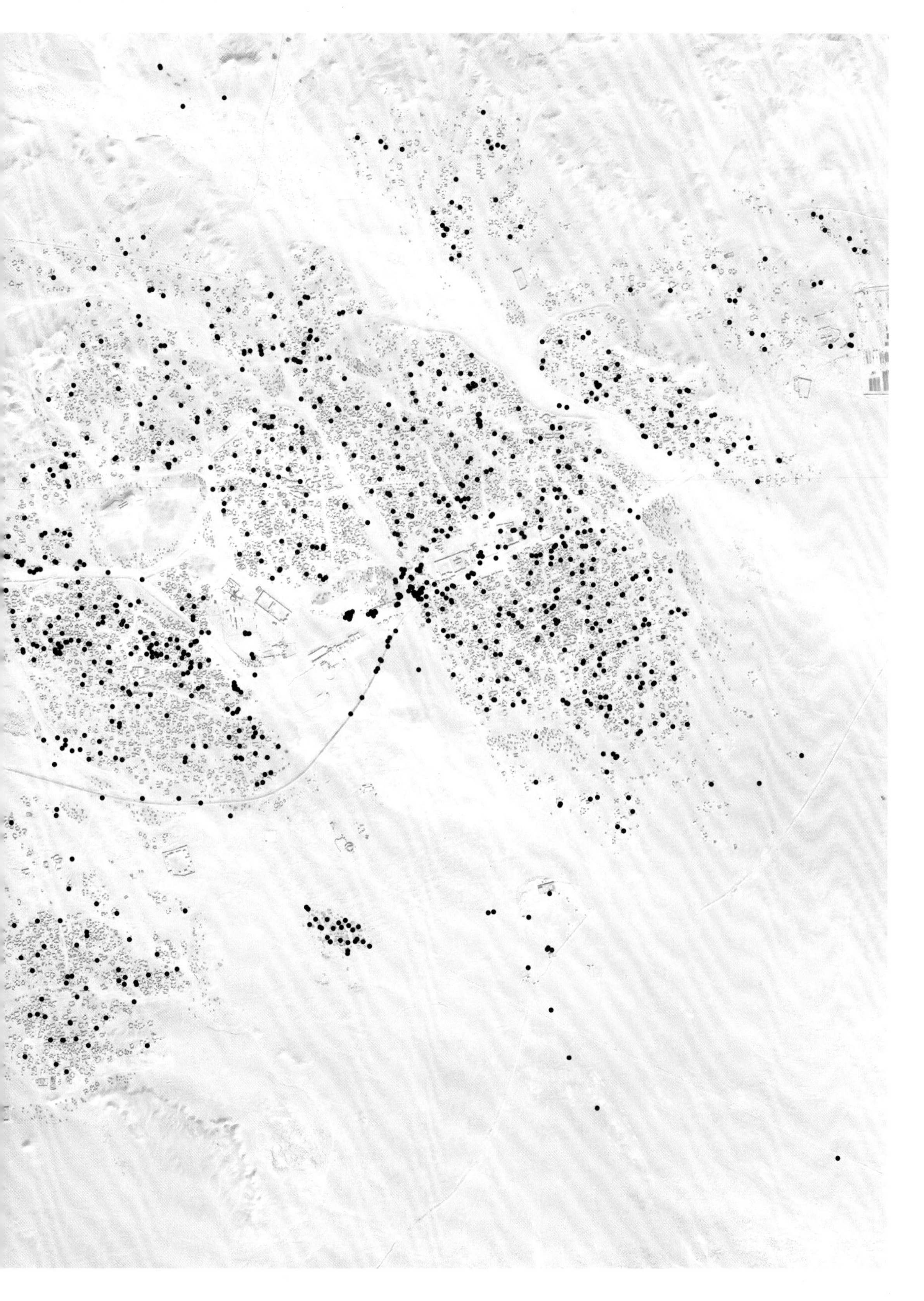

# Spaces of Movement

Roads are the some of the most permanent features of cities—certainly in developed nations, if not worldwide. While individual buildings can change, get torn down, or be rebuilt, with sometimes whole blocks being redeveloped, the layout and location of streets, once established, hardly ever changes. This is due to the investment into infrastructure and the placement of sewers, cables, and service pipes, but also the rigidity created by land ownership of precisely delineated plots and parcels. Furthermore, streets are imbued with a common memory and cultural importance that makes roads some of the most permanent elements in almost any urban fabric.

In refugee camps we are faced with a situation where buildings and sometimes even whole daïras are repeatedly rebuilt; where investment into road infrastructure is minimal if not mostly nonexistent; where land ownership does not exist; where the delimitation of parcels is never permanent; where the slow dynamics of the desert terrain reshapes topography; and where the overarching ideology of the Sahrawi refugees calls for the preference of the temporary in lieu of the permanent. Spaces of mobility therefore have a different status and spatial influence within the refugee camp. In the desert sand, ground conditions are also almost of a liquid nature. Nevertheless, more long-term constructions and institutions such as schools, administration buildings, hospitals, and markets form a network of stable nodes, which are connected by roads and pathways. By habit, routine, and practicability, a hierarchy of those routes has emerged, even though in theory all spaces between buildings and compounds can be used for driving and moving. The following pages will illustrate and analyze these different spaces of movement.

مواد غذائية
بالجملة والتجزئة
80

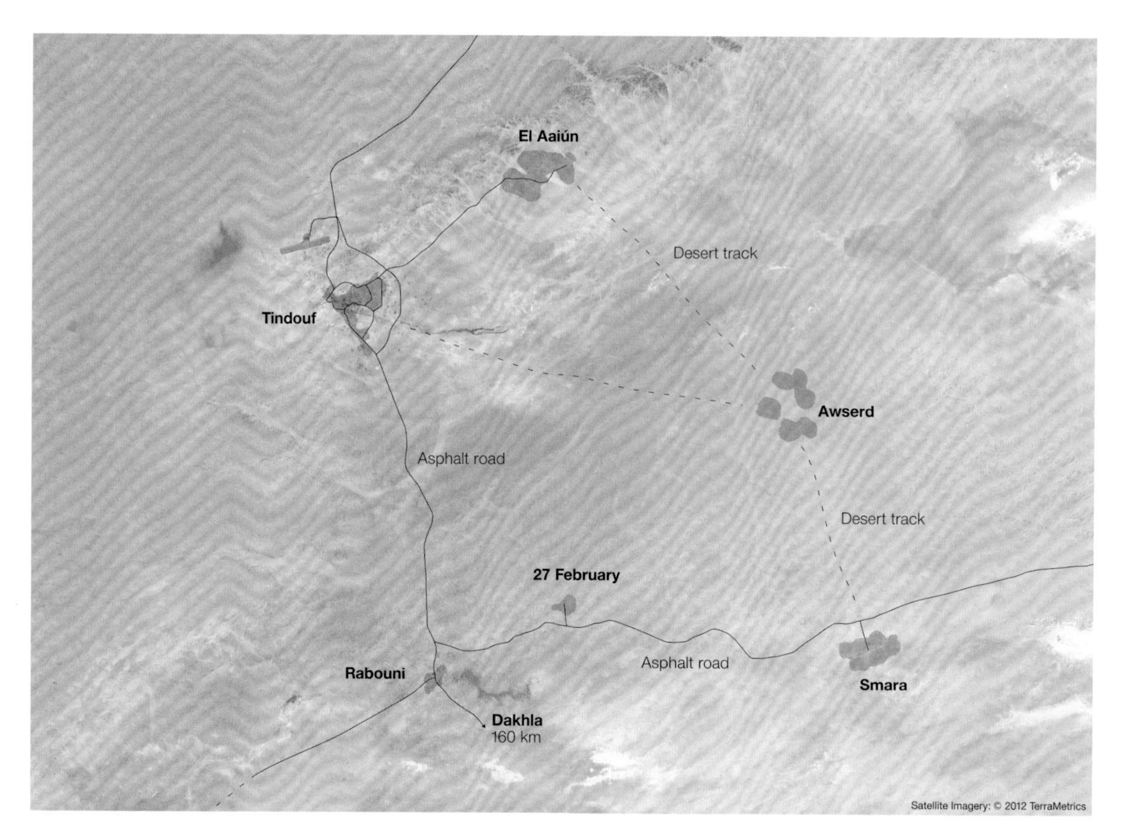


## Main Access to the Camps

The camps of Smara, 27 February, Dakhla, and El Aaiún are generally accessed by an asphalt road that leads to the middle of the camp, often ending in front of a *protocolo* or administration building. These roads are more comfortable to drive on than dirt tracks and are therefore the preferred route within the camp or when driving from one camp to another. Even though it represents a detour of approximately 30 km (and is therefore twice as long), the preferred route from El Aaiún to Smara follows the asphalt road, passing Tindouf instead of the more direct desert track via Awserd.

**Primary and Secondary Access Network**
Some of the primary roads are located in the original grid of the camp and therefore bear a trace of the early settlement structure. They are broad paths that are easily readable, both in situ and on satellite images. They divide daïras and barrios from one another simply by inserting a gap between them.

The secondary network infiltrates the neighborhoods and reaches out to every house. The proportion of the houses to the street makes the space inviting for different activities. Often children play on these roads and pedestrians use them for walking: the ground is much harder and one does not sink into the sand, making it easier to get around.

Asphalt road, El Aaiún

**From Temporary to Permanent**

The asphalt road in El Aaiún was realized in 2007 by the Algerian government. It follows one of the existing main sand paths, and was essentially the fixation of an ephemeral, volatile space. Apart from the access roads that have been asphalted for many years, this was the first permanent road within one of the Sahrawi camps and is one of the most permanent elements in the camps as a whole. It therefore represents a paradigm shift in the struggle and dilemma between the notions of temporary and permanent in the camps.

The added comfort and safety of driving on asphalt road is obvious and is appreciated and embraced by the community. But, by signaling a notion of settlement and permanence, it comes with a cost. It is an investment into the territorial space of the camp and its development, instead of an investment into the Sahrawi refugee population itself.

Regarding the concept of development, one would expect increased building activity to be triggered by the asphalt road. When we look more closely at the buildings that have been built after the construction of the road, however, we see that they are dispersed almost evenly throughout the spaces of the camp, with little relationship to the location of the road. The reasons seem to be of a pragmatic rather than ideological nature (such as the potential "denial" of the road). Even though it leads more or less centrally through the camp, it passes the daïras at their periphery, leading through the void space between the daïras instead of going through their centers. The commercial activities of the daïras take place in their respective cores, and this is where commercial construction has taken place. Residential compounds, on the other hand, usually expand in situ or, if relocating, do not necessarily choose to build near the road.

Zoom-in of figure-ground plan

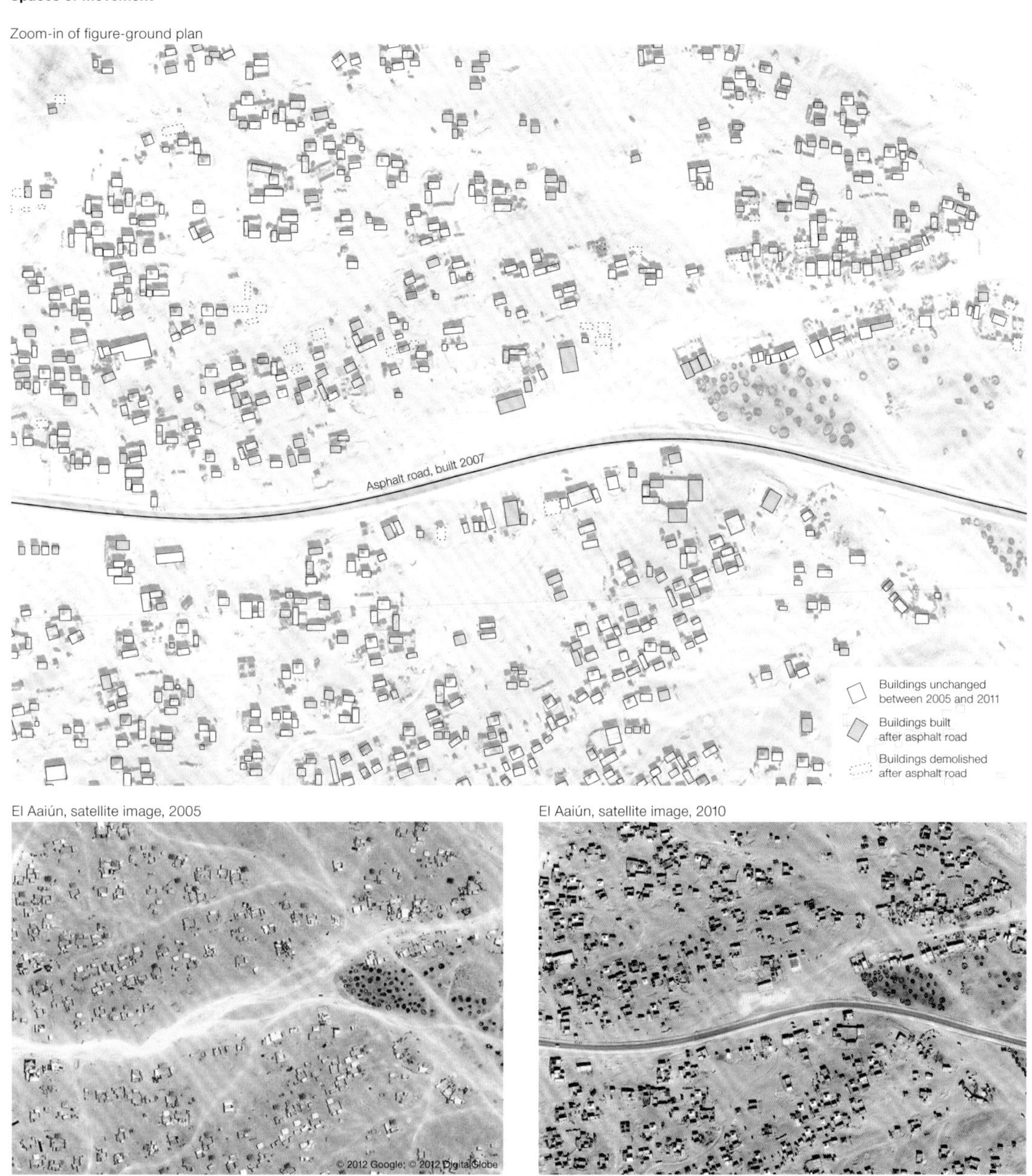


El Aaiún, satellite image, 2005

El Aaiún, satellite image, 2010

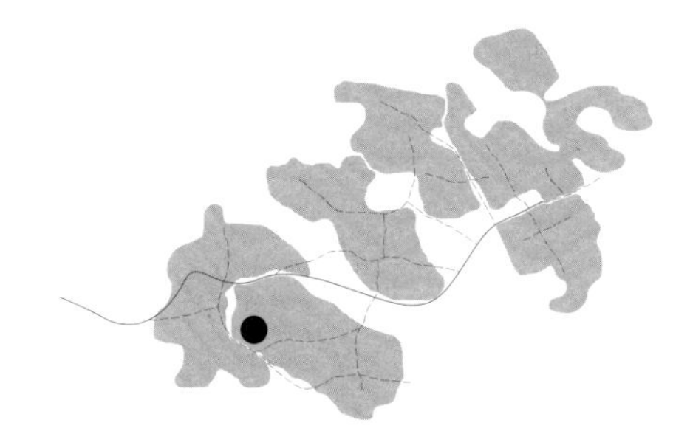

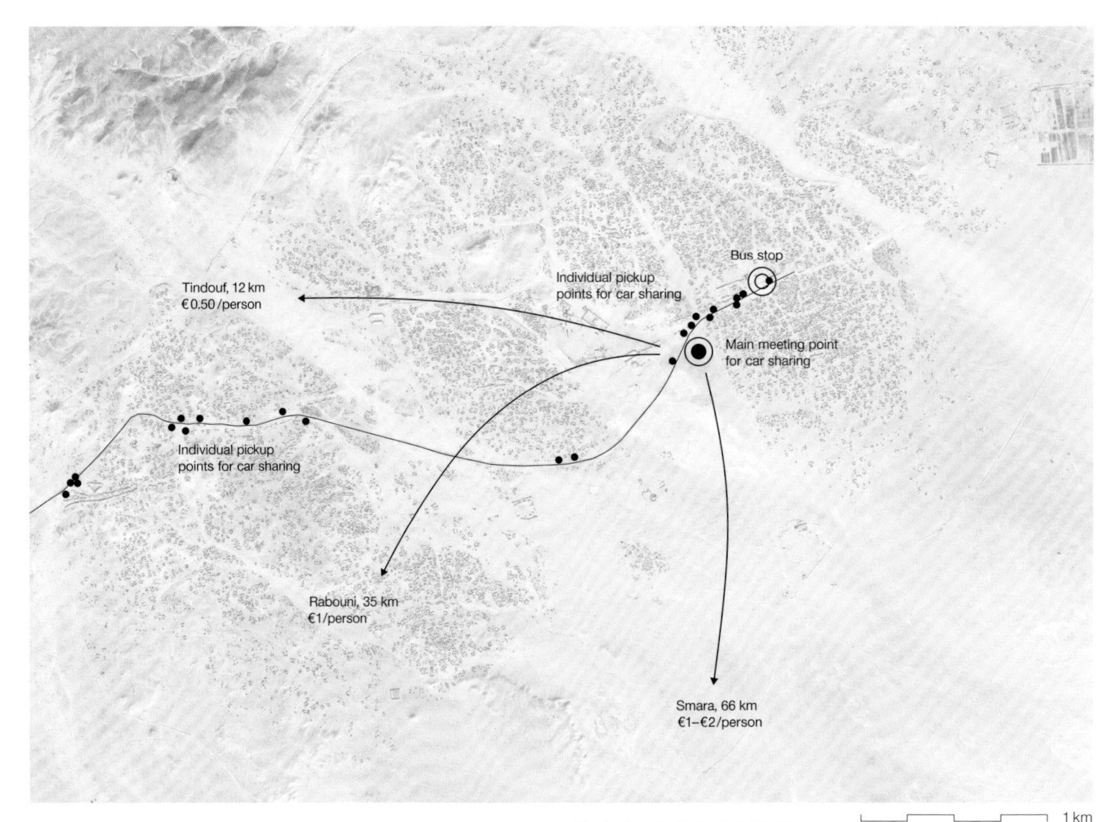


## Meeting Points

Private taxis and carpooling are common ways of moving from one place to another. Commuters working in Rabouni prefer to take a private taxi instead of waiting for the shuttle bus in the morning and evening. It is a symbiotic business: the driver is subsidized with the expenses of the car and the other party arrives more quickly and comfortably.

Within each camp there are usually one or two main points where drivers and passengers congregate before setting off on their journeys. In the mornings and evenings these places are usually busy and crowded with roadside vendors and stalls selling snacks and drinks. Such locations–where people of different origin and destination come together–are obviously also spaces for the exchange of news, information, stories, and gossip.

Costs for transportation by private taxi from Smara:

| | |
|---|---|
| to Awserd | € 0.50 |
| to 27 February | € 0.50 |
| to Rabouni | € 0.50 |
| to Tindouf | € 1.00 |
| to El Aaiún | € 1.00 |
| to Dakhla | € 10.00 |

Vendor by meeting point, Smara

# Means of Transportation

Cars and other methods of transport are ubiquitous in the camps. Mercedes, Golfs, all-terrain vehicles, buses, trucks, and vans can be seen everywhere. Although there is a relatively wide range of vehicles, two specific models dominate: Mercedes sedans and Land Rovers. Both have the benefit of being resistant to the tough environment of the rocky desert and the dry heat. They are durable, relatively easy to repair, and represent stable financial value. The predominance of just two models also has the advantage that only a limited range of spare parts and repair tools need to be available in the camps.

The Land Rover is obviously a practical vehicle for the terrain. It is robust and can deal well with the sandy, rocky dirt roads, and can be reliably used for overland travel between the camps or for farther distances. But beyond its practical value, it also symbolizes two important aspects of Sahrawi life. First of all, it represents the temporary nature of settling in the Algerian desert. The Land Rover is the logical consequence of the virtual absence of asphalt roads in the camps. Instead of investing in permanent roads, which would represent stability and a notion of settling permanently in the camps, investment goes into cars that are able to deal with the rough terrain of the dirt tracks. This investment is mobile and can potentially be taken back to the homeland. The other symbolic dimension of the Land Rover is its reference to the resistance against Morocco. The Land Rover was the preferred vehicle for operating in desert territory during the guerilla war against Moroccan occupation. Its robustness and the relative simplicity of its construction—and hence the ability to repair it—made it the ideal instrument for carrying out hit-and-run attacks against enemy positions. The car can thus be seen as a testimonial to the era of active and military resistance against the occupation. Not just a utilitarian object, the choice of car gains a political (and nationalist) dimension.

**Types of Vehicles**

Although there are several different modes of transport, cars are by far the most versatile and common vehicle for everyday life. In addition to private cars, we find trucks, buses, donkey carts, and bikes in the camps. Each vehicle is used for its own particular range and distance. Getting from one place to another is hardly ever a problem in the camps.

Communal ownership and usage of a car in the camps

## Import and Ownership

Cars are imported primarily from Spain and the Canary Islands by individuals who have either saved enough money themselves or borrowed the necessary sum from family members and friends. The cost of a used car in Spain is said to be between €2,000 and €3,000, an amount that is difficult to set aside in the camp without outside help. Ownership and use of the car is often shared among family members, sometimes including more distant relatives and friends. The concept of shared ownership makes the private means of transport available to the vast majority of the camp's inhabitants.

Surprisingly, there is hardly any market for used cars inside the camps. Cars remain in operation for many years–sometimes even decades. They are always repaired, and ownership remains within the same family. The car obtains symbolic value here and is seen as a status symbol. Maybe arising from a nomadic tradition, the car is cared for diligently, sometimes parked in its own garage, or exhibited with pride.

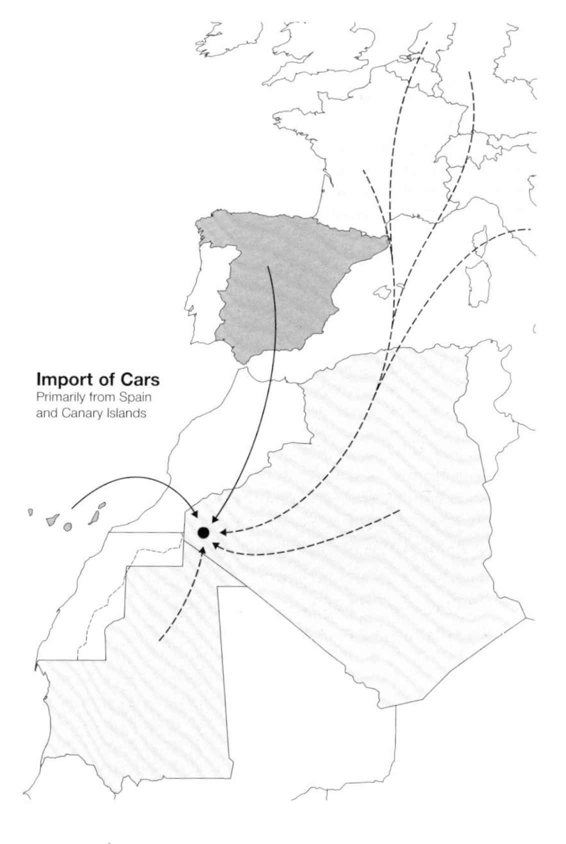

## Cars

Cars are the best-adapted and therefore most versatile vehicles available to Sahrawi refugees in the camps. The percentage of Mercedes in El Aaiún is striking and accounts for approximately eighty-five percent of all sedans. Mercedes owners claim they choose this model because they are sold at relatively low prices in Spain and are adequate for desert roads. The limited range of cars comes with a mutual benefit for car and garage owners, as the assortment of spare parts can be narrowed down to those necessary for the few car models present in the camps. This reduces the total amount of parts that have to be bought and stored as frozen capital.

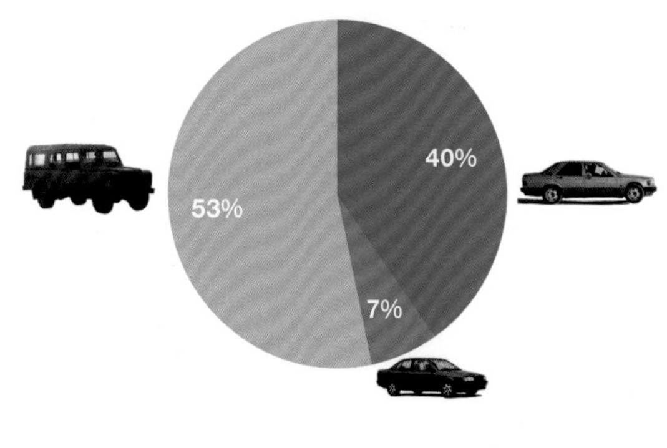

**All-Terrain Vehicles**

Aging Land Rovers and other four-wheel-drive cars are, to a certain extent, the replacement or antithesis of the asphalt road. On a pragmatic level they are more robust and resilient in the harsh climate of the Sahara and also make the whole territory more accessible. But giving it a more strategic reading, one can see them as an alternative to the improvement of the roads. Instead of investing in the road and thereby into permanence and the physical territory of the camps, the burden of dealing with difficult terrain is solved by investing in all-terrain vehicles. These cars are not fixed to the Sahrawi camps and theoretically could easily be taken back to the homeland if the opportunity arose. Beyond their practical use, the abundance of Land Rovers is compatible with the ideology of favoring the ephemeral and transitory instead of the permanent.

## Trucks

Trucks are often privately owned and used primarily to transport merchandise to the camps. They represent a possible form of income for the owners, who are paid by shop owners to bring goods from near Tindouf or from as far as Mauritania on an as-needed basis. As such, they act as motors of trade, connecting the camps to the wider region. A rather large investment of €6,000–€8,000 is needed to buy a truck, so the money generally comes from a Spanish pension or from family members who work abroad.

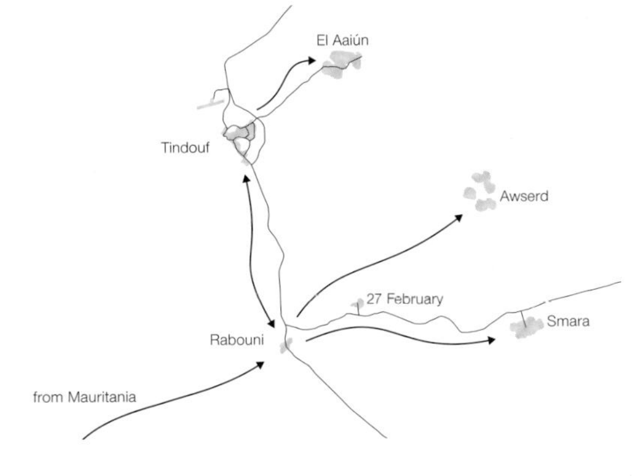

## Bus

As Rabouni does not offer any permanent residential accommodation, almost all of the workers commute daily between the camps and the administrative center. The government offers a daily shuttle bus to Rabouni in the morning and back to the camps in the evening free of charge to passengers. Other users include people needing to visit the regional hospital or people going to administrative offices in Rabouni.

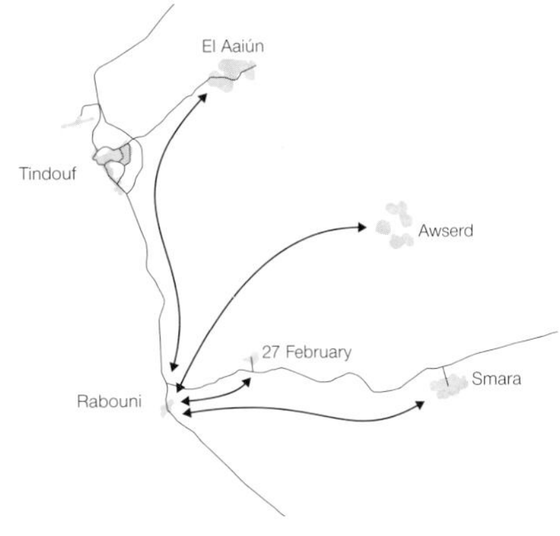

**Donkey-Drawn Cart**
Donkeys are a common sight, especially as pack animals and for pulling carts. They are a cheap and uncomplicated means of transportation for the distribution of humanitarian goods from a central distribution point to the neighborhoods, or for the delivery of clay bricks from their production area to the construction sites of houses.

**Bicycles**
Bicycles are often brought to the camps by NGO workers as gifts for children. The sandy and bumpy terrain prevents bicycles from being used for anything other than leisure and fun. Many children get bicycles after visiting Spain in the summer vacation, but the bike has still not become an especially popular mode of transport in the camps.

# Interrelated Infrastructure

The profusion of cars and trucks has given rise to a substantial economic infrastructure related to the activities of movement and transport. This infrastructure consists of car-repair shops, garages, petrol stations, and even a car wash. Economically, they seem to be the most profitable and active businesses in the camps, providing families with regular income and allowing for a certain financial independence. Because of the large number of such businesses, they also have a substantial spatial impact on the camps. Often located next to the main markets, garages and other services for cars and trucks form in large clusters or zones, sometimes sharing resources and equipment. Beyond the spatial and economical impact, this interrelated infrastructure also hints at the political dimension of movement and transport. Driving schools give lessons, teaching the rules and regulations of driving, as formulated by the Ministry of Transport. All vehicles are registered and carry license plates issued by the Sahrawi authorities. What might be regarded as an insignificant technical detail, driving schools and license plates actually give evidence to, and are a manifestation of, a level of political and administrative autonomy that is exercised by the Sahrawis in their camps.

Car engines in a garage courtyard, Smara

LES

### Repair Shops and Garages

Repair shops or garages represent a flourishing business, as there is a constant need to maintain the large number of vehicles in the camps. Needless to say, even rugged vehicles like Range Rovers and Mercedes become strained by the sand and the rough paths and potholes.

Mechanics working in repair shops are usually self-employed but organize themselves in cooperational networks, helping each other out with everything from workloads to tools and spare parts. This has a spatial consequence, with the garages forming clusters in the camps and thereby facilitating cooperation. It also makes them easier to find. Being one of the most profitable businesses, the garages are usually quite prominently located in the camps.

Although the building typology does not vary substantially, the spectrum of repair shops is wide, some being fascinatingly well organized, others seemingly chaotic or even abandoned. Some benefit from a large and well-stocked front yard, while others specialize in selling used parts.

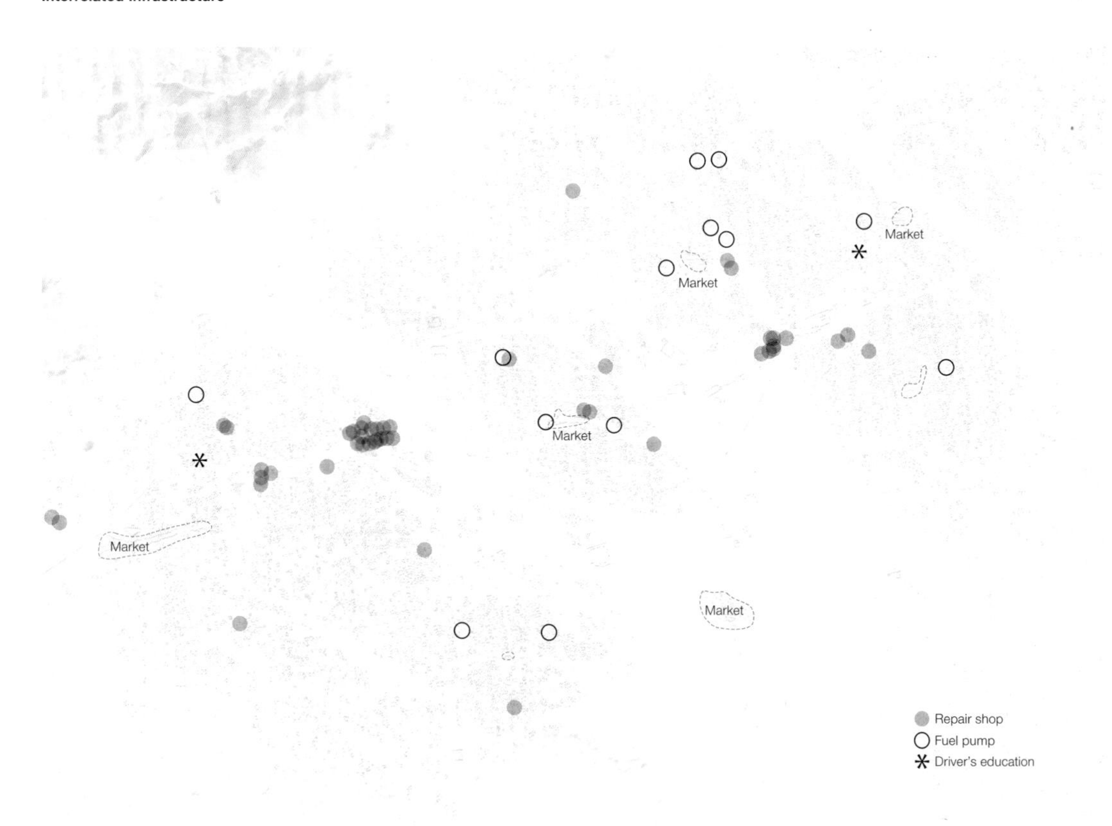


**The Car-Service Trade in El Aaiún**
Fuel pumps in El Aaiún can be found almost anywhere and are tucked away in the midst of residential compounds. Similarly, repair shops are scattered throughout the entire camp.

However, there are areas in which more than twenty garages form clusters and are gathered around large open spaces, exclusively framed by fuel pumps, repair shops, and car-part outlets. The areas of trade are notably also more spread out in El Aaiún than in Smara, showing a different organizational principle.

**The Strip–Repair Shops in Smara**
While in El Aaiún, repair shops and fuel pumps can be found spread out over the camp, sometimes even in the middle of residential areas. In Smara, however, they are all centrally located, flanking the two main market areas. The broad main road dividing Smara into northern and southern halves passes right through this car-repair area, turning it into a strip of car facilities. The strip turns into one of the busiest areas in the camp, especially in the evening. Shortly before dusk, cars drive past, obtaining fuel or picking up spare parts.

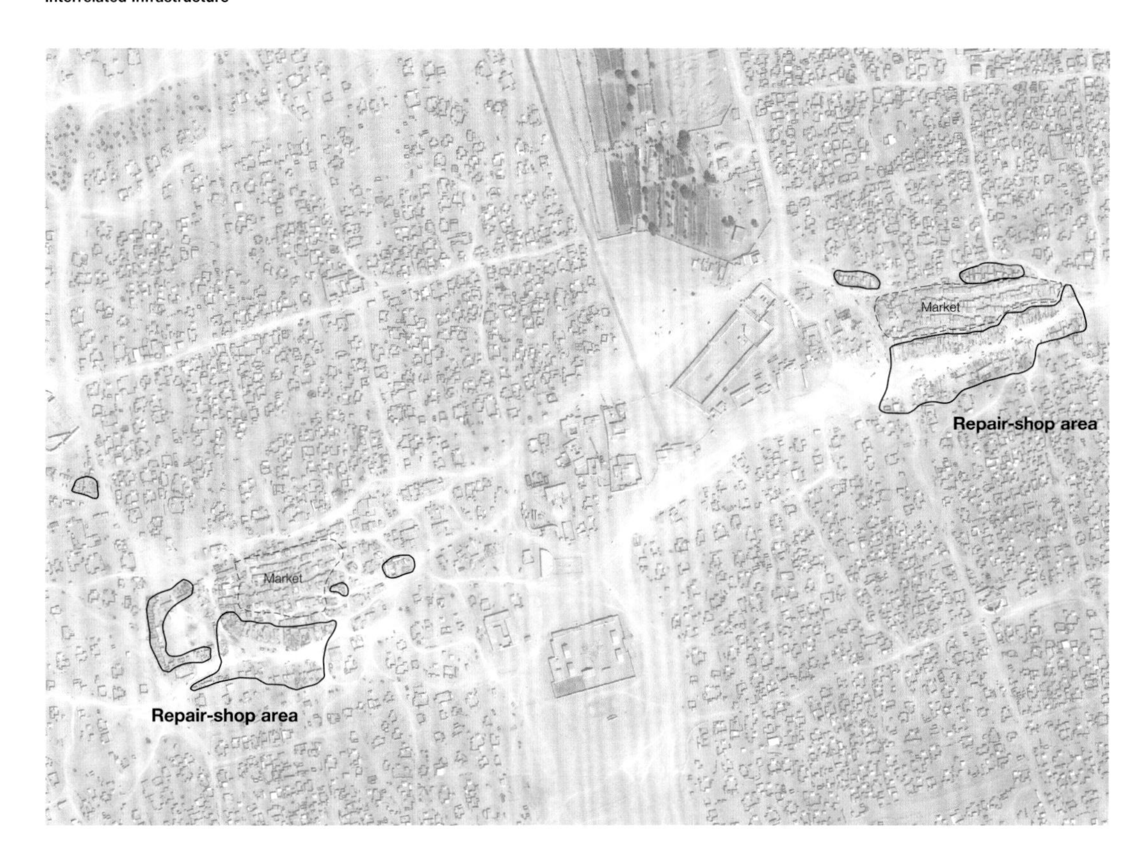


## The Car Service Trade in Smara

Unlike in El Aaiún, the repair shops in Smara are all centrally located. The two major areas are located south of the two main markets. Although the density of the built fabric is the same as that of the market, the market streets are clearly laid out to be accessed by foot, while the garages are flanked by a wide road space that basically frames the space in between. This typology is unique to the repair shops, where the open space has a direct relation to surrounding buildings.

**Petrol Stations**

Fuel can be bought at almost any repair shop, but there are numerous smaller, specialized fuel pumps that only sell diesel or gas. The fuel can either be bought in plastic bottles or filled directly into the car from elevated oil barrels with more or less makeshift pipes.

Price comparison:
1 liter gas: € 0.30
1 kg rice: € 0.80
1 bread: € 0.10

Fuel cost from El Aaiún to Smara, example:
Typical fuel consumption: 12 liters/100 km
Distance: 65 km
Fuel cost: 0.65 × 12 L × €0.30 = €2.34

## Car Wash

The only car wash in the Saharan desert! The importance of the car in the context of the camp is maybe best exemplified by the existence of a car wash. Although the dust and the sandy roads make it impossible for any car to remain clean for a substantial period of time, a number of car owners have their cars washed regularly. About seven to ten customers arrive every day, each paying €5. The water consumption of the car wash is significant and stands in contrast to the limited availability of this valuable resource.

**Driving Lessons**

In order to obtain a driving permit, Sahrawis of eighteen years or older must attend driving lessons and pass a driving test. What on first sight looks like an amusing oddity reveals an important aspect about the nature of the camps. Where one might expect a level of informality or an unregulated field, Polisario administration provides a set of laws to manage an everyday aspect of the refugees' lives. It reveals a striving towards normality in contrast to the predominant view of emergency and crisis.

The fact that the rules governing traffic and car use are not just adopted from Algerian law is another indicator of the (semi-) autonomy that the Sahrawis enjoy in the camps. In that sense, even if seemingly insignificant, the driving school gives testimony to the idea of self-determination for a nation in exile.

**Registration Plates**

The existence of Sahrawi registration plates follows a similar logic to the traffic laws. They are an indicator of an independent administration system, but they also operate on a symbolic level. All vehicles receive a unique Western Saharan license plate number. They are different from the Algerian style and are visible evidence of autonomous governance. These license plates not only allow them to circulate freely in their own territory, but also to Algeria and to pass the border into Mauritania.

The first two letters identify the overall status of the car: SH is for regular Sahrawi cars, while GSH denotes government vehicles. The first two digits indicate the specific camp–e.g. 30 is for vehicles registered in Smara.

SH - 30 - 8362

# Connecting the Camps with the World

If the isolation of the camps necessitates regional connections for the delivery of goods, information, and the transport of people, the lack of a nation-state is one of the main drivers for more distant and international connections. With no higher-level education system and few jobs with any substantial income as just two examples, Sahrawis need to travel to the large Algerian cities or other international destinations to fulfill needs that could otherwise be supplied by a state of their own making. Movement flows both ways, with Sahrawis leaving the camps (and later returning) and international visitors coming in. Every winter thousands of Spanish families visit partner families in the camps. Additionally, there is the constant presence of international NGO workers in the camps and frequent events that draw visitors from abroad. All this has made Tindouf Airport, formally only serving the small Algerian town, one of the larger airports in the country.

Photographer in Smara who studied in Cuba

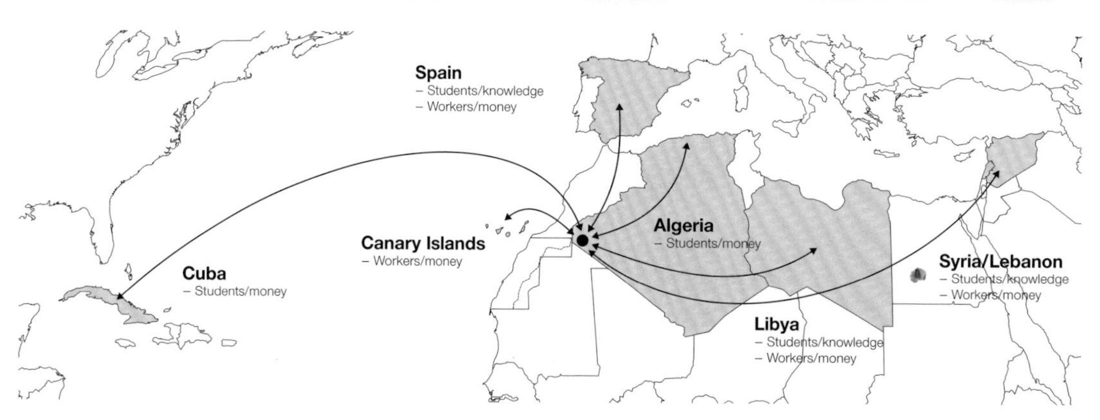


## Studying and Working Abroad

The Sahrawi refugee camps are able to provide a good level of basic education to all their inhabitants, and the illiteracy rate is one of the lowest of all of Africa, yet secondary education is not available in the camps. Many young students choose to go to SADR-friendly countries, especially Algeria, Libya, and Cuba, to attend university. The majority of the students choose to come back to the camps, although there are not many job possibilities.

As jobs and possibilities for earning money are scarce in the camps, many refugees find themselves forced to work abroad, especially in Spain and the Canary Islands, not least because of the language. They seldom chose this as a permanent solution, preferring to eventually return to their families. One of the main goals during this period is the financial support of family members in the camp.

Boarding a flight to the Western Sahara

Participants of the CBM program

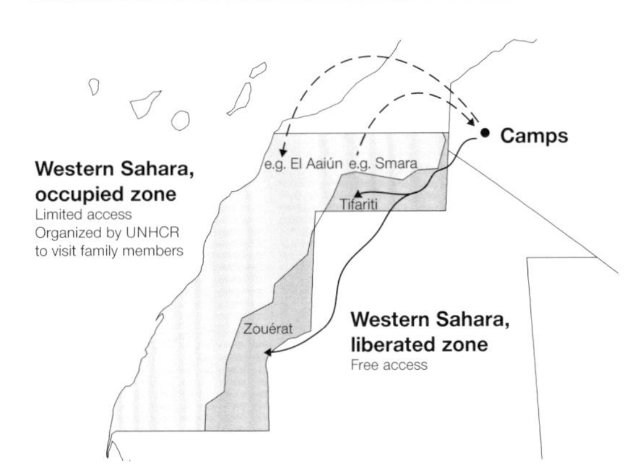


## Connections to the Western Sahara

As with all people with refugee status, the possibility of returning to their home is limited if not impossible. The liberated territories can be accessed without any major problems, but few people live in this region permanently. Often, trips and events are organized to underline a political statement, yet remain exceptional and temporary.

The UNHCR-organized CBM program allows refugees living in the camps and family members in the occupied territories to reunite, often after more than thirty years. Up to 2011, nearly 13,000 Sahrawis had benefited, and another 31,000 are on a waiting list. Each flight shuttles about thirty people both ways between Tindouf and Western Saharan cities, where the participants can spend five days in the camps or in the Western Sahara. Proposals have been made to expand the program through the addition of road transportation, thus allowing more people to participate.

Getafe Region holiday program

Vacaciones en Paz

Getafe-Sahara

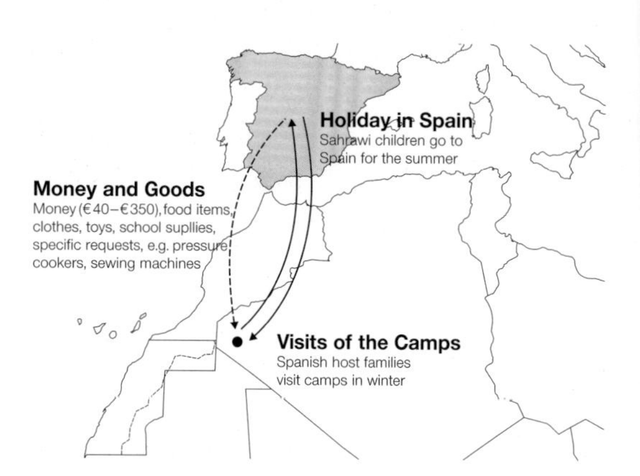


### Vacaciones en Paz

The annual holiday program began in 1988 and is organized by the Union of Sahrawi Youth (UJSARIO) and the Friends of the Sahrawi People, a collective group of about 300 associations throughout Spain. It allows between 7,000 and 10,000 Sahrawi children ages eight to twelve to spend two months in the summer with host families in Spain. Many of the children return to the same place each year, strengthening the bond between both families.

The Sahrawi children benefit not only from a relief from the unbearable climate of the Saharan summer, but they also receive support in the form of material goods and money. The children usually return with full suitcases, often responding to specific requests from their Sahrawi families. These gifts are often extended to regular economic support, which continues even when the children are not with the host families or are too old to participate in the program. Visiting Spanish families travel to the Sahrawi camps in early spring or late fall.

Tindouf Airport

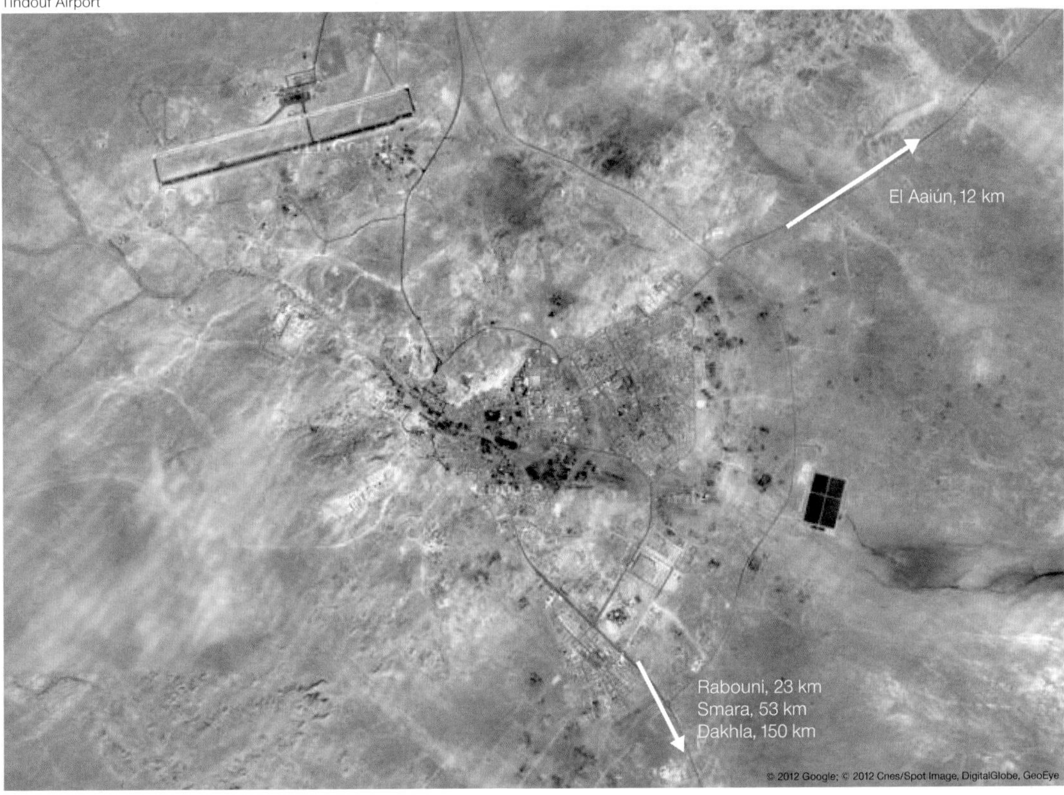


## Tindouf Airport

Tindouf Airport is the main access portal for all travelers coming to the camps from other countries. Although it is primarily a military airport, the influx of people to the camps has made it one of the busiest airports in Algeria, receiving the largest number of tourists per annum (Elena Fiddian-Qasmiyeh, 2011). Flights from Algiers to Tindouf are filled with NGO workers, people visiting the camps for academic and journalistic reasons, solitary tourists, and, in the summer, children flying to Spain.

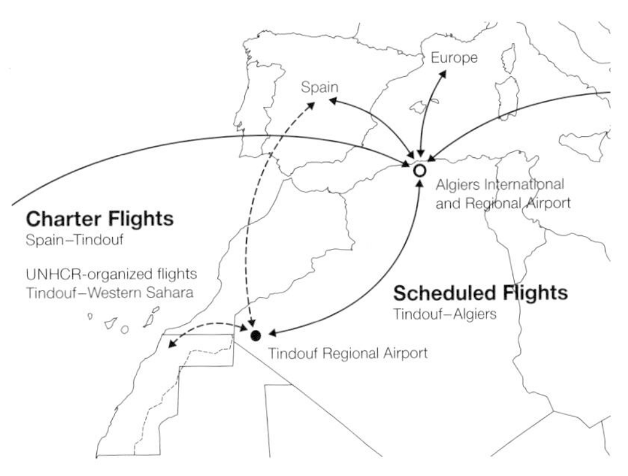

## Connecting through Communication

Where actual mobility is not possible, connections are established through media and communication networks. Media replaces missing links and makes it possible to bring spaces much closer than they physically are. In the case of the Sahrawi refugee camps, media plays an especially important role as a tool for exchange because of the refugees' otherwise remote location and high cost of access. The immediacy of communication that the TV, radio, mobile phone, and, to a certain extent, the Internet has allowed connects the camps to a global network of places and people, fulfilling personal needs, as well as strategic and political ones.

Mobile-phone shop in Smara

## Mobile Phones

Mobile phones started appearing in the camps around 2005, and the first antenna was installed in Smara that year by an Algerian network operator. Today mobile phones are widespread, despite often low network availability. Every family has access to a mobile phone, and most individuals own one. The use of the cell phone has become commonplace, and they have largely replaced the public phone facilities that were once more common but have recently fallen out of use. Phones are charged by the solar panels that supply electricity in the family compounds.

The profusion of mobile phones in the camps has also altered the landscape and silhouette of the camps, with several phone antennas dotting the scenery. Mostly located close to the center and to other central facilities such as administration buildings, they are the most iconic testimony of the connectedness of the camps.

## Internet

Despite a lack of broadband Internet access for the public (the only Internet cafés are in Smara and Rabouni), most refugees have an email address and use the internet sporadically. Networking services like Facebook and Skype are popular among the younger generation. In most cases, the email account is primarily used when studying or working abroad. When the network is up in the camp, the inhabitants use these tools to stay in touch with other refugees and friends outside the camps, or in other countries. The Internet is therefore used for long-range communication.

## UNHCR-Organized Phone Calls

To improve the possibility of staying in contact with relatives and friends in the occupied territory of the Western Sahara, UNHCR has organized several centers for phone calls, starting in 2004 with a link from 27 February school to the city of El Aaiún. Refugees can place calls here free of cost. The majority of the people using this service are women.

UNHCR call center

Café in Smara showing a soccer game between Algeria and Morocco

## Television

Five different channels bring the world's news and events into Sahrawi living rooms and cafés. Polisario operates a national channel, which serves as a link of information between the occupied territories and the refugee camps. Two of the channels are Algerian, with an additional sports channel and Al Jazeera providing international coverage.

Television is the main consumer of electricity in most households. The necessary electricity for powering it in the evening is collected all day and stored in a car-battery unit.

Editado por PRENSA Y PUBLICACIONES SAHARAUIS, S.A.

Inscrito en el Registro de los Servicios Informativos del Gobierno General de Sahara

الــواقــع

LA REALIDAD

DIARIO BILINGÜE DE SAHARA

تحررها صحافة ونشر الصحراء وهي مسجلة في سجلات مصالح أنباء الحكومة الصحراوية العامة

AÑO I *** NUMERO 99 *** VIERNES 24 DE OCTUBRE DE 1975 *** PRECIO: 5 PTAS.
Redacción y Administración: Calle del Este. 5 - Apartado 216 - AAIUN Telfs. 22 33 30 - 22 33 31 Director: PABLO-IGNACIO DE DALMASES

Parece próximo un acuerdo hispano - marroquí (según EFE)

**MULEY ABDAL-LAH, HERMANO DE HASSAN, RECHAZO CUALQUIER POSIBILIDAD DE AUTODETERMINACION PARA LOS SAHARAUIS**

**Y calificó al Frente Polisario como agente de Argelia**

**A España se le promete: el 60 % de los fosfatos y bases militares**

Martraquech, 23.-(Por Fernando Martínez Láinez, enviado especial de la agencia EFE).- «Marruecos y España están obligados a entenderse. Así lo exige el interés común de ambos países», dijo aquí el príncipe Muley Abdallah, hermano del rey Hassán II.

En una conversación en exclusiva para la prensa española el hermano del monarca alauita insistió en que los intereses de España en el Sahara y en el Norte de Africa sólo serían preservados si se llegara a un acuerdo global con Marruecos que reconozca la soberanía marroquí sobre el territorio saharaui.

La entrevista de Muley Abdallah con los periodistas españoles tuvo lugar en el palacio de Mullay Hassán, antiguo jalifa del protectorado español en Marruecos y actual gobernador del banco nacional de este país.

La charla fue en extremo cortés, y antes de iniciarse la misma se rogó a los periodistas que no hicieran «preguntas indiscretas» o que pudieran interpretarse «irrespetuosas».

DO UT DES

El hermano de Hasán II reveló que Marruecos ofreció a España seguir explotando el 60 por ciento de los fosfatos del Sahara e incluso la concesión de bases militares por tiempo indefinido para proteger las Islas Canarias. Si el gobierno de Madrid aceptaba la soberanía marroquí en el Sahara.

En el momento presente -añadió el príncipe-, la marcha es imparable y se llevará a cabo en las fechas previstas. Aún no es tarde para llegar a un acuerdo, pero éste, en caso de producirse, tendría que hacerse con el respaldo y la garantía de la ONU.

Muley Abdallah admitió que Mauritania tiene también derechos soberanos sobre algunas

(Continúa en la pág. 3.)

**WALGHEIM SIGUE CONSULTANDO ANTES DE DECIDIRSE A VENIR AL SAHARA**

Madrid, 23.-En las próximas 48 horas, llegará a España un alto dignatario marroquí con plenos poderes del rey Hassán para iniciar conversaciones con España en relación con el Sahara, según ha podido saber CIFRA en fuentes competentes.

Este es el primero y el más directo y espectacular de los logros conseguidos durante el vertiginoso viaje realizado anteayer por el ministro Secretario General del Movimiento a Rabat.

NO SE CONTRADICE CON LA AUTODETERMINACION

En círculos políticos se ha hecho saber a CIFRA que este viaje cuyos frutos podrán verse en los próximos días, no se contradice en absoluto con las tareas que la diplomacia española viene ejercitando en las Naciones Unidas a fin de conseguir la autodeterminación del Sahara.

En este sentido, se pone de relieve a CIFRA que la resolución planteada anoche en el Consejo de Seguridad, en la que se recomienda al secretario general de la ONU, Kurt Waldheim, la realización de entrevistas entre las cuatro partes interesadas en el problema del Sahara, esto es, Marruecos, Mauritania, Argelia y España, coincide plenamente con las línea seguida por el Gobierno español que, como es sabido, ha propuesto en varias ocasiones la celebración de esta conferencia cuatripartita.-(CIFRA).

**Nota de la redacción.**-El alto dignatario marroquí a que hace referencia esta información, según noticias llegadas a última hora, es el ministro de Asuntos Exteriores, Ahmed Laraki. Su llegada a Madrid está prevista para hoy por la mañana.

FRANCO: insuficiencia cardíaca

A primeras horas de la noche de ayer se divulgó un parte médico, firmado por todos los facultativos que atienden a Su Excelencia el Jefe del Estado, en el que se daba cuenta de un empeoramiento en la situación del ilustre paciente como consecuencia de la aparición de insuficiencia cardíaca.

A la hora de cerrar esta edición no se han recibido nuevas informaciones sobre la evolución de la enfermedad que aqueja al Caudillo.

**Barcelona, con el pueblo saharaui**

**Barcelona, 22.-Representantes de un grupo que se autodenomina «los amigos del pueblo saharaui» han entregado hoy en el Gobierno Civil de Barcelona una carta de petición para celebrar una manifestación el próximo sábado por la tarde de apoyo y solidaridad del pueblo español con el pueblo saharaui.**

**En el documento se especifica que los organizadores se comprometen a que la manifestación transcurra pacíficamente y en orden, ciñéndose exclusivamente al problema del Sahara, con una serie de consignas y con el recorrido y hora que se detalla en el escrito.-(EUROPA PRESS).**

## Print Media

The newspaper published by the SADR is directed at the Sahrawi population and also to people supportive of their nation. It is therefore written mostly in Spanish. *La Realidad* is a powerful instrument of the Frente Polisario, exporting statements to the outside world, although the paper is not widely available.

## Radio

A local radio program in the Hassaniya language is transmitted throughout all of the camps and also features an hour of Spanish in the evening. Political topics are mostly covered, broadcasting local news and events within the Sahrawi population.

SH 30 4312
Mercedes
250 D

# Movement in the Desert

Refugees are in a tenuous situation, where they see life in the camp as an extended transition period that forces them to point most of their efforts in the direction of the future, and often don't have the opportunity to ameliorate the present. In El Aaiún and the other Sahrawi refugee camps, a similar state of mind is expressed through the wish for temporary and mobile solutions: refusing to settle in a country that is not theirs; nor building a permanent framework of infrastructure. De-emphasizing permanent physical infrastructure gives more importance to the use of the space and its flexibility. Within the camp, traffic flows through the spaces set by buildings and compounds, which themselves are also only semi-permanent. Roads and main paths are not seen as the backbones for urban development and public centers, but are an integrated part of a networked body as a whole, or of the rhizome-like field of open spaces in the camps.

The links established by movement and communication are of crucial importance to the camps in their attempt to enhance political or economic development and cultural exchange, as well as establish an autonomous administration. Hence it comes as no surprise to see the abundance of vehicles and mobile phones in the environment of the camps. This omnipresence of spaces for movement is formative for the urban fabric and is further strengthened by the sheer quantity of cars, car parts, and infrastructure servicing mobility found throughout the camps, on all urban layers and scales. In fact, repair shops seem to be the most dynamic and flourishing businesses in the camps.

The ubiquity of cars and activities of transport arises from the spatial dislocation of the camps and the need for the refugees to move within and between the camps, as well as connecting with the region beyond. As such, taken at face value, there is maybe nothing too surprising about the cars in the camps. On the other hand, it seems strange to see ordinary cars in this environment of such isolation. The Mercedes sedan driving through the sand next to tents or huts that appear to be from a different century, or the freshly washed new VW Golf driving between daïras, brings the ideas of normality and exception into confrontation with each other. The clash of the condition of the camps on the one hand and the prosaic everyday scene of cars moving about seems extreme. Maybe, though, it is exactly this everyday quality that perpetuates the omnipresence of cars. It shows that life continues in spite of the exceptional conditions of the camps. To uphold or establish a level of everyday normality is one of the main narratives of life in the camps.

# COMMERCE AND WORK

Since the establishment of the refugee camps, there have been three distinct economic phases. Fleeing the war with Morocco and relocating to the camps in 1975, the Sahrawis' life became completely dependent on humanitarian aid. Life in the camps was initially characterized by a nonmonetary economy, based mostly on barter and exchange in-kind and relying on external aid. During the early 1990s this economy transformed to a money-based system. Small-scale commercial activities developed that resulted in the production of corresponding spaces within the camps, such as markets and workshops. This phase also coincided with the emergence of new work opportunities, as refugees started their own businesses or offered services. Even if still on a small scale, over time more money flowed into the camps, either from relatives working in Spain, through partnership programs, or international visitors coming to the camps. More recently, a third economic phase can be identified. This is marked by the emergence of a consumer mentality among the refugees and, though still cautious and timid, competition between businesses. The following pages look at how economic activities have shaped the camps physically, and whether the different economic phases have left specific imprints on the fabric of the camps.

Ropea
Ropea
طيور الجنة
Super Rose
Clere

Toudja
Fruits Méditerranéens
7 Fruits
JUPITER
JUPITER
JUPITER
12 MINI MUFFINS
MARBLE
gullón
Mega Duo
Campiello
Assala
yes
L'BEN
لبن

Campilé
Pulpe
Cocktail
JUPITER
candia
Cocktail de Fruits
candia
Cocktail de Fruits
Produit par Tchin Lait -Béjaia
N'GAOUS
Ramy
Coca-Cola
Milou
X-TRA
SALADE DE THON
Assala
MAGDALENAS
Campiello
Dialna
Yes

# History of Trade

One can identify distinct phases in the development of trade and the Sahrawi economy. While the precolonial period was marked by nomadic pastoralism and the cross-Saharan caravan trade, during the colonial era, trading links with Europe were established. At the same time, the nomadic culture transformed to a semi-sedentary one and Sahrawis began settling near cities for longer periods of the year. With the onset of the war against Morocco, the refugee camps were founded, and a nonmonetary economy was implemented. The camps were entirely dependent on foreign humanitarian aid.

A second phase of the camps commenced in 1991, when the Eighth National Popular Congress of the Sahrawis voted for the introduction of a free-market economy. At the same time, the Spanish government paid out pensions to Sahrawi families that had worked in the Bou Craa mines or in the Spanish administration during the colonial period. Over a short space of time a relatively substantial amount of money entered the camp, which was used to set up small businesses and shops or to buy cars. This period has continued until today, with low-level economic activities developing in the camps. More recently—influenced by the increasing number of international visitors, higher numbers of Sahrawis that have lived in foreign countries, and the availability of international goods—elements of consumer mentality and market competition are transforming the local economy.

## Timeline of the Sahrawi Economy

**Before the mid-19th century**
The economy is based mainly on nomadic pastoralism, trade, agriculture, and raiding. Sahrawis live in autonomous (often conflicting) emirates, confederations, and tribes: strong clans protect weaker ones, who are obliged to pay tribute to the strong ones, often by being mercenaries.

**1884: Spanish Sahara**
(Conflictual) Coexistence with Spanish settlements, trading ties with Spain.

**1958: Spanish Sahara becomes a Spanish province**
Spanish Sahara is administered as a Spanish province and becomes a tax-free zone. This sets the basis for the subsequent smuggling trade.

**1960s: Growing settlements**
A substantial proportion of Sahrawis had partially abandoned nomadism by 1974, and at that time approximatel
8,000 Sahrawis were wage earners.

**1969: Inauguration of the Bou Craa mines**
Spanish and Sahrawi worke
are employed in the mines.

### PASTORAL NOMADISM

### 1884: SPANISH SAHARA

TRADE

Local trade: camels, sheep, goats, milk, butter.
Export: dates, burnoose, woven strips of goat hair.
Import: tea, sugar, spices, guns, ammunition, knives, cotton cloth, leather goods, trinkets, perfume.

**1970s: First Sahrawi shops in Spanish Sahara**
With the growing urbanization, Sahrawis start setting up shops in towns and villages. There is a flourishing smuggling trade from the Canary Islands via the Spanish Sahara to neighboring African countries.

INDIGENOUS PRODUCTION

Nomadic animal husbandry was the basis of the Sahrawi economy. It led to the emergence of all other activities such as trade, agriculture, mining in the salines, and fishing.

**1959–1963: Drought**
A drought kills almost half of all Sahrawi livestock.

**1968–1974: Drought**
Another drought kills half of all Sahrawi livestock.

HUMANITARIAN AID

**1975: Refugee camps**
While Sahrawi men defend their territory in the Western Sahara, the Sahrawi women have to organize the provision of food and goods, and the administration of the camps. Life depends entirely on humanitarian aid.

**1991: Cease-fire**
After the cease-fire, Sahrawi men return from fighting and exile to the camps, with the hope of soon being able to go back to the Western Sahara after a successful referendum.

**1991: Eighth National Popular Congress**
A new constitution is adopted, calling, among other things, explicitly for the development of a free-market economy.

**1991: Introduction of money in the camps**
Spain pays out pensions to the Sahrawis who worked in the Bou Craa mines during the Spanish colonial period.

**1990s: Vacaciones en Paz (Holidays in Peace) commences**
This program places between 7,000 and 10,000 Sahrawi children with families in Spain for a two-month holiday over the summer. Children often return to the camps with presents and money.

## 1975: FIRST PHASE OF THE CAMPS

## 1991: SECOND PHASE OF THE CAMPS

**1980s: First (public-owned) shops open in the camps**
SADR opens one shop per daïra.

**1991: Pensions paid by Spain**
Spain pays pensions to Sahrawis who have worked in colonial administration or in the Spanish army (approx. €1,200).

**1991: First private shops in camps**
Families establish shops with money received from Spanish pensions.

**2005: Mobile-phones**
First mobile-phone antennas are installed in camp Smara. Phone shops start opening.

---

**1975: Keeping animals for family supply**
Goats and sheep are kept as a source of milk and meat by Sahrawi families.

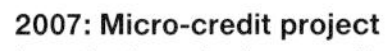

**2007: Micro-credit project**
Introduction of micro-credit program by Hegoa (Spanish NGO) to assist indigenous production and trade.

**1990s: Camel butchers open in the camps**
Camels from the liberated territory are used in the camp for food and milk supply.

---

**1975–1985: Algerian Red Crescent**
The government of Algeria provides the main source of assistance via the Algerian Red Crescent.

**1986: Involvement of UNHCR and WFP**
UNHCR and WFP assist the Algerian government in meeting the refugees' basic food and nonfood needs.

Aid organizations start employing refugees.

Caravan routes of 1887. The map shows Tindouf as one of the stops between the main centers of trade traversing today's Western Sahara

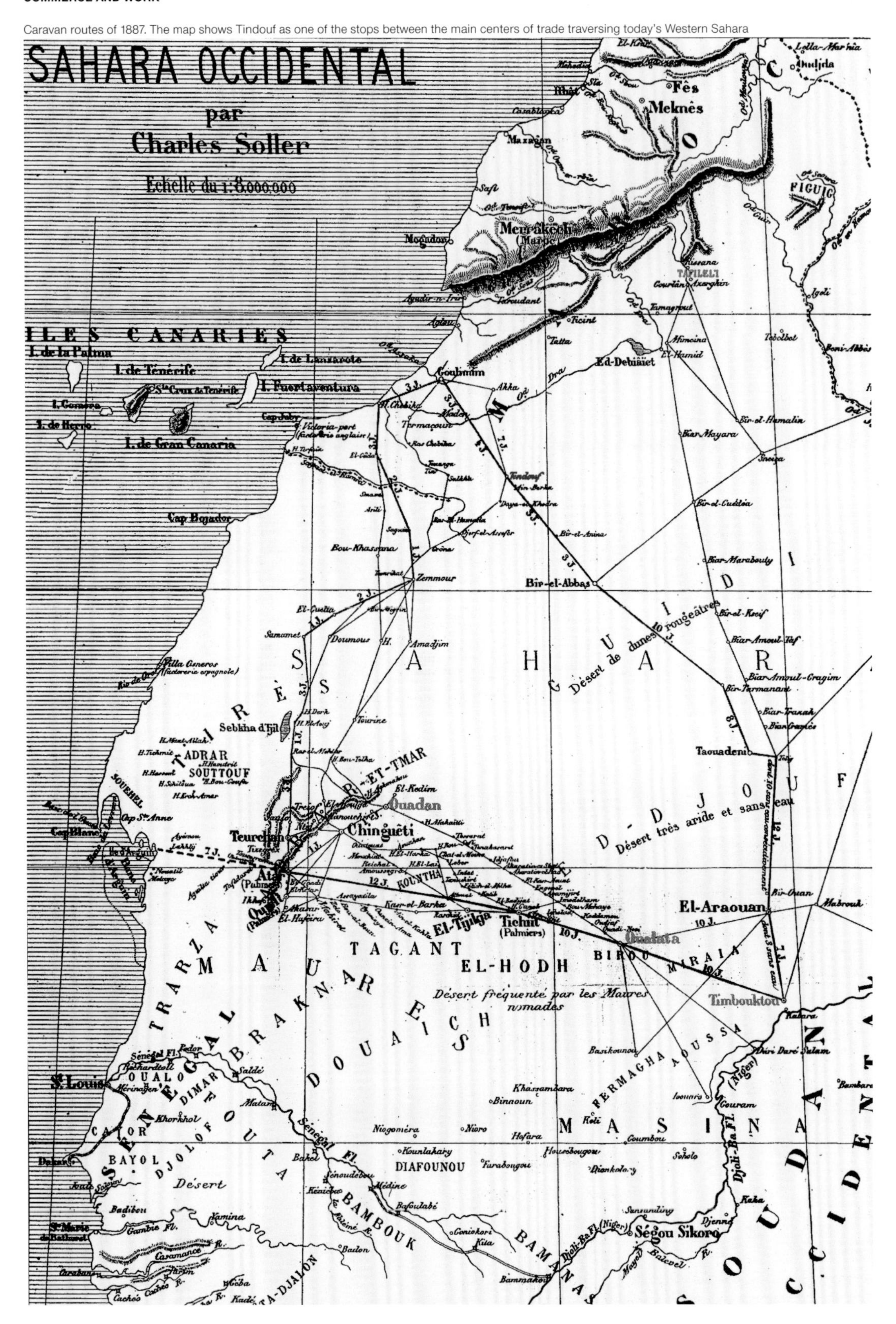

Camel caravan around Western Sahara

Market place of Ghardaïa in Algeria

Marketplace of Ghardaïa in Algeria as a center of trans-Saharan trade

**Nomadic Economy**

The economy of the nomads in the region of the Western Sahara consisted of nomadic pastoralism, trade, some agriculture, and raiding.

Trade had been one of the economy's most important sectors, both locally as well as caravan trade along the cross-Saharan routes. Sometimes consisting of a few thousand camels per caravan, this trade would not have been possible without animal husbandry, which was the basis for most economic development.

Camels, sheep, and goats were the livestock of the nomads and a sign of wealth. Social standing was not dependent on wealth, however. Nomads were able to advance their social position in the tribal system for reasons such as exceptional achievement in battle.

Local trade was principally based on the exchange of camels, sheep, goats, milk, and butter. The main products for export were dates and burnoose (long woolen cloak worn by Berbers), among other things. Import was much more varied and included tea, sugar, spices, guns, ammunition, knives, cotton cloth, leather goods, trinkets, and perfume.

Not all nomads were transient, and some settled at strategic locations to take advantage of the trading routes. These settlements were located either on crossroads, where the lateral branches met with the main north-to-south caravan routes like Tindouf, or in the large commercial centers such as Timbuktu. Nomads involved in trade were typically either freight carriers or shopkeepers.

During the early period of Spanish colonization, the Sahrawi economy remained little affected by the presence of European settlers. The Spanish occupied a few locations along the coastline and hardly dared to venture inland, while the Sahrawis remained in their traditional territories of the region's heartland and interior.

Trade between the Spanish Sahara and neighboring countries

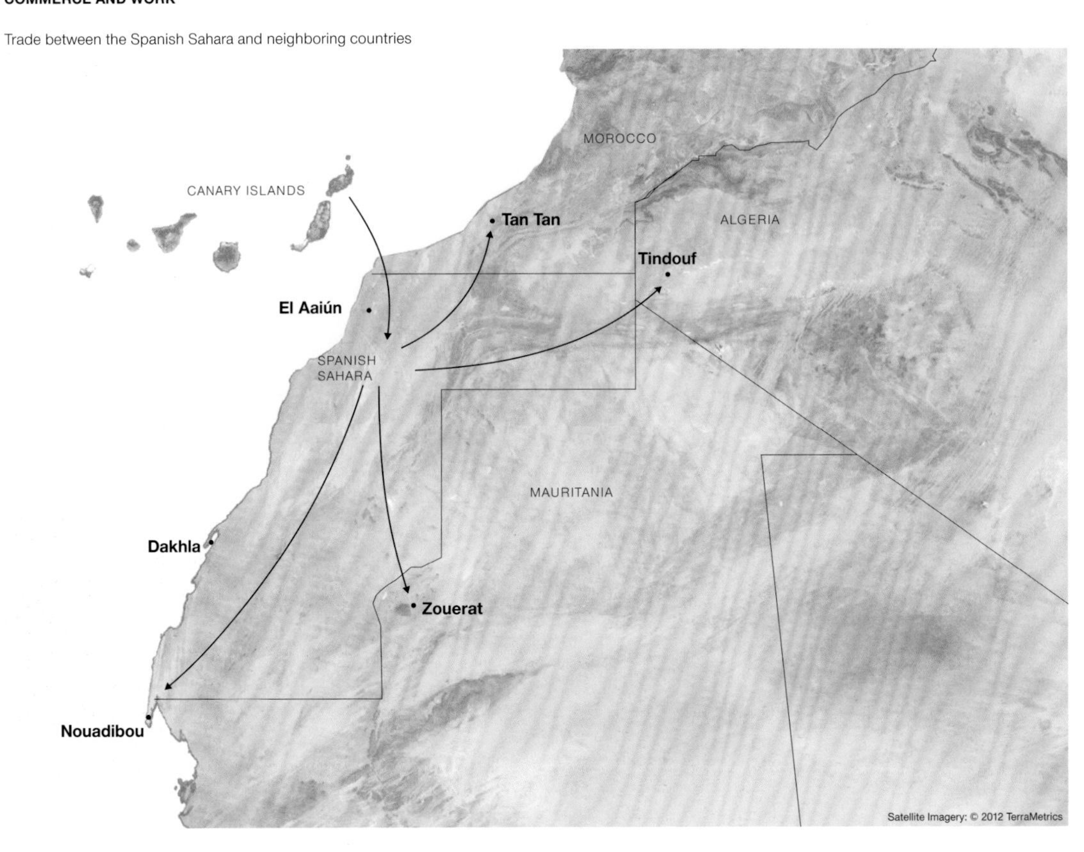

Market of El Aaiún, late 1960s

## Decline of Nomadic Pastoralism

A growing military presence and change in the political system in 1958 (which turned the Spanish Sahara into a province of Spain) resulted in a significant increase in the number of Spanish settlers during the 1960s. They were attracted by good salaries in public administration and tax benefits due to it being a tax-free zone, an outcome of the administrative change.

As a tax-free zone, the Spanish Sahara acted as a bridge between the Canary Islands and West Africa. A growing number of Sahrawis were able to accumulate personal wealth importing goods from the Canary Islands.

Because of business opportunities in the developing colonial towns, Sahrawi families became semi-sedentary and started setting up shops there.

By 1974, approximately sixty percent of the Sahrawis had abandoned nomadism and settled in one of the centers. This development was not only caused by trade, however. With the inauguration of the Bou Craa phosphate mine in 1969, Sahrawis began working for the Spanish. They also started taking on work in the colonial administration. This process was accelerated by two extended periods of drought, from 1959 to 1963 and from 1968 to 1974. Each drought killed approximately half of all the Sahrawis' livestock, thus eradicating the economic basis for nomadic pastoralism, trade, and agriculture. Though the nomads had experienced such periods of drought in the past, they were previously never faced with the opportunity to pursue a different source of income other than pastoralism, as had now become possible during the colonial period. Other reasons for the abandonment of pastoral nomadism in favor of a sedentary life were the better education and health facilities that existed in the towns.

With a significant increase of civilian inhabitants in the Spanish Sahara, spaces of trade became ever more important, and they were where the different ethnic and social groups met and exchanged goods. Trade between the Sahrawis and the Spanish took place in the markets of the Spanish colonial towns. They were usually arranged around a central plaza, as was the case in El Aaiún.

## First Phase of Camps, 1975–1991

**Living off Humanitarian Aid**
While the Sahrawi men were away fighting in the war between the Polisario and Moroccans, the women organized the provision of food and goods and the administration of the camps. Life depended almost entirely on external humanitarian aid, which was mostly supplied by Algeria. The only local source of food that families had were goats and sheep for a supply of milk and meat.

A very low-level trade existed among the Sahrawi families, with goods of humanitarian aid bartered or exchanged in kind. These goods were offered in an informal manner in front of huts and tents. In the 1980s, a limited number of shops were established, organized, and run by the SADR. Only one shop per daïra was set up, however.

**Sahrawi Red Crescent**

Even though goods came from international donors (mostly Algerian), it was always Sahrawi organizations, such as the Sahrawi Red Crescent, that were responsible for the distribution of the aid inside the camps. Although seemingly a formality, this represented a change from the way humanitarian aid was (and still is) usually distributed. Instead of an international humanitarian organization–such as MSF, Oxfam, or WFP–distributing alms to the refugees, a local refugee-led organization is responsible for sharing it out, turning it into a distribution of public commodities.

**The WFP Food Basket**

Refugees received supplies, first from the Algerian government and later from the World Food Programme (WFP), that covered basic needs and were meant to guarantee survival in the camps. Flour, vegetable oil, and pulses like beans or chickpeas formed the staple diet. Over the years, this food basket has not changed considerably, and still covers the basic food requirements of refugees in the camps.

"The key components of the World Food Programme food basket are: a staple such as wheat flour or rice; lentils, chickpeas or other pulses; vegetable oil (fortified with vitamins A and D); sugar; and iodized salt. Often these are complemented with fortified foods, such as Corn Soya Blend." (WFP 2011)

This food basket is usually distributed in the period immediately following an emergency. Based on the assumption that refugees are able to develop a level of subsistence after a certain time, aid is usually subsequently reduced. Due to the very harsh climatic conditions of the territory in which the camps are located, however, this level of subsistence cannot be reached.

| Food per person per day | Total value, kcal |
|---|---|
| 400 g of cereal flour/rice/bulgur | 1,400 |
| 60 g of pulses (legumes) | 186 |
| 25 g of oil (vitamin A fortified) | 225 |
| 50 g of fortified blended foods | 200 |
| 15 g of sugar | 60 |
| 15 g of iodized salt | 0 |
| Total nutritional value | 2,071 |

Source: WFP 2011

### Full Humanitarian Aid, 1975–1986

The government of Algeria was the main source of assistance via the Algerian Red Crescent. During the early years of the camp, refugees received the full humanitarian aid of 2,100 kcal per day.

- Algeria (Algerian Red Cross)
  – Basic food supply and other basic needs

- Bilateral contributions/NGO
  – Additional supply

### Humanitarian Aid, 1986 to Today

Since 1986, WFP and UNHCR have assisted the Algerian government in providing food and nonfood needs to the Sahrawi refugees. This aid program is ongoing.

- Algeria (Algerian Red Cross)
  – Additional goods, according to WFO, UNHCR

- WFP
  – Basic food supply

- UNHCR
  – Other commodities (tents, etc.)

- Bilateral contributions/NGOs
  – Fresh food, powder milk, cheese, etc.

## Second Phase of Camps, 1991 until Today

**Introduction of Money**

After the 1991 cease-fire agreement between Morocco and the Sahrawi People's Liberation Army, the Sahrawi men returned to the camps. At the same time, the Eighth National Popular Congress (held in the camps June 17–19, 1991) voted for the introduction of a free-market economy. This coincided with the inflow of money into the camps, coming mostly from three specific sources.

In 1991, Spain started paying pensions to the Sahrawis who had served in the Politica Territorial and Tropas Nomadas during the final months of Spanish rule. They had worked mainly in the mines of Bou Craa during the

Spanish colonial administration. A second inflow of money came from Sahrawis working in Spain, the Canary Islands, or other countries, and were sending money (remittances) back to their families in the camps. A number of these workers returned to the camps at this time, as the outlook for a resolution to the conflict and an eventual return to their homeland looked promising. The third source for money was the Vacaciones en Paz (Holidays in Peace) program that started in the mid-1990s. This program offers between 7,000 and 10,000 Sahrawi children a two-month holiday with families in Spain during the hot Saharan summer months. In reciprocity, Spanish families repeatedly visit their Sahrawi partner families in the camps. Through these personal ties, Spanish families often support the refugees with financial gifts.

With this inflow of money, the refugees are able to buy goods, build improved huts, and start up small-scale businesses such as shops or services. In the beginning, shops were informal and improvised, usually just a family selling food or textiles in their own house. Over the course of time, small clusters of shops have developed in the camps.

**Consumption of a Sahrawi Family**

This is an approximate list of goods for a family of ten people (grandparents, parents, and children). The goods come from humanitarian aid, indigenous production, or are purchased in the stores. Humanitarian aid is much reduced in comparison with the early years of the camp, which, in a protracted refugee situation, is standard practice. The small number of everyday goods that count as indigenous production is perhaps significant.

1 euro = 100 DZD (Algerian dinar)

This overview is meant to give an approximate idea of the regular (monthly, annual, or sporadic) expenses of a typical Sahrawi family living in the camps. It is based on data acquired from the NGO Hegoa and the author's interviews with Sahrawis in early 2011. It does not claim to be conclusive. Obviously, differences of income levels among families, which have increased in the past few years, have resulted in the development of different diets and consumption patterns.

| Monthly | Total Price |
| --- | --- |
| 15 kg of sugar | €12 |
| 100 L drinking water | €5 |
| 3 kg of tea | €24 |
| 8 kg of meat (mainly camel) | €24 |
| 10 kg of flour | €6 |
| 10 kg of lentils | €8 |
| 4 kg of beans | €4 |
| 25 kg of chickpeas | €5 |
| 25 kg of rice | €20 |
| 25 kg of pasta | €17 |
| 5 L of oil | €5 |
| 120 kg of bread | €15 |
| 10 L milk | €13 |
| Vegetables | €40 |
| 20 cans of tuna | €8 |
| 20 cans of meat | €12 |
| Telephone card | €20 |
| Other expenses (cooking gas, soap, etc.) | €35 |
| Transport (3 people × 20 trips) | €60 |
| Clothing | €35 |

| Annual | |
| --- | --- |
| There are three annual festivities: | |
| – Eid al-Fitr (meat, clothing) | €150 |
| – Birth of Mahoma (meat) | €40 |
| – Aid el-Kebir (lamps, clothing, etc) | €200 |
| Household equipment | |
| Kitchen equipment | €200 |

| Sporadic expenses | Price per unit |
| --- | --- |
| Cistern | €90 |
| Habitation | *dependent on size and facilities* |
| Kitchen | *dependent on size and facilities* |
| Bath | *dependent on size and facilities* |
| Carpet | €80 |
| Solar panels | €400 |
| Battery | €100 |
| Lamp | €12 |
| Fridge | €300 |

## Wage Earners in the Camp

Name: Ali
Job: Camel butcher
Wage: Up to €1,000 per month

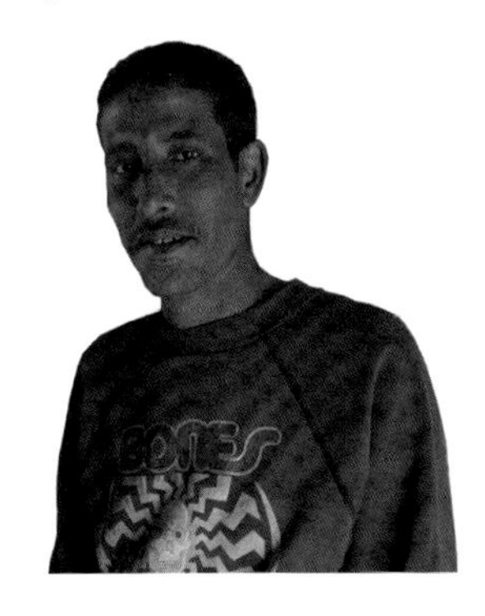

Name: Hamad Salem Daf
Job: Teacher
Wage: €140 per month

Name: Bechar Lamen
Job: Taxi driver
Wage: €250 per month

## Other inflows

Spanish pension

Work abroad

Relatives who work in Spain or the Canary Islands

Vacaciones en Paz (Holidays in Peace) program: Spanish families have Sahrawi children for a holiday and support the children's family

€200–€1,000 per year in cash and kind

Flour from WFP

Sardines from a Swedish NGO

Gas for cooking from UNHCR

### Reduced Humanitarian Aid Today

According to interviews with refugees, humanitarian aid has been reduced in the past years. The list of foodstuffs they receive is substantially below the 2,100-kcal daily allowance suggested by WFP.

However, it is considered standard procedure that humanitarian aid is reduced when an emergency situation stabilizes and turns into a protracted refugee situation. This is meant to reduce dependency on foreign aid and trigger economic activities among the refugees themselves so that they can generate an independent income.

Humanitarian goods in March 2011

| Values per person per day | kcal/100 g | Total |
|---|---|---|
| **WFP** | | |
| 250 g of flour | 350 | 875 |
| 35 g of lentils | 310 | 109 |
| 35 g of peas | 300 | 105 |
| 35 g of oil | 900 | 315 |
| 35 g of sugar | 405 | 142 |
| **UNHCR** | | |
| Green tea | 0 | 0 |
| 5 g yeast | 313 | 16 |
| **Bilateral contributions/NGO** | | |
| 15 g of sardines in can | 266 | 40 |
| 15 g of tuna in can | 347 | 52 |
| Total nutritional value | | 1,654 |

Source: Interviews in the camps

### Distribution

Food aid is first taken to storage facilities in Rabouni. From there it is distributed to the administrative centers in the individual daïras. Each family picks up its contingent in those centers. UNHCR demands that Polisario keep an accurate distribution list.

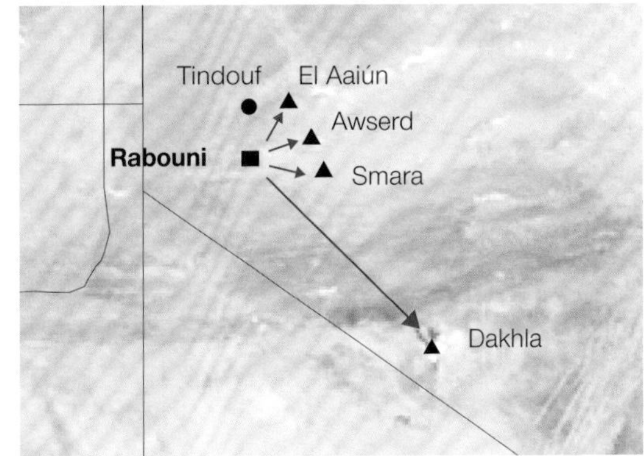

OR EXCHANGED
CONTRACT

**Baking Bread in the Sand**
A traditional way of making bread is to bake it in sand. The dough is prepared by kneading together flour, water, and salt. A fire is lit with wood on the desert sand. After the fire has burned down, the ashes are removed and the dough is inserted into the heated sand and fully covered by it. After approximately thirty minutes, the bread is baked. Once the sand is removed by peeling off the outer skin, the bread can be eaten.

**Sahrawi Diet in the Past**
Milk and milk products have always been a staple of the Sahrawi diet. Camel milk in particular was often the object of minor ritual observances. Cereals are important too, depending on the season. Goats and sheep are used mainly for milk, but are slaughtered for festive occasions like marriage, childbirth, or religious holidays. Camels are eaten after a lifelong service of transporting goods and producing milk. In colonial and precolonial times, certain tribes forbade the eating of poultry and eggs, but instead consumed various kinds of lizards as food.

Specialties such as tea, coffee, sugar, salt, and spices were imported via the trans-Saharan caravan trade, though the Sahrawi diet stayed simple. The main imports are tea, sugar, and salt.

Source: Briggs 1960

**Camel stew with vegetables**
The stew is eaten with pasta, rice, or couscous.

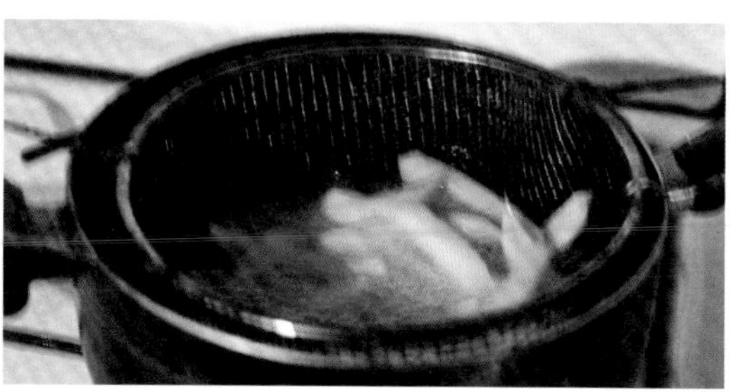

**Fried potatoes**
Sometimes in the shape of french fries or just cut and sliced.

**Potato pancake**
Prepared like a hash brown.

**Grilled chicken**
There is a poultry farm close to the camps, though it is not the Sahrawis' preferred meat.

**Grilled camel meat**
The shoulder is the preferred part of the camel.

**Vegetable stew with pasta or rice**
Meat is not eaten with every meal.

**Camel stew on bread**
Even though Sahrawis were involved in the spice trade, they prefer their meat unseasoned.

# Spaces of Trade

The first shops in the camps were set up by Polisario, and there was one in every daïra. These were often located on top of little hills for better orientation and visibility. This choice of location proved not to be successful, however, as centrality and the ability to expand in clusters turned out to be more important than visibility. Today, the derelict structures of some of the first shops have remained as lonely ruins throughout the camps. When families started opening individual shops as private initiatives, small commercial clusters developed in the immediate vicinity of the daïra centers. The adoption of a free-market economy at the Eighth National Congress in 1991 supported the establishment of these privately run shops. Even though shop owners need to apply for a license when setting up, few regulations exist to limit the size, location, or content of these shops. As land is free, everyone is at his or her liberty to decide about the dimension and location of their shop. Nevertheless, certain patterns in location, size, and appearance have emerged, with market streets developing a common look as a result of collective motivation.

Today we can identify three different shop locations. First, the camps usually have one or two central markets serving the camp as a whole, where the widest variety of goods are sold. Second, each daïra has its own smaller cluster of shops; and third, individual shops can be found on their own, in the middle of residential compounds, separated from other economic activity. Supplies for daily needs are most often bought at these individual shops or daïra clusters, while shopping for household goods or clothing is more often done at the central markets. The following pages illustrate the different shopping spaces and their influence on the camps.

Ruin of one of the first shops on a hilltop in camp El Aaiún

**Shopping Spaces in El Aaiún**

Each of the six daïras has a small market with between twenty and thirty shops. Since they provide most of the daily food supply, the markets have to be easily reachable by foot for the residents, hence their central location within each daïra.

The main market of the camp provides mainly nonfood products and is located on the western edge of El Aaiún, close to the entrance of the camp on the way to Tindouf. Most of the goods sold at the main market come from Tindouf or Mauritania. In the south of the camp an animal market sells goats, sheep, and camels. Because of the smell and noise, it is located at a distance from the residential areas.

■ Daïra markets
■ Main market
■ Individual shops
■ Animal market

## I. Main market

## II. Daïra markets

## III. Individual shops

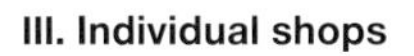

## IV. Animal market

## Main Market of El Aaiún

The main market of El Aaiún, located in the daïra of El Guelta, consists of approximately seventy shops that are built wall-to-wall. The long, continuous façade stands in contrast to the loose fabric of structures present everywhere else in the camp. The density and uninterrupted "street front" creates something akin to an urban environment. Small gaps between some of the shops create passages leading to the back. The social contact between customers and the shop owners is important, and most shop owners know their customers well. Because of a similar price level among the shops and a limited range of goods, customers often choose where they shop because of a personal connection to the owner.

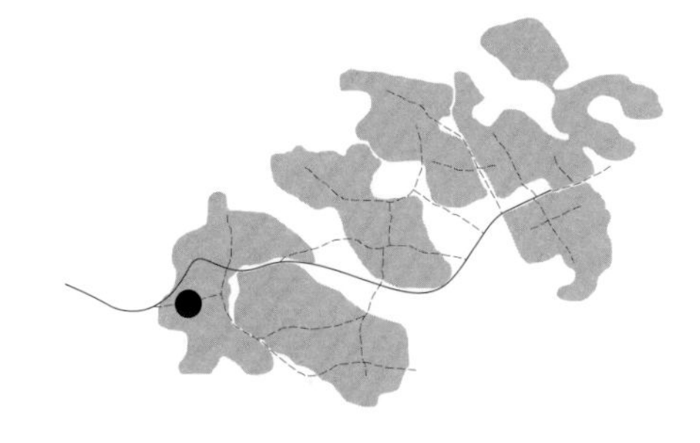

Continuous northern façade

Continuous southern façade

DOVE

**A Place of Urban Density**

There is no other place in the camp with a continuous street façade. The shops here have almost identical proportions arising from construction parameters and a common and routine process of building. Variations exist in the choice of doors and whether or not the outside is plastered or painted. There are no advertisements, and only rarely is the name of the business painted on the outside. Merchandise is not usually exhibited outside the shops. Although there is no master plan for the market street, it is apparent from the similar size and style of the buildings that there has been some kind of consensus regarding the design among the collective community of shop owners.

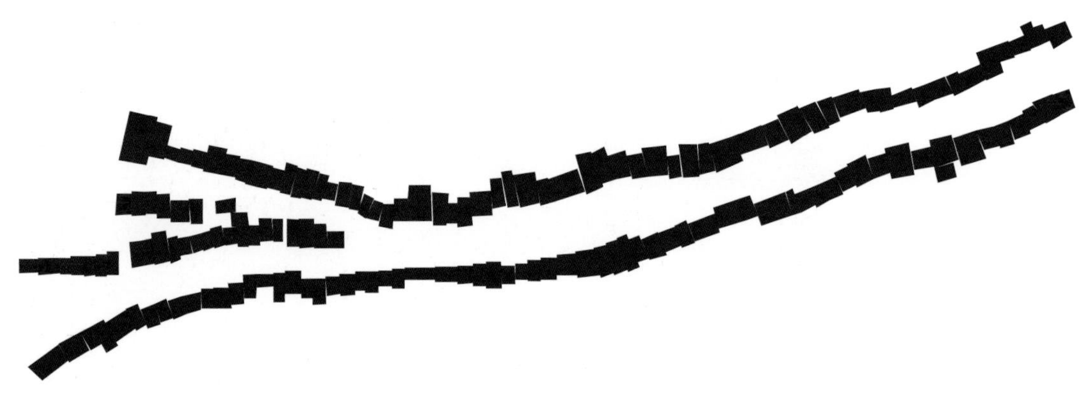

**Customers**
Customers come to this market from all six daïras because of its large selection of nonfood merchandise. Depending on distance and availability, they come on foot, by car, or in a taxi. During festival time, people buy new dresses and household goods, and the market becomes very busy.

**Typologies**
There are just three shops that sell food. The main focus is clothing, household articles, beauty products, and small pieces of furniture or carpets for the house. Shops do not usually specialize in one type of product but sell a wide range of goods.

- Clothing and household articles
- Food

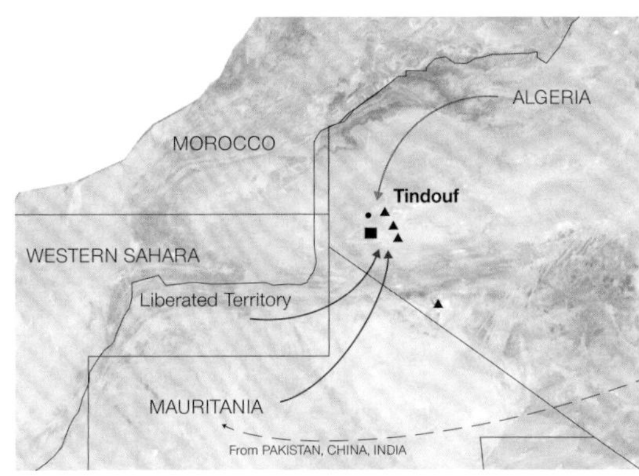


## Origin of Goods

With the opening of the shops, the Sahrawis restarted their trading connections with Mauritania. Products from Mauritania are preferred to ones from Algeria, because of their shared traditions and lifestyle–expressed in the way they dress and the animals they keep. However, fresh products are all bought from the market in Tindouf. Groups of shopkeepers organize collective transport to bring the goods into the camps.

## Trucks from Mauritania

Similarly, for the delivery of goods from Mauritania, trucks are organized by groups of shop owners.

■ From the market in Tindouf (Algeria)
- Food
- Household articles
- Toiletries

■ Direct import into the camps from Mauritania
- Clothing
- Textiles
- Beauty products

محل ملابس ووسائل التجميل

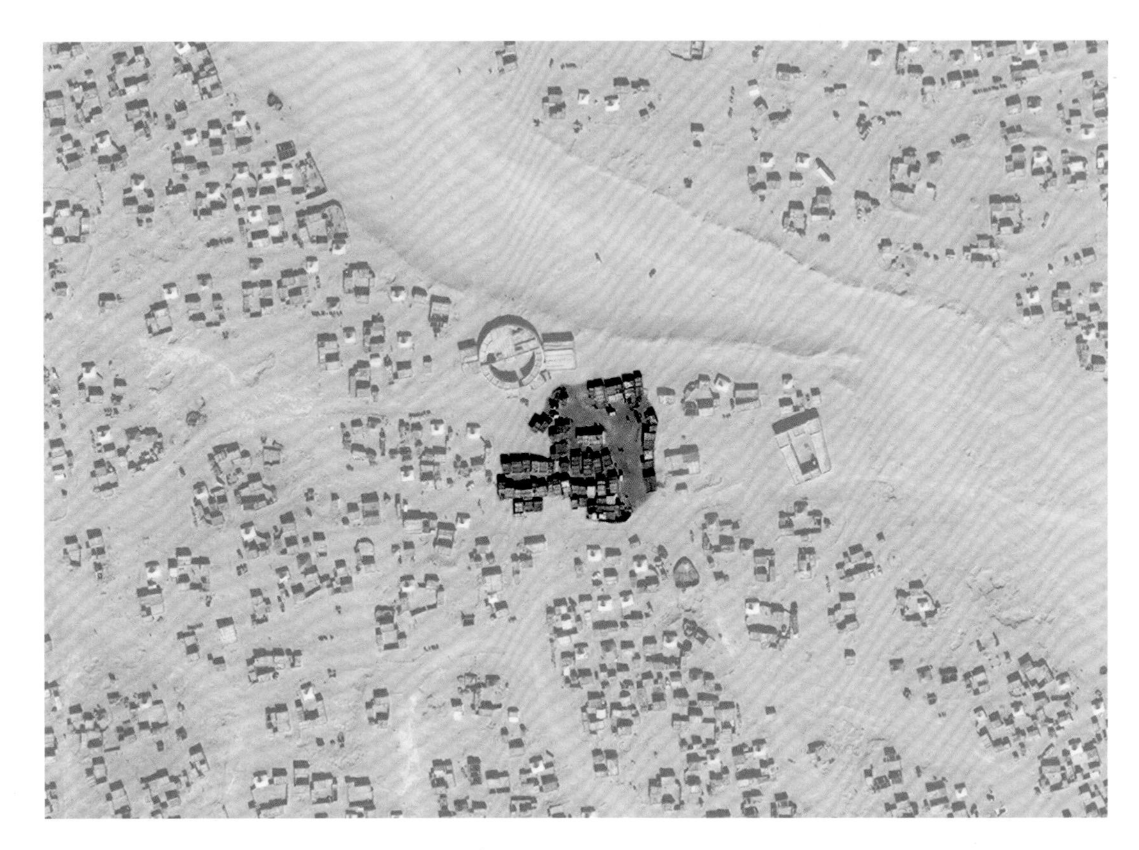

## Market of Edchera

The atmosphere of the market in Edchera is relaxed and intimate. Because of the convenience of its proximity and the familiarity and close relationship with the shop-keepers, inhabitants prefer to go to their local daïra market to purchase daily goods and food. The cluster of shops forms a dense unit, with one short, narrow street in which the shops are built wall-to-wall, similar to the main market of El Aaiún. Other shops form a little square around the corner or are located at a short distance from the cluster. Women and children move around the alleys, strolling and shopping or just lingering and talking to friends. The central plaza to the north is used as a social space for men to play games in the morning and evening.

## Typologies

The daïra markets fulfill everyday needs, with shops offering food and nonfood supplies.

- Clothing and household goods
- Food
- Butcher

**Strip of Connected Shops**
Three shops selling household goods, with a butcher for camel meat on the corner.

**Appliance Shop**
The appliance shop sells phone cards and electronic equipment. It only opens sporadically.

**General Store**
This shop contains a seemingly random mix of foodstuff, clothing, and household articles.

Boucra

Hagunia

Daura

### The Six Markets of the Daïras

The markets of the daïras differ significantly in size, layout, and the type of shops they offer. The market in Hagunia is said to offer the widest range of goods and has the best-kept shops. According to the shopkeepers, Hagunia is the daïra with the highest percentage of families with relatives in Spain, and hence receives the highest level of remittances.

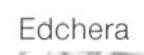

Edchera

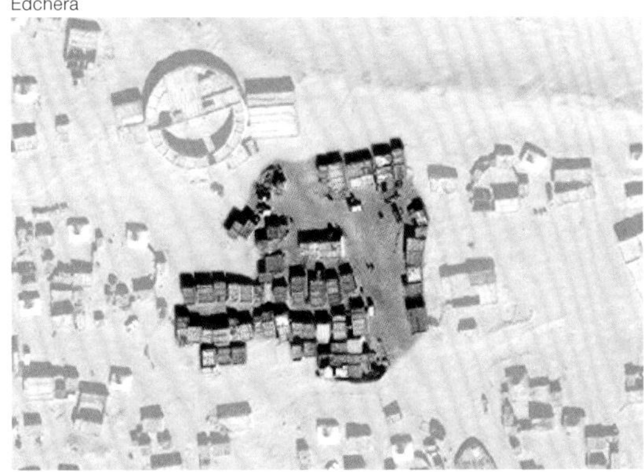

Amgala

El Guelta

**Individual Shops**

Spread around the camps, there are several individual shops that are neither part of the main market nor of the markets of the daïras. They are mainly placed along the asphalt road or the main thoroughfares. From Sahara-Foto to a hairdresser to a food shop, they offer different types of services and products.

Clothing store

Sahrawi pharmacy

Music store

Camel butcher

Cigarettes

Tailor's studio

Shop for soft drinks

Telephone box/house

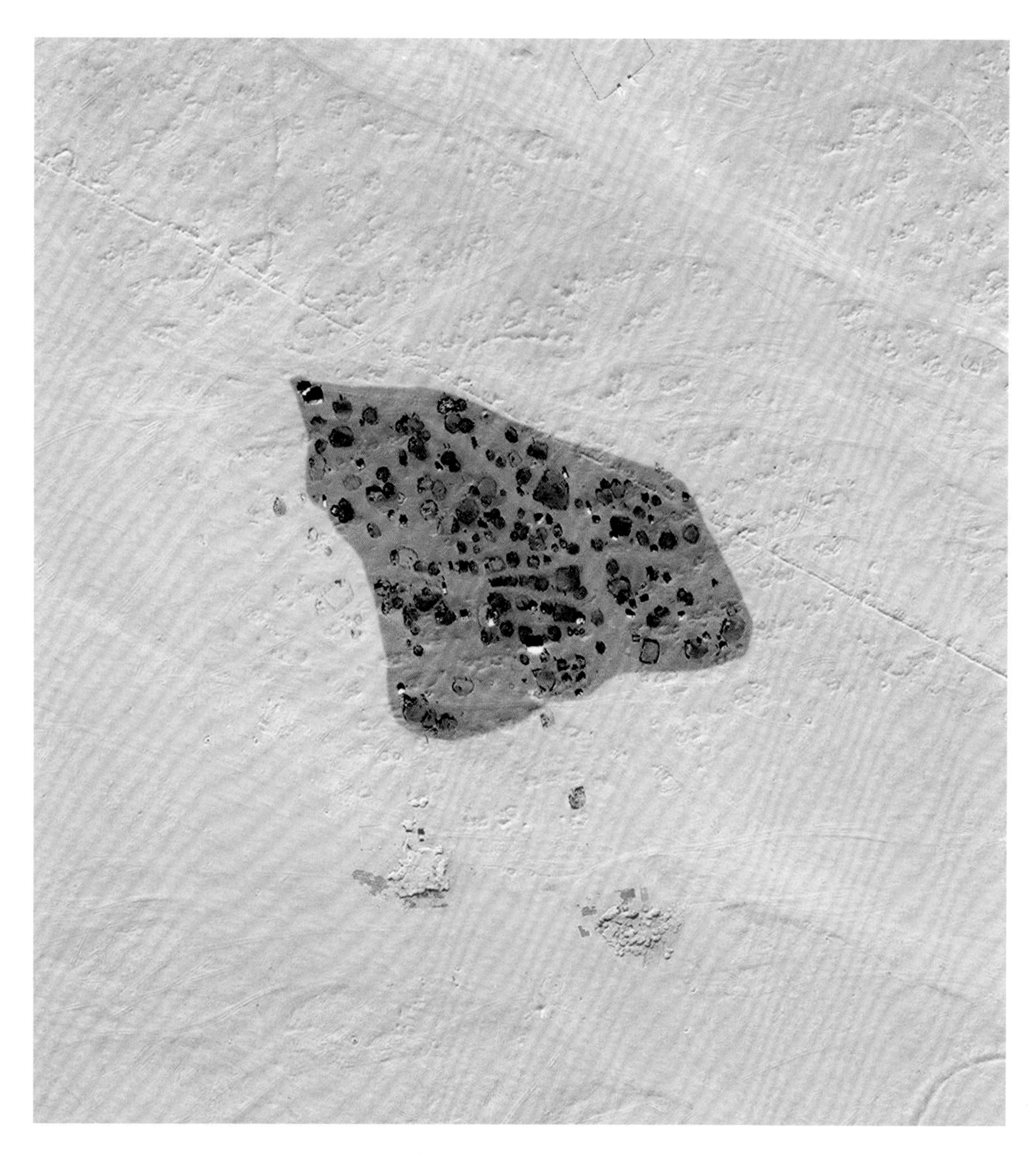

## Animal Market

The animal market is located beyond the southern edge of the camp. It is kept at a distance from the residential areas so that the noise and smell of the animals do not cause discomfort to the inhabitants. The market consists of circular cages, each housing a single or group of animals–either sheep, goats, or camels. Similar to the smaller enclosures built for goats in the camps, the cages of the animal market are made of a bricolage of metal and other recycled materials. The animals are kept in their cages all day and night. A veterinary keeps control of their health. The highest number of animals are sold in the run-up to important festivities, as they are used for the preparation of food.

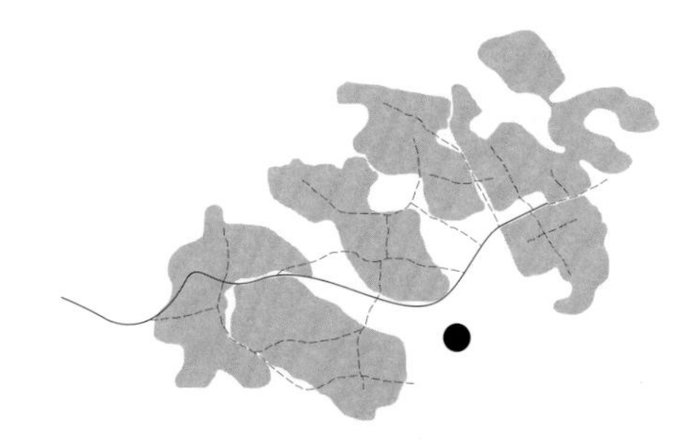

## Prices

The price of the animals depends on gender, age, origin, and physical condition. Considering the high prices, families only rarely have the funds to buy one. Occasions like weddings or childbirth call for celebration, which normally includes a sheep or a goat as the main dish, but this might be a significant financial struggle. The main customers of the market are butchers who sell the meat in their shops.

Sheep: €200–€300
Goat: €100–€140
Camel: €1,000–€1,200

## Indigenous Production

Animal husbandry has always been the economic basis of nomadic culture. The milk, meat, fur, and skin was used for many different purposes.

Today many of the animals still come from husbandries in the liberated territories of the Western Sahara. Others are imported from Mauritania. Every animal arriving at the camp must go through health checks to avoid bringing in diseases. Next to the vegetable gardens, animal husbandry is one of the few indigenous food productions in the camps.

# Shop Portraits

Walking into the shops of the refugee camps is a bit like looking into the personality of the shop owner. Some shops are very dense and organized, with shelves along the walls that feel like an elaborate storage system of every conceivable body-care product, canned food, or item of clothing. Other outlets treat the merchandise as exposition pieces, carefully laid out on top of tables and boards. Further shops are less organized, with merchandise arranged haphazardly, maybe because most of the goods have already been sold off. What is striking though is the large quantity of goods the shops contain. Many are stocked from floor to ceiling, with shelves along all walls, holding thousands of items of every kind. Considering the relatively low number of customers—sometimes as low as ten or twenty per day—one questions whether the large inventory will ever be sold or what kind of turnover the economic model of the shops is based on.

When setting up a shop, it is the acquisition of the first stockpile that represents the largest investment, often higher than the construction of the shop itself. This supply of goods is then slowly sold off, with only the more frequently sold goods being regularly replaced. There are some exceptions, however, with certain shops having a higher turnover of customers, higher revenue, and quicker replacement of goods. Aside from the camel butcheries, the most profitable businesses in the camps are petrol stations and shops selling phone cards. This is clearly based on the omnipresence of mobile phones and cars. Another obvious factor determining the rate of turnover for each shop is its location. Contrary to what one might expect, it is not always the central market of each camp that draws the highest number of customers. Whereas this is certainly the case for the markets of Smara, the central market of El Aaiún is less frequented than local markets in the individual daïras.

The market of Rabouni occupies a special and advantageous position within the economic landscape of the refugee camps. With no permanent residential population, Rabouni is frequented by many hundreds of workers and office employees who come every day to work in the administration and Polisario institutions. This mobile workforce is dependent on a daily supply of goods, food, petrol, and car-repair services, hence resulting in a well-frequented market and shops with a high turnover.

The following pages will look at three individual shops. One is a grocery store in Rabouni; the second is a typical general store in the daïra market of Edchera, in camp El Aaiún; and the third is a camel butcher, located in the same daïra.

إصلاح الأجهزة الالكترونية
0203

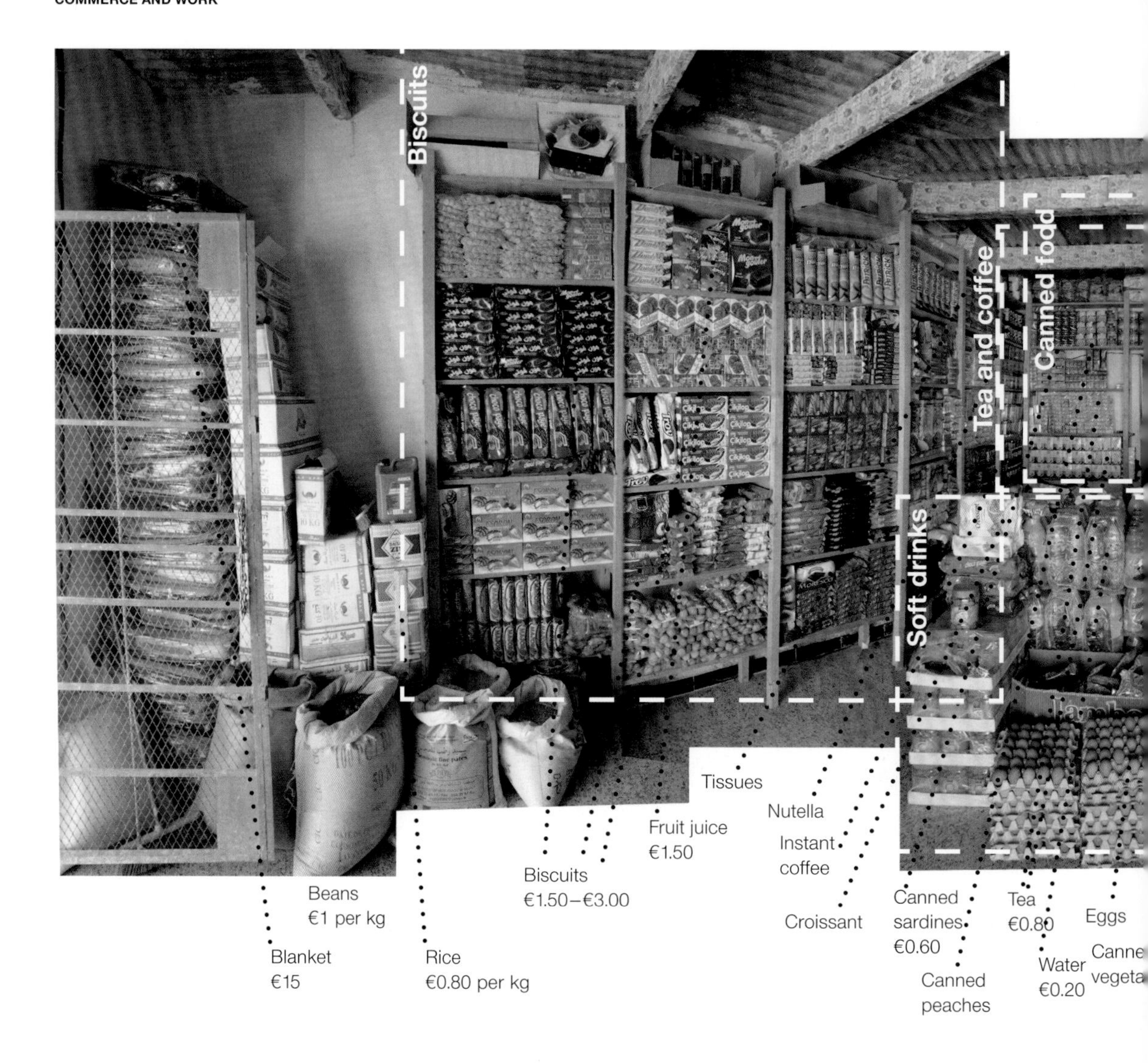

**Grocery Store**

Close to the main road in the market of Rabouni, this store has a high daily turnover of customers. It is equipped with a freezer and fridge offering cold drinks throughout the day, as Rabouni is connected to the Algerian electricity grid.

Name: Mahmoud
Age: Twenty-four
Customers per day: 100–200
Established: 2005
Construction: By the owners themselves
Funding: Spanish pension
Origin of goods: Mainly Tindouf market

Drinks

Bags with grain

Freezer

Fridge

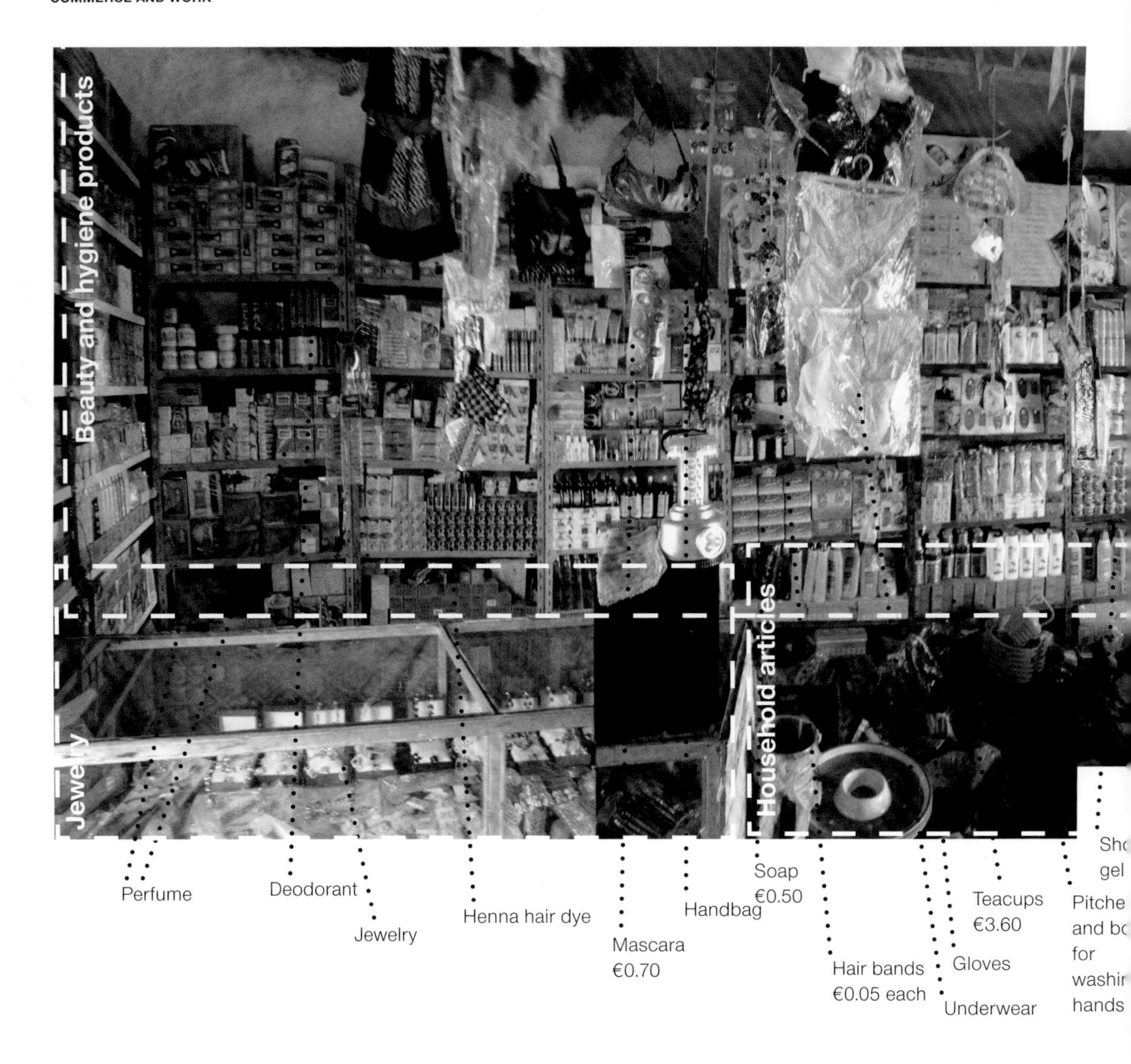

**Shop for Clothing and Beauty Products**
This is a small shop in the market of the Edchera daïra in El Aaiún. The sheer volume of beauty products is significant. Looking at the low number of customers, one wonders when Mohammed is actually going to sell all these items.

Name: Mohammed Salim
Age: Twenty-six
Customers per day: 10–30
Established: 2007
Construction: By owner with friends
Funding: Money from work in Mauritania
Origin of goods: Mainly Mauritania, some from Tindouf

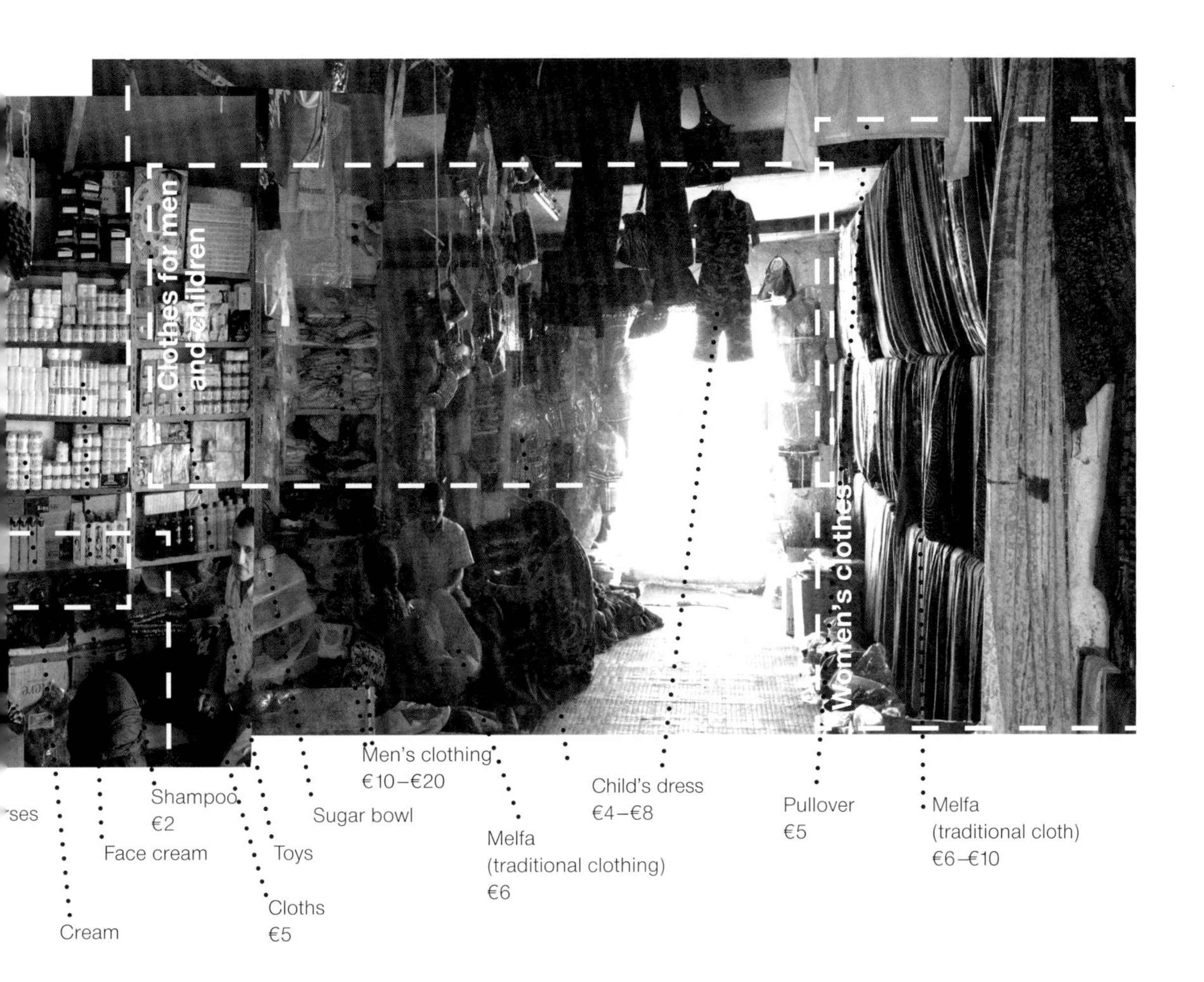
Clothes for men and children
Women's clothes
ses
Cream
Face cream
Shampoo
€2
Cloths
€5
Toys
Sugar bowl
Men's clothing
€10–€20
Melfa
(traditional clothing)
€6
Child's dress
€4–€8
Pullover
€5
Melfa
(traditional cloth)
€6–€10

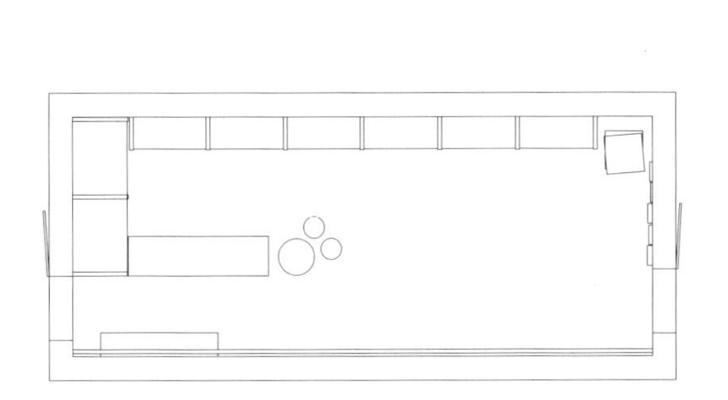

**Camel Butcher**

Being a camel butcher is one of the most profitable jobs in the camp. Very often, the first shops in the markets were the camel butchers. It is one of the very few products which can be considered indigenous, because many camels actually come from the liberated territories in the Western Sahara. The shop itself has a very simple layout. The most important features are the scales and hooks to put up the meat.

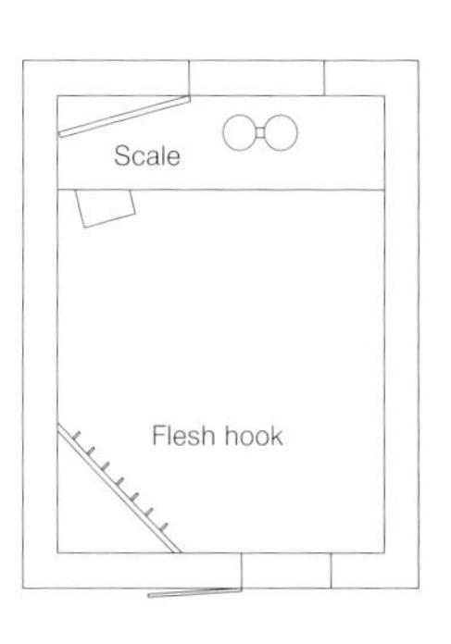


Offal
€3.50 per kg

Name: Ali
Age: Thirty
Customers per day: 50–100 (half a camel per day)
Established: 2007 (two butcheries)
Construction: Shop built by his boss
Funding: Through a friend who receives a Spanish pension
Origin of goods: Animal husbandries in the liberated
zone of the Western Sahara

**Advertising**

Walking through the markets of the camps, one sees many shops that are decorated with drawings of the goods they sell or the services they offer. Combined with the name of the shop often written in a calligraphic style, the appearance demonstrates a high graphic talent. This graphic quality seems to be the outcome of a conscious effort and intentional drive for layout and design. In an economy not based on branding and competition, the drawings put the objects of merchandise at the foreground, instead of a company name or the logo of a brand. Even though almost all Sahrawis are literate, the main purpose of the imagery seems to be about informing the customers about what items can be bought. Instead of announcing deals, bargains, or trade names, the advertisements function as decoration.

وسائل تقليدية
EXPO
Rami
جوبتر
كوكا
Yago
كوكا
NET
Dove
Royal
RECAMBIOS 4x4 ORIGINALES
قطع غيار 4 x 4 اصلية
ARTESANIA
EXPRES محل بابي
نسخ وتغليف الوثائق
بطاقات التعبئة
بابي
EXPRES
النصوير السريع
أدوات مكتبية ومدرسية
عند سيداحمد

# Diversity and Competition

Smara and El Aaiún were founded at the same time and have approximately the same number of inhabitants and population density. Their natural environment does not differ much, and both camps are located in the same stony, flat desert landscape. With these conditions in mind, one would expect the markets to have developed similarly, if not identically. Nevertheless, when we analyze the markets of both camps, the role they play within the camp economy, and their specific relationship to their respective camp as a whole, we can observe marked differences. The greater number of foreigners visiting Smara is a probable reason for its markets offering a larger variety of goods. But, as we will see, the background of the Sahrawi families, their connection to relatives living abroad, or the experience they bring back from trips to Spain has also shaped the local economy and shopping spaces. Competition between shops has started, and for the first time we can observe indications that, due to limitations of land in the markets, the notion of real estate has begun to enter the local economy and spatial management.

This comparison opens questions about how the differences in mentality and personalities of a local population can be a formative driver in the shaping of an urban environment. More fundamentally, though, it gives evidence to the question of how such differences arise in the first place.

**Main Markets in Smara**

Two main markets exist in Smara. One is located on the western side of the center and the other on its eastern side. The western market is the older of the two, having developed since the 1990s. Even though the eastern market existed in the early 2000s it has considerably expanded in the years since 2007. All shops in the latter have plaster façades, are painted white, and have metal doors in an identical blue. Some shops have a concrete base extending to the front from which goods can be displayed. Altogether, an aesthetic emerges that almost resembles a market in a Mediterranean holiday resort.

The older market is more haphazard, and most huts are unplastered, with a less regular layout. The paths between the shops are not as well kept and are often strewn with garbage. Because of the dilapidated look of the shops and paths, the market has a slight air of decay. The shops offer less variety of goods and seem to have fewer customers. In contrast, the eastern market is busier, with a wider range of customers. The shops also offer goods such as T-shirts or small items of local craft, which are attractive to foreign visitors.

■ Main markets
■ Shops in daïra

Old market in Smara

New market in Smara

**Space Limitations**

The eastern market is surrounded on all sides by streets, which limit its potential growth. In addition, all shops facing the perimeter roads are car-repair shops, further reducing the available space for other commercial activities. On the other hand, because of its higher standard, this market has proved to be more popular than its counterpart on the western side of the camp, resulting in more shop owners wanting to open their stores there.

The land in the market, like everywhere else in the camp, is free and can be claimed by anybody who has an interest in owning or operating a shop there. Nevertheless, because of the limitations of space, shop owners have started renting out their structures to other families who want to start businesses in the area. Other shops are sold when the original owner moves out or does not want to operate his business anymore. The limitations of space and the demand for retail facilities have created the first notion of a real estate market in the Sahrawi refugee camps.

■ Car-repair shops

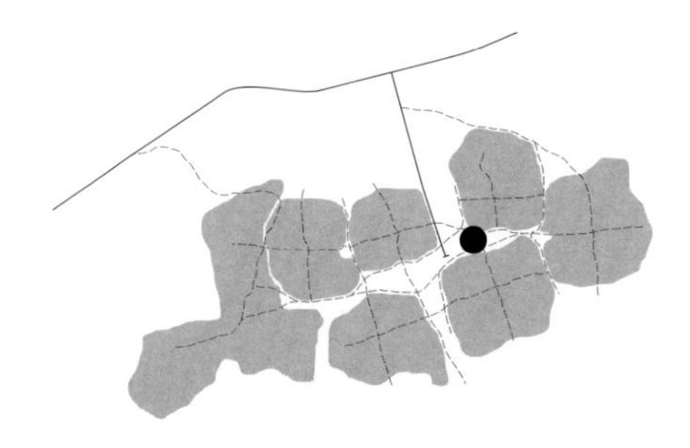

2007

2011

**Evolution of the New Market**

Since 2007, the appearance of the new market in the east of Smara has changed fundamentally. Many additional shops were constructed, and a common "look" was adopted for the façades, doors, and public spaces in front of the buildings. The market was cleared of rubble, containers, and dirt and has become the pride of the camp. In the close vicinity, an area with cafés and video-game stalls has developed (see chapter on recreation).

Mohammed is renting a shop

**Building Activities**
There is a constant level of building activity in the new market, with shop owners renovating or extending their shops and new owners constructing their stores from scratch.

**Buying a Shop**
The shoe shop used to house a camel butchery. When the previous owner did not want to continue as a butcher, he sold his shop to a friend who opened a shoe shop.

Price: €500

**Renting a Shop**
Mohammed is renting the building from a friend because he had no money to buy his own shop. He sells and repairs electrical equipment.

Rent: €30 per month

**International Influence**

Smara is the camp with the highest number of foreign visitors. In addition to participants in the Holiday in Peace program, there are a number of international NGOs based in Smara, as well as participants of other international events, such as the Sahara Marathon (see chapter on recreation). This higher presence of foreign visitors has created its own economy: shops for handcrafts and souvenirs, soft drinks, and even a café.

El Aaiún

Smara

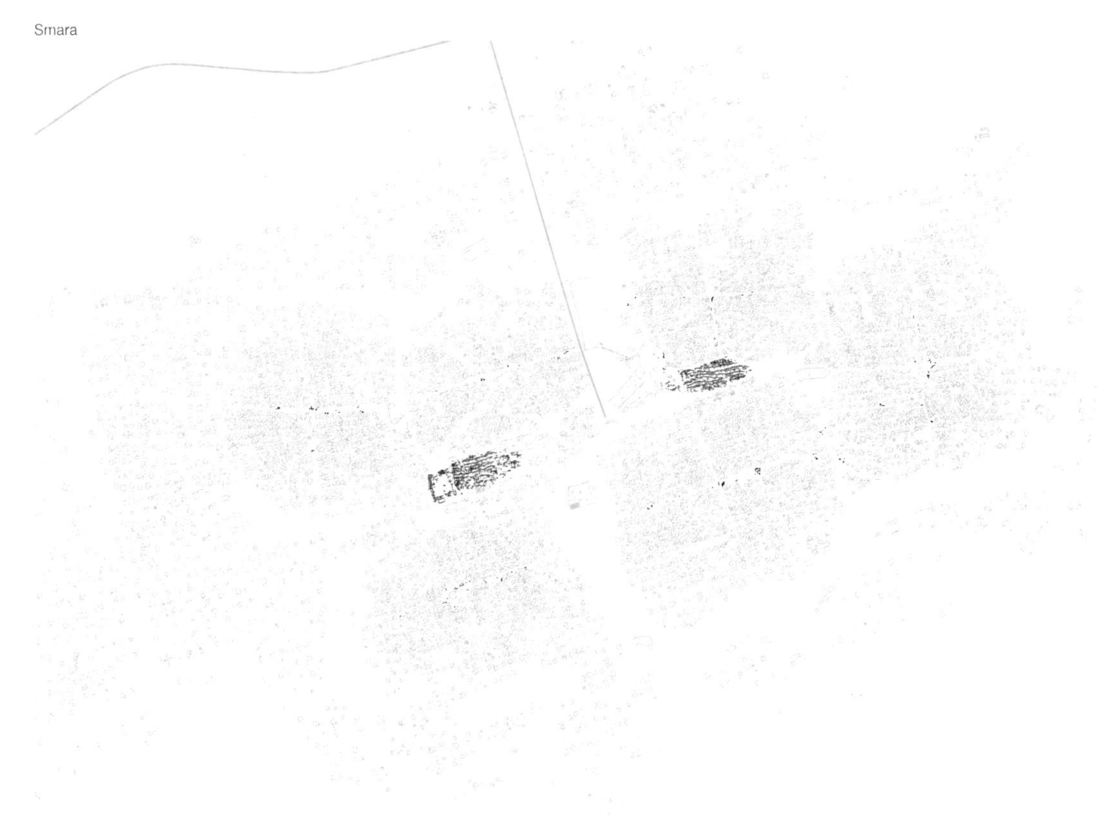

## Centralization Versus Decentralization

The difference in the way commerce manifests itself spatially in the camps of Smara and El Aaiún is considerable. The markets of El Aaiún serve each daïra separately, and the shopkeepers practice a close customer relationship, building on and enforcing the self-contained village-like character of each daïra. The main market is not frequented daily by the refugees, but acts more as an intermediary between Tindouf and the individual shops of the camps, and is conveniently located at the camp's western edge. El Aaiún's markets mirror the use and perception of space that prevails in the camp as a whole. The daïras and their centers are the first point of reference for the inhabitants and are where most of public life takes place. The spaces that could act as centers for the camp as a whole, for example, the zone of institutions along the asphalt road, do not attract a sufficient number of visitors to develop a life of their own.

In Smara, on the other hand, the individual daïra markets are practically nonexistent. Commercial life, with few exceptions, takes place within the two main central markets to the east and west of the camp center. Seen together with the cultural, administrative, and educational facilities that are located in between the two main markets, the camp features an extensive center where almost all public facilities and services can be found. In contrast to El Aaiún, which can be seen as a conglomerate of six more-or-less self-sufficient daïras, the structure of Smara can be described in terms that are more similar to a "normal" city. The center features the highest building density and combines administrative, cultural, recreational, and commercial functions. The daïras consist mainly of residential buildings, supplemented by educational institutions to be close to the local inhabitants. The central location of its main market means it is visited daily by most of the population. The main reference for the inhabitants is therefore not their respective daïras, but the camp as a whole. The concentration of shops in two distinct spaces consequently results in a larger specialization, in a notion of competition, and, being the main market of the whole camp population, a sense of the anonymous. Exchanges between strangers emerge, and this can be seen as one of the key elements of the urban condition.

# Working

In 2008, a group of international NGOs, together with the World Food Programme, conducted a survey in the Sahrawi refugee camps regarding nutritional and food security. Part of the survey was the attempt to establish income patterns and livelihoods. The resulting data showed that three percent of the refugees pursue formal work, one percent pursue informal work, while more than half of the refugees didn't want or didn't know how to answer the question. The remaining proportion responded that they were living off savings or loans.[1] This rather distorted range of answers exposes some of the dilemmas and difficulties of life in the camps, but more than that, it exposes the absurdities of trying to capture the economic dimension of life in the camps with categories that seem intended for a more Western context. Most obviously, there is little distinction between formal and informal work in a setting where no taxes are paid, only a small amount of money is in circulation, and the state itself is not firmly established. But beyond this "technical" aspect, and maybe more substantially, the whole concept of work seems to be of a different nature to large parts of Sahrawi society.

When walking through the camps, it quickly becomes obvious that many, if not most, Sahrawis are involved in some kind of work. This is evidenced by the large number of market stalls and car-repair shops, i.e. work that in a different context would be classified as "private sector." But refugees also work as nurses and doctors in the hospitals, as teachers in the many schools on the camps, in the administration of the daïras, or in the ministries in Rabouni, and several other occupations that would conventionally be seen as representing the "public sector." Many of these jobs, though, are unpaid, as teachers, doctors, or staff of the Polisario institutions receive very little or no salary. Their livelihood is secured by payment in-kind and by the food aid they receive through WFP. Work in these cases is seen as being a service for society and not necessarily connected to the Western notion of "earning one's living." All of this maybe results in the impossibility of answering the above-mentioned questionnaire.

The refugees are also faced with a different dilemma. While education in the camps is of a high standard, and many refugees have the chance to go to Algeria, Spain, or Cuba to pursue higher education and university studies, there are only a few opportunities to use their expertise when they return. There is little demand for engineers in the camps, and only a small number of politics, social studies, or history students find employment in the Polisario ministries or as journalists. This leads to a situation where many overqualified Sahrawis find themselves running petrol stations, having studied engineering.

The following pages show a cross-section of the range and possibilities of work and employment in the camps. It does not claim to be comprehensive nor representational in the strict sense, but gives an insight into the jobs that refugees pursue, and the spaces that are produced thereby.

1 Nutritional and Food Security Survey Among the Sahrawi Refugees in Camps in Tindouf, Algeria, October 2008

ENMTP

Construction worker

Agricultural engineer

Shopkeeper

Brick maker

Butcher

Cook

Gardener

Radio moderator

Nurse

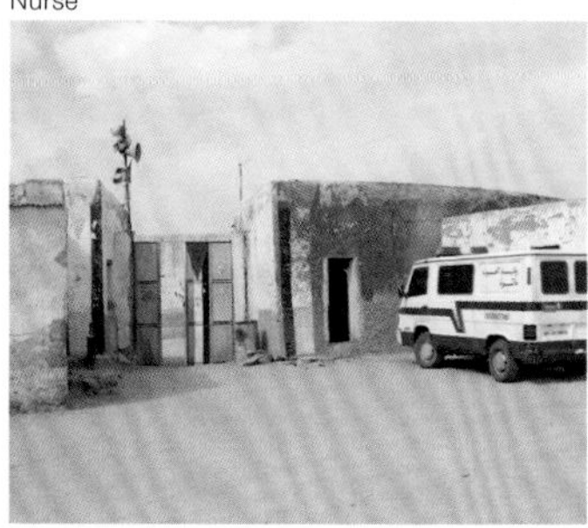

Tire mechanic

Chauffeur

Construction worker

Construction worker

Petrol-station owner

Chemist

**Working**

Appliance repairman

Shopkeeper

Gendarmarie

Mechanic

Hospital director

Hauler

Petrol-station owner

Car mechanic

Donkey herder

Archivist

Student/builder

Photographer

Shopkeeper

Mechanic

Construction worker

Toyota Land Cruiser of the El Aaiún *protocolo*

**Driver**

Bechar Lamen was one of the first drivers that Polisario employed. He is assigned to drive international visitors such as journalists, researchers, or students.

Polisario assists and houses international visitors to the camps. Initially, there was a single guest house in Rabouni. From there the driver drove the guests to the locations they wanted to visit.

Today every camp has its own guest house. Bechar works in the camp El Aaiún and drives visitors around. His car is a Toyota Land Cruiser, which is supplied by Polisario. Work hours are irregular and depend on the requests of the guests. He has to be on duty throughout the day, but apart from the drive to and from the airport, he does not work during the night.

| | |
|---|---|
| Name: | Bechar Lamen |
| Age: | Fifty-two years old |
| Civil Status: | Married, one son |
| Address: | El Aaiún, daïra Edchera |
| Education: | No formal education |
| Language: | Hassaniya, basic Spanish |
| Working hours: | Dependent on guests and clients |
| Employer: | Polisario |
| Income: | Up to €250 per month |

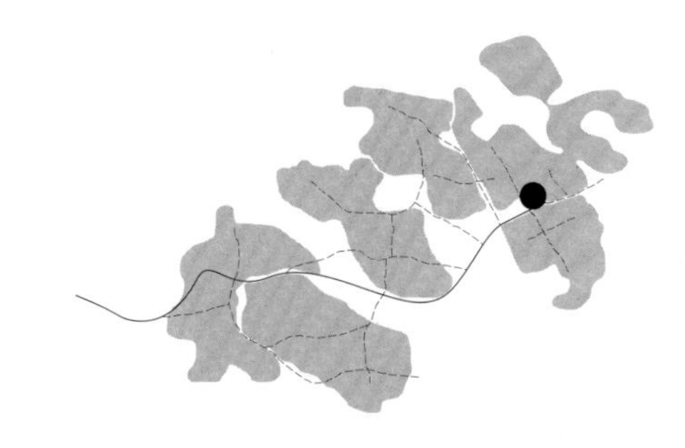

Family garden project in El Aaiún

## Agricultural Engineer

Taleb Brahim studied agricultural engineering in Syria. After his graduation, he remained in Syria for an additional year, working in several orchards and vegetable gardens. In 1998 he returned to the refugee camps, settling in Smara, where he tried to plant a vegetable garden in 2003. His attempts did not prove successful, as the amount of water required was high and the yield was very low. A Belgian agricultural scientist, Willem Van Cotthem, introduced him to a soil conditioner that increases plant growth and reduces the need for watering. After several tests with different plants, Taleb succeeded in growing garlic, courgettes, beans, tomatoes, watermelons, canary melons, lettuce, and sweet peppers. In 2006 Taleb launched the project Family Gardens in the Refugee Camps with UNICEF. The main objective of the project is to provide fresh food to refugees and supplement the food offered by WFP.

| | |
|---|---|
| Name: | Taleb Brahim |
| Civil Status: | Married |
| Address: | Smara |
| Education: | Studied agricultural engineering in Syria, Mauritania, and Libya |
| Languages: | Hassaniya, French, English |
| Employer: | Polisario, works with approximately twenty-five gardeners |
| Income: | Not specified |

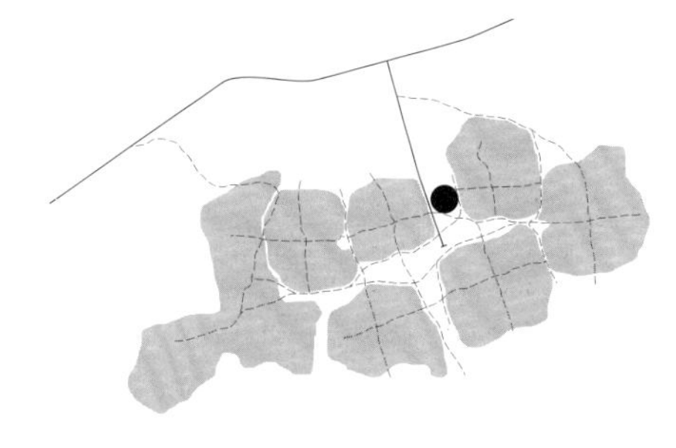

**Brick Maker**

Hassan started to produce bricks in 1995. Before then, families produced their own bricks for building. Hassan needs mainly sand and water from wells. His main investment was for the tools he uses for digging the sand and shaping the bricks.

The best time for construction is from March to May. During winter, bricks need four to five days to dry, while in the summer it takes only one to two days. During the busy spring months, Hassan usually gets support from friends. He also uses someone to transport the bricks to the construction site–a service included in the price of the bricks.

| | |
|---|---|
| Name: | Hassan |
| Age: | Forty-five years old |
| Civil status: | Married with children |
| Address: | El Aaiún, daïra Amgala |
| Education: | No formal education |
| Language: | Hassaniya |
| Working hours: | Morning to midday, depending on temperature |
| Employer: | Self-employed |
| Income: | 100 bricks = 1,000 dinar |

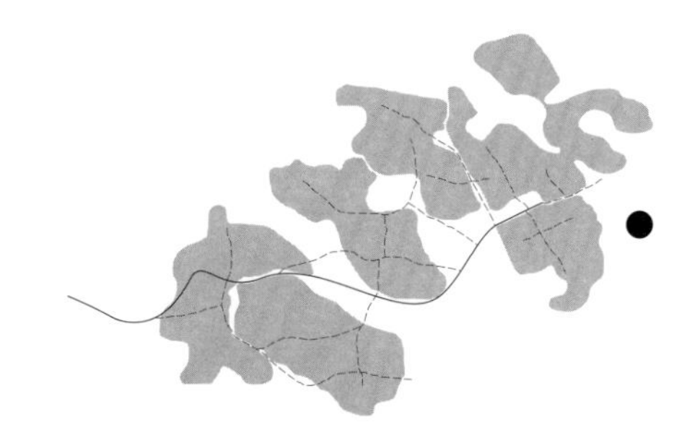

**Chemist**

Fatima Lessen studied pharmaceuticals in Algeria. Her pharmacy sells Western medicine as well as traditional herbs and treatments. She lives in the same building and often closes the shop when she is playing with her children.

Fatima's husband, Mouhamed Embarek Saleh Deihan, travels frequently to Mauritania or Algeria to buy herbs and medications.

| | |
|---|---|
| Name: | Fatima Lessen |
| Age: | Twenty-seven years old |
| Civil status: | Married, three children |
| Address: | El Aaiún, daïra Amgala |
| Education: | Studied pharmaceuticals in Algeria |
| Language: | Hassaniya, French |
| Working hours: | Morning to evening, but closed in the middle of the day |
| Employer: | Self-employed |
| Income: | Not known, but "sufficient to feed family" |

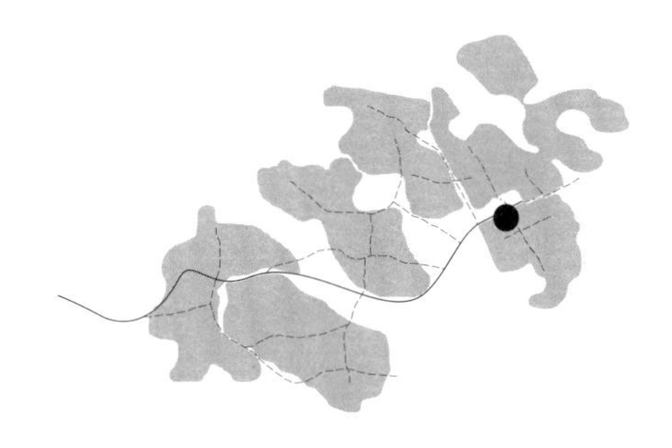

**Hospital Director**

Nayem Mohamed Ali works mainly with women, whom he teaches nursing. One of his other main responsibilities is the distribution of medicine to the refugees and the administration of the hospital.

Nayem lived in the Western Sahara until his eighth school year, when the war against Morocco broke out. He was then sent to Algeria by the Polisario government in order to gain higher education in nursing.

Name: Mohamed Ali
Age: Fifty-one years old
Civil status: Married, with children
Address: El Aaiún, daïra Hagunia
Education: Studied nursing in Western Sahara and Algeria
Language: Hassaniya, Spanish
Working hours: Daily, 8:30 a.m. to 1 p.m. and 4 p.m. to 6 p.m.
Employer: Polisario
Income: No regular income

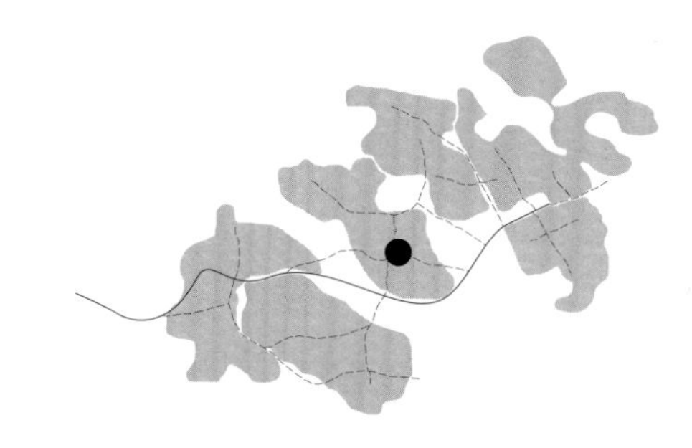

## Nurse

Because of the need for nurses in the camps, Nayem Ali decided to study nursing in Cuba. He is the only one in his family who was sent abroad to study. Upon returning, he started working in the hospital. He mostly cares for children and pregnant women.

Nayem Ali sees his work as part of the liberation movement. He doesn't expect an income and enjoys his job.

| | |
|---|---|
| Name: | Nayem Ali |
| Age: | Thirty-eight years old |
| Civil status: | Married with two children |
| Address: | El Aaiún, daïra Amgala |
| Education: | Studied in Cuba for ten years |
| Language: | Hassaniya, Spanish |
| Working hours: | 8.30 a.m. to 1 p.m. and 4 p.m. to 6 p.m.; Fridays off |
| Employer: | Polisario |
| Income: | No regular income |

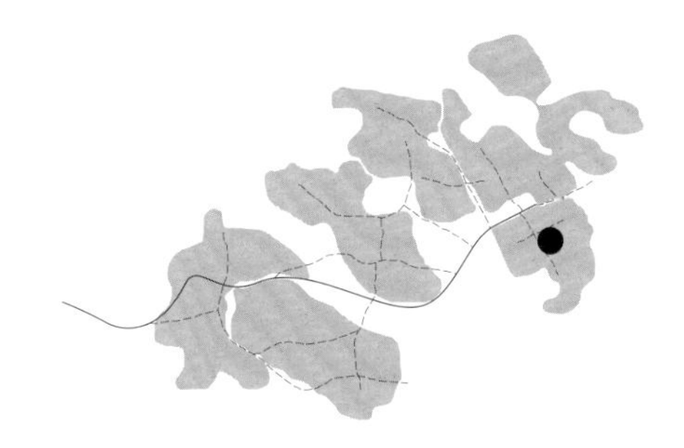

**Petrol-Station Owner**
Mohamed has a petrol station with an adjoining shop. He sets his own working hours, usually operating from morning until evening, with a long break during the middle of the day when temperatures are highest.

Mohamed built his shop with the help of friends. He travels to Tindouf at least once a week to buy his supplies and goods.

| | |
|---|---|
| Name: | Mohamed Moctar |
| Age: | Twenty-seven years old |
| Civil status: | Single |
| Address: | El Aaiún, daïra Amgala |
| Education: | Studied literature in Algeria |
| Language: | Hassaniya, French, some English |
| Working hours: | Irregular, usually morning to evening |
| Employer: | Self-employed |
| Income: | Not known (approx. forty percent of petrol price) |

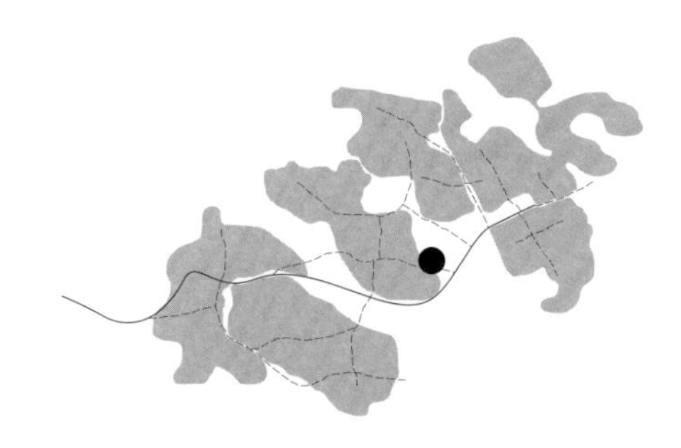

**Garage Owner and Mechanic**

Mehedi built a garage with two friends. They mainly repair cars, but also sell them from time to time. Apart from the garage, they also own a petrol station.

Mehedi gets most of his merchandise and spare parts in Algeria. He takes a car to Tindouf, buys the parts, and returns by truck. Some of the parts are also imported from Mauritania or Spain. The cars he sells are also imported from Spain.

| | |
|---|---|
| Name: | Mehedi |
| Age: | Twenty-three years old |
| Civil status: | Single |
| Address: | El Aaiún, daïra El Guelta |
| Education: | Secondary school in Libya |
| Language: | Hassaniya, Spanish |
| Working hours: | 9 a.m. to 1 p.m. and 4 p.m. to 7 p.m.; closed on Friday |
| Employer: | Self-employed with three friends |
| Income: | Up to €1,000 per month |

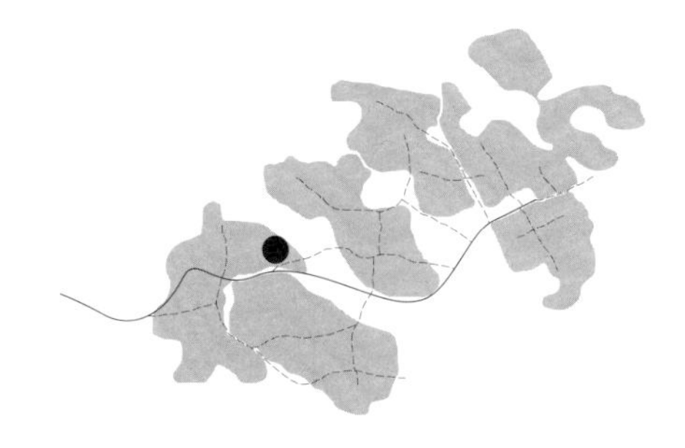

**Gendarmerie**
There is no longer obligatory military service for Sahrawi men. Joining the military is voluntary and can last for any period of time. Some of the soldiers have been in the army since the initial fight for liberation and are now more than sixty years old. They see their service as a continuation of the struggle for independence.

The military academy of El Aaiún trains soldiers in civil defense and fire protection.

| | |
|---|---|
| Name: | Balsa Salam |
| Age: | Fifty-two years old |
| Civil status: | Married with two children |
| Address: | El Aaiún, daïra Boucra |
| Education: | Two years in military academy in El Aaiún |
| Language: | Hassaniya |
| Working time: | Two weeks on duty, followed by two weeks off duty |
| Employer: | Polisario |
| Income: | No comment |

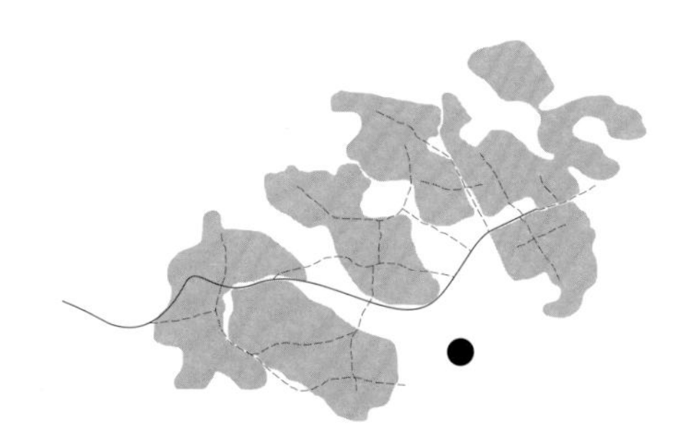

## Radio Moderator

Lala works for a youth radio program that was founded in early 2011. This radio station only broadcasts in El Aaiún. Lala works in the morning and has to prepare programs that deal with the topics and problems of everyday life for the camp's youth. There are plans to introduce similar radio programs in Awserd and Smara.

| | |
|---|---|
| Name: | Lala |
| Age: | Twenty-two years old |
| Civil status: | Single |
| Address: | El Aaiún, daïra Hagunia |
| Education: | Primary school |
| Language: | Hassaniya, Spanish |
| Working hours: | 8 a.m. to 1 p.m. |
| Employer: | Radio Nacional de la RASD |
| Income: | None |

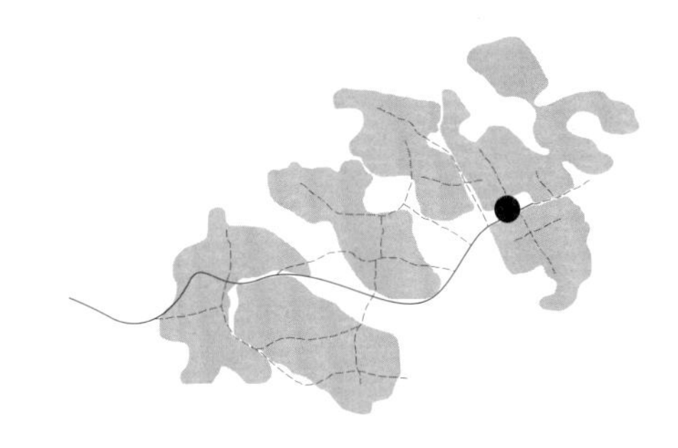

**Photographer**
Foto-Sahara is located in Smara, next to the new market. It is run by Mohamed, who had previously studied in Cuba. When he returned to Smara, he opened this photo studio. Mohamed's main job is to take pictures and print them. He also offers photocopying and laminating services, as well as a currency exchange.

The interior of the shop is very colorful. The walls are decorated with various posters, pictures of famous people, and a big Cuban flag.

| | |
|---|---|
| Name: | Mohamed |
| Age: | Forty-three years old |
| Civil status: | Married, with children |
| Address: | Foto-Sahara, daïra Mahbes, Smara |
| Education: | Studied in Cuba |
| Language: | Hassaniya, Spanish, French |
| Working hours: | 8 a.m. to 1 p.m. |
| Employer: | Self-employed |
| Income: | No information |

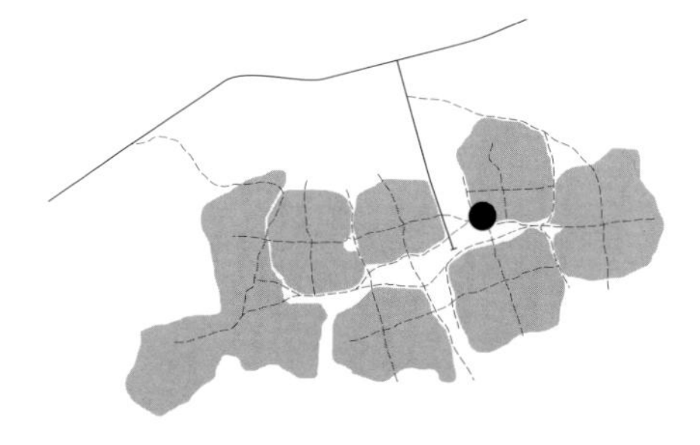

## Journalist

Bechir studied Arabic literature in Algeria. After graduation, Bechir returned to the refugee camps and started working in the Ministry of Information. For several years he was employed in the Information Center. In 2010 he started working for the national radio and television station.

The range of topics Bechir reports on is very wide. He feels a responsibility to inform refugees about international news, health topics such as vaccinations, distribution of resources such as food or gas, human rights, and other topics.

| | |
|---|---|
| Name: | Bechir |
| Age: | Forty-two years old |
| Civil status: | Married, with two children |
| Address: | Works in Rabouni, lives in Awserd |
| Education: | Studied Arabic literature in Algeria |
| Language: | Hassaniya, French |
| Employer: | Government |
| Income: | Approx. €40 per month |

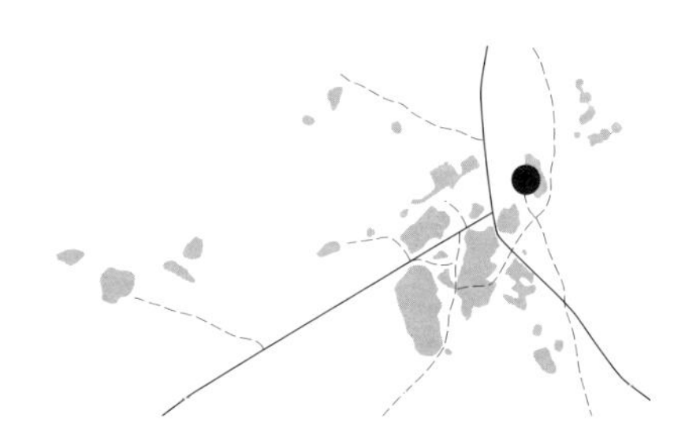

# Goat Barns

Goat barns in Smara

**Goat Barns**

Goat barns are one of the most striking features in the refugee camps, and one of their most particular spaces. Mainly located in the larger open spaces between daïras or on the periphery of the camps to avoid inconvenience and conflict with the residential zones, they are nevertheless ubiquitous and can be found in almost all areas of the camps. Approximately forty percent of all households keep livestock[1]–in most cases, goats and sheep. Both are kept for their milk and meat.

It is mostly women who take care of the goats. In the morning the goats are let out of their barns. They are fed with leftover food, or they roam around independently feeding on whatever they find in the camp. In the evening they are rounded up and returned to the barns.

The barns are usually circular, of varying size, and employ a wide range of different materials in their construction. The most common construction technique starts with wooden planks or posts that are fixed into the ground, and wire mesh forming a fence. In order to provide shade for the goats, this wire mesh is then covered with a variety of objet trouvé: rusting car doors, oil barrels and their lids, traffic signs, corrugated sheets of metal, window frames, and even the skins of goats and other animals.

The goat barns can be seen as a catalog of the discarded objects of camp life. Their impressive aesthetic is similar to an Arte Povera installation that would be envied by Mario Merz.

1 www.vastsaharaaktionen.se/files/Nut.surv_.Version%20EN%20oct_08.pdf; downloaded May 8, 2011

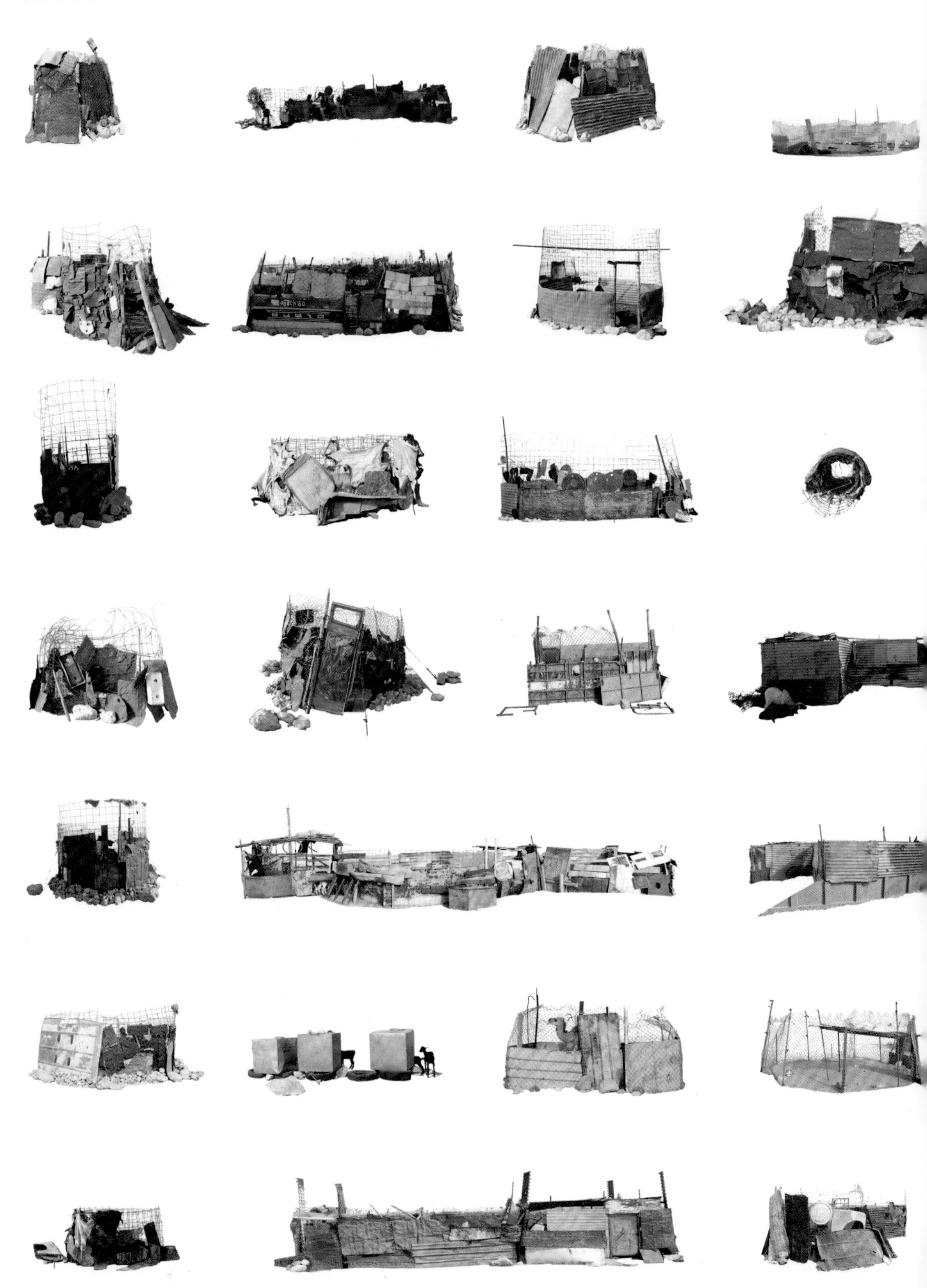

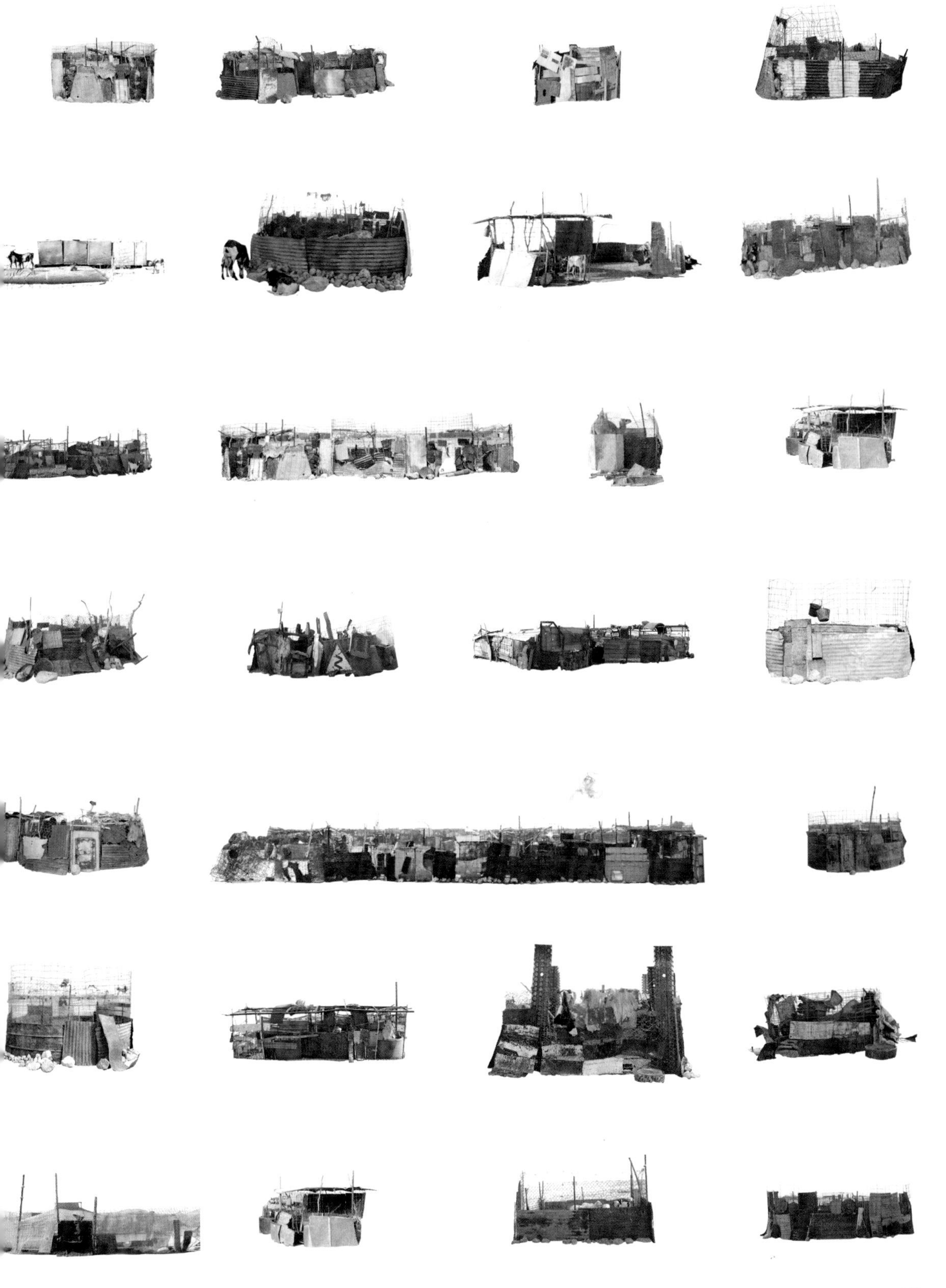

# From a Utopian Ideal to a Market Economy

When the camps were established in 1976, an idealistic, almost utopian, agenda guided their formation. Land should not be private property and could neither be bought nor sold. The camp economy was based on a nonmonetary system and trade consisted mostly of an exchange in-kind. Being fully dependent on humanitarian aid meant that all food supplies were shared and that hardly any differences in income or wealth existed. Few people had anything of material value anyway. Services like teaching or medical care were (and still are) available for free. Even though Polisario and the Sahrawis never officially subscribed to a leftist ideology, a proto-communism was practiced out of necessity and also by intention. The corresponding spaces of commerce were few and hardly impacted the spatial organization of the camps.

The second phase, beginning in the early 1990s, introduced a market economy to the camps and led to the establishment of a large range of small businesses and their corresponding spaces: individual shops and markets; garages and petrol stations; snack bars and cafés; goat barns and animal markets. The amount of money circulating in the camps increased considerably, though most families still didn't spend much more than a few hundred euros per month.

Nevertheless, recent years have witnessed the growth of competition as well as widening differences in income and wealth within the camps. While families working for official institutions such as the ministries, hospitals, or schools receive only very minimal pay, families owning shops or other kinds of private initiatives can sometimes make the equivalent of several hundred—sometimes more than 1,000—euros per month. These differences are likely to increase further in the future. So far the situation has remained surprisingly peaceful, and no conflicts or tensions (at least not visible to the authors) have arisen from the disparity. Whether this peace can be sustained remains to be seen.

Nonetheless, today the camps are still largely dependent on external aid. Even though some agricultural and livestock production takes place locally, the output is not large enough to sustain the population. Most food therefore needs to be imported, along with other resources and products such as petrol, building materials (other than the clay bricks), household goods, appliances, most clothing, and obviously cars. Hence, there is a constant outflow of money. Accordingly, the camp economy also relies on a steady inflow of money in the form of financial donations and remittances, as the camps, apart from very few handicraft and souvenir items, produce literally nothing exportable (and camel meat has yet to become a globally recognized delicacy).

While money is circulating in the camps, however, it gives rise to a wealth of areas of commerce, markets, shopping, and transport. What is interesting is how these spaces materialize differently in the individual camps. As we have seen in the preceding pages, the markets of Smara are organized centrally for the camp as a whole, while the markets of El Aaiún emphasize the neighborhood quality of each daïra. Commerce and its spaces thus become indicators of, or reveal underlying differences in, the relationship between the camp's parts and its whole, indicating what sense of urbanity exists there.

Ruin of one of the first shops on a hilltop in El Aaiún

Interior of a grocery store in camp 27 February

# HEALTH AND EDUCATION

In a refugee camp, health and education are two activities usually organized by humanitarian organizations. In a paradigmatic way they symbolize what is perhaps the central ethos of humanitarianism: educating and healing people. Both fields are also fundamental to the common concept of quality of life and are considered key factors when assessing human development. Hence, international NGOs are often at the forefront when it comes to delivering health services and establishing educational facilities.

In the case of the Sahrawi camps, however, in contrast to other refugee conditions, these services are administered and managed by the refugees and their representatives themselves, instead of international NGOs. Health and education are not just technical services, but become means of shaping a national identity and carry the understanding of a common destiny. At the same time, life in the camps shows the spatial and territorial dimension of health and education: the camps offer different ways to organize activities that were not possible in the homeland, thus exposing some of the dilemmas of the refugee status.

# Health and Education in the Colonial and Precolonial Era

The question of how to establish education and medical facilities within a nomadic and semi-sedentary culture, consisting of several tribes and spread out over a vast desert territory, must have always been a challenge. The spread of Islam in the Berber region of North Africa during the eighth and ninth centuries brought about a new concept of teaching that was based on the Koran. Even though some of the earliest formal schools were established in the Maghreb (for example, the University of Al Karaouine in Fez, Morocco, in 859), schools with a fixed location rarely existed because of the nomadic lifestyle. Instead, traveling teachers moved around the territory, teaching several families.

The area of today's Western Sahara was inhabited by the Sanhaja, a local Berber tribe, during the early Middle Ages. The Sanhaja converted to Islam during the ninth century and formed a strong, cohesive trading and military union. With the disintegration of that union during the eleventh century, the Almoravids gained control of the Maghreb, later extending their rule to cover the area from the Iberian Peninsula in the north to today's Senegal in the south. Though short-lived, it had a lasting impact on the culture of the territory. The Beni Hassan tribe that migrated to the Maghreb in the twelfth century lead to an Arabization of Berber culture and brought a more semi-sedentary lifestyle to the region. While so-called Zawiyahs (Arabic for "assembly" or "group") were established in the north as formalized places of learning and religious study, a new caste or tribe developed among the Sahrawis carrying the same name. These Zawiyahs were responsible for education and teaching.

During the colonial period, the Spanish set up a formalized education system, with schools catering to either Spanish or Sahrawi children. For the latter, education was mostly limited to primary level, with very few Sahrawis being able to continue to secondary school, and virtually none to higher-level education such as university.

The health system showed a similar pattern, with modern medical facilities being introduced by the Spanish colonial power. Even though historical statistics hint to the fact that this health system compared favorably to other countries of the Maghreb, access was unevenly distributed between the Spanish and Sahrawi population. For Sahrawis pursuing a nomadic lifestyle, many facilities remained out of reach.

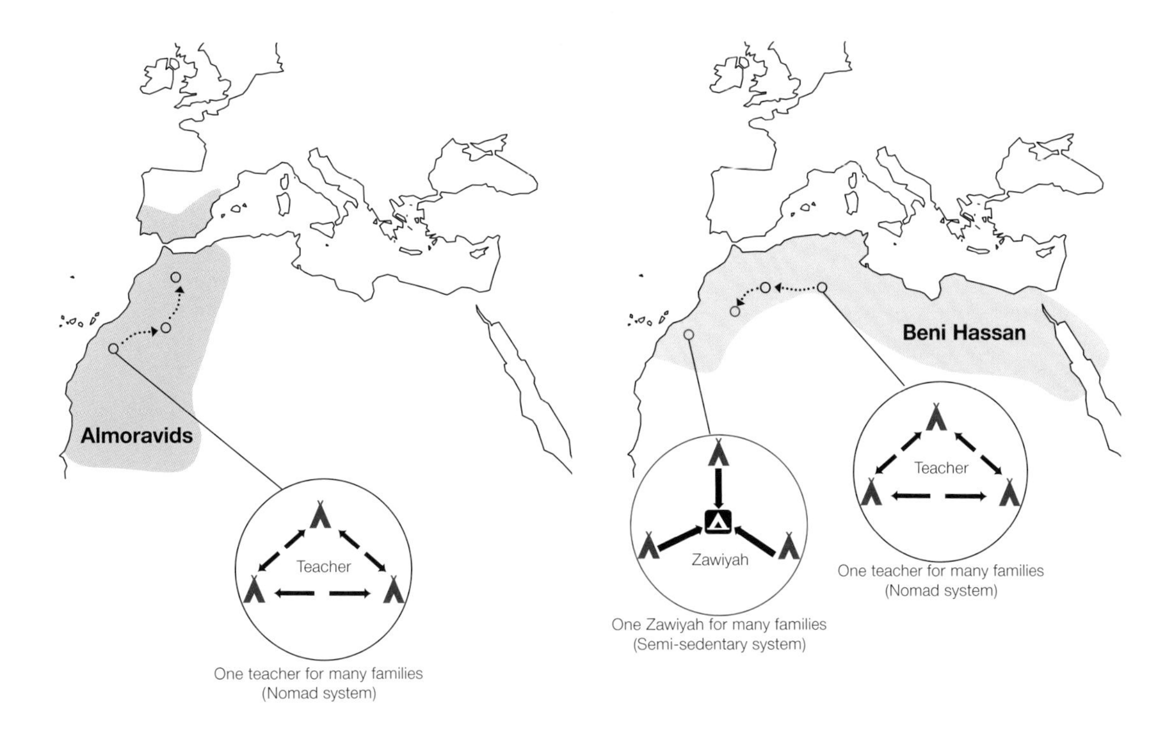

**The Almoravids**

Almoravids were a Berber dynasty that ruled and governed the areas of today's southern Spain, Morocco, and Western Sahara, extending as far south as today's Mauritania and Senegal during the eleventh and twelfth centuries. They had a lasting influence on the Sahrawi culture, with the implementation of the Koran together with the first nomadic schooling system, in which one educator would teach several families. The notion of a fixed school did not yet exist among the Sahrawis.

**The Beni Hassan Tribe**

The Beni Hassan was an Arabic tribe that migrated to the Maghreb and into the territory of today's Western Sahara during the twelfth and thirteenth centuries. Despite being nomadic, they brought a semi-sedentary way of life into Sanhaja culture, allowing for an improved school system. At the same time, the first fixed schools were established by the Zawiyah caste. The Beni Hassan also brought the Arabic language to the area. Giving testimony to this, the dialect spoken by Sahrawis today is called Hassaniya.

City of El Aaiún, 1958–1959

School in El Aaiún, 1963

Demographics of the Spanish Sahara

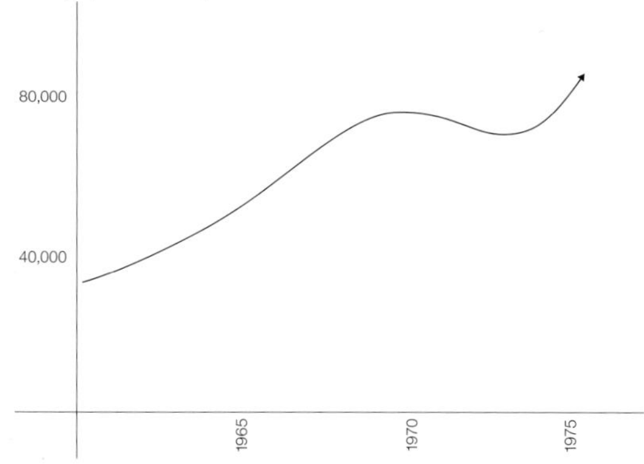


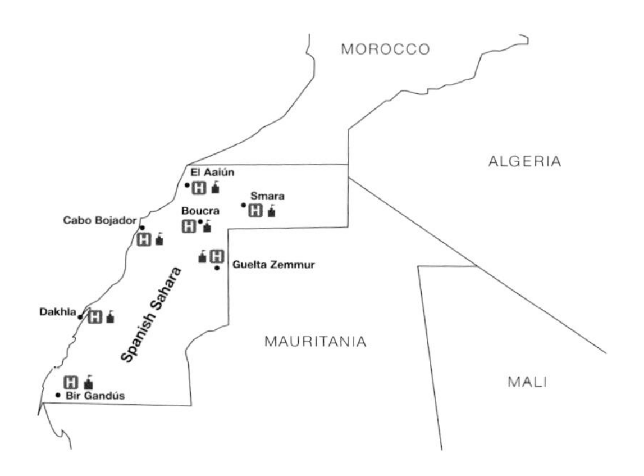


## Education in the Colonial Era

With the establishment of new cities, the Spanish colonial system also constructed hospitals and schools. Even though the school system was partially accessible by the Sahrawi population, the level of education remained low. At the end of the colonial era the illiteracy rate was still in the range of ninety percent, and only twenty Sahrawi students pursued higher education at university level. The few with access to Spanish universities were limited in the fields they were allowed to study. They were prevented from studying subjects such as political sciences, sociology, or journalism.

The small number of Sahrawis holding a university degree in 1975 was due to the fact that Spain only started allowing Sahrawis to study at Spanish universities in 1968. By the end of the colonial period only two Sahrawis had completed their university studies, and only twelve had advanced technical diplomas.

| | |
|---|---|
| Educational units | 44 |
| European teachers | 37 |
| Sahrawis | 15 (Koranic lessons) |
| | |
| Primary students: | |
| European | 850 |
| Sahrawi | 1,162 |
| | |
| Intermediate (secondary): | |
| European | 370 |
| Sahrawi | 82 |

All data from 1965

El Aaiún, 1972

El Aaiún, 1971

Hospital El Aaiún, 1975

## Health

With several dispensaries, two hospitals, and approximately thirty medical doctors, the Spanish Sahara had a far better health system than the neighboring territories. An average of one doctor per 2,150 inhabitants compares favorably even to the rate of contemporary Morocco. Nevertheless, the health infrastructure of the colonial Spanish Sahara primarily served the Spanish army and its civilian population. Concentrated in the larger cities of El Aaiún and Dakhla, the health infrastructure was often inaccessible to nomadic Sahrawi society.

Two hospitals for the entire population

| | |
|---|---|
| One bed per | 239 people |
| | 4.65 doctors/10,000 inhabitants |

All data from 1972

(WHO 2011):

| | |
|---|---|
| Mali | 0.5 doctors/10,000 Inhabitants |
| Algeria | 12.1 doctors/10,000 Inhabitants |
| Mauritania | 1.3 doctors/10,000 Inhabitants |
| Morocco | 6.2 doctors/10,000 Inhabitants |

# Overview of Health and Education in the Camps

Fleeing the war with Morocco and first arriving on the Algerian border, the refugee condition exposed the fragility of life in the desert. Medical conditions were problematic in the early days of the camps. The first refugees, arriving in late 1975, were often injured in the war against the Moroccans and were weak and exhausted from their flight. The hamada (Arabic for "stony desert") around Tindouf proved to be exceptionally barren, and the refugees were exposed to the rough winter climate with little shelter. During the first few months only a single doctor was available to treat the whole refugee population. Medical teams sent by Cuba and Médecins Sans Frontières were unable to control a measles epidemic that ravaged the camps in early 1976, killing more than a thousand Sahrawi children.

On the other hand, the camps became a turning point for Sahrawi society to reorganize its health and educational facilities. For the first time, large numbers of people were living in close proximity, allowing the establishment of health and education services that could reach the whole society. The refugees saw and understood the opportunity open to them and developed a novel system of public services that coincided with the organizational structure of the camps.

Ministry of Public Health, Rabouni

Medical eduction in the early years

## Setting Up the Camps

After the initial crisis of the camps' early days, the situation improved with the establishment of clinics and the delivery of increased food aid the following year. However, one of the most important reasons for the improvement of the health situation and general living conditions in the camps was the refugees' emphasis on education.

From early on, schools were established that granted an extensive education to virtually all young Sahrawis, both men and women. Cuba also offered free secondary and university education to the refugees. Over time, more than 5,000 Sahrawis, including 200 doctors, have graduated from Cuban universities.[1] Combined with over 1,000 nurses, this has given the refugee camps a medical system that is almost unequaled in the Maghreb and Saharan Africa today. A rate of approximately one doctor per 1,000 inhabitants puts it far above Morocco, which has just half that number.

But the emphasis on education not only served the medical system. From the very beginning, Polisario set up education committees and developed its own school curriculum. In the first fifteen years of the camps–up to the armistice of 1990–the camps were largely inhabited by children, women, and older people, as most of the men were fighting in the guerilla war against Morocco. Women therefore figured (and continue to figure) very strongly in the education sector, leading to an overall emancipation of society.

Similar to the health system, and because of a lack of higher education during the Spanish colonial era, only a handful of teachers existed among the Sahrawi population when the camps were first set up. To start this process, adults who could prove a sufficient level of reading and writing in an Arabic or Spanish test were admitted to further exams in specific fields chosen by the Commission of Education and Teaching. From these humble steps, a general education system developed, supported by countries such as Cuba, Algeria, Libya, and others that offered to train young teachers.

Today the Sahrawi camps are able to offer all children an extensive and free primary and secondary education. The refugee population now has a illiteracy rate of less than ten percent, again comparing very favorably with neighboring countries such as Algeria, Mauritania, or Morocco, which lie significantly higher.

1 Alejandro Garcia: *Historias del Sahara,* 2001; as quoted in Pablo San Martin: Western Sahara, 2010.

A lesson in Arabic

One of the first schools

An early camp committee meeting

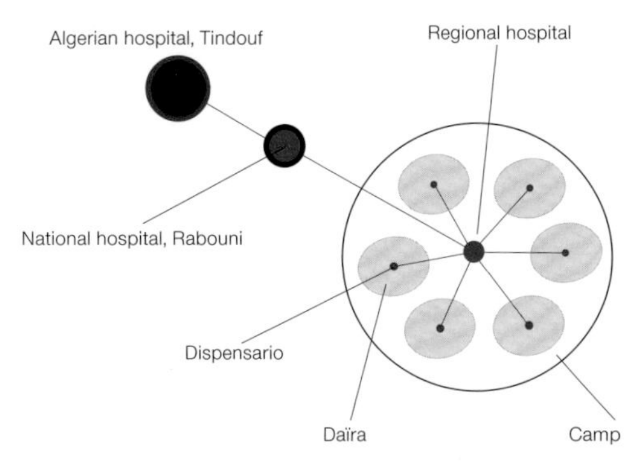


Hierarchy of medical institutions

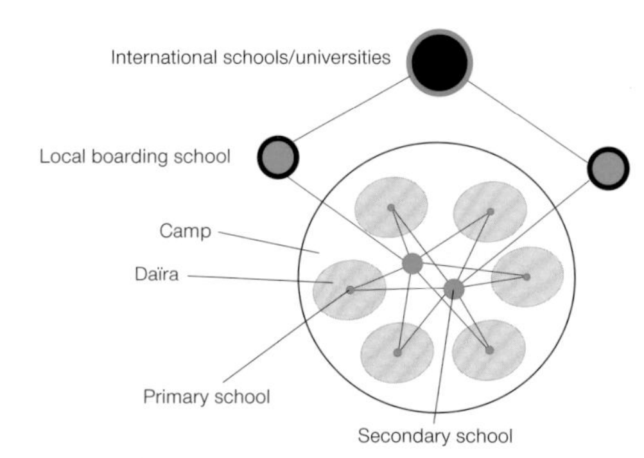


Hierarchy of educational institutions

| | Rabouni | El Aaiún | Smara | 27 Feb | Awserd | Dakhla |
|---|---|---|---|---|---|---|
| ● | 1 | | | | | |
| ● | | 1 | 1 | 1 | 1 | 1 |
| • | | 6 | 7 | 2 | 6 | 7 |
| ● | | 2 | 2 | 1 | 1 | 2 |
| • | | 6 | 7 | 2 | 6 | 7 |

Health and education facilities in the camps

**Education and Health in the Camps Today**

The health and education system follows the organizational structure of the camps. Camps, also called "wilayas" are organized in "daïras" or districts, which are subdivided into "barrios" or neighborhoods. Every daïra features a "dispensario," or dispensary, that supplies medication to its inhabitants, offers basic medical services, first aid and nutrition advice, as well as child care. These are mostly staffed by nurses.

Each camp also has a regional hospital that provides more extensive diagnostic and medical services and has limited operation facilities. The regional hospital offers outpatient as well as inpatient treatment, has a number of patient rooms, and is staffed by nurses and doctors. In addition, some more specialized clinics exist in the camps, such as a new maternity center in El Aaiún.

For more serious cases, patients are transferred to the national hospital in Rabouni, which offers more extensive treatment and is connected to the Ministry of Health. The national hospital also serves as an educational facility for nursing and medical education. All treatment and medication is free of charge and is offered not only to the Sahrawi population but also to foreigners. Likewise, Sahrawis receive free treatment at the Algerian hospital in Tindouf, where they are transferred if the national hospital does not have the facilities to treat them.

The education system mirrors this pattern, with a primary school in each daïra and one or two secondary schools located in each camp. The boarding school 12 October and the women's school of 27 February, which has grown into a settlement in its own right, offer additional education facilities and vocational training.

On a national level, health and education are administered by the Ministry of Public Health and the Ministry of Education, which are located in Rabouni. The ministries are responsible for securing resources such as medication or teaching aids. They also set the national health strategies and education curriculum.

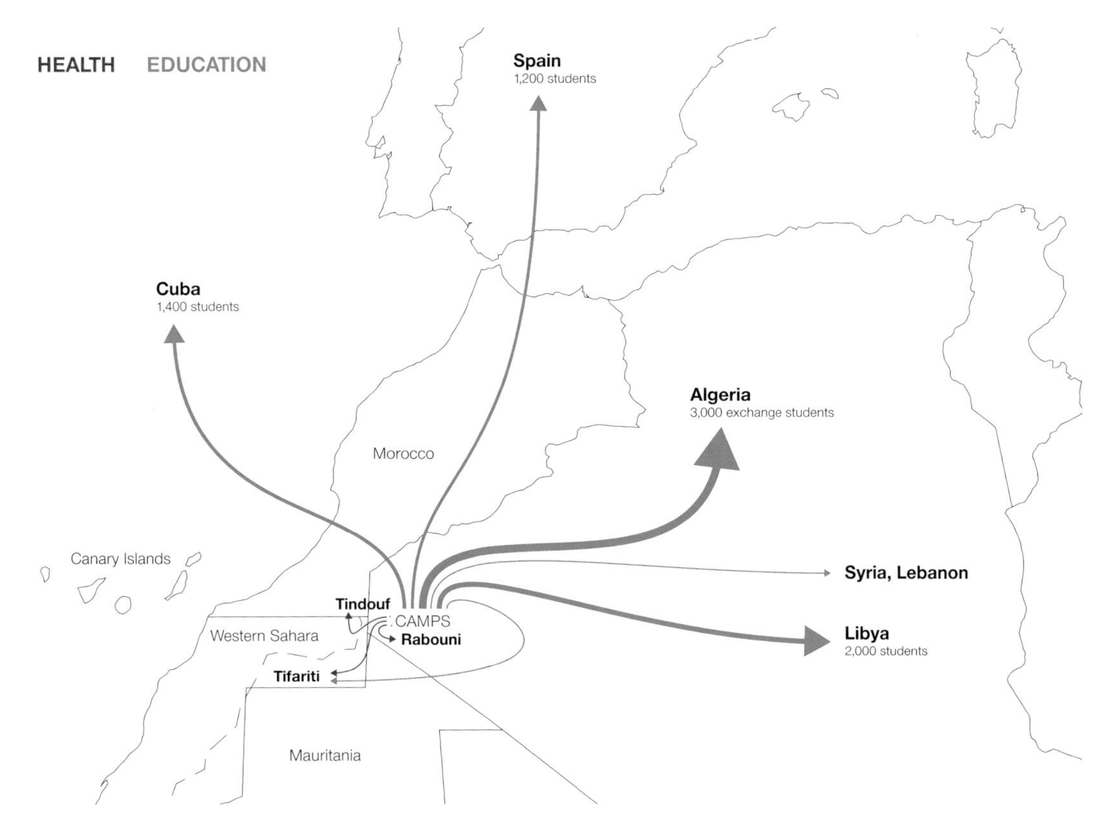


## International Dimension

For higher education beyond secondary level, Polisario has established a number of international programs. Young Sahrawis move abroad to Cuba, Libya, or Syria, and also Algiers, to study at universities. These programs are funded by the host countries, with Polisario providing a limited stipend for the basic cost of living.

Some Sahrawis have also been invited by private or public organizations to study in European countries such as Spain, Germany, or France. In most cases, students return to the camps after completing their studies abroad. The education situation is likely to change in the near future, when Algeria completes the construction of a university campus in Tindouf, bringing higher education within closer reach of the camps. At the same time, the so-called Arab Spring, with revolutions and unrest in countries like Libya and Syria, have profoundly affected Sahrawi students studying there.

Sahrawi students abroad in 2003:

| | |
|---|---|
| Libya | 2,000 |
| Algeria | 3,000 |
| Cuba | 1,400 |
| Spain | 1,200 |

Source: Coggan 2003/Datos del Ministerio de Educación y Ciencia. Oficina de Estadística, Spain

# Hospitals

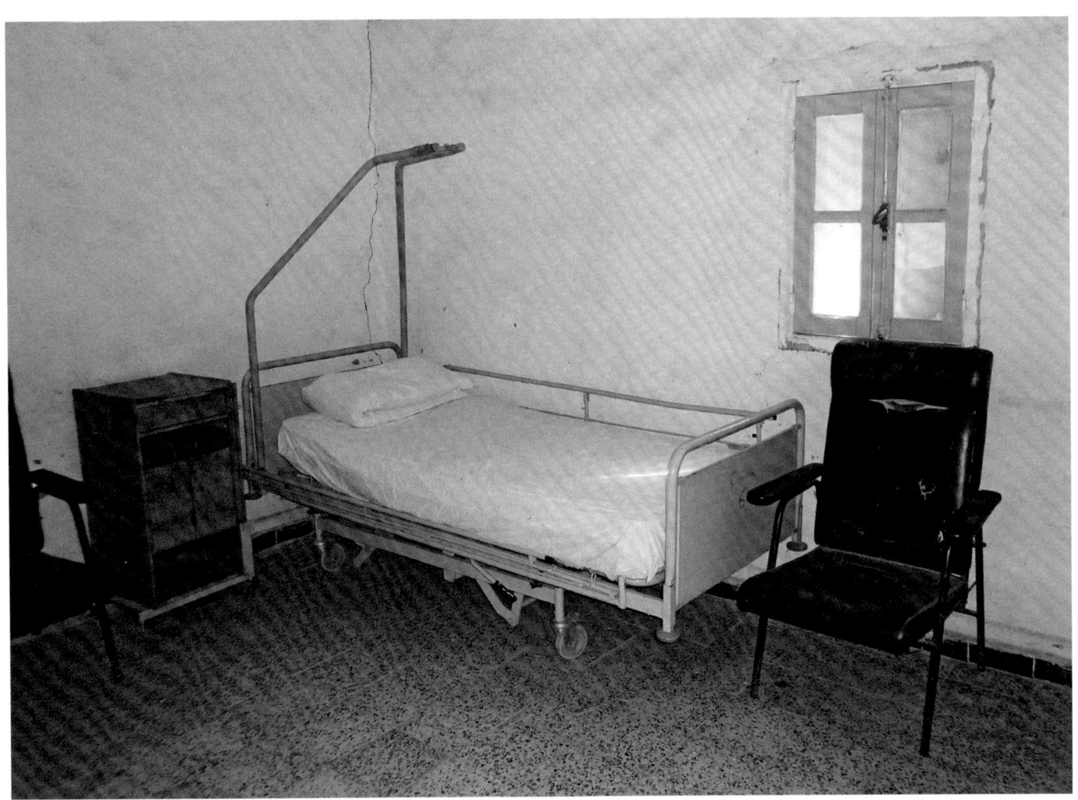

Patient's bed and examination room in the regional hospital of El Aaiún

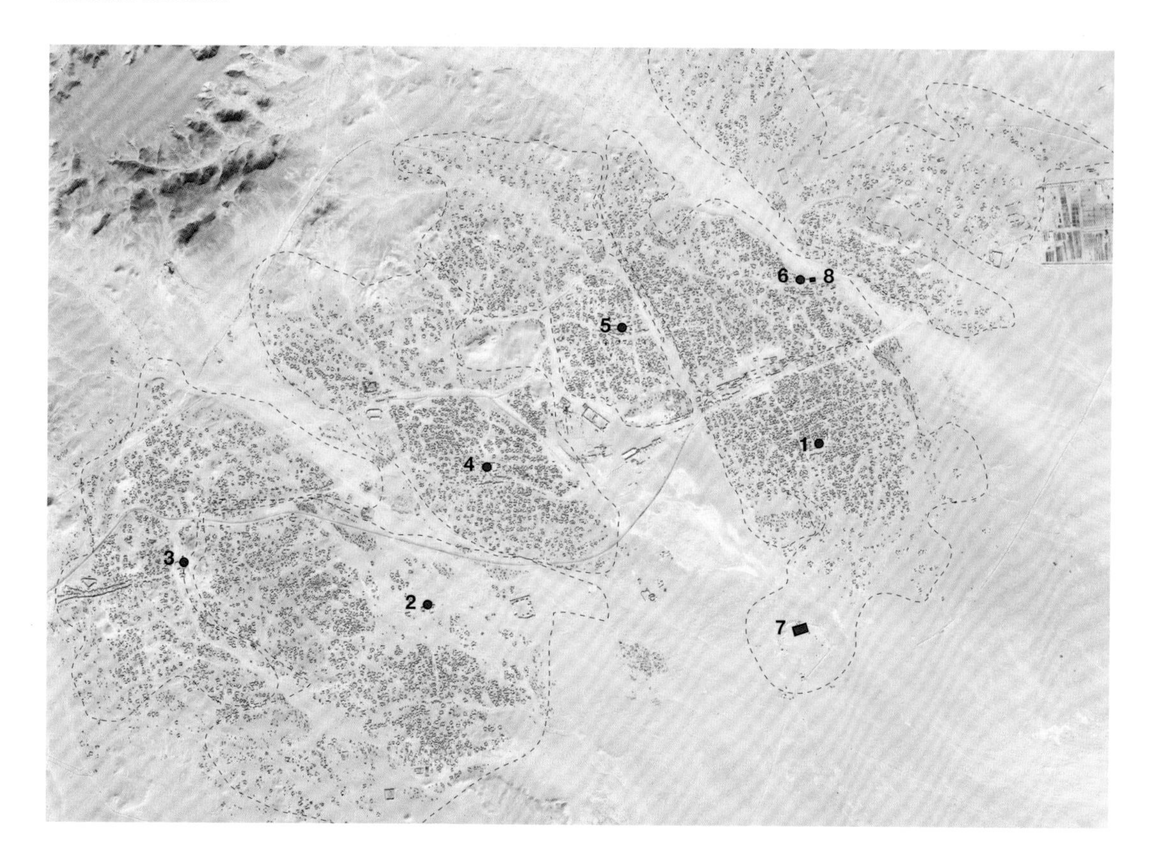


**Hospitals and Dispensarios in El Aaiún**
The organization of medical services in El Aaiún follows a simple logic, based on the urban structure of the camp. Every daïra has its own dispensario or distribution facility, which is part of the daïra center. It acts as a small clinic, providing medical assistance for nonserious cases, nutrition control, and other services such as the distribution of medication.

The regional hospital is responsible for the camps as a whole and offers treatment facilities for patients. Among other things, it features a pharmacy, X-ray machines, small operation facilities, and various departments such as psychology or physiotherapy. The regional hospital registers all patients that are treated. It also keeps track of health statistics for the camp as a whole.

For more serious cases, patients are transferred to the national hospital in Rabouni, or, for cases requiring specific or specialized treatment, to the hospital in Tindouf, where Sahrawis receive free medical care provided by the Algerian government.

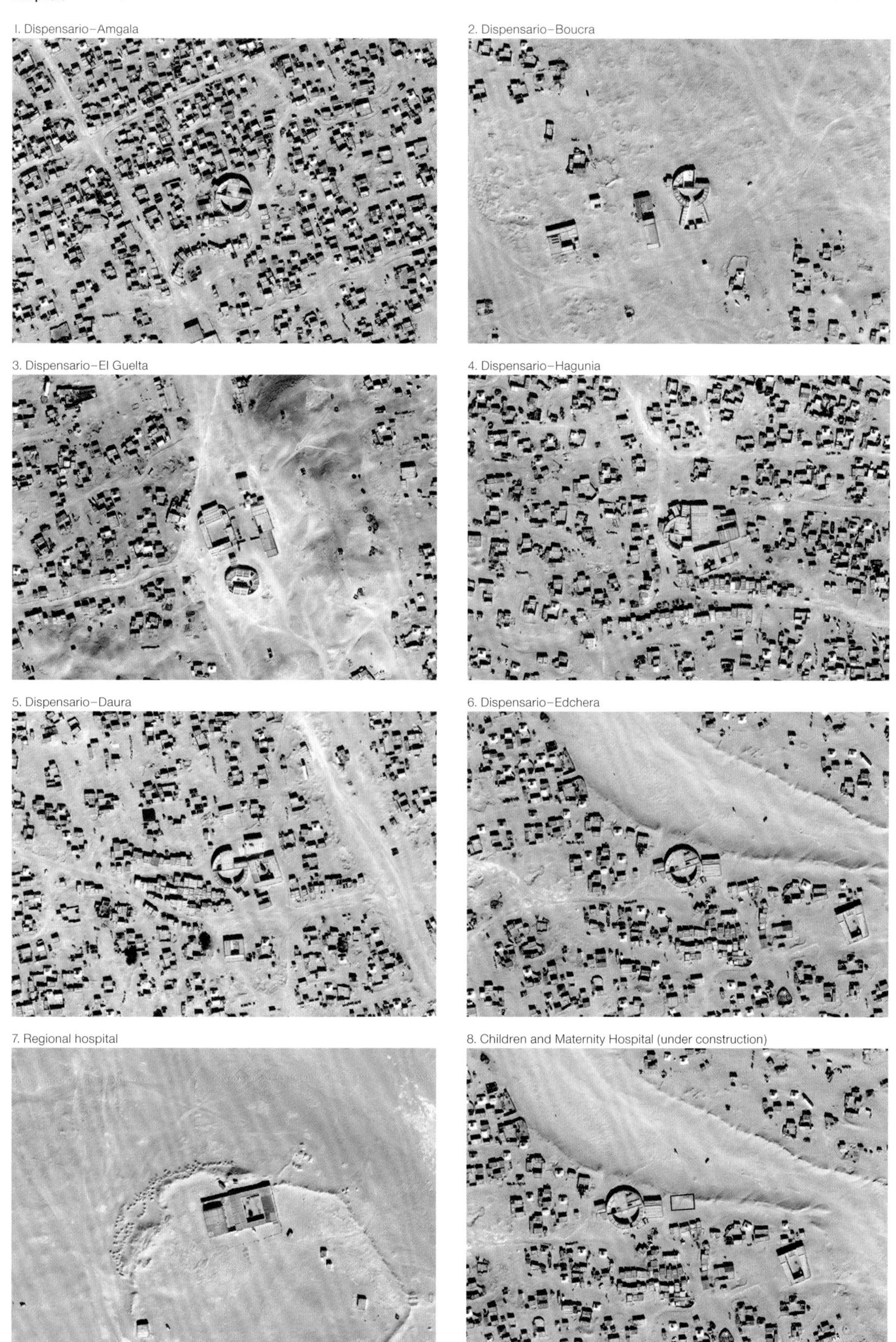
I. Dispensario–Amgala
2. Dispensario–Boucra
3. Dispensario–El Guelta
4. Dispensario–Hagunia
5. Dispensario–Daura
6. Dispensario–Edchera
7. Regional hospital
8. Children and Maternity Hospital (under construction)

Courtyard within the dispensario

Consultation room

Waiting area

## Dispensarios of El Aaiún

The dispensarios are part of the daïra centers. Within the circular layout of the center they occupy one quarter, usually consisting of three or four rooms with a small waiting area. The dispensario is operated by a nurse, sometimes assisted by a doctor.

Functions: first aid, distribution of medication, nutrition control
Location: one in each daïra

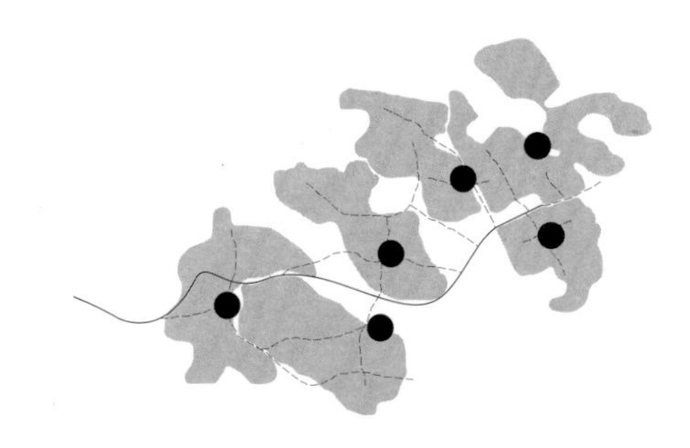

Entrance

Sponsor's plaque

Water supply

## Maternity Clinic

This clinic was constructed in 2010 and funded by the NGO Médicines du Monde. It treats women and children and specializes as a maternity clinic. Instead of being located in the center of the camp, it is situated in Edchera, which is one of the newer and faster-growing daïras of El Aaiún. The building is prominent in the fabric of the camp due to its unusual color and the little parapets that decorate the roofline. The regional hospital of El Aaiún also features these parapets.

Location: daïra Edchera

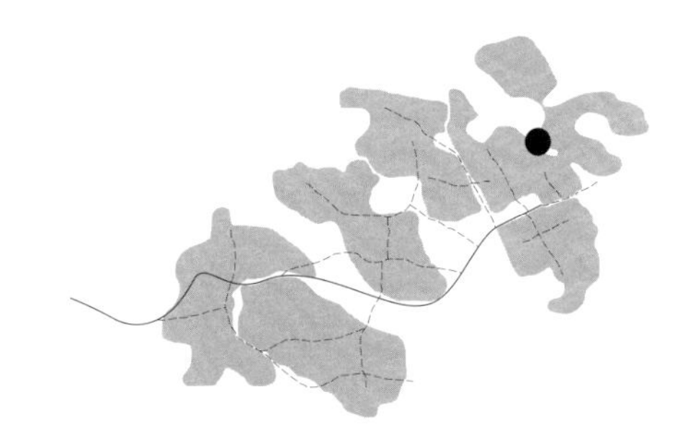

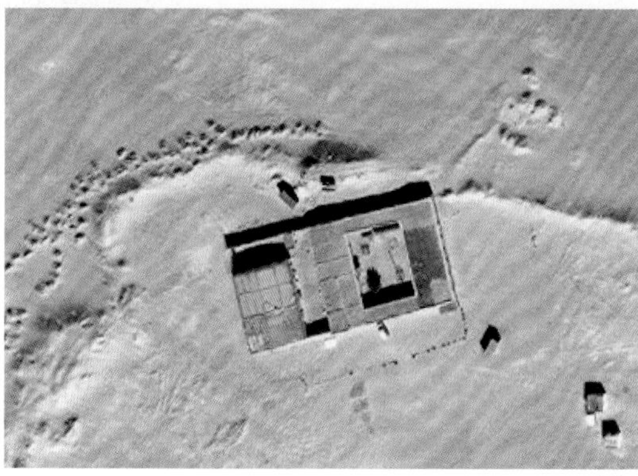

**Regional Hospital, El Aaiún**

The regional hospital in El Aaiún is a large complex that is detached from the continuous fabric of the camp. The hospital consists of several buildings merged into a single compound. Its solitary location and the compact composition of its different functions and spaces gives it a heterotopian quality. Treatment in the regional hospital requires leaving the camp and withdrawing from its density and bustle.

Location: south of daïra Amgala

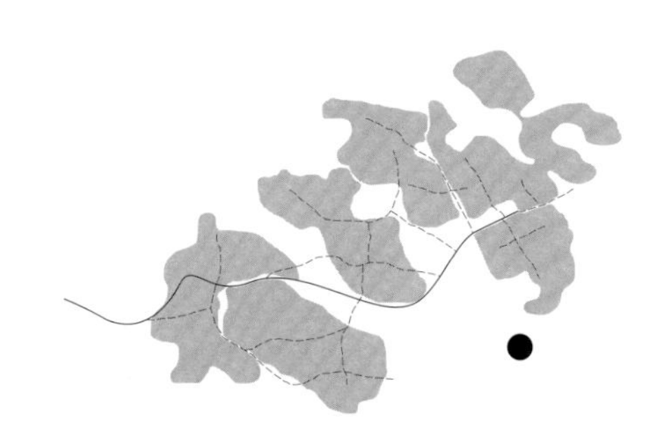

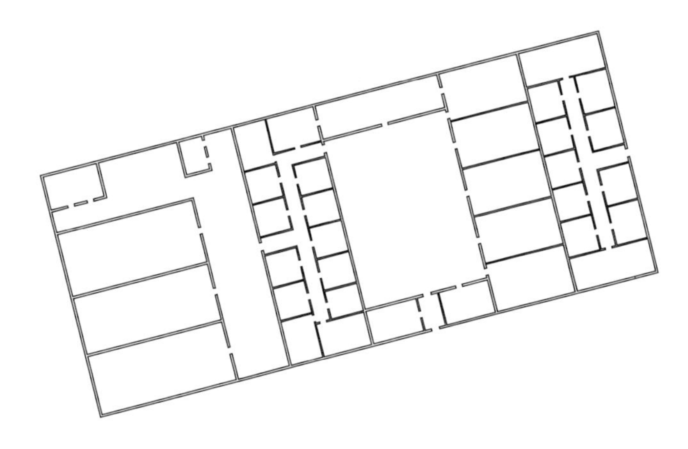

25 m

**Name:** Minatu Mohame Salama
**Age:** Thirty-three
**Address:** El Aaiún, daïra Edchera, barrio 1
**Civil status:** Married
**Children:** Two
**Education:** Secondary school in the camps, medical studies, nursing and laboratory training in Cuba.
**Position:** Chief doctor of the maternity hospital, El Aaiún.
**Schedule:** From Saturday until Thursday, Fridays off.
**Summer:** From 8 a.m. to noon, and from 5 p.m. to 7 p.m.
**Winter:** From 9 a.m. to 3 p.m., and from 4 p.m. to 6 p.m.
**Salary:** No formal salary: "I don't work for the money." She receives a honorarium every three months from the government.
**Languages:** Arabic and Spanish.

**Why did you become a doctor?**
To help the Sahrawi community, my people!

**What are your duties as chief doctor?**
Everything from administration and maintaining the medical statistics to direct treatment of patients.

**Who initiated the hospital?**
It was founded by Doctors of the World (Médecins du Monde) and was inaugurated in February 2011.

**Who finances the hospital?**
Several NGOs. Every type of help has to first be approved by the government. The medicine comes from Rabouni.

**What kind of services do the local hospitals and dispensarios provide?**
We supply first aid, mainly for women and children, and sometimes also for men. We also do periodical controls on chronic patients and provide their necessary medicine. Although we mainly offer an ambulatory service, we also carry out childbirths and postpartum cases. Each patient is treated individually and has their own medical file. People come here for their first diagnosis. In case of emergency we send patients to the regional hospital.

**What are the most common illnesses?**
We differentiate between chronic and nonchronic illnesses. Chronic conditions include diabetes, asthma, epilepsy, or celiac disease (inability to eat gluten). And the nonchronic include fever, diarrhea, inflammation of the tonsils, and arthritis.

**What are the priorities for the Sahrawi population in terms of health?**
There's a lot of "brain drain." Many young professionals study abroad and don't come back. A doctor's salary is very good in Spain, and quality of life is better too. We need more specialists and more doctors to work in our camps to avoid or counteract this brain drain.

**What about contraception?**
The religion, as well as the government, prohibits birth control. We are a small nation that needs to grow. Condoms or contraceptive pills would need to be bought in Tindouf, but this is not allowed. Nonetheless, some people use them in secret. The worst thing to happen to a young women is to become pregnant before getting married. According to government rules, she then has to go to jail until the child's father promises to marry her.

**How has the medical system changed over the years?**
It is difficult to say ... Before the war, there wasn't any real development. During Spanish colonial times all houses were equal and cities looked the same. In the beginning of the camps, there were just the tents, nothing else. Many things have improved since then. I think these recent years have been good years for the Sahrawi population.

**What about the future. What are the plans or strategies for an eventual return to the Western Sahara?**
Well, the idea is to continue working in our homeland in the same way we have been working here. We should apply the same system we have here.

**Name:** Nah Lahse Ranban
**Age:** Fifty-two
**Education:** Trained in nursing and medicine during colonial times in El Aaiún (city) hospital.
**Background:** After two years of fighting in the war, he fled to the refugee camps. "I haven't seen my family in the occupied territories for thirty years. When I speak to my mother, she prefers me to be in the camps instead of losing my dignity living under Moroccan repression."
**Position:** Director of the regional hospital in El Aaiún, and nursing trainer, as appointed by the Ministry of Health in Rabouni.
**Activities:** Administration, nursing, and training.
**Salary:** No formal salary; receives a honorarium every three months from the government.
**Languages:** Arabic and Spanish.

**How was the health system organized in the past?**
During the colonial era, Spain built hospitals in the cities and the system was centralized. We were trained at the hospital where we received our education. The first hospital built in the camps started with just six khaymas (tents). It was called Badir Saleh and was put up in 1977 by the women of the camp, while men where at war. Today the health system is centrally organized from the Ministry of Health in Rabouni and its national hospital, which also offers a three-year educational program for nurses.

Each wilayah has a regional hospital, and each daïra has its own dispensario, but all financial aid and medicine has to pass through Rabouni beforehand. The Ministry of Health is in charge of administration. Medical supplies come from the national hospital in Rabouni. We handle up to thirty cases a day. Our hospital has several departments, such as physiotherapy, psychology, ultrasound, and X-ray facilities, a laboratory, a pharmacy, and staff facilities.

We even provide odontological and veterinary services. We also work with a specialist in gynecology, who rotates from camp to camp. And, finally, we operate a children's health program, the PSI (Programa de Salud Infantil).

**What are the relationships between the camps and other countries in terms of health?**
We have good relations with Cuba, Libya, and Algeria. They know what it means to be a colony. They have lived through revolution and therefore understand our situation. There are agreements with Cuba allowing some of us to study medicine at university level. We have a very good relationship with Algeria, from where we often receive blood donations via Tindouf. They are like brothers to us. If one of us falls seriously ill we can go to Tindouf anytime and receive health assistance for free.

**What are the principal needs or priorities?**
The lack of medical supplies and specialists is the most urgent thing. We especially need to focus on prevention. This means vaccinations. We are working to prevent tetanus, polio, hepatitis B, and tuberculosis. We also need to improve hygiene in the camps. Another very important fact would be to have access to information without having to leave the camps, for example, via the Internet.

**Do you think what has been learned in the camps can be applied to the homeland?**
We have definitely learned a lot from the camps. We are more united. If you need something to eat, you can go to a house or tent anytime and someone will offer you food. We share everything with everyone. We have also improved hygiene conditions considerably and have gained knowledge about water consumption and how to raise animals. There have been many meetings and conferences organized by various organizations and NGOs. We have gained a lot from them.

Talking about the future, we need to apply what we have learned from this time in the camps. But we also have to modify our system to improve the quantity and quality. We need more specialists per capita and a larger variety of specialists in all areas of medicine to achieve a higher coverage. If we resettle, there is a plan to keep some administrative structures, for example El Aaiún camp would go to El Aaiún city, together with its doctors and health administrators. This is a way to make the process of resettlement easier.

# Schools

View of typical classroom and courtyard of Abda Mohammed School in Smara

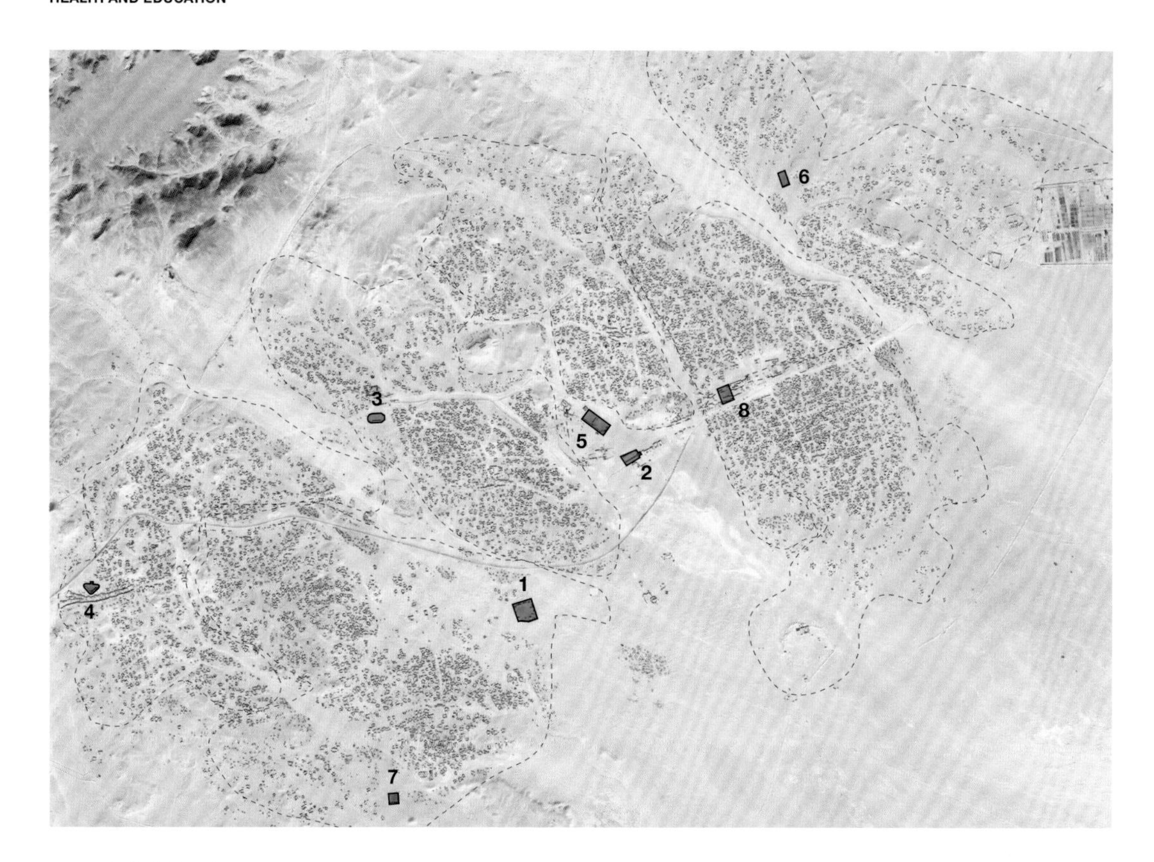


**Schools in El Aaiún**
The organization of the educational facilities follows the spatial structure of the camp. Each daïra has its own primary school, where the children of the neighborhood are taught in mixed classes, their sizes ranging between twenty and thirty. Additionally, two secondary schools exist (Umdraiga and Said), as well as a few specialist schools.

The Olof Palme School is a women's school specializing in higher education and vocational training. It offers courses in handicrafts, information technology, foreign languages, and nursing, among other things. The camp also has a school for handicapped children, teaching them carpentry and other manual crafts.

In the beginning, the few schools in each camp were named after martyrs or locations in the Western Sahara. Later, when more schools were established with the help of foreign partners, schools started to carry names of the region of funding, for example, Cordoba or Cantabria. As its name implies, the Olof Palme School was funded by the Swedish Social Democratic Party in 1989, three years after the assassination of its name bearer.

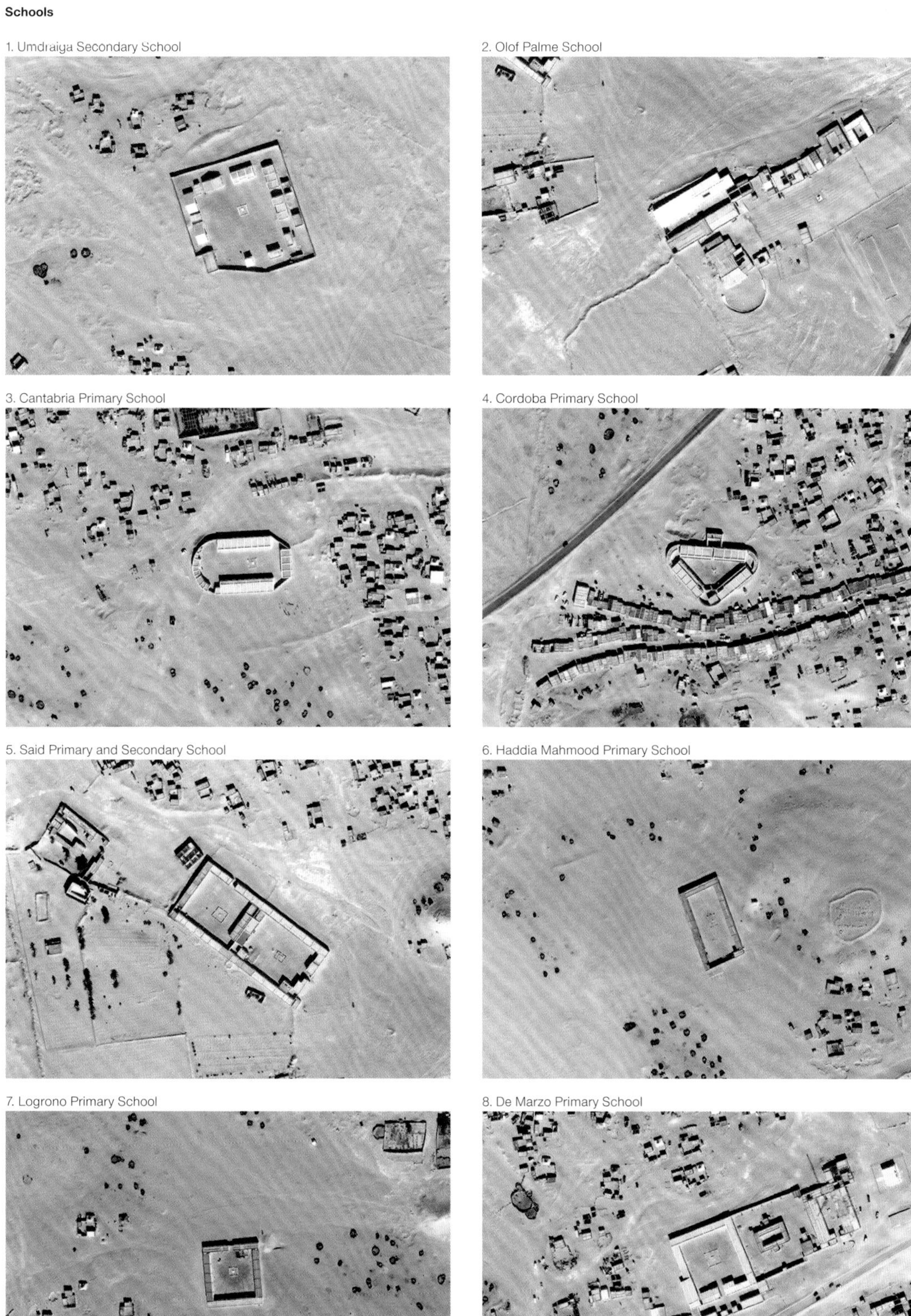

1. Umdraiga Secondary School

2. Olof Palme School

3. Cantabria Primary School

4. Cordoba Primary School

5. Said Primary and Secondary School

6. Haddia Mahmood Primary School

7. Logrono Primary School

8. De Marzo Primary School

**Olof Palme Women's School**

The Olof Palme School was founded 1989 in cooperation with the Swedish Social-Democratic Women's Organization. The school focuses on adult education and the teaching of craft and vocational training, thereby encouraging self-reliance and economic activities for the women. The school consists of two wings, each approximately 70 m long, sharing a long central open courtyard. The school is a single-story building (like all other buildings in the camps) and has walls plastered with cement and painted in ochre colors.

As it is a women-only school, Olof Palme also has a small nursery and day-care room, where children can play while their mothers attend lessons. The subjects taught include computer science, filmmaking and video editing, foreign languages, sewing, carpet-making and other crafts, as well as accounting and bookkeeping.

The school lies next to a number of other cultural and educational institutions, such as a small gallery, youth center, and school for disabled children. It overlooks a large open square that is used for celebrations, processions, and other larger public events, thereby marking it as one of the main spaces of the camp.

Founded: 1989
Number of students: approx. 160

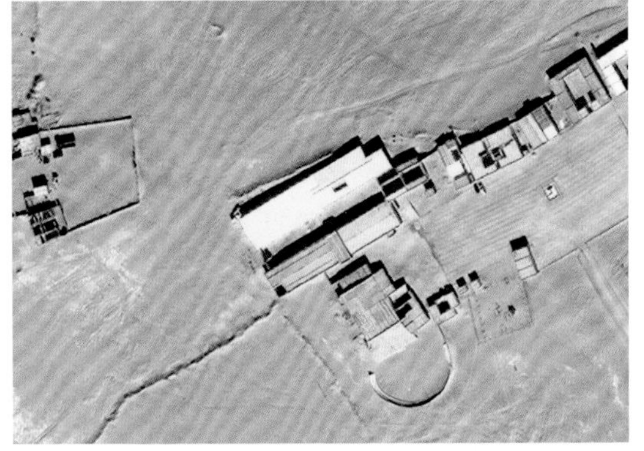


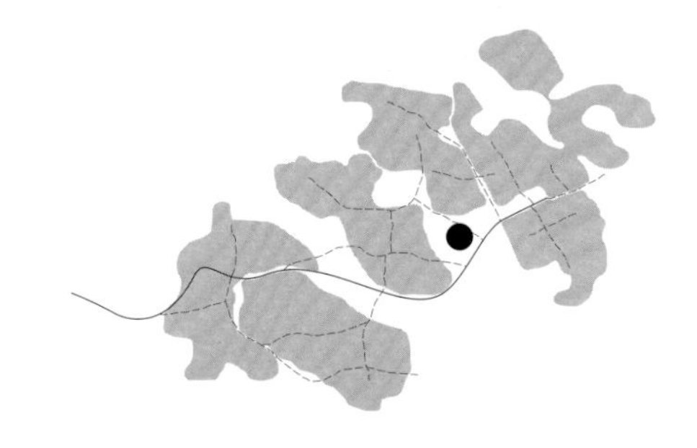

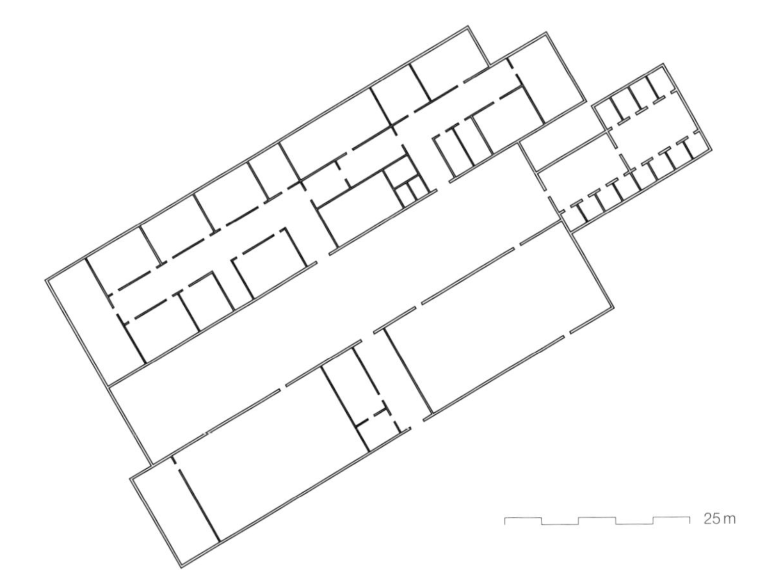
25 m

## Umdraiga Secondary School

The school is different from the other schools in the camps as it is composed of a series of identical buildings, each housing two or three classrooms. The arrangement around a large central square creates something akin to a small school village within the perimeter walls.

The other main difference is that it is built with OSB wood and roofing made of Eternit boards. According to the teachers the material is better suited to the extreme climate conditions of the Sahara Desert.

Founded: 1984
Location: between daïras Boucra and Hagunia
Number of students: approx. 1,000

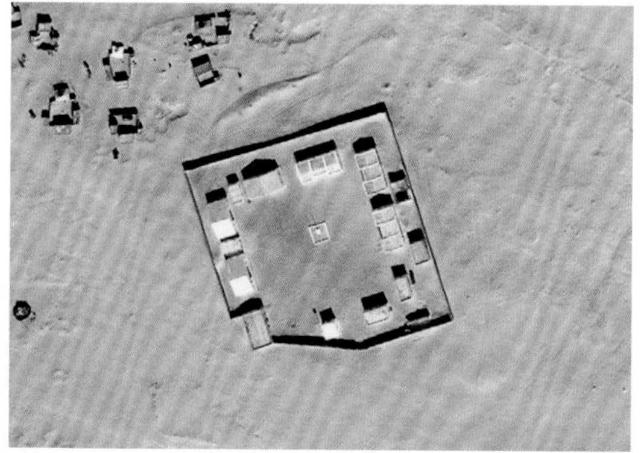


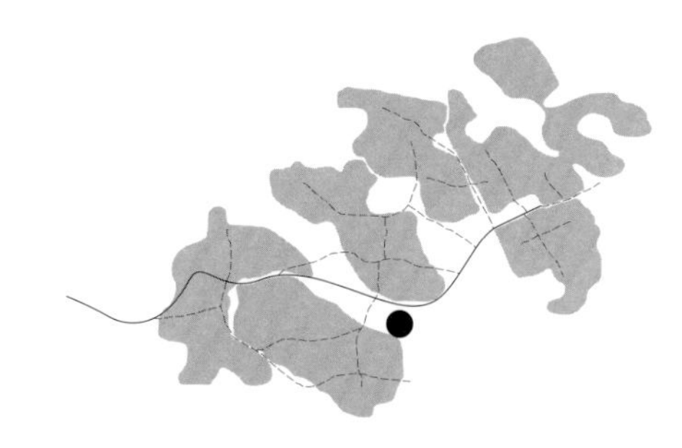

**Sadia Secondary School**

This secondary school is the largest in El Aaiún, encompassing a compound of approximately 140 × 60 m, so is almost one hectare in size. The layout consists of a compound with multipurpose spaces located in the middle and classrooms around the perimeter. This creates two large open spaces approximately 40 × 40 m in size, which are used for sports, games, and events. The vast open spaces obtain an almost agoraphobic quality, especially in the heat of the summer sun.

Location: daïra Hagunia

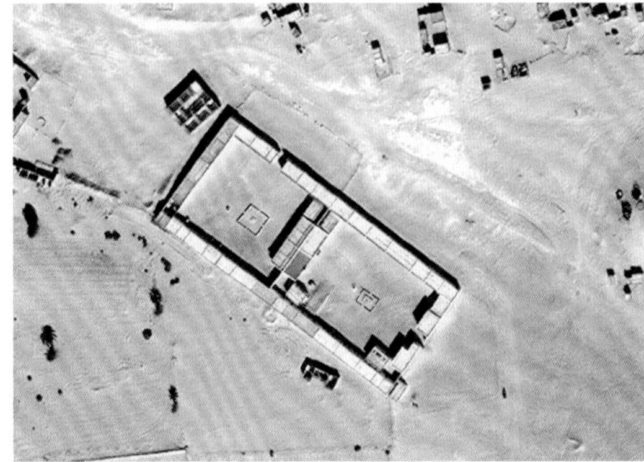

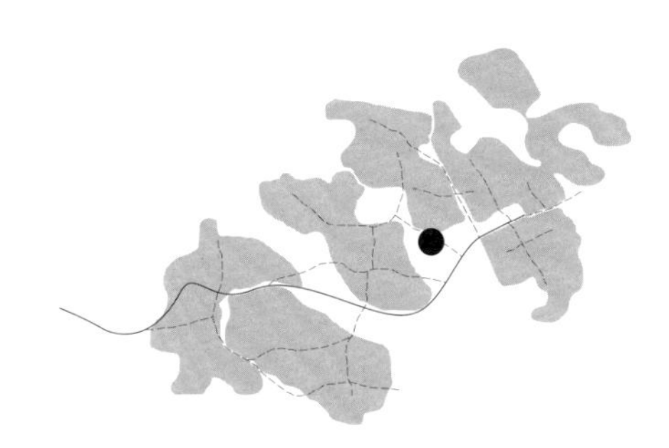

**Cantabria School**

The school consists of two long wings containing classrooms, which face a central courtyard. Additional classrooms and school facilities are located in smaller wings, one of which forms a half-circle, giving the whole arrangement an iconic quality.

The schoolrooms in the larger wings are separated from the courtyard by long corridors, improving the acoustic and climatic conditions of those rooms.

Location: daïra Hagunia

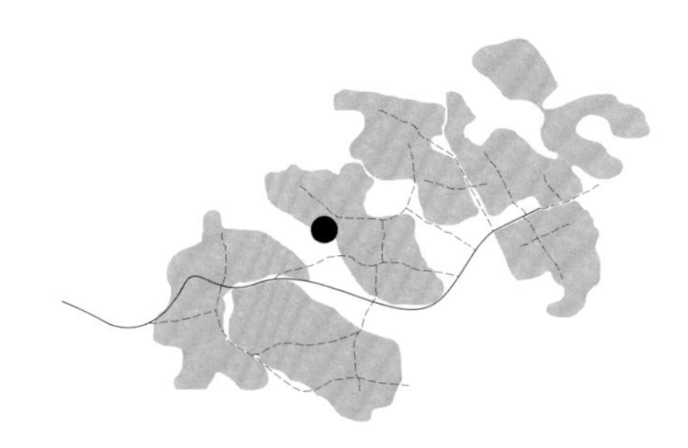

## Cordoba School

Cordoba features a unique triangular layout, with the school rooms arranged along the perimeter, leaving a triangular court in its center. The corners open up to smaller, intimate courtyards, giving a good combination of spaces on different scales. Like all other schools, the central courtyard is dominated by a flagpole with the Sahrawi flag. Similar to the Cantabria School, the internal corridor shields the rooms from the courtyard.

Location: daïra El Guelta

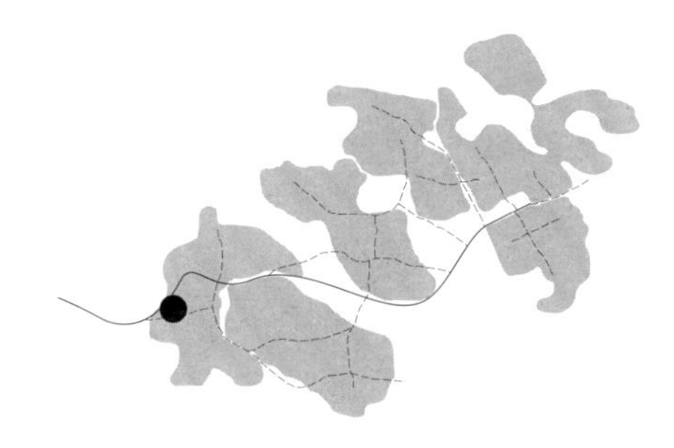

**Haddia Mahmood Primary School**

This school presents a typical courtyard typology, measuring approximately 70 × 40 m overall. It includes the classrooms from first up to fifth grade, with additional school facilities such as the administration office, volleyball field, playground, and toilets.

Located in one of the newer and faster-growing daïras, Haddia Mahmood School was built in 2006. The overall layout of the school is slightly skewed, creating a rhomboid shape, though this is only perceivable from an aerial view.

Location: daïra Edchera

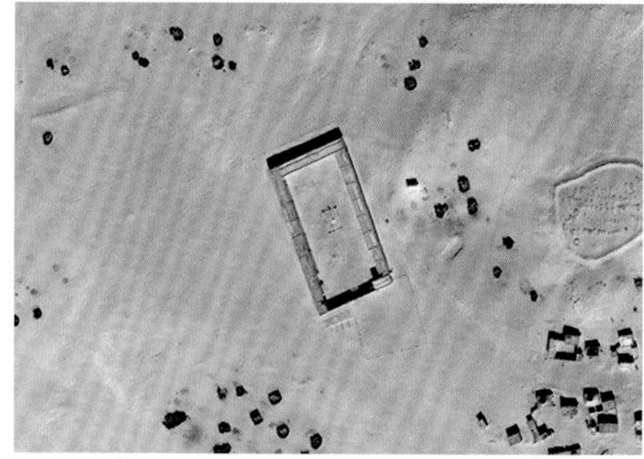


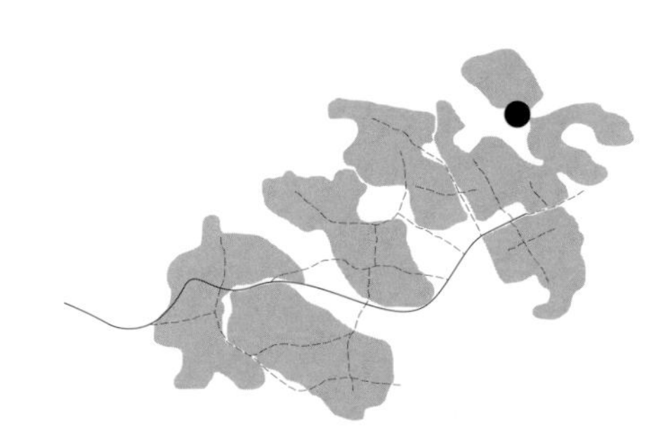

**Logrono Primary School**

Logrono Primary School is the most recent school in the camp and was established in 2007. It is also the smallest of the schools in El Aaiún. Over time, the schools constructed in El Aaiún seem to have adopted a simpler typology, and this school has a perfect square layout of approximately 45 × 45 m in size. It does not offer any of the additional design features that the other schools have–for example, an access corridor or alcove-like spaces. The courtyard has a central platform with the Sahrawi flag.

Location: daïra Boucra

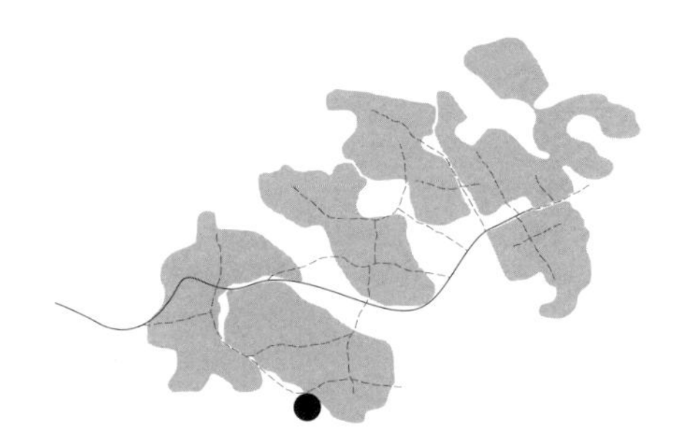

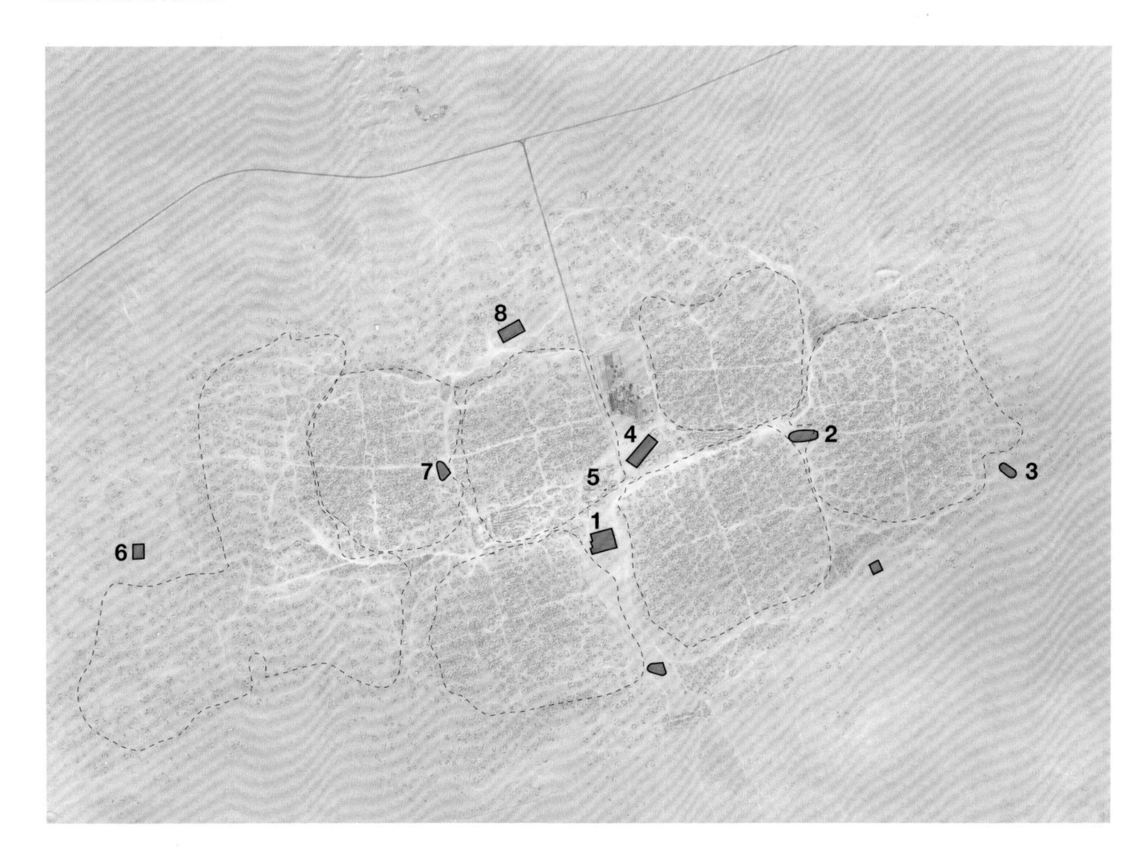


**Schools in Smara**
Similar to the other camps, each daïra in Smara has its own primary school. There are two secondary schools for the whole camp, the school of 17 Junio and the Abda Mohammed school. Additionally, there are some independent schools and educational facilities like the Essalam English Center. This aims to provide English lessons to the Sahrawi population in order to support and promote scholarly or family exchange with the United States. Compared with El Aaiún, we see different typologies and architectural elements employed in the school buildings, for example, domes as roof structures and courtyards with seating facilities.

1. 17 Junio Secondary School

2. Abda Mohammed Secondary School

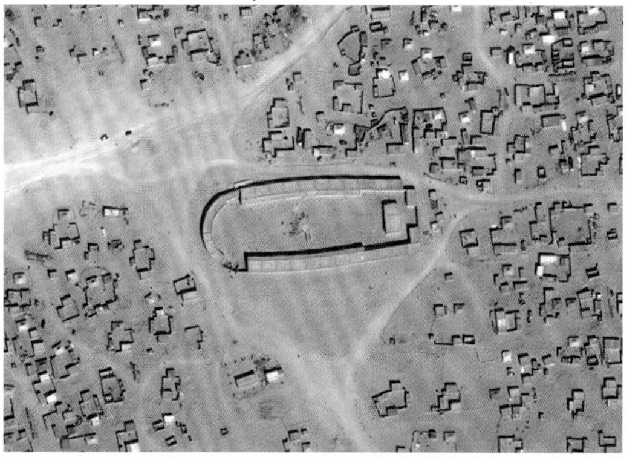

3. Mustafa Mohammed Dachmid Primary School

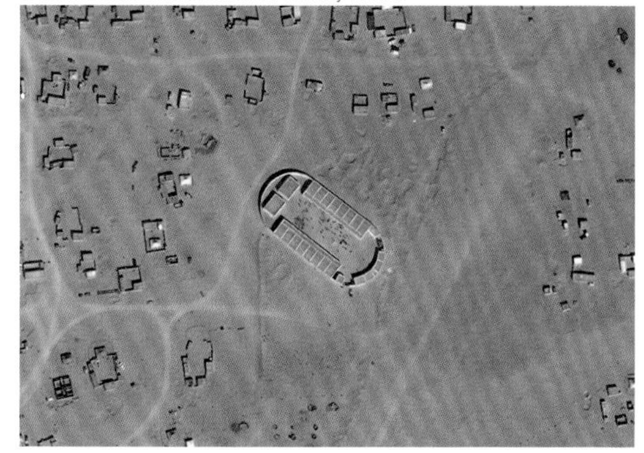

4. Balla Haezned Zaed

5. Essalam English School

6. Nachna Primary School

7. Valencia Primary School

8. Castilla y León Primary School

### 17 Junio Secondary School

The school of 17 Junio is located in the center of Smara, close to the camp administration and markets. It is similar in design and construction to the Umdraiga school of El Aaiún and was built around the same time. It also features the OSB wood and Eternit roof, which is supposed to offer better climate conditions within the rooms. It is the only school in camp Smara that has its own sports facilities, with a hard-surface court located within the school walls. Unlike its El Aaiún counterpart, which is situated at the periphery of the camp, the centrality of its location gives it an important urban role, acting as an organizing element for its context.

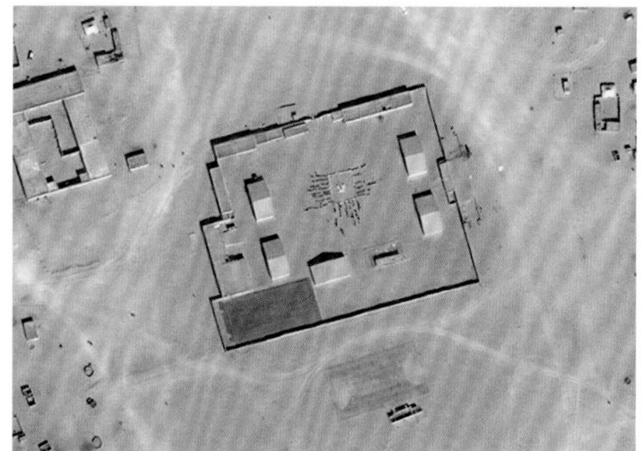


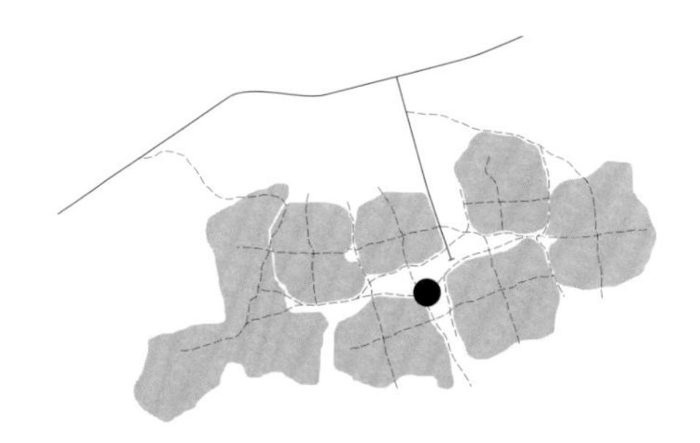

## Abda Mohammed Secondary School

Abda Mohammed School has a long, horseshoe-shaped arrangement and is the largest school on the camp. The wings of classrooms, forming long sections of the compound, feature a corridor separating the rooms from the central compound. The main entrance to the school is not located at the short, flat end of the horseshoe layout as one might expect, but in one of the curved segments.

South elevation

West elevation

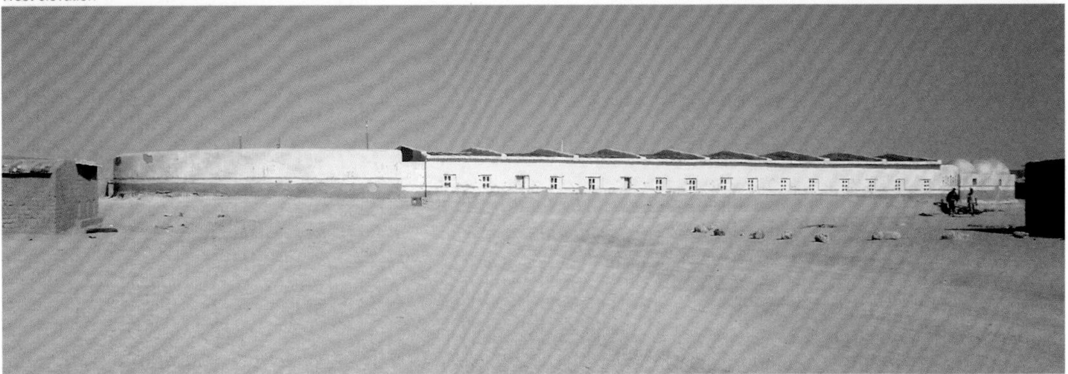

### Valencia Primary School

Compared with other schools on the camps, Valencia Primary School features a unique layout. It has an asymmetrical triangular shape and two of its corners consist of circular elements. Two classroom wings, arranged at an oblique angle, open up to a large central courtyard. Its smaller end consists of a circular amphitheater structure. Along its southern side the compound features smaller classrooms that are roofed with half-sphere domes. These domes give the building an iconic appearance and are instantly recognizable from a distance.

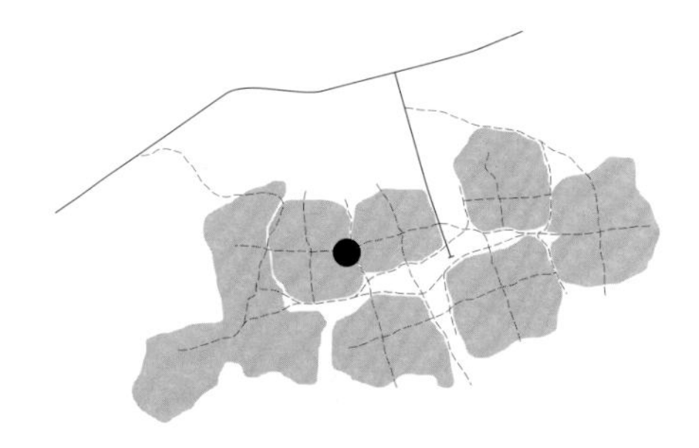

Domes and façade details of southern corner

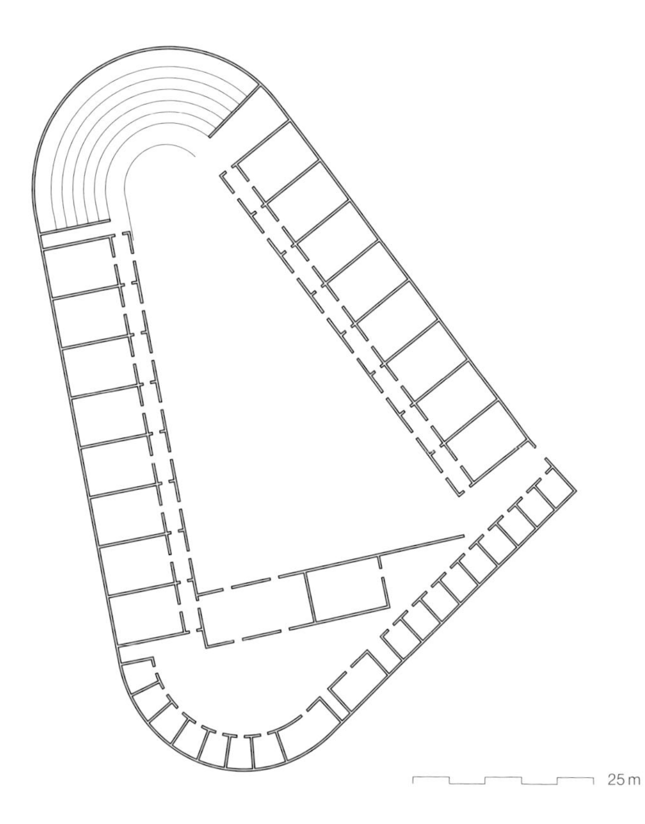

View of entrance area in internal courtyard

View of internal courtyard from stage (above) and from entrance (below)

Access to domed classrooms (above) and internal corridor (below)

# The School as an Urban Agent

When looking at the urban context of schools in cities, we can often identify a relationship between the school as an element of urban infrastructure and urban development itself. For instance, a neighborhood or suburb with a large volume of new housing will often result in the establishment of a new school. And we can also observe the opposite dynamic: a school with a good reputation will attract young families into a neighborhood, affecting the availability of housing and potentially even triggering the construction of new homes. Schools are therefore not just educational institutions, but also urban agents in a wider sense, being susceptible to urban transformation processes.

When looking at the Sahrawi refugee camps, a picture emerges of the relationship between schools and the urban fabric. We can see how newly constructed schools attract new residential compounds in their vicinity. The construction of additional institutions, such as youth clubs and radio stations, also follows the building of a school. Obviously it is difficult to establish a clear causality, but looking at a series of satellite images allows us to determine a chronology in which the schools are built in empty areas, and shortly after, other construction, including residential, follows.

The most extreme case of the school as an urban conductor was in the camp 27 February near Smara. This settlement did not start off as a camp, but as a boarding school and adult education center for women. After the school had been established, the families of the women attending were allowed to live in its environs, resulting in the growth of a small settlement. This settlement continued to grow and later also offered facilities such as shops, so that the area around the boarding school grew into a camp in its own right. Today it is considered a fully functioning Sahrawi camp, though it is administered by the administration of camp Smara.

**Olof Palme School**
Developing an educational and institutional axis

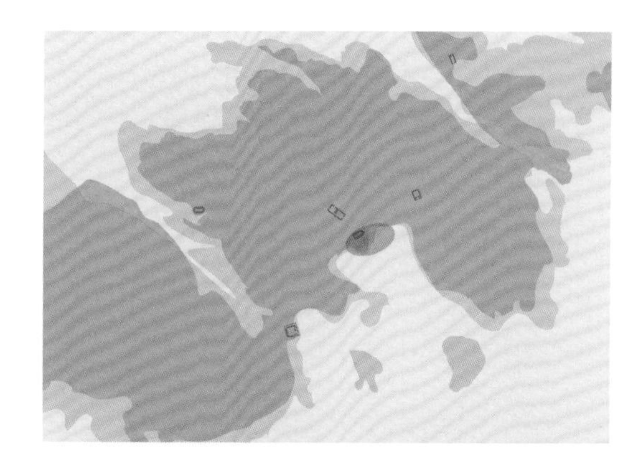

**De Marzo Primary School**
Commercial and institutional densification

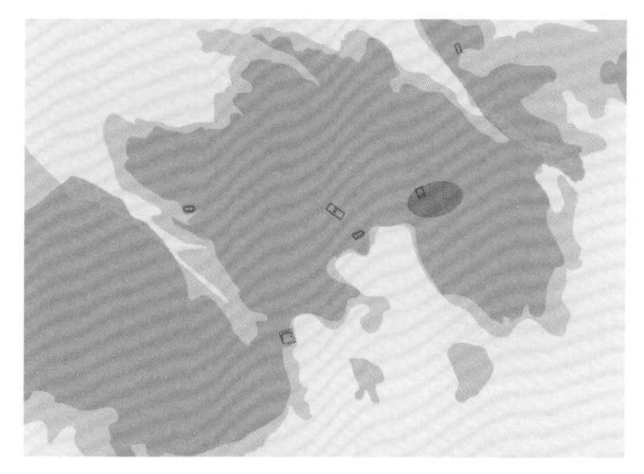

**Umdraiga Primary School**
Residential growth around a school

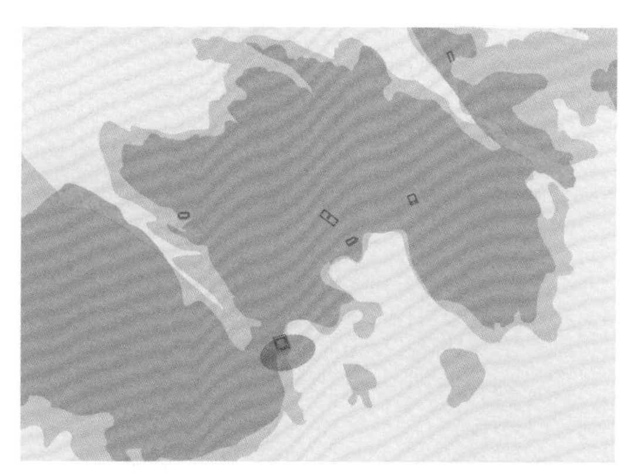

**Schools as Urban Agents: El Aaiún**

Established in 1989 near Sadia Secondary school, Olof Palme School was a solitary building in 2003, with the exception of an exhibition space close by. By 2010, the area around the school had fundamentally transformed, with the construction of a school for handicapped children, new sports facilities, a youth club, and radio studio. Along with the construction of a large, hard-surfaced square that is used for big public events, celebrations, and ceremonies, the area had turned into one of the main public zones of the camp, all aligned according to the layout of the Olof Palme School.

Showing a slightly different development, the area around the De Marzo Primary School developed into one of the main commercial and institutional zones of the camps, with the subsequent construction of offices for the camp's mayor and the establishment of several shops. Finally, within the past decade, the Umdraiga School saw the construction of several residential complexes in its immediate proximity, as well as a general densification of the barrios in its surroundings.

We can deduce from the first two examples that the development did not take place in a haphazard way, but were conscious acts of master planning.

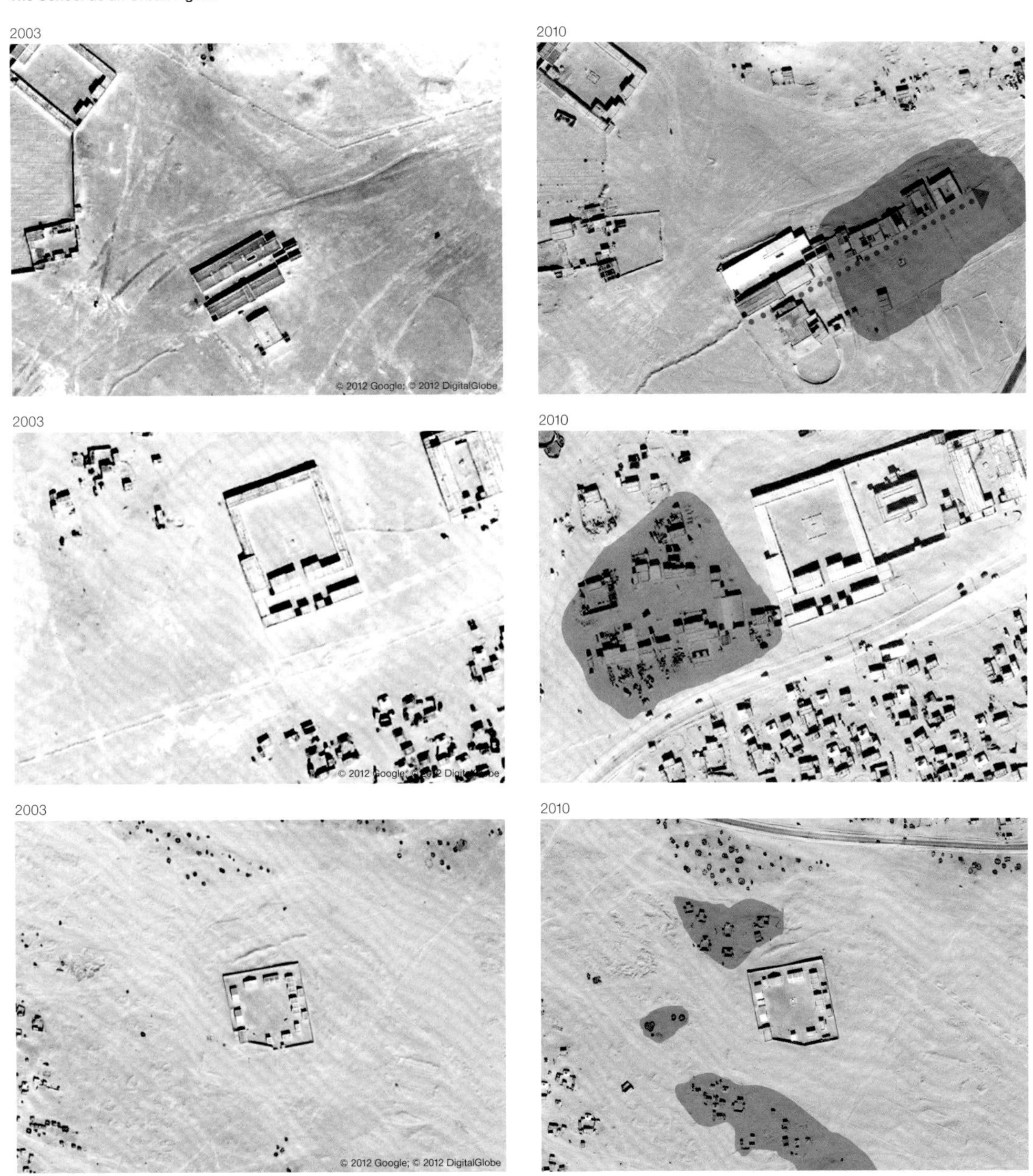


The schools are understood to be the seeds for additional development, especially within the public and commercial sectors.

**17 Junio Secondary School**
Urban void

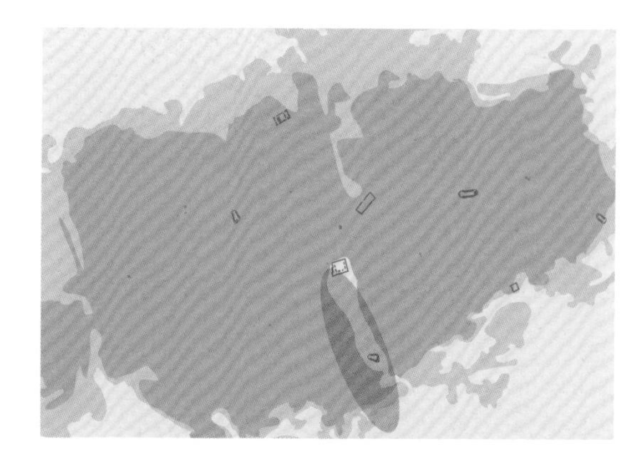

**Nachna Primary School**
School as an urban attractor

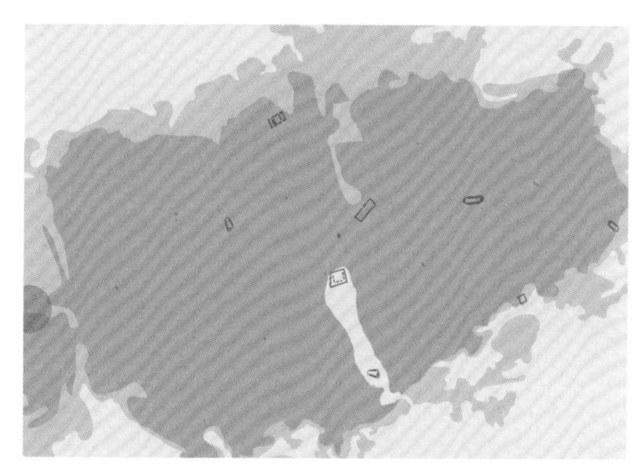

**Mustafa Mohammed Dachmid Primary School**
Development of peripheral zone

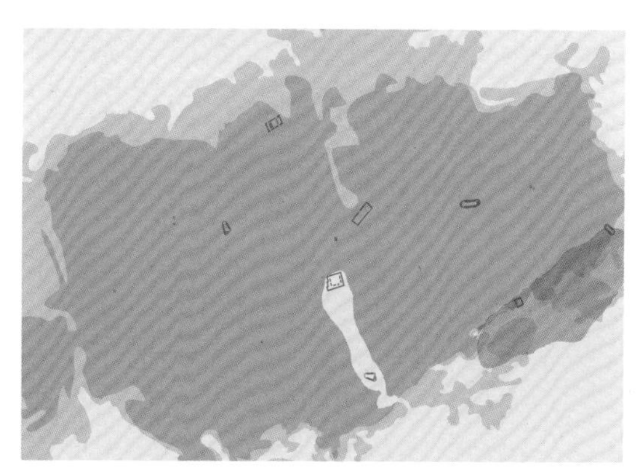

### Schools as Urban Agents: Smara

One of the most noticeable features in Smara is a large open zone at the center of the camp, separating it into eastern and western halves. This zone, more than 600 m long and approximately 200 m wide, is completely void of housing or any other construction and stretches between the two largest schools of the camp. The area is used for recreational purposes, such as playing football, and sometimes for celebrations and ceremonial purposes, but mostly remains vacant. Even though the neighboring quarters have experienced densification and growth in the past decade, there seems to be a general consensus that the area between both schools should not be developed.

The opposite process can be identified when looking at the schools located at the periphery of the camp. Each has seen the building of several new residential compounds in its immediate proximity over the past few years. They act as attractors, triggering residential growth and also some commercial development.

All in all, the schools in the Sahrawi camps seem to adopt a role that goes beyond their educational purpose. They often act as seeds of further urban development or form a nucleus for later public and commercial zones to emerge. This growth can take place informally or independently of a master plan, in the case of residential units around the schools on the periphery of camp Smara. In the more

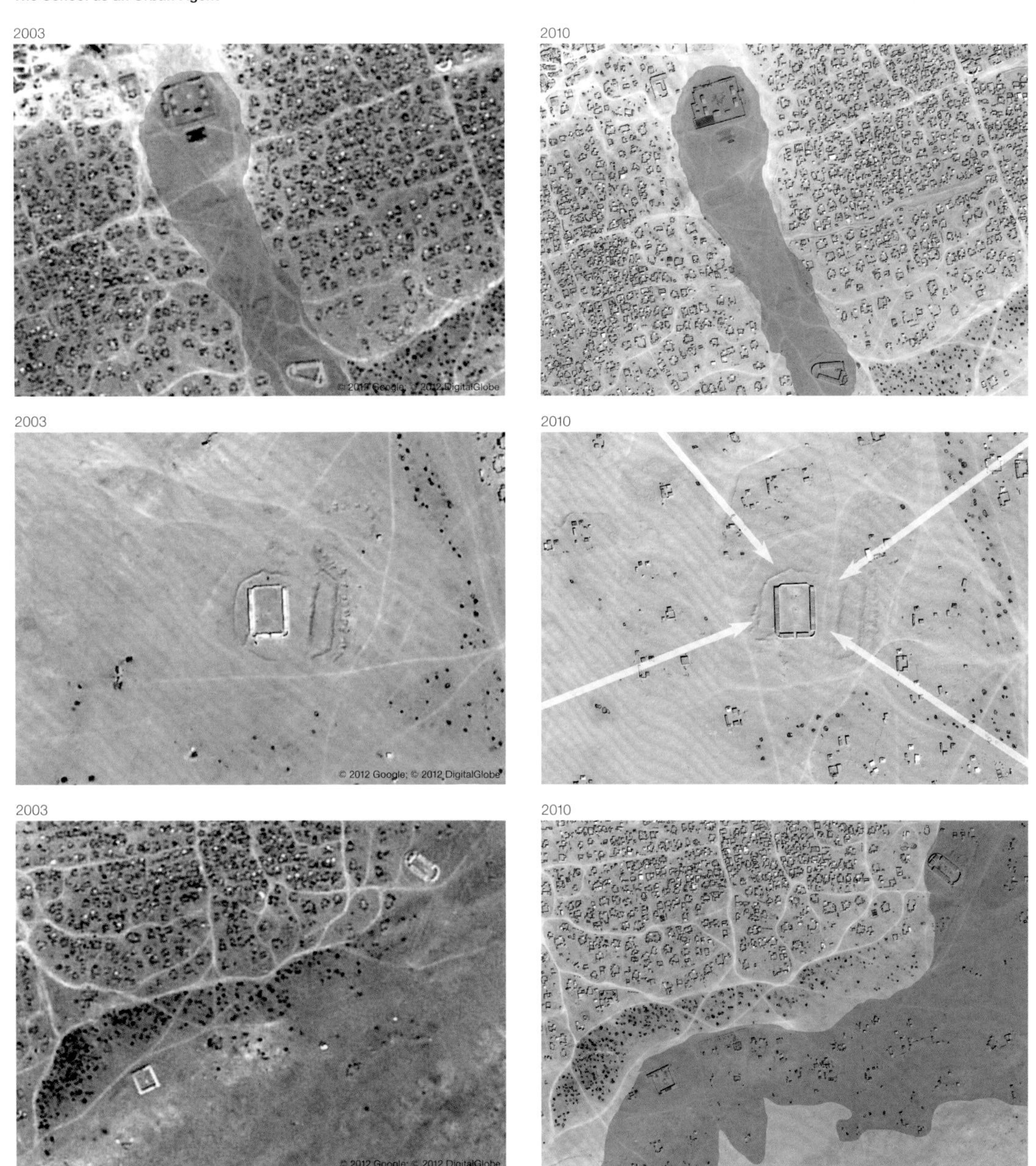


central areas of Smara and El Aaiún, top-down planning decisions are the core reason for the development of new institutional zones, or, as is the case in the center of Smara, preserving an area as an urban void and preventing construction from taking place.

View of 27 February camp

Entrance of 27 February school, 2011

Urban development around the school, 2004

**27 February: One School, One Camp**

Nowhere is the relationship between schools and urban development more obvious than with the 27 February school. Founded in 1976 as a women-only boarding school, it is located midway between Rabouni and Smara (which at the time had just been set up). With Awserd and El Aaiún to its north, 27 February has retained its central location amid the four major camps of the region.

The school was founded as an adult education center, teaching women vocational knowledge and specific crafts such as weaving and carpet-making. Today it has expanded and also offers courses in technical and artistic subjects such as computer science, filmmaking, administration, and bookkeeping. The school has been important to the refugee society in developing an emancipated generation of women who are able to pursue their own economic activities.

Over time, based on the fact that women were living with their children for extensive periods in the school, and small-scale economic activities brought about by the presence of the school, 27 February slowly developed into a settlement in its own right. Starting with a few tents and huts, more and more families started to move to the area around the school, settling there permanently. The central location of the school, relatively close to the administrative center of Rabouni, aided this development.

Camp 27 February with newly installed power line

The school is centrally located within the camps, 2006

High densification west and east of the main street axis, 2010

By the 1990s, the settlement had grown far larger than the school itself and had taken on a life of its own. With approximately 8,000 to 10,000 inhabitants, it is now larger than a typical daïra in one of the other camps.

Recently, 27 February became the first camp with electricity, supplied by Algeria via an overland powerline. This powerline, installed in 2010, has allowed the establishment of air-conditioning systems and more extensive electric lights within the residential compounds. In the tough climate of the Sahara, the availability of electricity without reliance on solar cells or generators is a major benefit. This will lead to additional growth as families move from other camps to take advantage of the development.

# Shaping the Nation through Health and Education

## The Camp as Catalyst for Health and Education

During the Spanish colonial era, the Sahrawi population was transformed from a traditional nomadic society to a semi-sedentary one, and approximately half of the population lived in or near a city by 1975. With the start of the war against Morocco and the flight through the desert to the camps in Tindouf, Sahrawi society underwent an abrupt transformation and basically became fully urbanized overnight. The low standard of health and education services during the colonial era was not just caused by the racially segregated Spanish system, but it was also a result of the traditional tribal structure of Sahrawi society itself. Furthermore, it can be traced back to spatial or territorial causes. The Western Sahara—a country larger than the United Kingdom, but at the time inhabited by approximately 100,000 people—is too thinly populated to be able to provide medical and educational services of reasonable standard for the whole territory. The relatively dense settlement of the refugee camps gave the Sahrawis the territorial preconditions to set up services that, for the first time, could reach the whole population.

Health and education are considered to be the “core businesses” of international humanitarian organizations. By improving the physical well-being and by providing education and knowledge to a disenfranchised group—whether they be refugees, disaster victims, or the poor—these organizations express a central spirit of humanitarianism. These principles are based on the idea of assistance and empathy across national, cultural, and social boundaries. On the flip side, more often than not, they result in control and an uneven power relationship between donor and recipient. The beneficiary is reduced to being a recipient of aid and is often not in control of how this aid is distributed and whose interests are served.

Sahrawis understand that health and education are not merely technical fields where service needs to be provided in an efficient way. By organizing health and education independently, the Sahrawis were able to develop their own understanding, curricula, and approach to these central dimensions of society. Obviously, the Sahrawi refugees are, however, still dependent on outside help. This can be seen by the fact that higher education can only be pursued outside the camps, and by the fact that they rely on donations of medication and teaching aids. But it is the refugees themselves who organize and administer these fields with their ministries of education and health. Hence, they are the ones who decide which curriculum is followed, which aid organization is granted access to the camps, and where to send students to receive their higher education.

Health and education became a national agenda, and not just in the sense of improving the conditions of refugees' daily life. It is also seen as an investment into the formation of a new country. The fact that the first schools were named after the dates important in forming the nation (27 February, 18 October, etc.) show that these schools are embedded in the construction of a national narrative that forms the new Sahrawi identity.

Education became a means of transforming a traditional society organized by tribal structures and fixed power relationships into a modern society allowing emancipation, not only of the women, but of all its social groups. While traditional society was characterized by a strict and impenetrable tribal order, education allowed the emergence of a modern nation with social mobility. Health and education thus expose the dilemma of the Sahrawi refugee condition. Having experienced the tragic loss of a homeland and their arduous existence as refugees, it is precisely this condition of living in the density of the camps that allows a new health and education system to be developed. And it is this health and education system that, among other things, facilitates the modernization and emancipation of Sahrawi society.

CENTRO DE SALUD

## Learning from the Camps

The self-organized system of health and education has resulted in considerable improvements in the living conditions of Sahrawi society. In spite of the harsh climate, the geographical remoteness of the camps, and their weak economy, life expectancy, literacy rate, and the general level of education are among the highest of all North African nations. Through their respective ministries, the refugees have not only learned how to provide health and education, but also how to administer and organize these services that are of strategic importance to any nation. Thus, one of the central questions is whether, and if so how, this experience can be brought back to the Western Sahara, if the opportunity arises to return. Can the refugees use the time in the camps as a learning period and apply this organizational and administrative knowledge to their original homeland if political transformations allow them to resettle there?

One scenario for effective resettlement is to translocate administration and infrastructure in a one-to-one relationship. The facilities, manpower, and administrative system of camp Smara would, for example, move to the city Smara, while those of camp El Aaiún would move to the city El Aaiún, and so on. While the literal nature of this system might facilitate the first period of such a return to the homeland, it would still struggle with the local specificities of the cities in Western Sahara, some being coastal cities, some inland cities, some well connected with roads and airfields, and some remote and isolated.

The main challenge, however, lies in the size of the country and its low population density. Whereas now the camps themselves have a population density of around 10,000 inhabitants per square kilometer—of comparable density to cities in general—and, with the exception of camp Dakhla, the distance between the camps is no more than 30 or 40 km, a return to the Western Sahara would mean a population of 200,000 inhabitants in a country larger than the United Kingdom. Already, the logistical difficulties of operating in a country this size with such a small population are immense. But beyond the logistical difficulties, it would mean a substantial reconsideration of the relationship between rural and urban, or between cities and their hinterland.

Whereas increasing self-sufficiency would mean making the territory productive and hence occupying it at least to a limited extent, a high urbanization rate and concentration of the population in the cities would also be needed to reach the level of health and education services that the Sahrawis currently enjoy. Furthermore, the health and education system in the camps presently relies on a very limited monetary economy, where the provision of most services is based on an exchange in-kind, and doctors, nurses, or teachers are willing to work for very little financial remuneration. When resettling in the homeland of the Western Sahara, and establishing a working economy, this would be difficult to uphold.

المكتبة
BIBLIOTECA

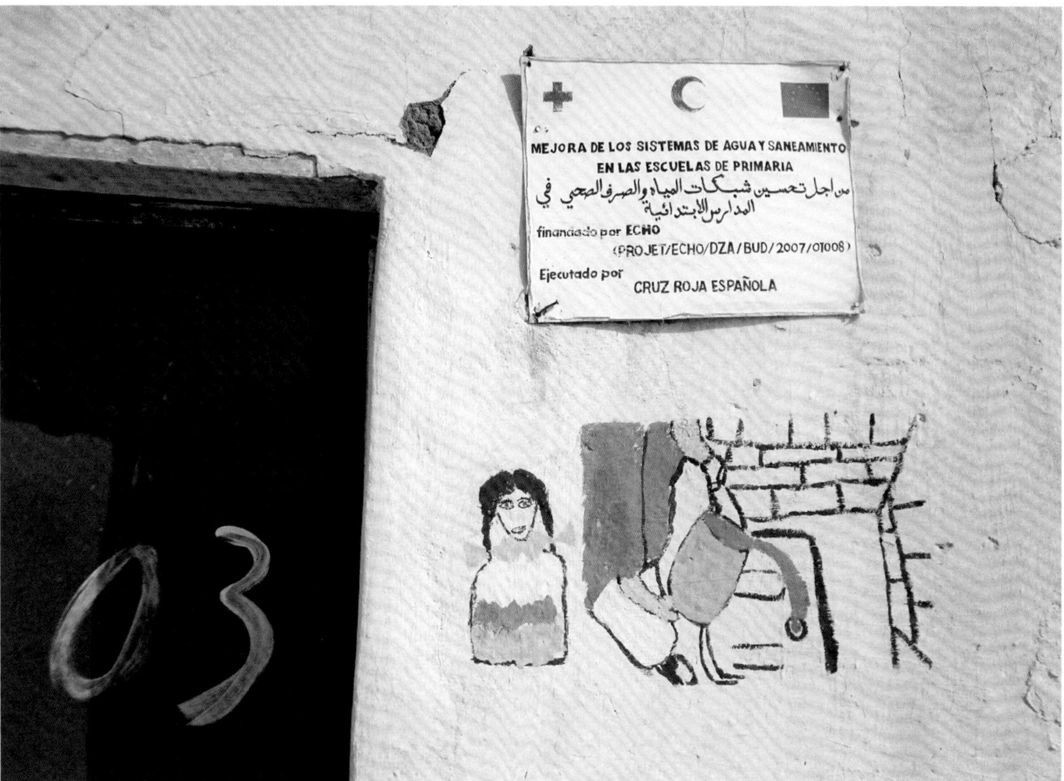
MEJORA DE LOS SISTEMAS DE AGUA Y SANEAMIENTO
EN LAS ESCUELAS DE PRIMARIA
من اجل تحسين شبكات المياه والصرف الصحي في
المدارس الابتدائية
financiado por ECHO
(PROJET/ECHO/DZA/BUD/2007/01008)
Ejecutado por
CRUZ ROJA ESPAÑOLA
03

# RECREATION AND LEISURE

In the planning of a refugee camp and its discourse, recreation is something that rarely receives attention. It is somehow a common understanding that "when lives are at stake," activities pertaining to leisure are considered frivolous, and seemingly more fundamental activities are prioritized. The UNHCR handbook for emergencies, containing the main planning guidelines for refugee camps, makes no mention of the notions of leisure or entertainment. It seems to be human nature, however, that the supposedly trivial activities of recreation nevertheless emerge everywhere, together with their corresponding spaces. This chapter will look at a wide variety of leisure activities, ranging from personal and family-related rituals, via the use of public spaces and sports activities, to the establishment of green spaces. Even though some of these might not be considered recreational in the conventional sense, they all share the characteristic of going beyond the basic necessity of sustaining existence, instead encompassing the social dimensions of everyday life.

# Private Spaces

Tea is of great cultural and social importance to the refugees. And the Sahrawis regularly point out that they developed a tea ceremony that differs from other North African cultures, specifically highlighting the difference from the Moroccan tea ceremony. Drinking tea happens everywhere and is an element that accompanies everyday life. It allows the maintenance of social relationships and slows daily life down to a speed more comfortable for the desert environment. The spaces where the tea-drinking ceremony is performed thus take on a central role in the private spaces of the family compounds. WFP and UNHCR pay homage to the significance of the Sahrawi tea culture, and they are the only refugees that receive green tea as an official part of their food aid.

Family occasions in the refugee camps—especially weddings and other festivities—are very important in maintaining relationships with family and friends across longer distances. As the distance between some of the camps is relatively large, these events offer the chance for reunion. Additionally, because of the Islamic background and a tradition-based separation between men and women, weddings offer the opportunity to meet potential partners from the opposite gender. Festivals thus play an important role in social life on the camps. They are colorful celebrations with music, dancing, and food. Their presence spreads across the whole camp, creating a pleasurable interval from the repetition of everyday life.

## The Ceremony of Drinking Tea

Tea culture has its origins in the nomadic and semi-nomadic life that existed before the refugee camps. But the form as it is practiced today has been developed in exile. The principle is to drink three rounds of tea. Apart from for the most urgent reasons, this basic rule is never broken.

Each round is given a symbolic significance:

*The first round is strong like life.*
*The second, sweet like love.*
*And the third, smooth like death.*

The whole ritual of three rounds can easily take an hour or two. The preparation of the tea is elaborate and has a ceremonial quality:

Boil up water and green tea in a pot on hot coal.
Pour a single glass of tea from the teapot.
Boil up new water with the remaining green tea.
Pour a large amount of sugar into the pot.
Pour tea from glass to glass to create a white foam.
Pour the boiling tea from the pot into the glasses.

This is repeated three times with the same tea leaves. The preparation of tea is a social event but can also accompany debates or political events.

**Family Tearoom**

Every residential compound has a lounge where the family prepares tea and sits together, as well as with neighbors or guests. Most often the floor is carpeted and usually there is a shelf for a TV, radio, and the utensils needed for tea preparation. The windows are decorated with curtains. Normally, everybody sits on the carpet, although in more wealthy families, cushions or seats are available. The tearoom is one of the most important rooms in the daily life of the Sahrawis. Sometimes it also doubles as a bedroom.

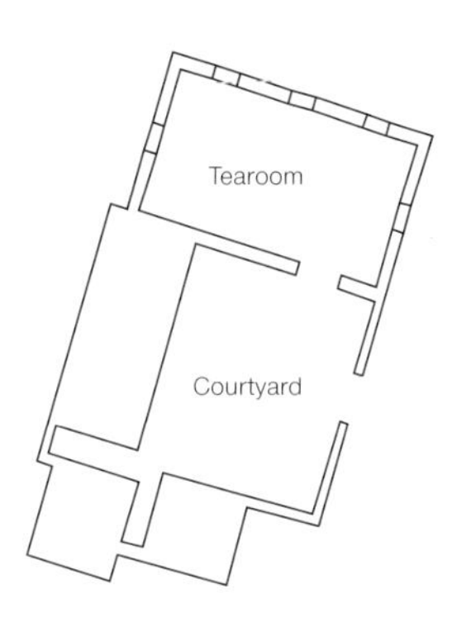

## Tea Break

The tea ceremony requires patience and calm. Its slow, drawn-out process is compatible with the environment of the desert, which slows everything down. If there are no customers, it is time for tea. Some shopkeepers have a tearoom next to their shop where they can relax. This small room is usually equipped with a TV, radio, and carpet. The most beautiful space for a break is beneath a tree in the market garden, where the gardener invites his family to drink tea with him.

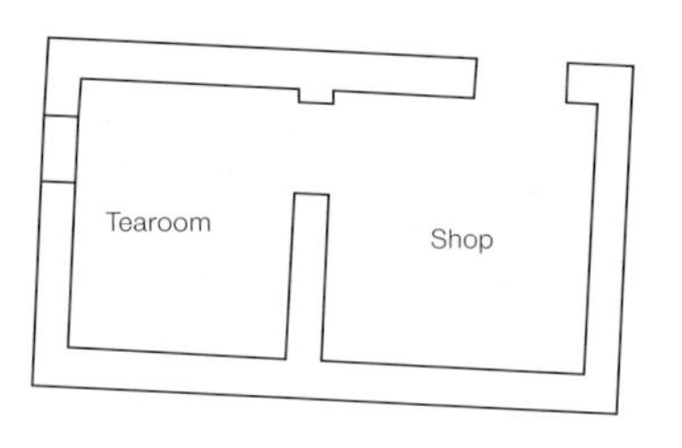

## Drinking Tea as an Engine for Daily Life

Drinking tea is central to Sahrawi culture. Even though it is most often performed in the central room of a residential compound, the tea ceremony can take place anywhere and has a huge influence on the quality of life in the camps. It is a good excuse to get in contact with people, so it becomes an important engine to maintain relationships in the social network. Additionally, the sweet, sticky tea cleanses the throat from the dust of the desert.

Although tea is a traditional and central ritual in the life of the Sahrawis (and most of the Maghreb), it is not a local product. The tea consumed in the camps is usually imported from China, or sometimes India. This gives evidence to the fact that even in the most remote locations and in conditions of limited resources, settlements are still inscribed in a global network of exchange and trade.

**Festivals and the Mobile Tent**
Weddings are colorful events, and there are often many visitors from the other refugee camps. It is therefore a convenient opportunity to re-establish connections between camps. A mobile tent, which moves from wedding to wedding across the camp, becomes the receptacle for this mode of exchange. Set up next to the house of the bride's family, this large, rented tent is pitched in an open space. The sides of the tent are open, indicating that everybody is welcome to join the celebration.

A wedding usually takes place over two days. The first day of the wedding is organized by the family of the bride, and the second by the family of the groom. During the two days, many friends and neighbors visit the festival. All guests are sprayed with perfume, creating an olfactory experience that can be perceived from afar. The festival consists of the wedding itself and much dancing, tea drinking, laughing, and talking. Guests come and go whenever they want. The important guests, especially the groom's family, drive to the celebration in decorated cars, honking loudly, and with music blasting from the stereo systems.

The festival becomes a strong, sweet presence in the camp–you can hear the music and shrill howls of women borne by the wind throughout the locality.

# Common Spaces

Leisure activities not only take place within the private realm, but also in a number of "common" spaces. Beyond the private habitat of the home or family, these common spaces are about interaction with the inhabitants of the camp at large. They are spaces where social interactions take place beyond the family and close circle of friends, and an exchange with strangers or more distant acquaintances becomes possible. The range of spaces and activities performed in them is fairly wide. Among them, we can find cultural spaces, such as galleries or stages for performances; as well as the daïra centers, with their distribution and meeting areas; and also the cafés and sandwich stores that have sprung up in recent years. Some of these are not necessarily spaces of recreation in the strict sense of the word, and it could be debated whether they should be included under this heading.

Daïra centers, in particular, are purpose-built buildings that serve other needs such as administration, health services, and the distribution of goods. Nevertheless, they also act as spaces of leisure and recreation, and attract these activities to take place in their immediate environment. People come to meet friends, relax, play games, and listen to music. Often, these activities occur informally and spontaneously. What is important for the camp and for its urbanistic reading is that a sense of commonality emerges in these locations. The areas in and around the cultural spaces, daïra centers, and cafés have an openness and do not restrict who has access to them. They are cared for and used by the general population, and are often open in their use or "programming."
It is this openness that gives these spaces their sense of an urban quality and makes them so important in the overall fabric of the camp.

جزر أولاد

**Typology of the Centers of the Daïras in El Aaiún**
The centers of the daïras exhibit a conscious and precise planning intention, and the circular shape comes close to being an example of iconic architecture. With its external ring of small rooms, large semicircular courtyard, smaller wedge-like courtyards, and the adjacent assembly hall, it is an almost exemplary model of how to deal architecturally with the platonic form of the circle. The color scheme, originally dark red with blue doors, is striking and enhances the iconic quality of the building in contrast to its environment.

This archetype of a daïra center has been used all over the camp. Over the years, the centers have often been transformed or extended, but the strong basic form is still clearly visible. The centers have several tasks. One of these is to act as a location for relief supplies to be distributed. While this has originally taken place in the large semicircular courtyard, today distribution takes place in the larger space to the front of the center. The centers also have a small health care station that provides first aid, and a meeting hall, used for political events. Individual rooms around the perimeter function as offices for administration or are used for storage.

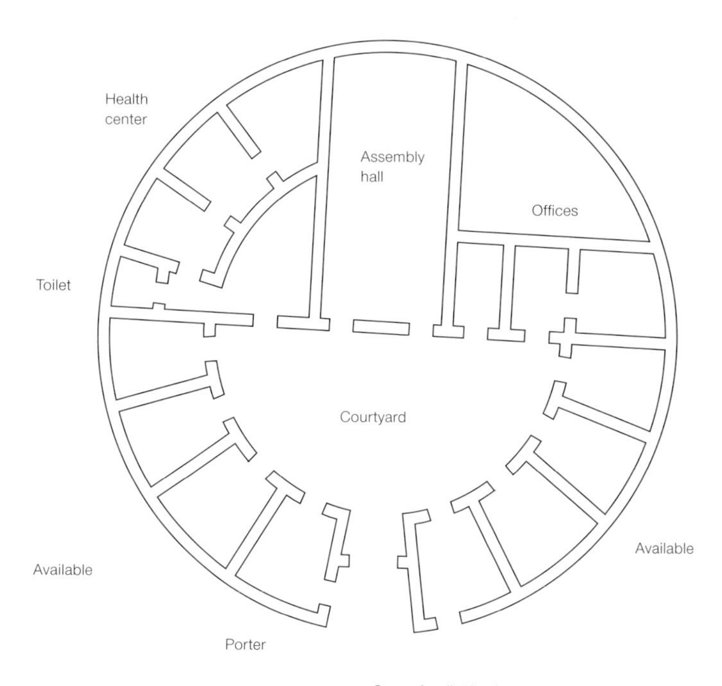
Health center
Assembly hall
Offices
Toilet
Courtyard
Available
Available
Porter
Space for distribution in front of the center
25 m

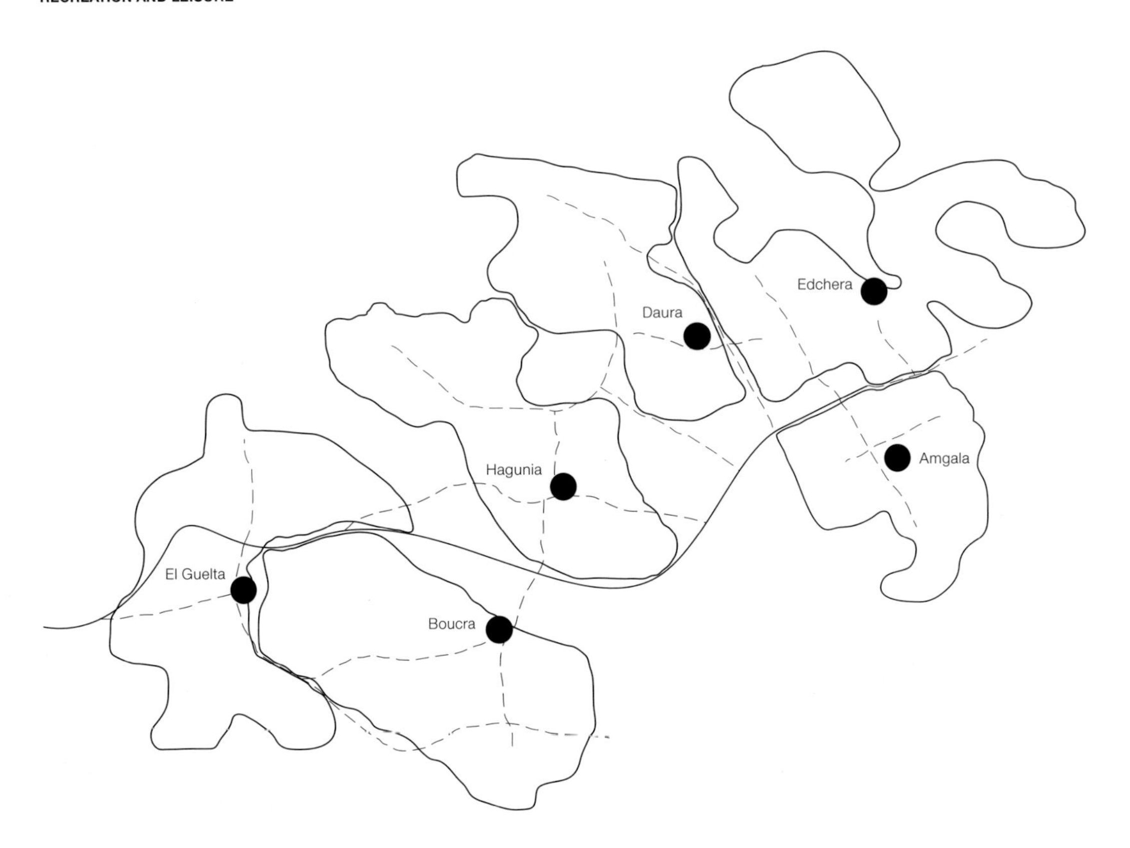


**The Daïras of El Aaiún**

Because of several floods, the structure of El Aaiún has changed over the years. El Guelta–which was previously located between Amgala and Boucra–was moved to the western edge of the camp. Other daïras have also been heavily modified. The previous location of El Guelta, south of the center of the camp, has since remained empty and fallow.

In most cases, the daïra centers are located in the heart of their respective daïras. Building density is relatively high, and other facilities such as shops attract inhabitants, making these centers easily accessible by most residents. The daïra centers of Edchera, Amgala, Daura, and Hagunia also act as engines of public life. Social activities, games, and informal gatherings take place in the spaces around these centers. The daïras of El Guelta and especially Boucra have developed areas of public activity that are spatially independent from their respective centers. El Guelta is home to the camp's main market, which acts as the daïra's busiest zone of activity. In Boucra, the center is located outside the residential area, and only few buildings have developed in its vicinity. Public life accumulates around the central shopping zone, which is several hundred meters to the south of the center.

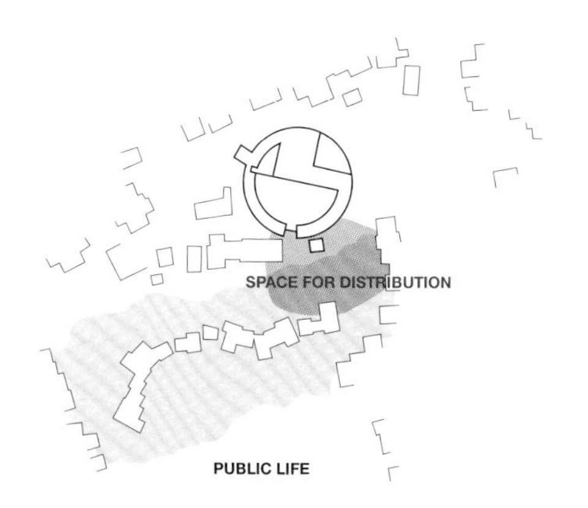


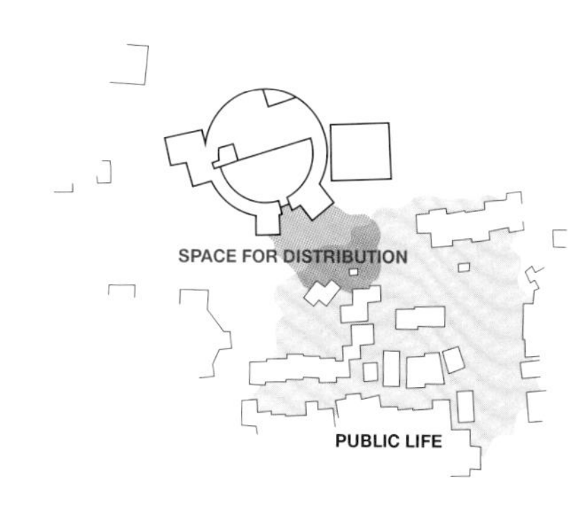

**Amgala Center**
Of all the daïra centers, the one in Amgala has remained closest to its original condition. With the exception of two small extensions, the round building seems to have survived without any major alteration. Also, the floods have left no significant trace. The center is located in the middle of the daïra, which has developed all around it. Compared with other daïras, Amgala has a higher density of structures and population. Close to the center, a street and square with shops and commercial activity have evolved.

**Edchera Center**
The center of Edchera is situated along a wadi-like basin that divides the daïra into two parts. The section to the southwest, and towards the center of the camp, has a high density of structures and population. On the other side of the wadi, the daïra is much more sparsely populated and extends far into the desert. In front of the center there is a large open area used for the distribution of supplies. Beyond is a cluster of shops selling everyday necessities.

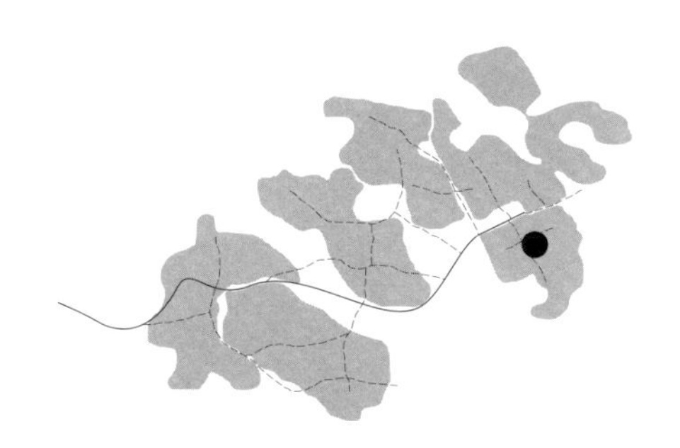

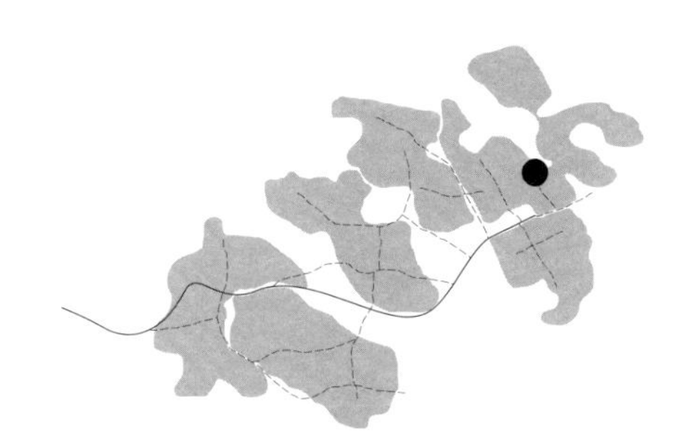

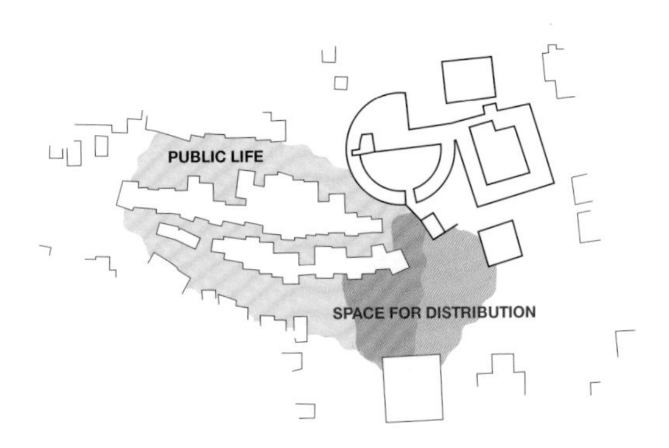


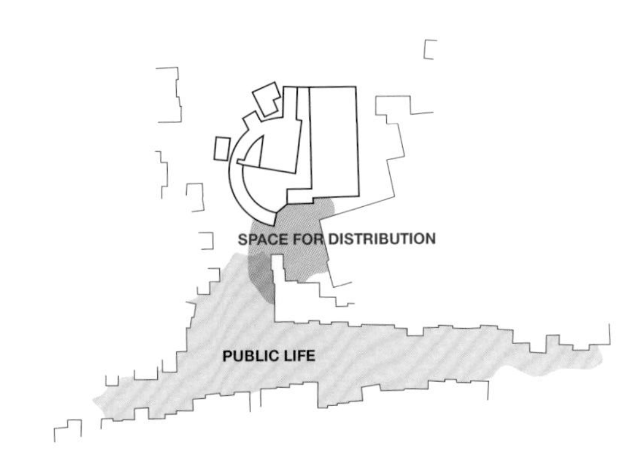

**Daura Center**

The area for the distribution of relief supplies is located on the main road. The round center of Daura is located next to it and has been rebuilt or transformed several times. The round shape of the building is not clearly visible any longer because of interventions to its exterior, and because other buildings have been constructed in front of it. Close to the center, a handful of shops have developed. A few palm trees stand in the sand next to them. Potentially offering a pleasant place to rest with plenty of shade, the trees are blocked by barbed wire protecting them from goats.

**Hagunia Center**

Hagunia is a lively daïra with a large cluster of shops along a street located next to its center. The street was once the main access route to El Aaiún and is still a central location for the camp as a whole. Today the character of the road remains, and residents from other daïras come shopping here, increasing the number of shops and the range of goods offered. The center has changed significantly over time. Large parts of the round building have been broken down and replaced by other buildings, though from one side the general form has been preserved and is still visible.

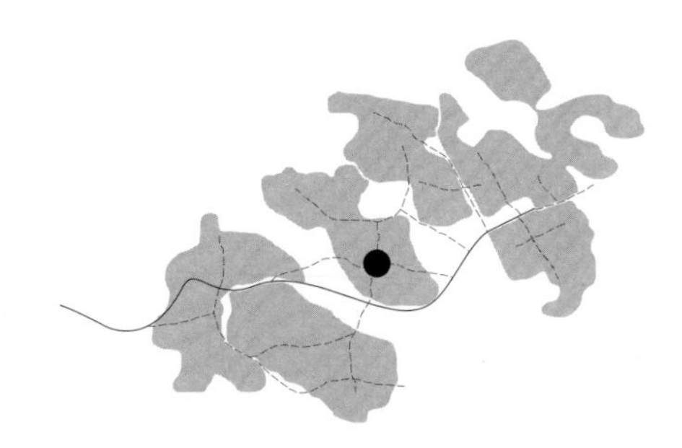

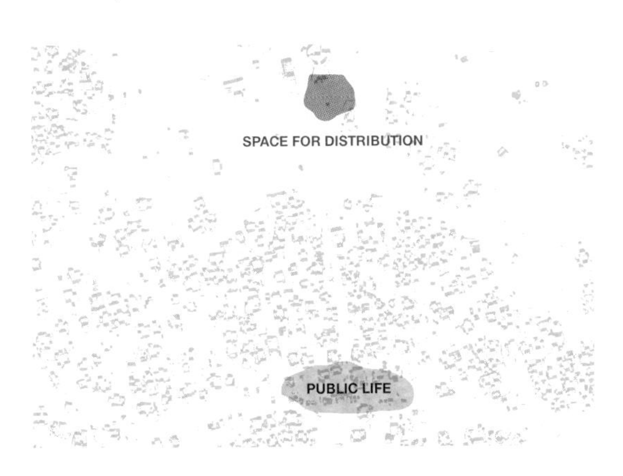


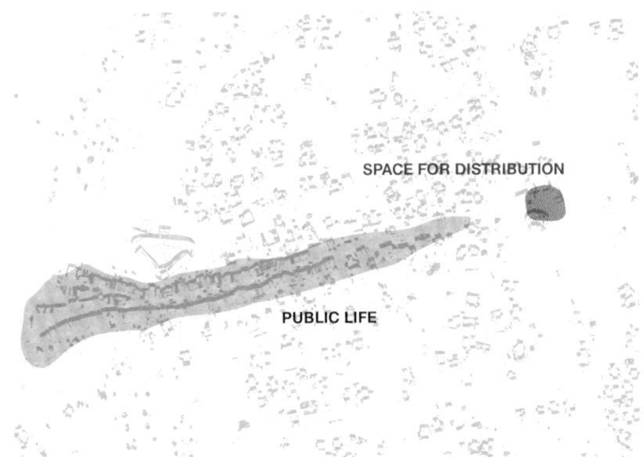

**Boucra Center**
The daïra Boucra was altered by the floods of 1994. Today the center building is located at the edge of the daïra and has not attracted the formation of much public life around it. Although it serves a technical function, with the output of relief supplies and medical care, the center of public life has shifted and is located farther south near a scattering of shops. The original building has changed in only one of its quarters. The building was supplemented by a striking wedge-like addition that was built on the southern side of the existing structure.

**El Guelta Center**
El Guelta, which was previously located between Amgala and Boucra, was completely destroyed by the floods of 1994. Today its old center is used as a police station. The new El Guelta was reconstructed to the west of Boucra. The new daïra center is the only one that does not use the circular typology, but instead consists of several separate units. The only building with an iconic shape is an oval storage building. The biggest shopping street in El Aaiún, used by the whole camp, extends from the center of El Guelta to the entrance road of El Aaiún. This is where most people gather throughout the day. The daïra center itself is only visited for special events or the distribution of goods.

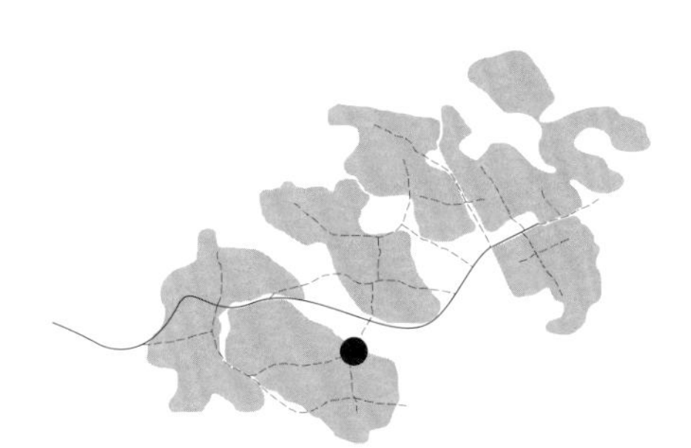

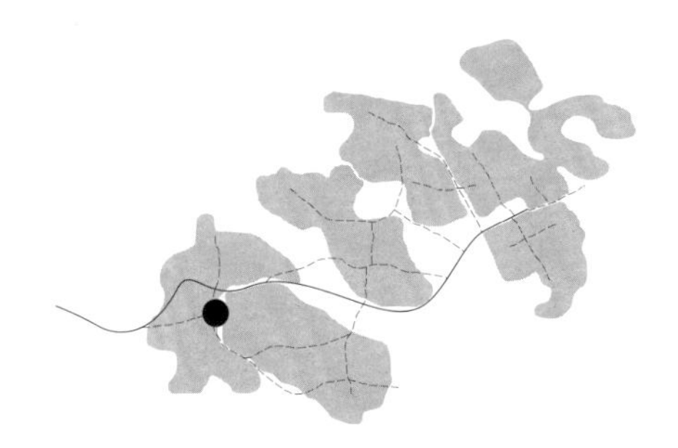

**The Daïras in Smara**

The structure of Smara has not significantly changed over the past ten or even twenty years. The original organization of the camp still prevails, though it has grown in size. Only the borders of the camp show a certain elasticity, with an ever finer grain of construction merging with the surrounding desert. Looking more closely at Smara, one can observe the similarity of the daïras, which form the twin-like pairs of Jederia and Hauza, Mahbes and Farsia, and finally Tifariti and Bir Lehlu. One can assume that they were all established at the same time. Only the daïra Emheriz has a different configuration. It was created recently as a new extension and has a low density of inhabitants and physical structures.

In contrast to the centers of El Aaiún, those in Smara are used mostly as aid distribution points or for administrative purposes. Most communal and public life takes place around the central area of the camp itself, instead of in the daïra centers. The centers of Smara also do not share a standardized building typology. Apart from the centers of Jederia and Hauza, which are also circular buildings, the other centers consist mostly of rather nondescript rectangular buildings.

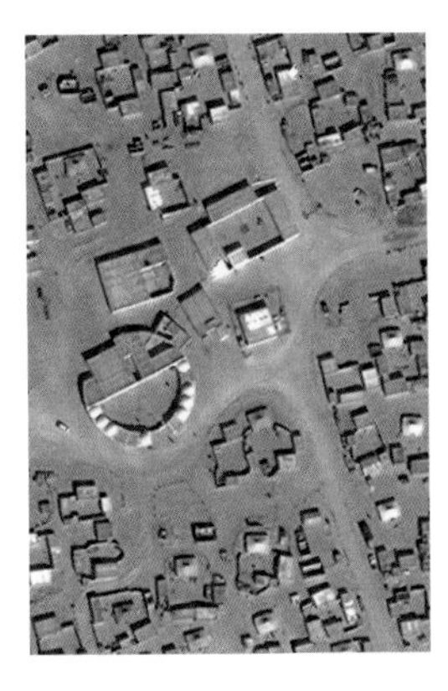

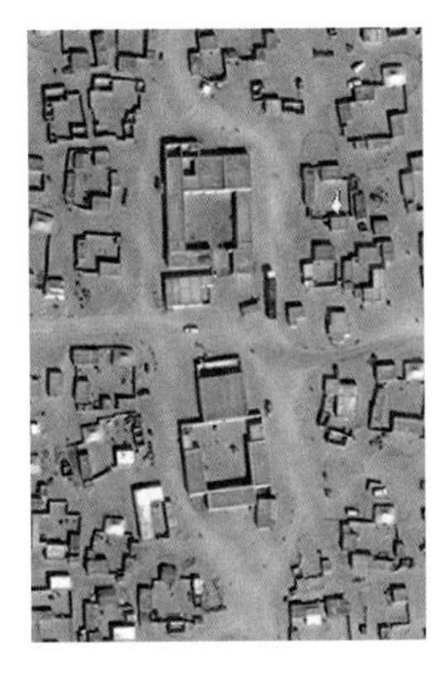

**Centers Jederia and Hauza**

With the traditional spherical-shape roofs–which can also be seen in old photographs from the Spanish Sahara–made of clay bricks, the centers of Jederia and Hauza have a very striking design. Their plan and layout is similar to the daïra centers of El Aaiún, but they seem to have been changed and transformed over time. In contrast to El Aaiún, there are no other public spaces or shop clusters around these centers.

**Centers Bir Lehlu and Tifariti**

The centers Bir Lehlu and Tifariti have a simple rectangular structure. Everything seems to be built in a very practical and pragmatic style. With a courtyard building of approximately 60 × 30 m in Bir Lehlu and two structures of 40 × 25 m in the case of Tifariti, the compounds are larger than those in El Aaiún. Aid distribution takes place in the inner courtyards. This means that less activity occurs outside the compounds, preventing them from acting as engines of communal life.

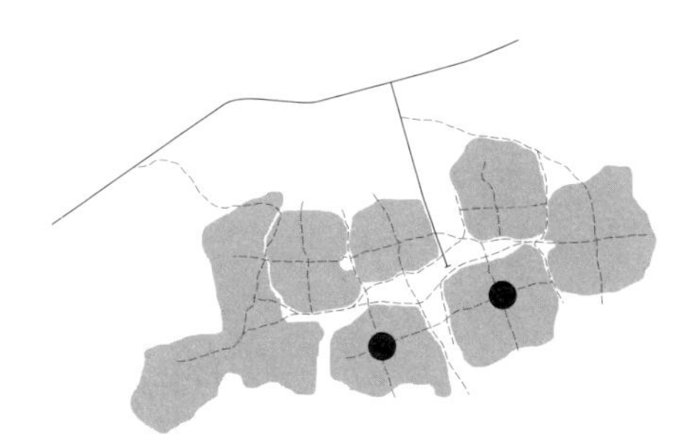

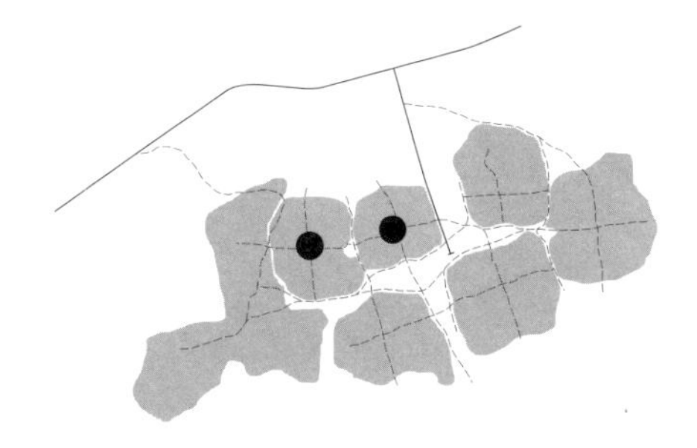

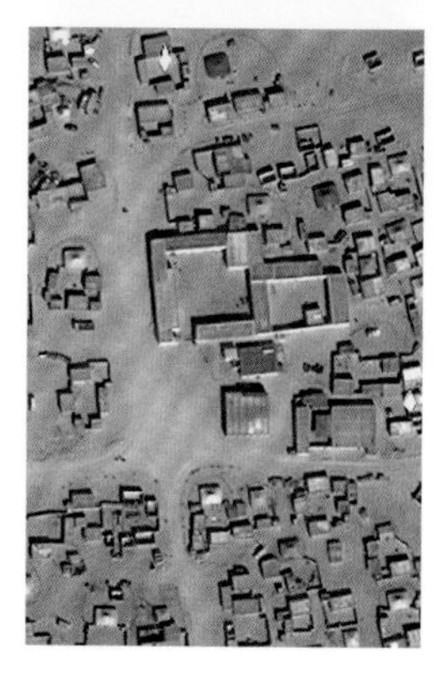

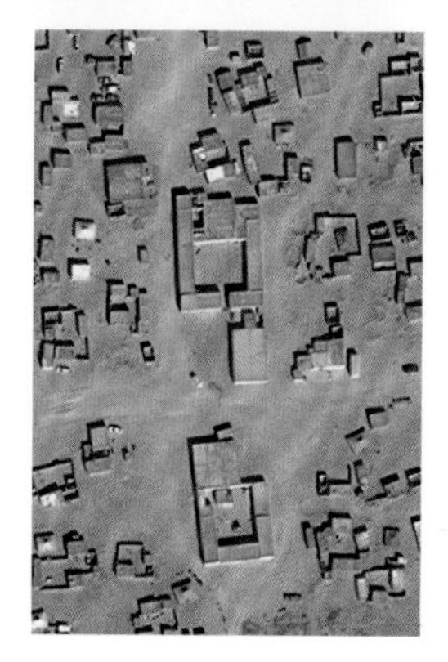

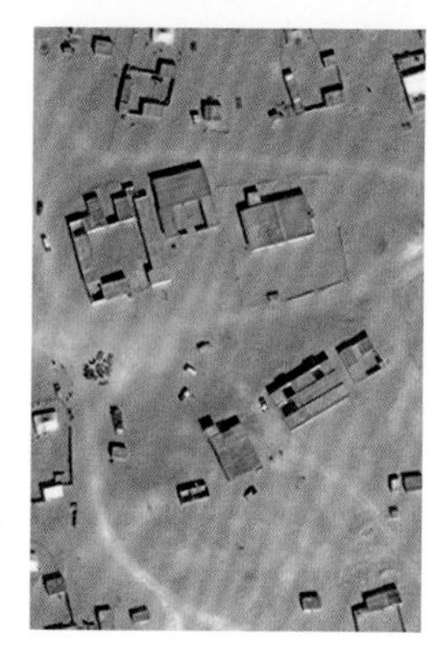

**Centers Mahbes and Farsia**
The daïra centers of Mahbes and Farsia share the same pragmatic rectangular structure as Bir Lehlu and Tifariti, though with a different layout. There are also no public spaces outside the compounds, nor hardly any shops.

**Center Emheriz**
Emheriz was set up in 2002 and has continuously expanded over the following years. The design seems more pragmatic than in the previous examples, which seemingly lacked a coherent urbanistic approach. In addition to the buildings forming the daïra center, a few other huts have been constructed. They were probably meant as shops, but have since been vacated and are currently unused. The compound is located on a small hill, making it visible from further afield. The daïra as a whole is characterized by its low density and a seemingly haphazard arrangement of structures.

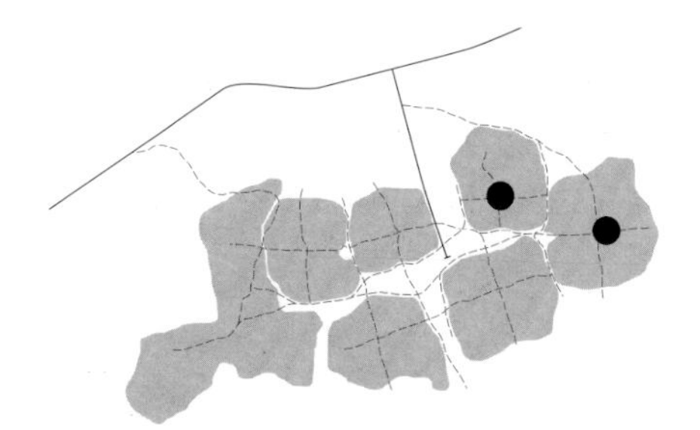

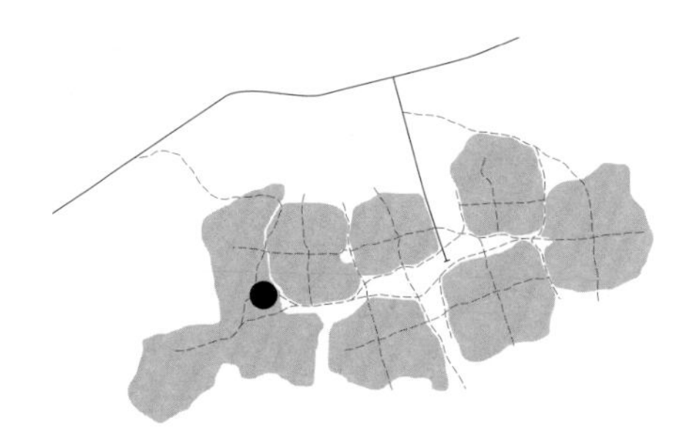

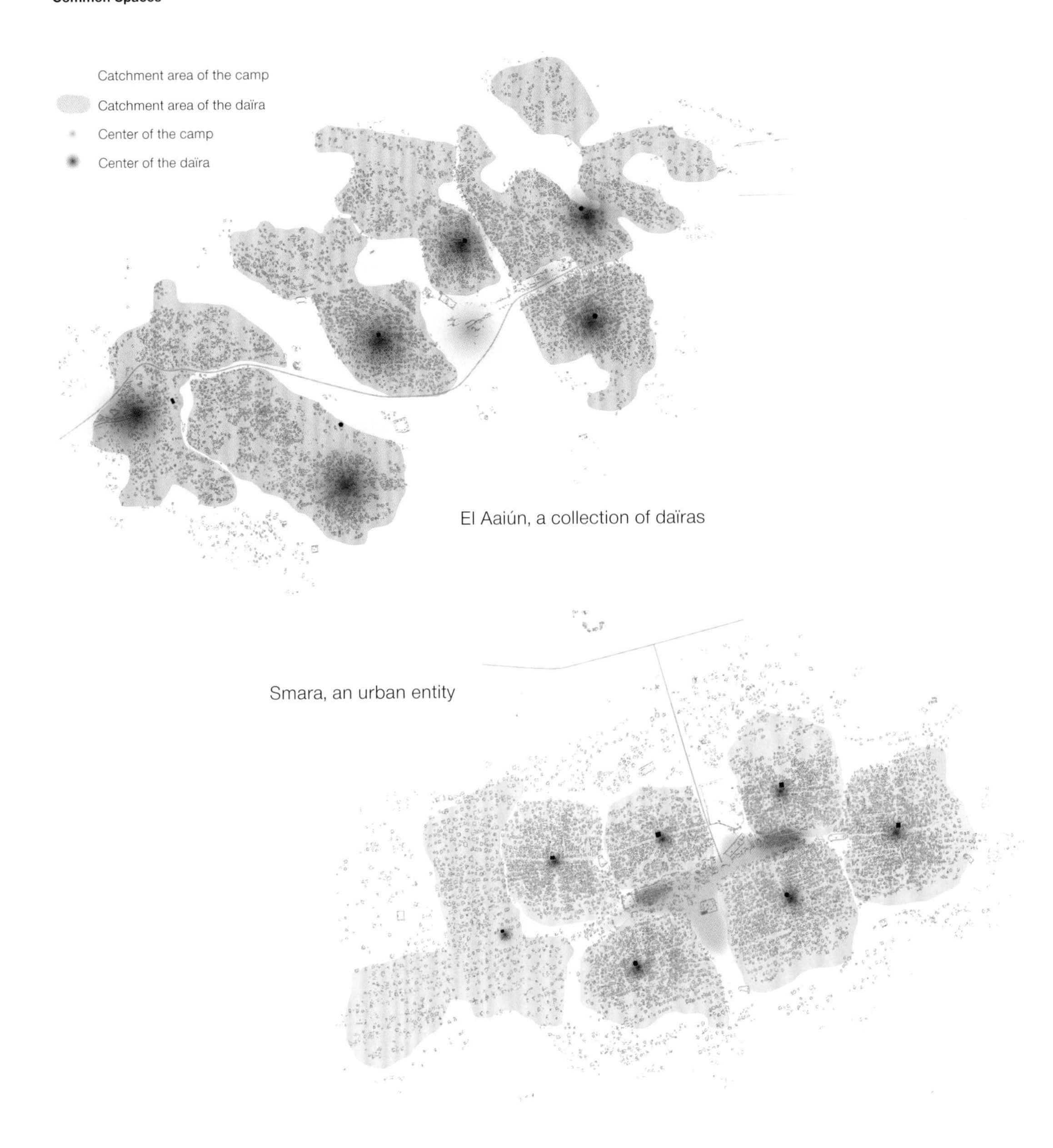


## Understanding Differences in the Centers

**Comparing the centers of El Aaiún and Smara reveals a difference in how daïras are used as a unit of identification, and as organizers of communal life. In Smara, the centers are predominantly used for the distribution of aid supplies, for political events, and for some administrative functions. Compared with El Aaiún, the space around the centers is used less for social and commercial activities. In Smara, most social and commercial activity takes place in the center of the camp, with its main facilities and two large markets. In El Aaiún, meanwhile, the daïra centers are used as an engine of public and social life. Small shops and facilities have developed close to these areas. This allows the emergence of a social and political space for each daïra and creates a level of autonomy. While El Aaiún could be understood as a collection of small villages, the concentration of facilities in a central location lends Smara a more proto-urban character.**

**Spaces for Games**

Every morning and evening, one can see men sitting in the sand near the daïra centers or shops, preferably in the shadow of a building. They play cards, a special form of checkers, or dominoes. The utensils of the game are often created using simple means. The board of checkers is drawn in the sand, and the pieces are twigs and small stones. The domino pieces tend to be slammed with great force on to the board, indicating the excitement and enjoyment of the players. A group of spectators surrounds each game being played, commenting on every move.

### Assembly Hall and Political Events

Each daïra has its own constituency and sends its representatives to the national assembly. For this process, each daïra needs its own assembly hall–located in the center buildings. Political gatherings are passionate events, with intense speeches accompanied by loud applause and shrill howls of the women in the audience. The high proportion of women involved in the organization of the camps results in their keen political participation.

During political events, a Sahrawi band plays music between the speeches. People sit on carpet on the floor, swing flags, clap their hands, and move their bodies to the beat of the music. Despite the often sharp and vociferous speeches, there is a happy and cheerful atmosphere. Politics is like a festival: it directly connects every refugee with the common aim of a future in the liberated homeland. These gatherings also give testimony to the politicization of everyday life, where most elements of the daily routine are imbued with a political dimension.

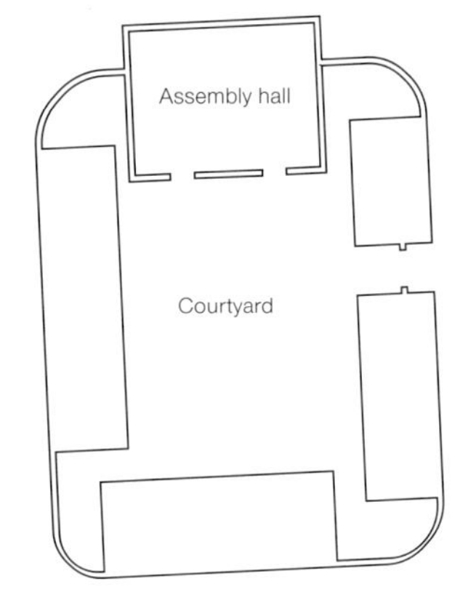

مطعم
Dove

## Distribution of Relief Supplies as a Social Event

Every week, different supplies, such as foodstuff or gas, are distributed in the daïras. It is usually women who are tasked with picking up the goods. If gas is distributed, the old gas bottles must be returned, and they are often rolled and pushed by foot towards the center. Arriving at the center, the women sit on their empty gas bottles to chat. Even having received the new gas bottles, they remain, showing that the distribution of relief supplies performs an important social function. Sometimes someone will bring a CD, and music is then played through a megaphone. Together with the colorful clothing of the women, the bell-like sounds from the gas bottles, and the constant coming and going of people, it could easily be mistaken for a festival. This shows how utilitarian events, such as relief distribution, are immediately augmented with a social and recreational dimension, and with an "everyday" quality.

**Mosques**

The Sahrawi are Sunni Muslims, and even though most describe themselves as being observant, religion and its visual practices are not overly present in the urban environment. Each daïra has a mosque, which is generally a rather small and simple structure, often indistinguishable from other buildings. Only the call of the muezzins and sometimes a small, dome-like construction on the roof indicate the special function of the building. A considerable proportion of the refugees prefer to pray at home instead of going to the mosque.

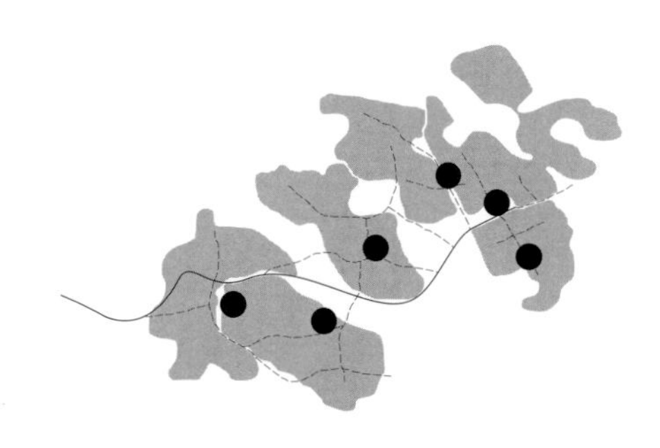

## Cultural Life

Each Sahrawi refugee camp has a number of spaces for cultural activities. Smara and El Aaiún, for example, have central stages with spectator stands, where bigger events take place. Live music is performed whenever people come together for social and political events and festivities. In youth centers, children learn to act, dance, and broadcast over the radio. Painters can exhibit their pictures in small art spaces, such as the Museo de Arte in El Aaiún. In spite of the wide range of cultural expression there is a common theme connecting almost all artistic production: the lament of life in exile, the memory of the lost homeland's beauty, and the call for a return home.

**Central Stage El Aaiún**

Next to the central sports field and Olof Palme School is a relatively unimposing open-air stage. The seating is arranged in a half-circle facing the stage, with the neighboring building as its backdrop.

| | |
|---|---|
| Stage: | 22 m wide, 8 m deep |
| Stand: | 60 m long, 3 steps |
| Capacity on stand: | approx. 300 spectators |
| Flat ground: | 40 m wide, 15 m deep |
| Capacity ground: | approx. 1,000 spectators |
| Capacity total: | approx. 1,300 spectators |

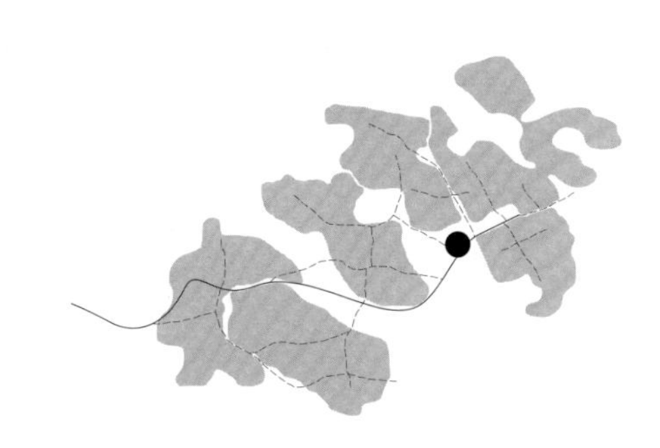

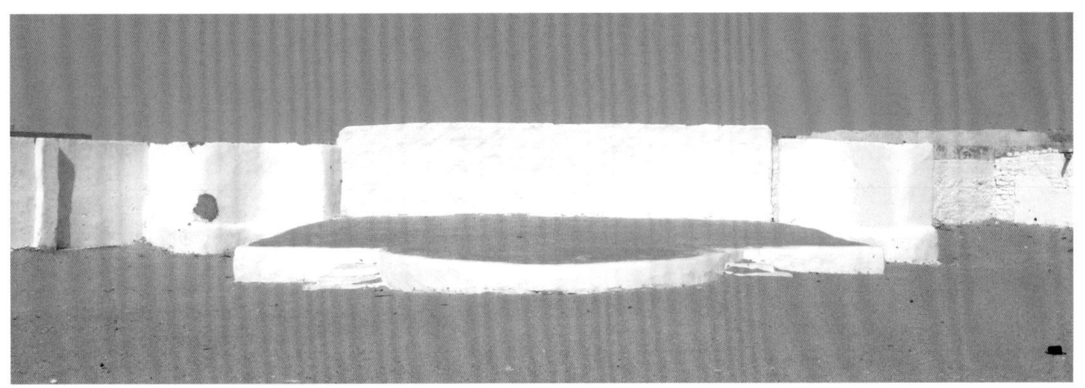

**Central Stage Smara**
The central stage in Smara is located in a larger courtyard, next to buildings of different uses in the center of the camp. It features a curved stage backdrop with secondary back access.

| | |
|---|---|
| Stage: | 10 m wide, 6 m deep |
| Stand: | 50 m long, 10 steps |
| Capacity on stand: | approx. 500 spectators |
| Flat ground: | 30 m wide, 20 m deep |
| Capacity ground: | approx. 1,000 spectators |
| Capacity total: | approx. 1,500 spectators |

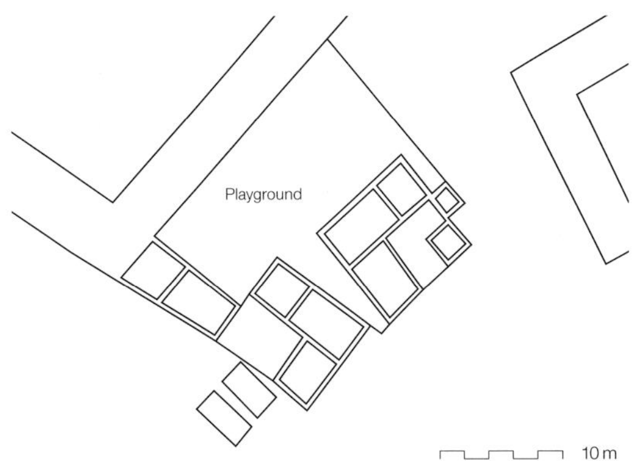

## Youth Center in Smara

The youth center has a playground, as well as rooms and spaces for kids. There is also a practice room for children's theater. Here, accompanied by a keyboard, the kids rehearse a play. The drama is about the life of hardship they are confronted with in the camps and the dream of a future in their homeland. The teacher reminds the young actors to show their emotions with credibility and intensity, and to be expressive with their gestures and voices.

**We want to live in peace,**

**We are here in exile,**

**How long we must remain?**

**We have never seen our homeland,**

**We have never heard the sea–**

**Please help us!**

Excerpt from youth theater

## Culture with a Mission

After thirty-five years in exile, the second generation of Sahrawis have grown up in the camps and never seen their homeland. Images of the Western Sahara as memorized by their grandparents are fading, but need to be passed on to the current generation. Cultural production preserves these impressions, and also constructs a new common memory of the idealized homeland. Theater plays tell the story of the comfortable climate of the Western Sahara, which is at odds with the fierce summer and frequent sandstorms of the camps. Paintings depict streets with trees and an urban life that contrasts with the dusty environment of their current living conditions. For the collective memory, it is essential that the refugee society is imbued with an idealized notion of the homeland, thereby keeping alive the ultimate aim of a return as a broad and unquestionable consensus. Cultural production, whether in the guise of painting, singing, or acting, is never innocent, but reinforces this construction of a common memory, supporting a universal mission, and hence is deeply political.

-Restaurant
-Sagua-
حل بولوتاد للمواد الغذائية

Restaurante

## Nightlife in Smara

Close to the center of Smara, cafés, restaurants, and other shops occupy a side street in the market. In contrast to other areas in the camp, the shops are open in the evening and sometimes even into the night. They are lit by colorful lights and have advertisements powered by electricity from generators. As well as the restaurants and cafés with TVs playing movies or broadcasting football matches, a few video-game shops give off the computer-generated blasts and roars of their arcade games. The youth of the camp hang out here or in the cafés next door. Cars come and go, picking up sandwiches from the Restaurante Bulautad and driving back into the darkness of the camp.

The area might have the atmosphere of a roadside petrol station with facilities attached, and is somewhat limited when compared with any other settlement of approximately 40,000 inhabitants. It is influenced by the refugees' experiences during visits to Spain or other international destinations. Independent of its modesty and simplicity, the simple fact that there is some sort of nightlife and amusement area gives evidence to the normality of urban life within the environment of the camp.

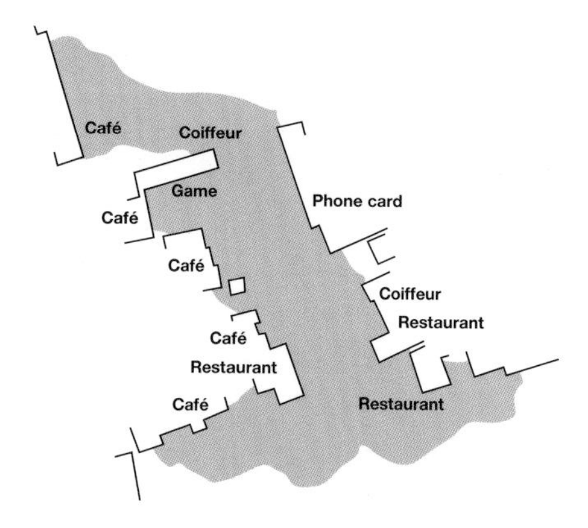

## Restaurante Bulautad

Situated at the entrance to the market and square with the cafés and game shops, the Restaurante Bulautad–named after an area in the south of Western Sahara–enjoys one of the best commercial locations in the camp. It serves cold soft drinks and sandwiches with camel meat or chicken–which maybe stretches its designation as a "restaurant" a little. It predominantly serves as a takeaway, and is as much a testimony to the fact that many Sahrawis absorb Western influences during time abroad as to the fact that Smara is the camp with the largest number of foreign visitors.

The international audience has created a demand in its own right, which is serviced by Restaurante Bulautad and a few neighboring venues. The owners are fluent in English, play Western pop music, and serve items popular with visitors from Europe and America. Such visitors are there to work with one of the NGOs; are journalists; or are involved in the visiting program of Spanish families. It is therefore visible proof of the cultural and economical impact–if only on a relatively small scale–that foreign exchange and networking has had on the refugee camps.

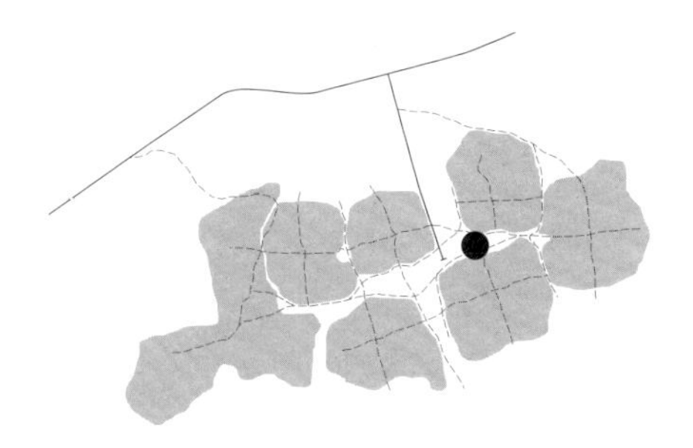

El Aaiún

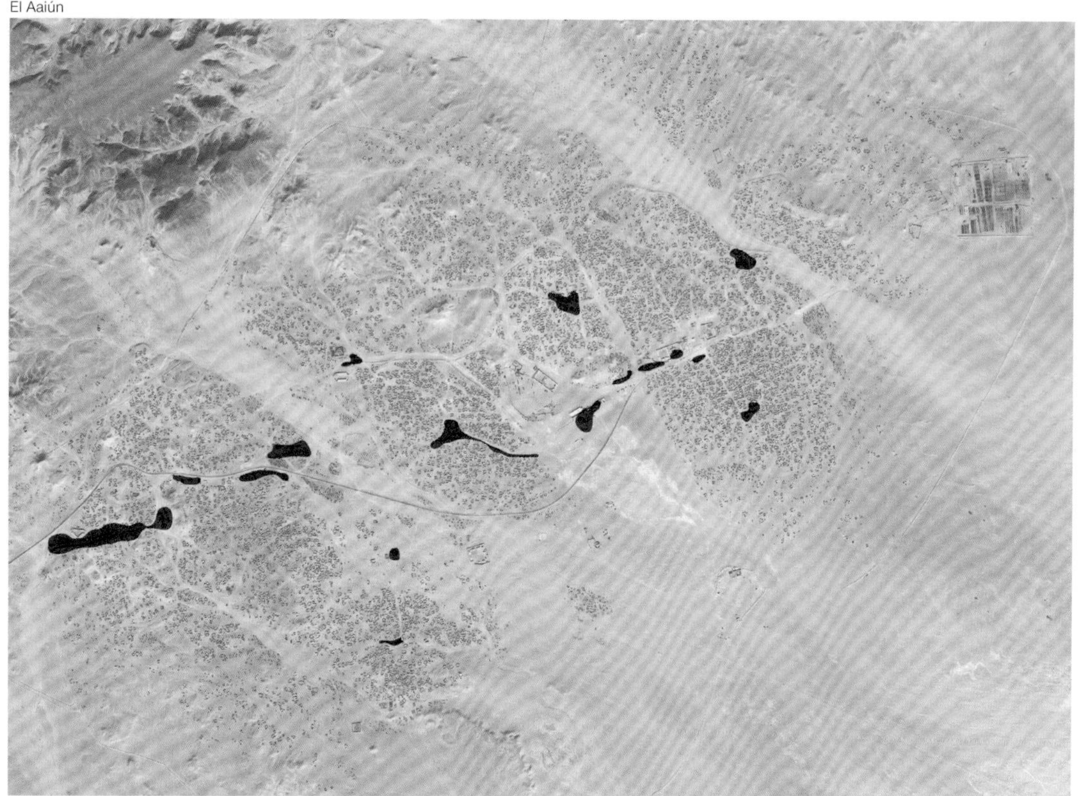

Smara

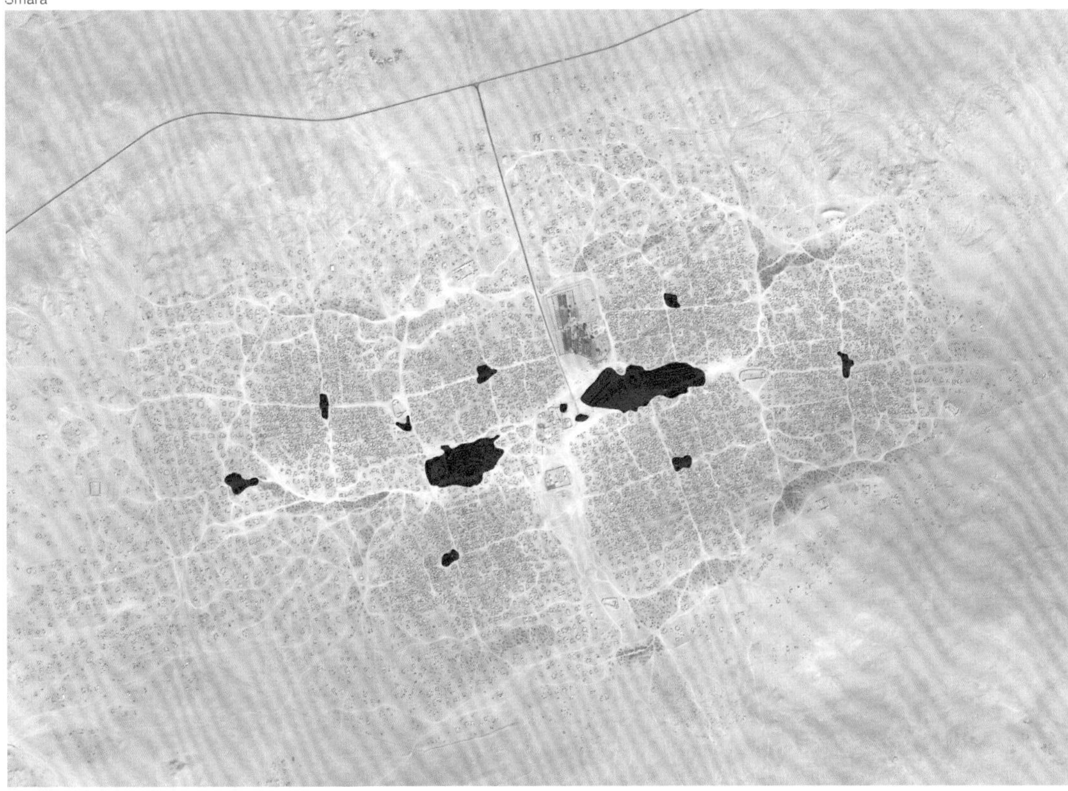

## Public Spaces—How Difference Emerges

Looking at public leisure spaces in the camps of Smara and El Aaiún highlights the key differences between the two camps. In El Aaiún, the centers of the individual daïras take on an important role in the daily lives of the camp's inhabitants. They serve as the spatially concentrated locations for social interaction, shopping, and recreation. The camp's central functions are, on the other hand, spread out over a long linear stretch of land, with the main market located in the far west, cultural institutions in the middle, and administrative services in the east. Maybe counterintuitively, the greater importance of the daïra centers might be connected to the destructive floods that El Aaiún experienced, leading to the relocation of complete daïras. Instead of forming a common center as a reaction to the floods, the development focused more on the entity of the daïra, making these units of the camp more self-sufficient. Based on their respective histories, each center has developed differently. The intimacy of the inhabitants and the tight-knit local network results in a village-like atmosphere, where every daïra is more or less independent of each other.

Smara, on the other hand, is characterized by a strong twofold center, where most public functions, markets, cultural institutions, and areas of recreation are located. The corresponding hubs in the individual daïras offer only the most basic functions and are not used as social meeting points or areas of recreation. The center serves the camp for the daily needs of its population as a whole. It is also the place offering nighttime activities for the younger inhabitants. International visitors meet there, having the market nearby as well as some facilities, though limited, for recreation and for eating and drinking. The center is thus marked by its greater complexity and develops into a place where different groups can meet and interact—a feature we usually connect with urban life.

# Spaces for Sports

One can observe sporting activities taking place everywhere in the camps. It is mostly team sports that are played, such as football or volleyball. For obvious reasons of climate and terrain, endurance sports like running are not popular, nor are sports that require sophisticated or expensive equipment. For the youth especially, sport is an important activity that allows for an active daily life. The kids and adolescents mostly play football, though at school they have to participate in other sports such as gymnastics. In general, sport creates a defined framework for competition. In this context it is also possible to establish social contacts within one's peer group.

Due to the nature of football and its flexibility and simplicity, children can be seen to be engaged in football games everywhere in the camp. It is played on purpose-built football pitches, in the open fields between daïras, or in between houses or small courtyards. Although most plots are not marked, and fences or other types of enclosures are few and far between, football is flexible enough to squeeze itself into almost any kind of space. In the way that it infiltrates the fabric of the settlements, using certain interstitial spaces and disregarding others, football can also be seen as a means of indirectly reading and assessing the spatial dimension of the camps. And it is not just an informal activity, either. Every daïra has its own football team that plays against other daïras in an organized tournament. The overall camp champion then goes on to play against the teams from the other camps. The best players of each camp are also selected for a "national" team. This national team has never played an international match, however, as it is neither member of the international football association (FIFA), nor of its African counterpart, the Confederation of African Football (CAF). Thus, politics enters the field of recreation and sports, just as it affects and shapes all other spheres of camp life.

Two other sports explicitly bring out the extreme, and sometimes absurd-seeming, conditions of the Saharan refugee camps: swimming and marathon running. Probably unique among refugee camps, at least in this part of the world, El Aaiún features a communal swimming pool that was constructed by an NGO in 2003. El Aaiún is located above an underground water source, and the pool is used during the hot summer months, giving welcome refreshment to the children of the camp. The seemingly innocent playfulness of the swimming pool clashes powerfully with the politically charged nature of the camps originating from violent conflict, just as the abundance and seemingly wasteful use of water clashes with the extreme climate of the desert and scarcity of the resource. The marathon, on the other hand, is organized for European runners who come to the refugee camps for a few days in February each year. The runners start in camp El Aaiún and run via Awserd to Smara, over 42 km of desert terrain. The intention is to raise awareness for a forgotten conflict and create images that will be circulated in the global mediascape. In this case, it is maybe the naivete of the European runners, who often come with the intention of "doing good," that clashes with the reality and political gridlock on the ground.

**Central Sports Field in El Aaiún**

In El Aaiún, the central sports field is located just next to the big stage, near the art museum and the Olof Palme School. At 140 m, it is longer than a regular football field (usually 105 × 68 m). The complex also consists of an additional fenced and illuminated hard court and a small service building. A mound of sand separates the football field from the adjoining area. The field markings are indicated by stones, but during official games the goals are equipped with nets.

Dimension of the main field: 140 × 60 m
Dimension of the small field: 50 × 25 m

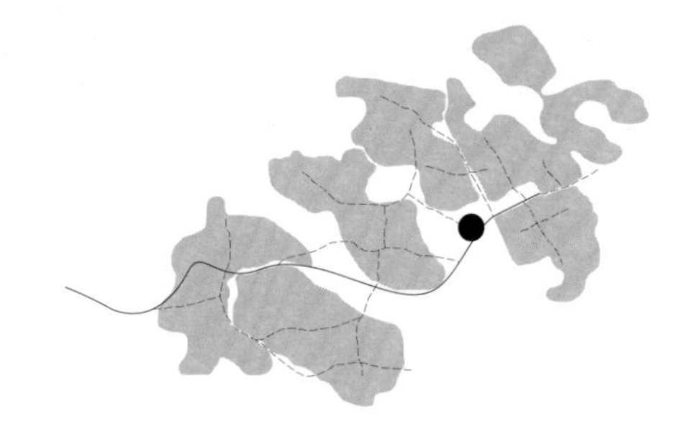

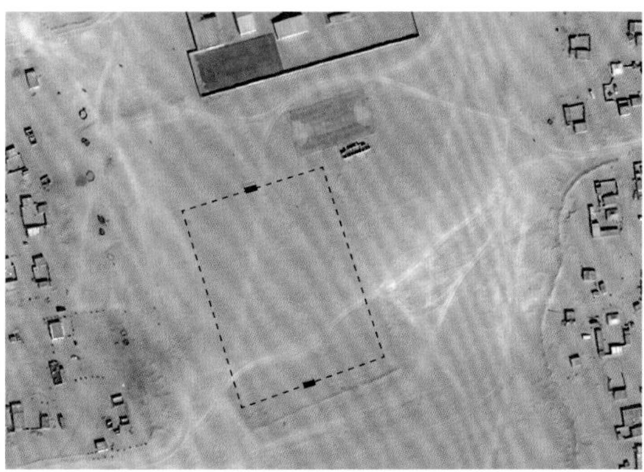

## Football Field in Smara

Smara's central football field is situated in a large open space between the daïras Jederia and Hauza. Because of the absence of boundaries, the road connecting the two daïras leads directly over the football field. The limits of the field are indicated by stones. In the past, a smaller fenced and illuminated pitch existed next to the large football field. This pitch was moved closer to the center of the camp in 2009. The remaining hard surface is still visible in the ground.

Dimension of the field: 130 × 80 m

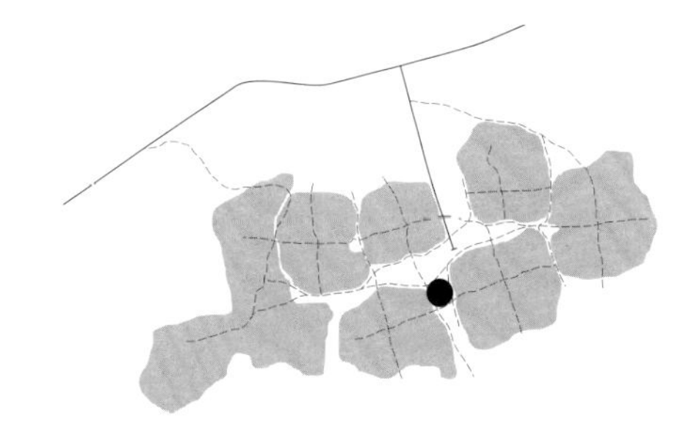

**1**
Permanent
Length: 43 m
Width: 22 m
Goal: wooden poles
Ground: sand

**2**
Temporary
Length: 48 m
Width: 17 m
Goal: stones
Ground: sand

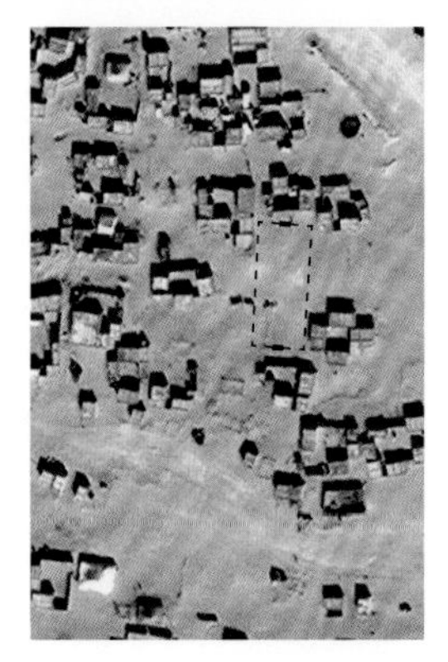

**3**
Temporary
Length: 44 m
Width: 16 m
Goal: shirts
Ground: sand

**Football in Interstitial Spaces**

In their spare time, the Sahrawi boys play football with a passion. Everywhere in the camp, one can meet groups of boys from five to fifteen years old playing football in a multitude of spaces. The fields exist in all variations, from permanent to temporary, some with proper goals and others with more spontaneous pitches defined by T-shirts in between houses or daïras. On one hand, the omnipresence of football and the kind of spaces sought by the children appears to mirror the pattern of other cities worldwide. Children act as "urban pioneers," seeking out locations in cities and villages that lend themselves to alternative use. On the other hand, the omnipresence of football points to two related phenomena that distinguish the Sahrawi camps. It is an indicator of the relative low population density and the fact that land doesn't have the status of property, as it isn't owned by anyone. Football can insert itself into multiple places within the camps because the huts and tents are located at such a distance from one another, and because abandoned plots often remain uninhabited. The absence of land ownership means that many vacated plots are not reused, as the ground constitutes no economic value. It also means that its usage by others (in this case, the kids playing football) is not controlled. The children might be chased away because their noise is disturbing to the families living close by, but not because of the unauthorized use of someone else's property.

**4**
Permanent

| | |
|---|---|
| Length: | 40 m |
| Width: | 33 m |
| Goal: | tires |
| Ground: | sand |

**5**
Permanent

| | |
|---|---|
| Length: | 100 m |
| Width: | 50 m |
| Goal: | metal frame |
| Ground: | sand |

**6**
Temporary

| | |
|---|---|
| Length: | 54 m |
| Width: | 18 m |
| Goal: | shirts |
| Ground: | sand |

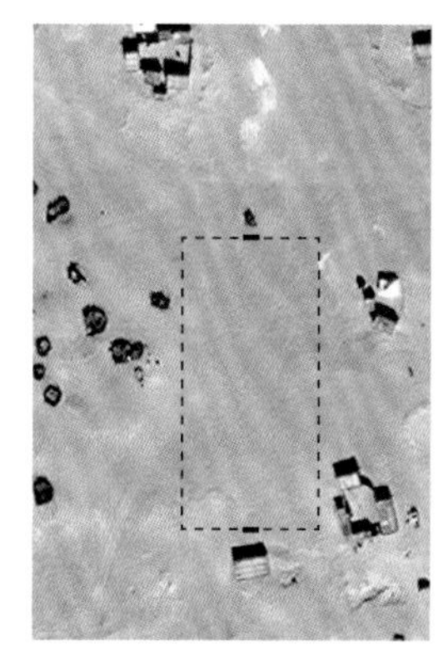

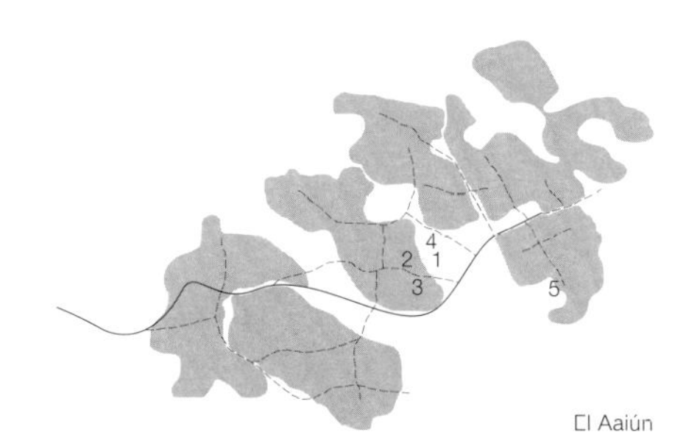


El Aaiún

Smara

F.S.F.
R.A.S.D.

## The National Football Team That Has Never Played

No sport is practiced more in the camps than football. It has become something akin to a national sport. On average, the technical skill of the players is high, especially when considering the poor equipment they struggle with (many do not have sports shoes, let alone special football boots) and the lack of practice. Given the nature of the environment, games mostly take place on sand, but smaller pitches are available with hard concrete surfaces. Every daïra has its own team that competes against the other daïras in a championship. A selection of the camp's best players form teams that play each other in a "national league." Finally, the best players are selected into the Sahrawi football team—the only national football team that has never competed in an international tournament. The FSF (Fédération Sahraoui du Foot Balle) is not a member of FIFA, nor of the CAF (the Confederation of African Football). Lacking these memberships, the team has been unable to play in international competitions, aside from occasional friendly games against Algerian teams. The formation of a national team is testimony to the national aspirations of the Sahrawi people. It is an attempt to fulfill the elements that constitute a modern nation-state.

**Polysportive Center, Smara**

The center has a playing field of 18 × 28 m, while a larger building provides space for table tennis, offices, and meeting rooms. The center organizes the sporting activities for Smara, and also the other camps. In addition to the Sahrawi football league, where the daïras of the camps play each other, it also organizes the bike race through the desert to Tifariti and the Sahara Marathon from El Aaiún to Smara. While only football is played in El Aaiún, young men in Smara meet in the evening to play basketball or volleyball at the polysportive center. In the other camps, sports are mostly done by younger children, while in Smara the adults are more active in sporting activities, not just restricted to football.

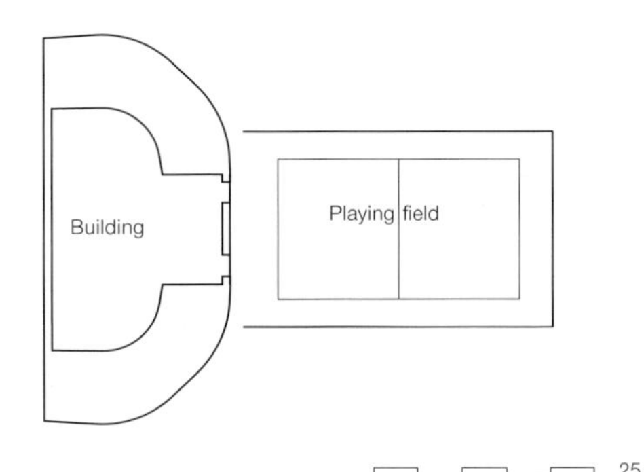

### A Humanitarian Marathon

By chance, the distance between the camps of El Aaiún and Smara via Awserd is a little over 42 km, the precise length of a marathon run. Since 2001 a humanitarian marathon has been organized by a joint European group, consisting of Spanish, Italian, British, and German organizations, in collaboration with UNHCR. Every year in late February, approximately 400 runners from a variety of European countries travel to the Sahrawi camps to participate in four different races: the full marathon, half marathon, 10 km, or the 5 km race. The event is meant to educate and inform the participating Europeans about the situation of the Sahrawi people, and, more importantly, create awareness in the general population of Europe through media reports on the event. The participating runners also contribute money that is used for upgrade projects, such as the renovation of schools.

The marathon is another illustration of the inherent dilemma of the Sahrawi refugees: 400 sweaty Europeans hoping to do something "good" while pursuing a sport of stamina and perseverance, raising awareness for a noble issue, and improving the local situation. The biggest beneficiary, however, is probably Air Algerie, which flies the runners to Tindouf. On the other hand, it is exactly these visits and exchanges that allow the Sahrawi people to connect with the world at large and make their cause known.

**A Refugee Camp Swimming Pool**
Standing in the central part of El Aaiún, one can observe a mysterious-looking building. Approaching the structure, one can be mistaken for thinking it is some sort of defense facility, a bomb shelter, or maybe even a prison. Walking around the windowless structure, one comes to a locked metal door–its only access. Glancing over the entrance, one then looks into what is most likely the world's only refugee camp swimming pool, and maybe also the only one in the middle of the Sahara. The swimming pool was built by a Spanish NGO in 2003 and is open during the hot summer months, from mid-April to mid-September. It is filled with the water obtained from the aquifer located beneath the camp. Restricted by severely limited resources, yet symbolizing luxury and exuberance, the swimming pool epitomizes the bizarre nature of life in the camps.

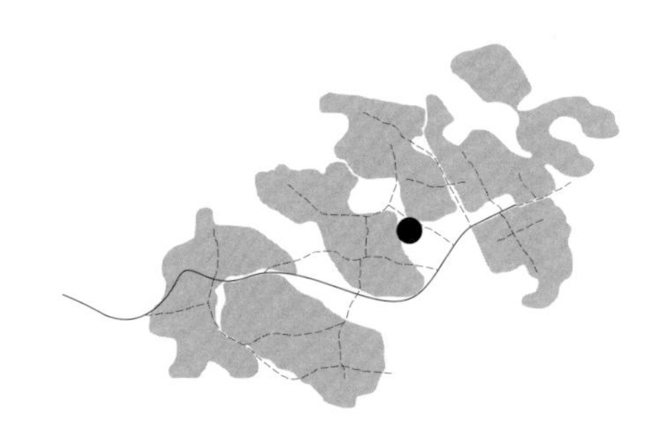

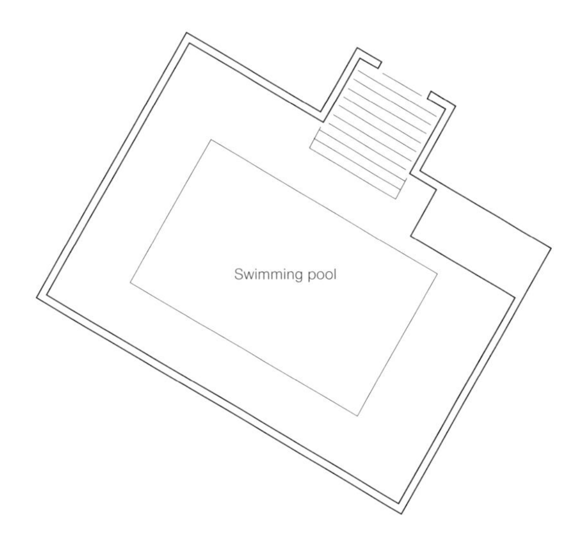


5 m

## Sport as a Litmus Test

Of all recreational activities, sport seems to be the most "innocent" of all—benign games played mostly by children. The sports are shared by most cultures and nations, thus supposedly showing the commonality and similarity of people around the globe. Beyond this positivistic and naive conception of sport, we can use the activity to reveal underlying processes or characteristics active in the Sahrawi camps. On a most literal level, sports are not innocent, but are inscribed within the Sahrawi project of a nation-state, with the Sahrawi national football team being an important symbolic element in the construction of the nation. Its symbolic value is more important than the potential benefit of the actual games, in that it does not matter whether the team actually gets to play or not. On a spatial level, we can use sporting activities as an "interpreter" or reading device for the spaces existing in the camps. The choice of places football is played and the overall abundance of those spaces points to the way that space is negotiated within the camps and to the economical and practical value of space in an environment that is, uniquely, not endowed with a monetary value.

# Gardens

Similar to the other camps, the region of El Aaiún is arid, with one of the most unforgiving climates in the world. In the winter, the temperature drops below zero degrees Celsius, while during summer it easily reaches forty-five degrees in the shade, and considerably higher in the sun. The ground varies between coarse sand and dusty gravel. This dry and barren soil produces no life, and one can walk for miles without passing so much as a blade of grass. Nevertheless, in almost uncanny proximity, just one or two meters underneath this parched landscape lies a huge water reservoir. Accessing it is relatively easy: an hour of digging with a shovel creates a well deep enough to reveal the water below. This reservoir is the water source for the inhabitants of the camps El Aaiún as well as Awserd, where it is transported by truck. The contrast between the scorched terrain overground and the profusion of water underground could hardly be more striking and unsettling.

Apart from being used for drinking and washing by the camps' inhabitants, the water has also been used to set up several gardening projects in El Aaiún. These range from individual trees within the fabric of the camp, to small family gardens that provide vegetables for private consumption, to a park-like arrangement of public greenery in the central area of the camp, to a large market garden at the eastern edge contributing to the food provision for the camp as a whole. In spite of the profusion and proximity of water, setting up gardens in the camp is a difficult and often frustrating endeavor. The sandy, rocky soil carries few nutrients and is overly salty. Plant growth remains weak, with many species not developing at all, while the produce of the plants that do grow is often small and meager. The extreme heat of the summer months burns many of the plants and trees, and intense maintenance—as well as green fingers—is required to keep the vegetation alive. The existing gardens tell a story of the sometimes successful, sometimes futile attempts to bring greenery into the camp. In most cases the gardens are set up as spaces for producing food rather than spaces of recreation. Nevertheless, they hold the potential to be used as spaces of leisure, offering shade, smells, and the sounds of the chirping of birds, which are available nowhere else in the camp. Whether these green spaces are indeed utilized as spaces of leisure and recreation will be discovered on the following pages.

Irrigation system

Wells

**Traditional Garden**
When entering the traditional garden, one is transported into another place. Compared with the dusty and sandy world outside the walls, the plants and palm trees produce a unique atmosphere. The garden was initially planted eighteen years ago, and the owner's family has cultivated it ever since. The irrigation system is traditional, with ditches watering the vegetable beds. The garden is enclosed by a head-high wall of clay bricks. The residential spaces of the family compound are constructed within the enclosure and face the garden.

| | |
|---|---|
| Dimensions: | 70 × 30 m |
| Crops: | dates |
| | tomatoes |
| | onions |
| | corn |
| | beets |
| | turnips |
| | cabbage |
| | herbs |
| | peppermint |

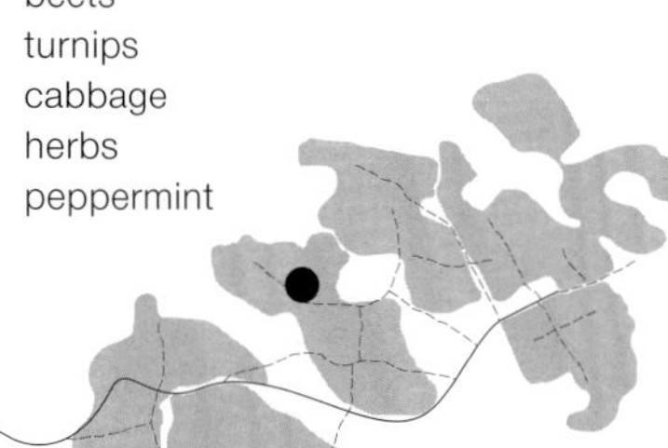

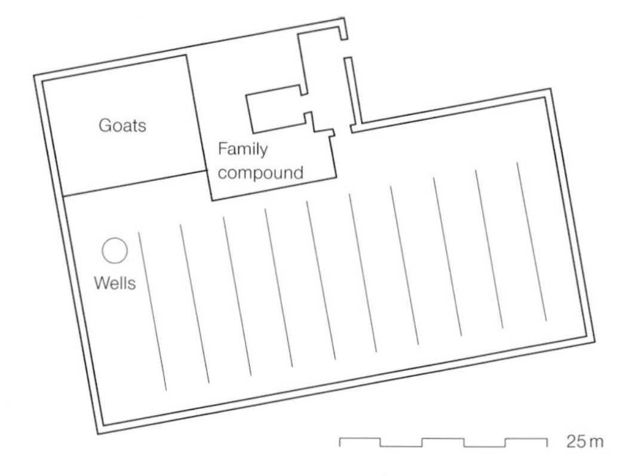


25 m

## New Garden

Recent gardens are more simple and do not create the spatial quality experienced in the traditional garden. Instead of elaborate irrigation with ditches, the plants are watered with plastic pipes that are laid out between the vegetable beds. Water is obtained with an electric pump from self-dug wells. The gardens are smaller, and gardening is more like a hobby for the families. They are happy when anything at all is growing–even if it is only a weed.

Dimensions: 8 × 8 m
Crops: lettuce
tomatoes
beets
onions
turnips
cabbage
carrots
cilantro

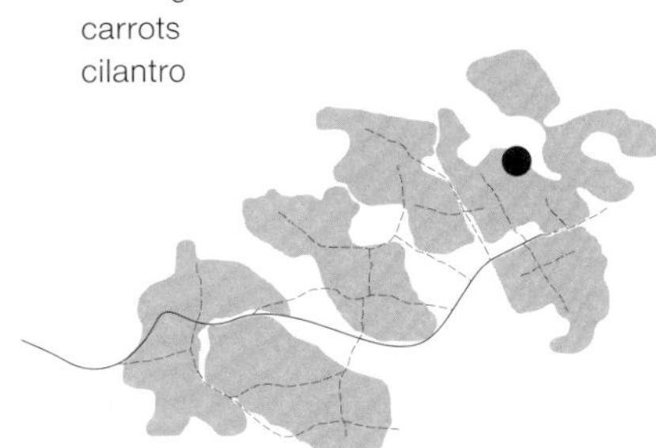

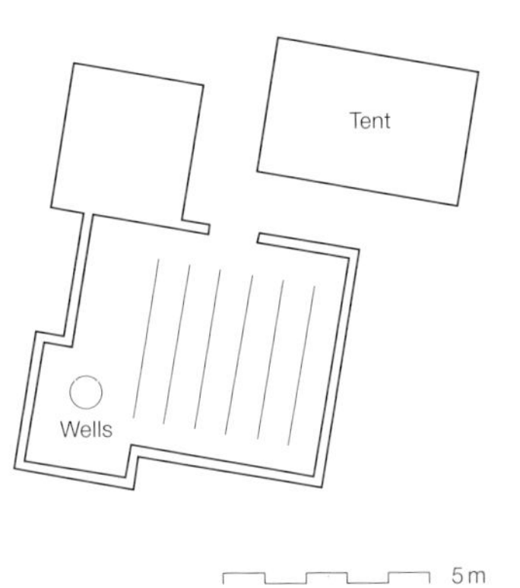

## Small Family Gardens

The small family gardens, usually around 20 to 30 m², are supported by the administration of the camp with funding from NGOs. They often contain a simple greenhouse for growing tomatoes. With these gardens, the administration aims to establish a culture of gardening. Because of a lack of gardening knowledge and poor, salty soil, the crops are often of low quality.

| | |
|---|---|
| Dimensions: | 6 × 5 m |
| Crops: | tomatoes |
| | onions |
| | herbs |
| | turnips |
| | cabbage |

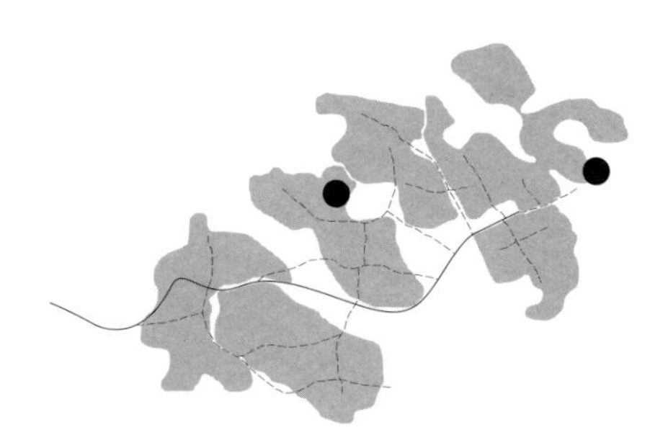

5 m

## The Gardener's Private Garden

A few hundred meters from the houses of the camp stands an isolated residential compound: the house of the gardener. Here, in the desert, the gardener of the El Aaiún market garden has created a real work of love–his own private garden. Surrounded by sand and fed by a self-dug well, he grows vegetables, beets, and herbs in abundance. Standing in the garden, one can suddenly smell nature.

| | |
|---|---|
| Dimensions: | 70 × 40 m |
| Crops: | chard |
| | lettuce |
| | melons |
| | onions |
| | beets |
| | turnips |
| | cabbage |
| | herbs |

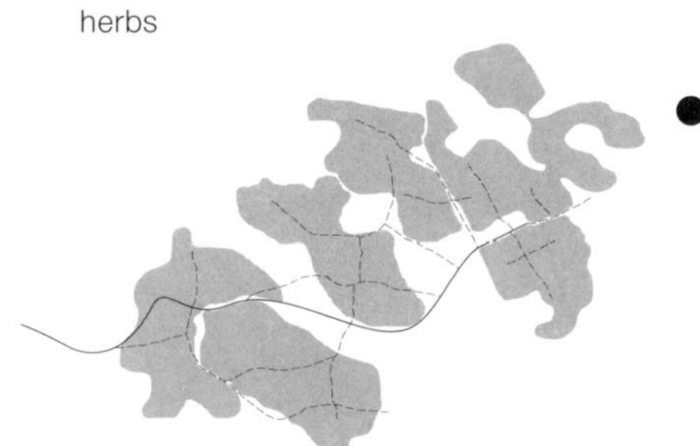

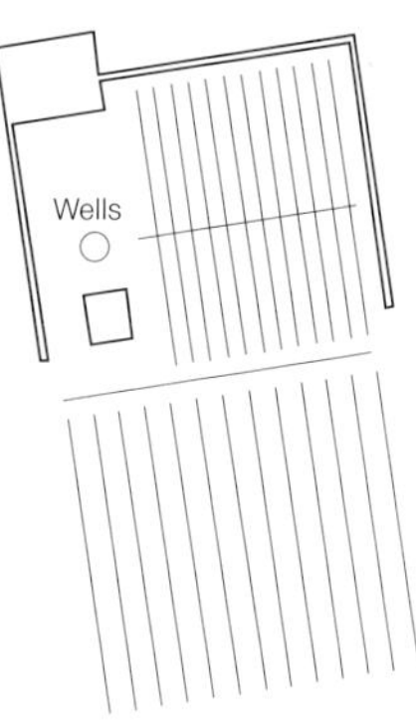


25 m

## Making the Desert Bloom

To the foreign visitor, the gardens seem impressive. But, in conversation, the gardeners often note that the work is connected with hardship and patience. The soil is poor and salty, and the climate extreme because of the excessive wind and heat. It takes patience and knowledge to achieve even meager results. However, working with one's hands, the visual effect of seeing things grow and the pleasure of harvesting and eating their own produce gives satisfaction to the families. In the Arab world the color green is also the color of hope. The work in the gardens is therefore bound up with learning and enhancing knowledge for a future in the homeland.
In the common imagination, the homeland is a fertile territory with a favorable climate. In this sense, gardening is a political symbol. Even though the establishment of a garden might seem like move towards settling down permanently, the work is connected to the common idea of returning home and as a preparation for a self-sufficient life there.

**Market Garden, El Aaiún**
Beyond the eastern edge of the camp, the market garden stretches over an area of 168 hectares. The garden was founded ten years ago, and the area is divided into three organizational units. Water is pumped from a well outside the garden and distributed via tubes. One of the three units has a separate pump. Tomatoes grow in greenhouses, giving the plants a hot and humid microclimate. Onions, beets, beans, and cereals are planted in the open fields. A few trees and reed-like plants protect the crops from sun and wind. Approximately half of the total area is unplanted. One of the biggest problems is the salty and poor soil, which lacks nutrients.

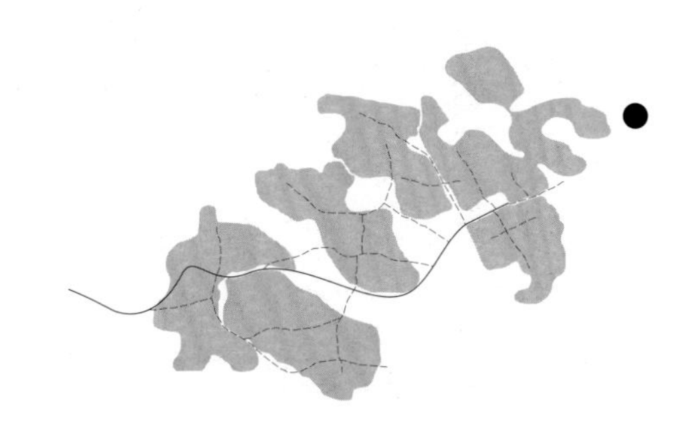

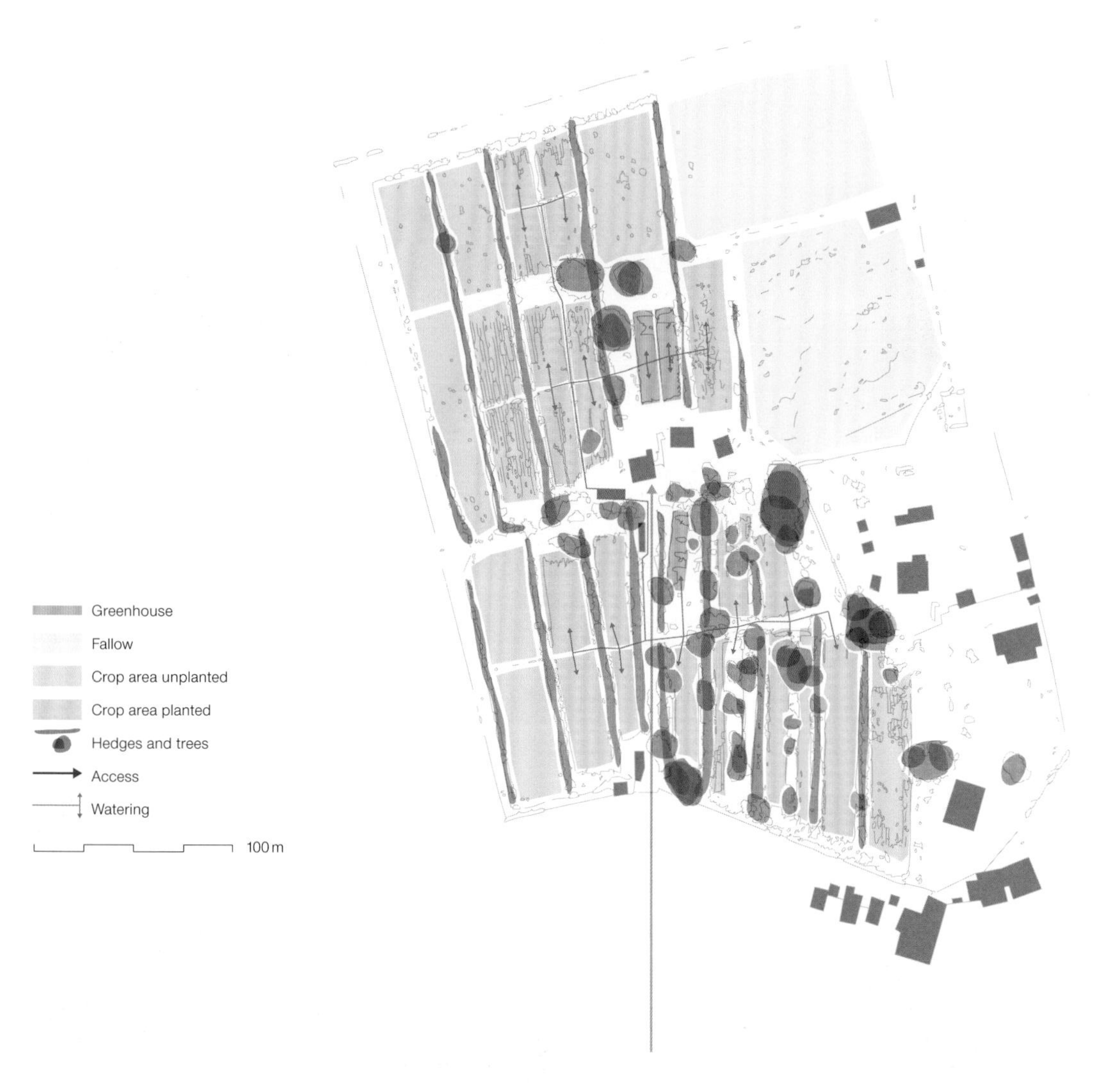


## Market Garden, Smara

Located directly next to Smara's main access road, the market garden extends over an area of 75 hectares. The garden has developed since the 1980s to a size that today employs fifteen to thirty part-time gardeners. Because there are no wells in Smara, the water for irrigation must be brought in by truck. In addition to tomatoes in the greenhouses, the main crops are onions and lettuce. The large trees create shade in the center, attracting birds that can be heard twittering in the branches. Even though it is located close to the center of the camp and could be conceived as a place of relaxation, the garden is not used for lingering or strolling by the inhabitants.

**The Failed Promise of a Central Park**

Next to the swimming pool, central sport field, and large stage in the middle of El Aaiún, some palm trees stand in the dusty sand. A closer look reveals the decaying leftovers of an irrigation system made of cement drainage channels. This is the site of a former planted garden. Satellite images from 2003 show areas of greenery with planted gardens and palm trees giving shade to vegetable beds. The present-day satellite image shows only sand, with a few palm trees remaining. The planted garden was the attempt to establish a kind of "central park" that could have been used not only for harvesting produce, but also for the enjoyment and recreation of the inhabitants. The salinity of the sand, however, prevented the garden from growing. Today the few remaining palm trees and crumbling fragments of the irrigation system remain as evidence of this urbanistic plan. With the exception of a few kids lingering in the shade of the trees, no one visits it.

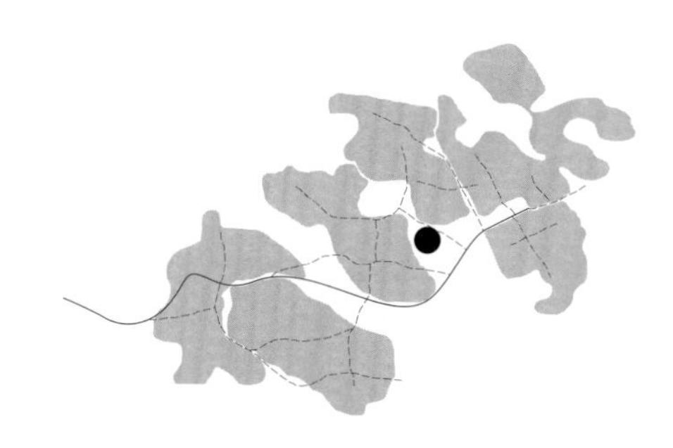

2003

© 2012 Google; © 2012 DigitalGlobe

2004

© 2012 Google; © 2012 DigitalGlobe

## Lingering in a Garden Must Be Learned

An obvious function of gardens on the camps is the production of food. They are meant to deliver produce and make the Sahrawi refugees more self-sufficient, reducing their dependency on humanitarian aid and imported food. Coincidentally or not, the gardens also often offer a relatively high spatial quality. The shadows of the trees create a more amicable climate, and the gardens are the only places birds can be heard and the different smells of plants can be perceived, in contrast to the otherwise ever-present smell of dust and sand. Although hard to understand from a Western point of view, such places are hardly ever used for lingering or recreation. It would be so easy to pack up a teapot and roll out a blanket beneath the shade of a beautiful tree, but this happens only very rarely. If the time in the refugee camps can be understood as a period of learning, the quality of leisure and the social potential of a family garden could be one of the elements of this learning.

Tindouf, Algeria

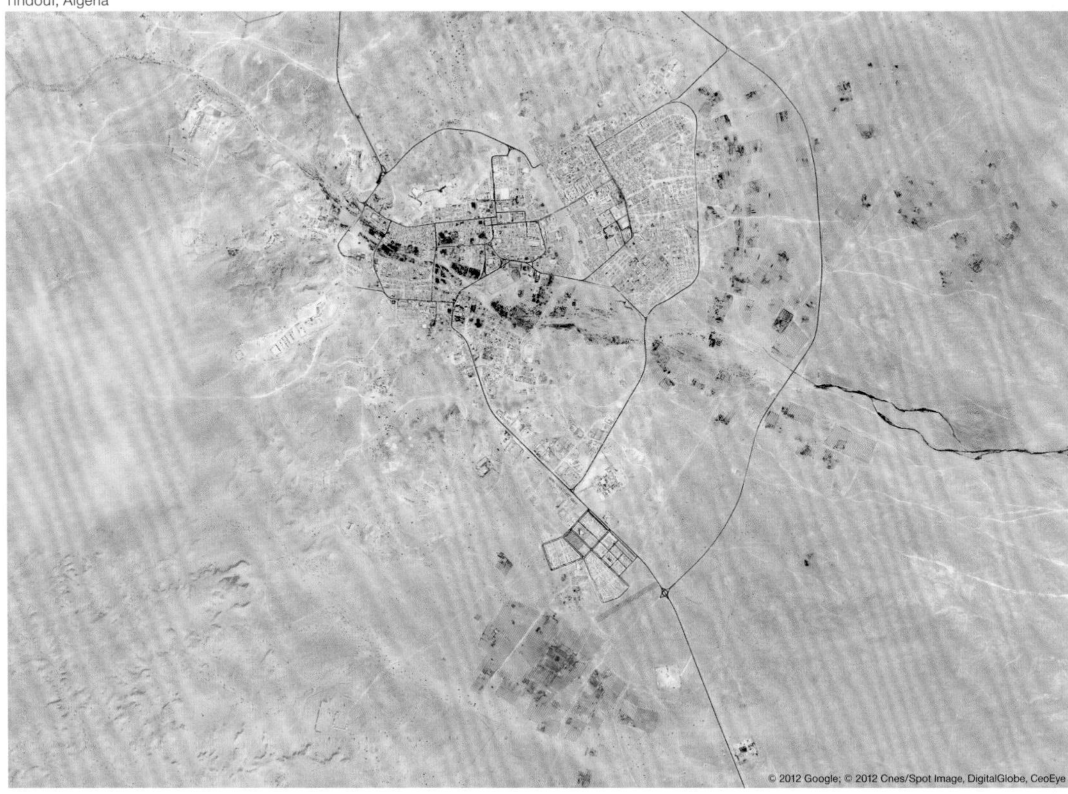


**Gardens in the Desert**

Gardens are an important part of any city, and one would assume that in desert cities they obtain an even more central role, by providing shade, affecting the microclimate, being a source of food, and enhancing the general quality of life. Other cities in the region show how strongly local conditions influence the way a population deals with nature in an urban context.

The Algerian cities of Tindouf and Adrar, and to a lesser extent Smara in the Western Sahara, are oasis cities with sources of fresh water. And, indeed, these cities feature urban gardens and parks in addition to agricultural areas. Nature is understood as not just utilitarian, but something that also lends itself to the quality and pleasures of life. What often seems to be missing, however, are small courtyard gardens or little pocket parks that bring nature to a domestic or private setting.

Without a local source of water, the camp Awserd features no gardens whatsoever and hardly has a single palm tree in the whole area. This is testimony to the huge–sometimes impossibly huge–effort necessary to keep nature in bloom.

Adrar, Algeria

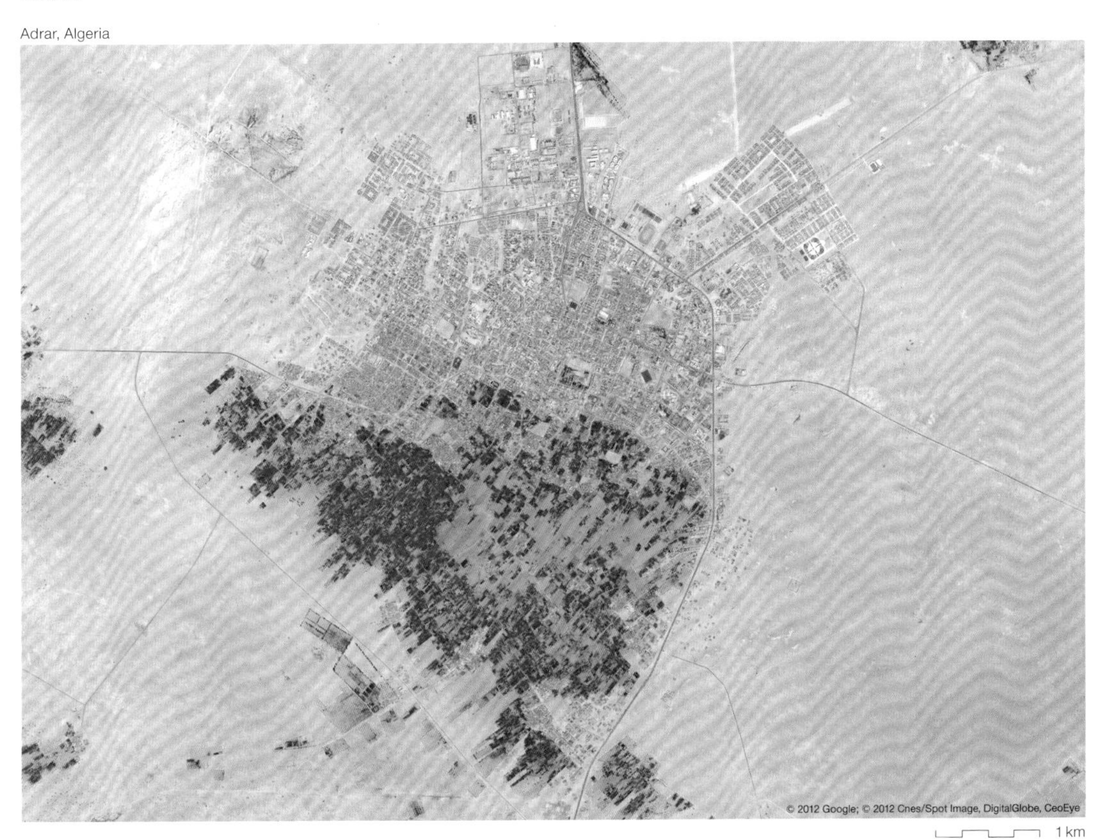


Smara, Western Sahara

# The Significance of Recreation

Activities of recreation and leisure are hardly ever considered in the discourse on refugee camps. UNHCR, in its 600-page *Handbook for Emergencies*—the central planning guide for dealing with refugee cases, makes no mention of recreational activities. When assessing the needs of refugees, it focuses exclusively on requirements of water, food, and health-related services, at times also taking education into consideration. Refugees are not considered to be in need of leisure activities, aspects that, after all, have a fundamental impact on the quality of life. The gravity of the refugee condition, often triggered by war or internal conflict, and accompanied by suffering, loss of life, and severely limited resources, means that the highest priority is given to keeping people physically alive. Thoughts of recreation and leisure are taken to be trivial or frivolous, if not even immoral. In that sense, refugees are reduced to recipients of aid, and to purely physical and biological notions of life (or to "bare life," as Giorgio Agamben would say) instead of being seen as social beings. Given the fact that refugee camps often exist for far longer periods than originally envisaged, the view of refugees as biological beings with few social needs seems like a significant misrepresentation of the human condition.

In the Sahrawi refugee camps, we can observe a wide range of leisure activities taking place, and the corresponding spaces shaped by them. Contrary to the above view, activities of recreation abound and are a central feature of the camps. We can see this in the private spaces of the refugees' homes with their purpose-built rooms for the tea ceremony, as well as in the galleries and theater stages, on the sports fields, and even the "nightlife area" of Smara. As frivolous as they might be, these spaces perform a crucial function in enabling social exchange, offering moments and spaces for debate, enjoyment or grief, and introducing a notion of the "everyday" to this condition of exception.

Similar to the commercial activities covered in one of the preceding chapters, we can use the activities of leisure and recreation as indicators of how space is utilized differently in the individual camps. This difference can be shaped by environmental factors, such as the availability of the water reservoir beneath El Aaiún manifesting itself in the presence of small gardens and trees throughout the camp, while hardly existing in Smara (with the exception of the central market garden). Looking at other communal areas, such as social meeting spaces around the daïra centers or the use of sport facilities, we see how each camp has developed a different approach based on the patterns of its inhabitants' social engagement.

Smara exposes a centralized structure where the main markets, the football and volleyball courts, and the central nightlife area become the focal point of recreational activities. El Aaiún, on the other hand, emphasizes the daïra centers, which become the attractors for social life, with the central cultural and sport facilities being used less intensely. Social exchange in El Aaiún could thus be described as being based on the local and personal relationships of the individual daïras, while in Smara this exchange takes place across the camp as a whole, bringing into contact residents not only from the immediate surroundings, but also from further afield. Looking at the activities of recreation and leisure reveals a mode of interchange in Smara that could even be described as "urban." Beyond this specific assessment, what is interesting is that it is specifically the activity which is largely ignored in refugee discourse that allows for this analysis in the first place. Maybe it is precisely the self-organized nature of these types of activity, often occurring spontaneously and arising out of a particular approach or condition, that lets these specificities and differences emerge.

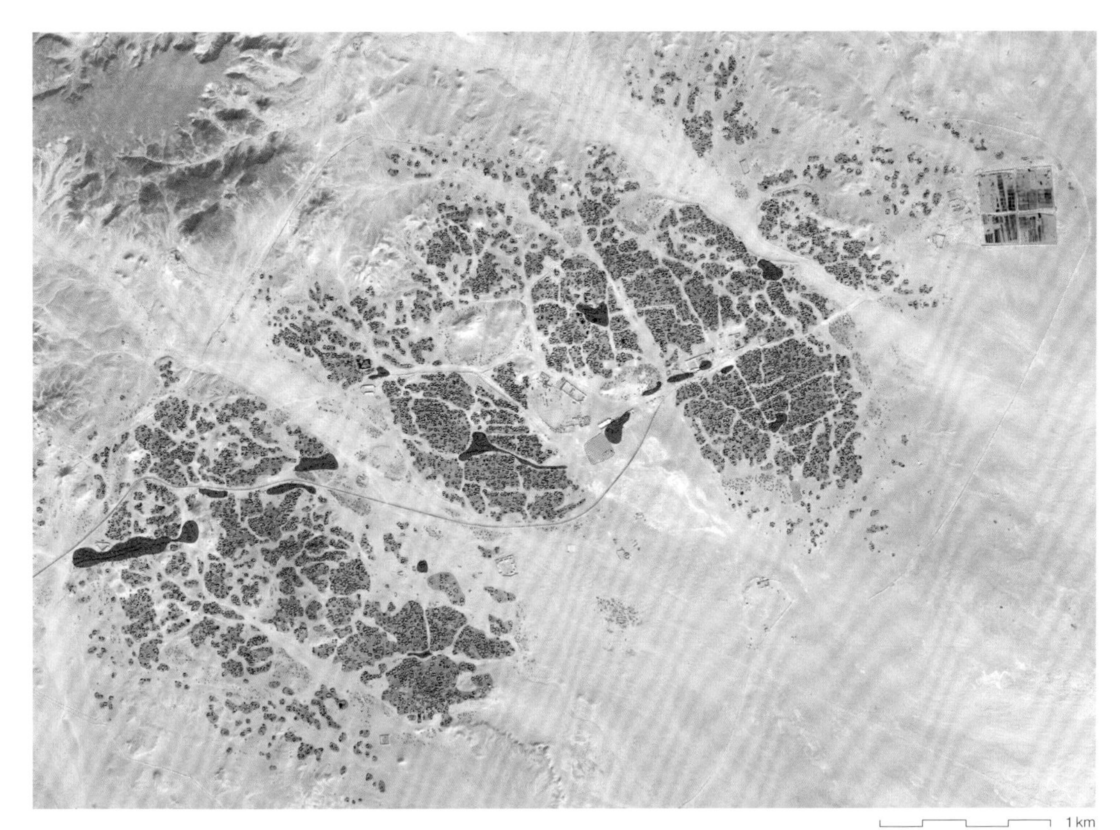

1 km

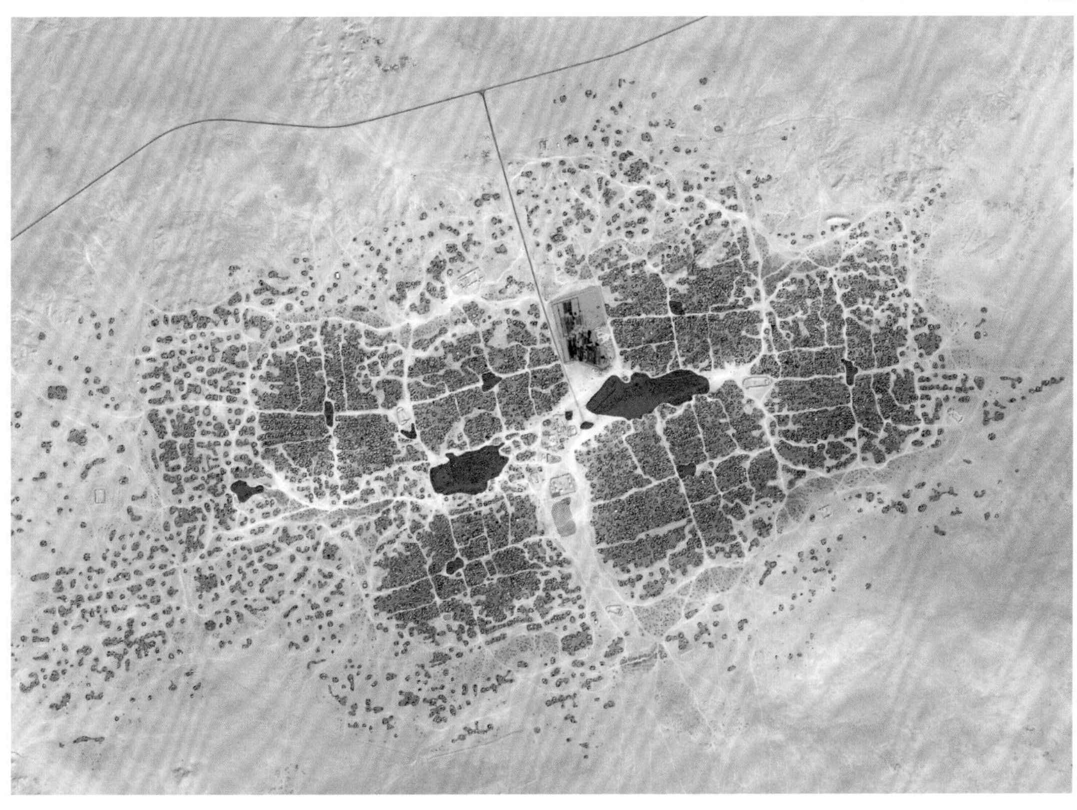

Activities of recreation and leisure perform an important communal function within the camps and allow for the development of a cohesive social network. Looking at the paintings exhibited in the small galleries or watching a play performed by children, we can see how these cultural and recreational activities not only touch upon the social, but also upon the political dimension of life as a refugee. Beyond their artistic value, every work of art, play, or song performed carries a political message. The work is never innocent. It is inscribed with a political agenda and a national narrative claiming the right to the homeland and demanding a return. Even the tea ceremony—consciously altered after the expulsion from their homeland to mark their individuality and cultural difference from the Moroccans—carries a political message. Sports cannot escape these implications either.

Setting up a national football team is not just the logical conclusion of enthusiasm for the sport and a mirroring of the spatial and organizational structure of the camps and their respective administrative units. Assembling a national team encompasses the same claim for international recognition as a proper nation and the rightful bearers of the Western Sahara territory. The fact that this national team has never played an international match is a reminder that the conflict remains unsolved. Kicking a ball as part of the national team thus becomes something akin to making a political statement and an assertion of sovereignty.

VENTA
2009
LA RELIGIO

# URBAN LABORATORIES

# From Camp to City

## On Public and Private

The inscription above the entrance gate to the administrative building in Rabouni, which manages all health issues in the camps, reads, "Ministerio de Salud Publica," or, Ministry of Public Health. Being aware of the fact that "public health" is an established scientific and technical term with its own specific meaning, the use of the word "public" in the context of refugee camps is nevertheless striking. What are the implications of using the word in relationship to the camps? What or who constitutes the public that is referenced thereby? What rights, common agenda, or shared identity does this public possess? Who protects and guarantees this public? Thus, the use of the word allows us to ask if a notion of the public, or, by extension, the notion of public space can exist at all in the camps.

Public and private are categories that can normally only be conceived of in relationship to a state. Ideally speaking, the state takes care of public space and public property, while guaranteeing its population a right to own private property (and in most cases also private space), safeguarding the entitlements and rights, as well as the responsibilities and duties that come with private property. Furthermore, the notion of the public can only be thought of in connection to a state, as the state defines citizenship, and hence the rights of access and usage of public space and property.

In the case of refugee camps, the question of the state is thoroughly problematic. Having fled their homeland and crossed a national border, the refugees' nation of origin cannot (and is not willing to) guarantee the rights of private ownership, nor provide and cater for public property in the camps, as these are located in another country. The refugees have, in most cases, fled from their home country, as it could not afford them protection in the first place. The hosting nation, on the other hand, accepts the refugees only temporarily and, with few exceptions, does not grant them civil rights. Refugees are not allowed to own real estate, nor does the hosting nation bestow the spaces of the camps with rights that are usually connected with public spaces, such as the right of assembly, of free expression, or political agency. Thus the hosting nation grants refugees temporary shelter and protection from threat, but does not grant them the rights that their own civilian population enjoys. Also, humanitarian organizations such as UNHCR or NGOs, being nonstate actors, cannot guarantee the rights of refugees, as a state could. Hence, in absence of the home country and with the hosting nation unwilling to grant civil rights, we can say that the categories of public and private do not apply in refugee camps.

Ministry of Public Health in Rabouni

Entrance gate to the ministry

In the case of the Sahrawi refugee camps, however, the situation is different. The Sahrawis founded their own state, the SADR, in February 1976. Not being able to reign over its own territory of the Western Sahara, the state institutions of the SADR govern the daily lives of the refugees in the camps. Having been granted a far-reaching autonomy by Algeria, the Sahrawis were able to set up national ministries and other institutions that control aspects such as foreign affairs, economy, health, education, and even defense. The Sahrawis, through political representation, are able to formulate their own laws, as well as to implement and enforce them. This ability to formulate laws and control their enforcement within the territory of the refugee camps makes permissible the use of the categories of the private (guaranteeing the safeguarding of private property with its privileges and responsibilities) and the public (providing public services and property by and for the inhabitants). The Sahrawi refugee camps are therefore probably the only camps worldwide where the concepts of public and private exist. On the level of everyday life, this results in processes and activities of participation and representation.

## The City Versus the Camp

When we think of the idea of a city, we like to think of qualities such as heterogeneity, openness, and empowerment. In our modern world, cities are places where enough knowledge, capital, and infrastructure come together to allow for creativity and a richness of daily experience. These are some of the notions that thinkers in the field of urbanism have developed to describe our understanding of the city. In his seminal essay *Die Großtadt und das Geistesleben (The Metropolis and Mental Life)* in 1903, the German sociologist Georg Simmel writes about the intensity of impressions that influence the inhabitants of cities, which lead to a specific "intellectual character" of urban residents. Along the same lines, in his essay *Urbanism as a Way of Life,* written in 1938, the American sociologist Louis Wirth dismisses the conventional quantitative factors that are used to define a city, such as size, number of inhabitants, or population density, and proposes a specific way of life that can be characterized as being urban. It is a life based on the abundance and multiplicities of exchanges, meetings, and connections between people that do not rely on personal acquaintance and that end up allowing for social, economic, and cultural mobility. Thus, even if at that time the city is pictured against a perceived threat of uncontrollable industrialization and capitalism, as well as the unfavorable aspects of anonymity and superficiality that characterize the exchange of people in an urban context, it is also seen as a place of potential and fulfillment, where people can be in control of their own lives.

Camps, on the other hand, are seen as the exact antithesis of cities. Camps are described as places of exclusion and complete control. They are places where, governed by others, a homogenous group of people have no command over their own lives. Camps are not about empowerment and exchange, but about dependency and limitation.

Much of the academic, as well as the technical, literature pertaining to camps focuses on this aspect of control and dependency. Giorgio Agamben sees camps as being the spatial manifestation of a state of exception that has become permanent. The state of exception—i.e. the moment when normal rules of governance are suspended and measures of direct, and mostly totalitarian, control are enforced, limiting the mobility of people, their rights of expression, and their overall ability to make decisions regarding their own lives—according to Agamben finds its spatial counterpart in the camp. Refugees caught behind barbed wire, waiting in miserable conditions for years on end for a chance to return that is unlikely to come, seem to be the visible evidence of this powerlessness and absolute control by others.

View over daïra Hagunia in El Aaiún

Football game in El Aaiún

In more profane language, a multitude of scholarly and technical literature analyzes the camp as a site of danger and risk (Sarah Kenyon Lischer, *Dangerous Sanctuaries*), as a place where aid is seen as being hazardous (Mary B. Anderson, *Do No Harm: How Aid Can Support Peace—or War*) and where refugees are caught in an endless circle of waiting (Gil Loescher et al., *Protracted Refugee Situations*). We need to ask, though, whether this simple relationship of diametrical opposites—the city as a place of openness and potential, and the camp as a site of absolute control—needs to be rethought. If we take the starting point and the prevalent view of the relationship between city and camp as one of antithesis (with certain other typologies of settlements like gated communities occupying an intermediate place along the spectrum that is opened by the two paradigms), one can approach this questioning from two ends. Is the city really a place of openness? And can the camp only be seen as a site of dependency? This book is not the place to reassess the concept of the urban. Much has been written by academics and practitioners describing qualities of contemporary urbanity and "its way of life" in view of, and under the influence of, globalization, so I will not even attempt to add to this comprehensive and often insightful body of work. Nevertheless, and precisely because this large volume of urban thinking exists, it seems valid to bring other voices into the debate.

It is Michel Foucault (maybe not surprisingly) who shows us that the history of the city cannot be divorced from the notion of control. In his 1977–1978 lecture series at the College de France, published as *Security, Territory, Population,* Foucault describes a series of towns from the late Middle Ages to industrialization and their relationship to sovereignty, discipline, and security. Each town represents a specific generation of urbanism. While the town of the Middles Ages is characterized by a clear separation between the urban space within the city walls and the rural (mostly uncontrolled and wild) space beyond its walls, the town of the sixteenth and seventeenth centuries had to incorporate techniques of control to this countryside. It therefore had to open up the walls. Foucault gives three examples, the first one being an idealized concept of a metropolitan city that through its location, its connections via roads, its function as a marketplace, and its accumulation of wealth, is able to govern the territory around it. Interestingly enough, the second example is the "ideal city" of Richelieu in France, close to the Loire Valley, which follows the plan of a Roman camp. Here, the gridded city plan is used to spatially organize and separate different groups of society, trade, and the guilds, as well as to control the flow of people, material, and goods within the city, trying to enhance the trade between the town and countryside and within the town itself. Foucault's last example from the late eighteenth century involves a development plan for Nantes, with the aim of first increasing hygiene, ventilation, and reducing overcrowding; second facilitating trade within the town by improving infrastructure; and third facilitating trade and exchange between Nantes and other cities, while at the same time reducing the danger of unwanted elements such as criminals and beggars. Thus again, city planning is seen as an instrument for consciously controlling the flow of people and merchandise within the city, as well as to and from, with the aim of "maximizing the good circulation by diminishing the bad."[1]

Maybe anecdotal, but nevertheless revealing, Foucault shows that the planning principle of the Roman camp was seen as a way of facilitating the flow of people and goods within a city. More important, though, we see that the notion of urbanity cannot only be conceived as representing openness and exchange, but that this exchange, trade, and heterogeneity is always connected to measures of control, discipline, and to the idea of security. One could say that cities have always been places of exchange, providing the potential for self-reliance and enabling mobility. But this mobility and exchange has, in most cases, been carefully controlled, whether it be by the gates and walls of the medieval city, their cautious opening in the Renaissance, the introduction of permits of residency and civil registration offices in the early modern era, or the installation of CCTV equipment in our contemporary cities.

Daïra center in Smara

Daïra market in El Aaiún

If, on the other hand, we look at the case of the Sahrawi refugee camps, we can observe a scene that on first sight seems to fulfill all the parameters of what we imagine the typical condition of the helpless refugee to be. Tens of thousands of refugees living for many decades in a foreign country in the middle of one of the most inhospitable deserts in the world, fully dependent on external aid, and with no hope of returning any time soon to their original homeland, having become a small pawn in the game of larger global interests. But having looked more closely, we see that in the case of the Sahrawi camps, our usual notion of disempowered refugees cannot be sustained. First of all, we can observe a camp that isn't set up and run by an international humanitarian organization or by UNHCR, but by the refugees themselves. Although still dependent on external aid, the decisions about how to organize their lives, what forms of administration to develop, and the freedom to express themselves politically, culturally, and socially represents a condition of empowerment that we do not usually associate with camps. The camps are not only the site where this empowerment is practiced, but they are the very tool with which it is achieved. The camps allow the Sahrawi refugees to set in motion a social transformation process that has emancipated the Sahrawi society, brought education and media, as well as inscribing them in an international network of exchange and knowledge transfer. The Sahrawis have set up their own administration and established ministries and national institutions in anticipation of creating a "proper" state within the boundaries of their homeland. In short, the camps are understood as a political and social project. In this sense they are not the antithesis of the urban condition, but could be described as being hyper-urban: not in the sense that the camps are excessively urban, but that, at least in certain aspects, they are consciously employed as an instrument to achieve emancipation, self-control, social exchange, and mobility, eventually to be realized permanently in the homeland.

In recent years, we have observed that the difference between the public and the private in our cities, especially of the Western world, has been increasingly undermined. Public spaces have become more controlled and restricted in their use or have been given over to private bodies altogether. The rights of free expression, just as the right to assemble, have been curtailed, often as a consequence of the war on terrorism. At the same time, commercial spaces like shopping malls, hotel lobbies, or privatized parks perform a number of functions that were previously associated almost exclusively with public spaces. Furthermore, the protection of the private space has also been undermined in the name of security, especially in the wake of new technological and economic developments. The rapid increase of state-sanctioned phone and email tapping, and our willingness to disclose the most intimate details on commercial websites, give testimony to the blurring of the categories of the private and public. But if we deem the spatial manifestation of these two categories to be one of the fundamental building blocks of a city and of urban quality, their erosion in our contemporary city becomes crucial. The Sahrawi refugee camps, on the other hand, allow us to speculate that today it is in these camps where such notions are upheld, reasserted, or reformulated. Going back to the initial question of whether the camp and the city represent binary opposites, we can tentatively state that the notions of homogeneity, limitation, and control (by others) that we usually connect with the camp has become (or perhaps has always been) an integral part of our cities. The alleged openness of our metropolitan life only exists in response to, or as a result of, enclosures, limitations, and areas of controlled access. The Sahrawi camps are a case study in which this controlled access has been turned around and enabled a project of social emancipation and political autonomy. Rather than being binary opposites, the city and the camp can be described as conditions that are always contained within, and necessitate, each other.

View over camp February 27

## Beyond the Western Sahara

Beyond their specific case, can the Sahrawi camps tell us anything about camps in general? One might justifiably assert that the conditions that gave rise to today's situation are largely bound to the fact that the Sahrawis were provided semi-autonomy by Algeria. It allowed the Sahrawis to take control and manage the camps themselves and to develop their own institutions such as the ministries in Rabouni, the state archive, and structures of political representation. And it is exactly this semi-autonomy that in today's world one will be hard pressed to persuade a state to grant. The image of the refugee has changed dramatically since the 1960s and 1970s. Whereas in that period the refugee was connected to the figure of the independence fighter, struggling against colonial domination, dictatorship, and ideology, today's image of the refugee is seen against a backdrop of economic migrants, competition over limited resources, and the overall weakening of the nation-state. Instead of being seen as a potential ally in the fight for a common (ideological) agenda, as was often the case in the 1960s and 1970s, today the refugee is seen as a threat. A number of countries in the Western world, just as in Africa itself, have passed laws in recent years constricting the movement of refugees, limiting their economic activities and rights of expression. But it is against the backdrop of these changes that the case of the Sahrawi refugee camps becomes so significant. They are proof of the fact that affording refugees with a semi-autonomy does not result in reduced resources for the host nation, or unfair competition. They are further proof of the fact that the time spent living in camps is not just a period of futile waiting, with protracted refugee cases often being described as refugee warehousing, but as potential spaces of agency and instruments for political projects.

## Why Should We Be Interested?

Why is it interesting or relevant for architects and spatial practitioners to look at camps? Why does the relevance of this study go beyond the circle of humanitarian workers and people involved in refugee camps? For one, refugee camps house millions of people in many parts of the world. The sizes of these camps is significant, often reaching tens of thousands of inhabitants. For this reason alone, there is a need to look at and assess these spaces, not only with the vocabulary of technical solutions but with categories of the urban. The planning guidelines of UNHCR, even if efficient and effective as an immediate response to people fleeing conflict and violence, are too limited in grasping the complexity of the local situation and the consequences of refugees living for longer periods of time embedded in a specific regional context. They reduce the refugee to being a recipient of aid rather than grasping the larger connotations of the human condition, with its social, cultural, economic, and political dimensions. In the case of the Sahrawi refugee camps, we have seen that these settlements are where a significant number of people are exposed to urban conditions, in one way or the other, for the first time in their lives. The camps represent their introduction to urbanity, with all the dilemmas, opportunities, hardships, and transformations of one's lifestyle this brings about. This was not only the case for the Sahrawi refugees in the 1970s, but continues to be the case, whether it concerns refugees from Darfur, Afghanistan, or the Central African Republic. If these camps represent the refugees' introduction to a notion of urbanity, we had better start looking at them carefully with a vocabulary of urbanism.

Secondly, in the camps we can observe how difference and specificity emerges. The Sahrawi camps were all founded at the same time, are inhabited by a homogenous population with, at least initially, identical economic power, and are located in the same geographical region, featuring the same topography, ground conditions, and climate. Nevertheless, in spite of these virtually identical starting conditions, differences have emerged.

Residential compound

Smara and El Aaiún expose two contrasting approaches to organizing public and social life in the fabric of the camps. While the center of Smara is the main reference point for its population to perform daily errands and come together to pursue sports and other recreational activities, in El Aaiún the center does not have this importance. In fact, unlike in Smara, a concentrated center, where the main markets, administrative, and recreational facilities are located, does not really exist in El Aaiún. Instead, the functions are dispersed over the length of the asphalt road, acting as a spine for the camp. Meanwhile, it is the daïra centers that act as attractors for social and commercial activities. The camps can thus be seen as a laboratory where the emergence of differences and complexity from very simple and almost identical starting conditions can be observed. Small differences in the proximity to Tindouf, the connections to different parts of Spain or other international networks, the number of international visitors a camp receives, or the accessibility of water result in each camp's having developed its own identity over time. To observe this emergence of difference, specificity, and identity is also to observe a fundamental aspect of urbanity.

Last but not least, we can witness the discipline of architecture and planning engaged in one of the most conflictual and tense situations. While being an extreme context to pursue planning, instead of thinking of the case as an exception for the discipline, on the contrary, it might reveal a certain truth about planning that is otherwise often cloaked or made opaque. The camps could be described as the "ground zero" of the profession. In the environment of the camps, we can see how every aspect of planning and construction holds additional significance beyond their functional or aesthetic value. No building detail is innocent; no employment of a building typology or construction material is neutral. We can observe how architecture, beyond its function and aesthetic, is always also political. And, finally, we can observe how the discipline of architecture and planning itself can be a means of understanding, or a specific way of assessing a political situation, as it plays out in space.

1 Foucault, Michel: *Security, Territory, Population:* Palgrave, 2007, p. 18

Smara at dusk

# CAMP SMARA, 2007–2011: A PHOTOGRAPHIC SURVEY

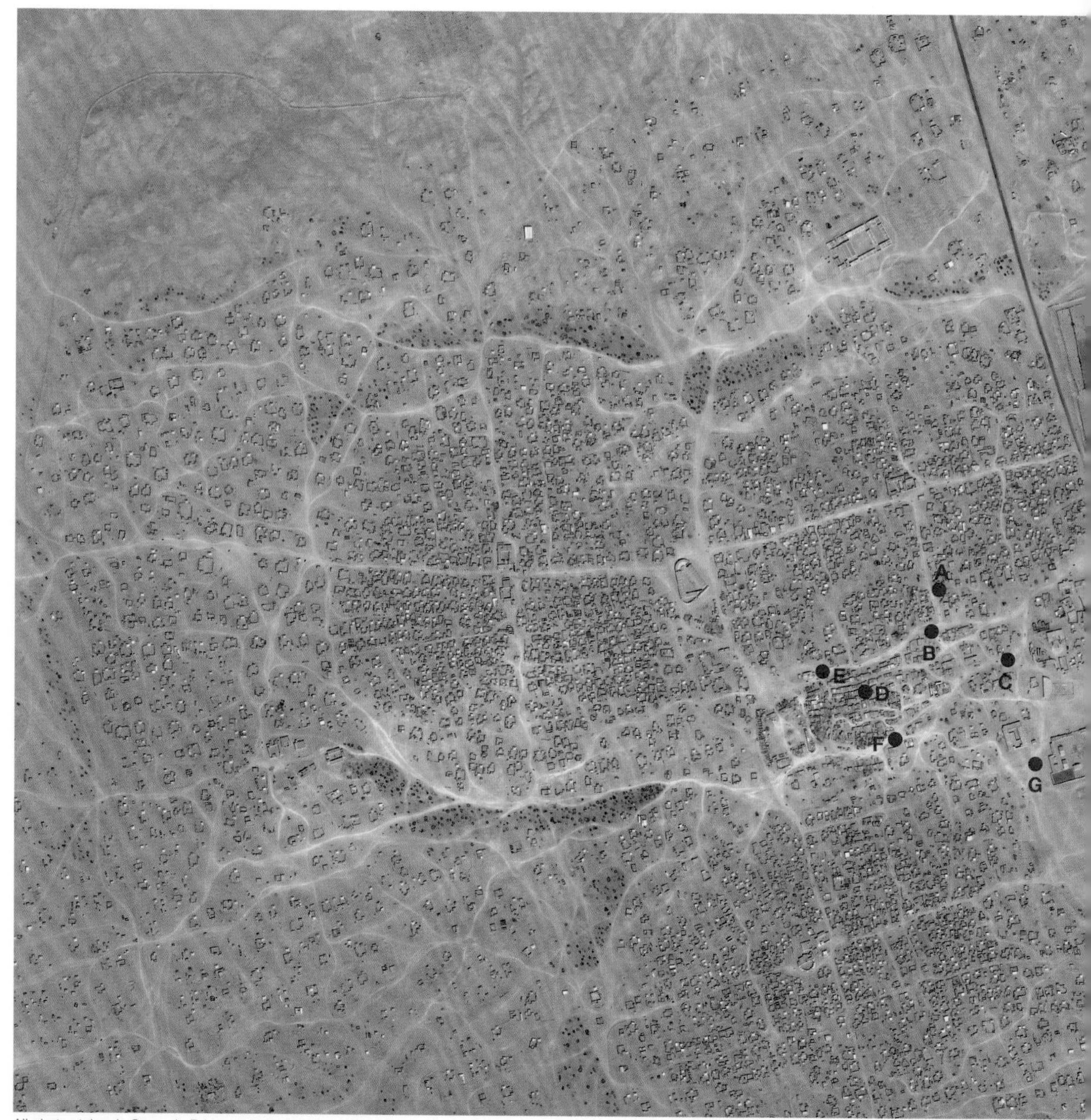


All photos taken in Smara in February 2007 and March 2011

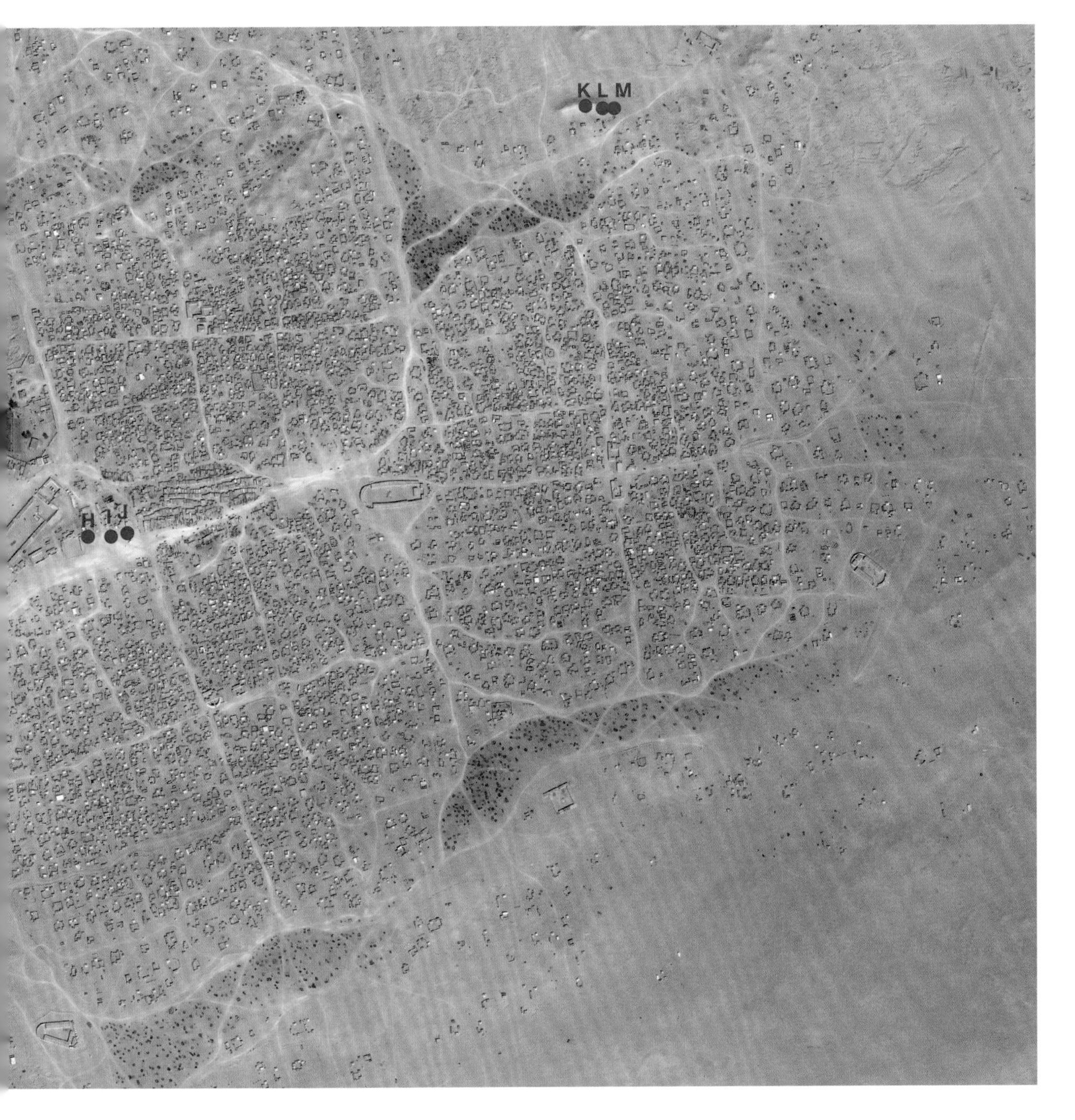
K L M
H I J

2007

2011 (A) View of mosque near the western market

2007

2011 (B) View of the northern parts of camp Smara

2007

2011 (C) View towards the *protocolo* and administration buildings

2007

2011 (D) Shop in western market

2007

2011 (E) View towards the western parts of camp Smara showing Valencia Primary School in the background

2007

2011 (F) Shop near western market

2007

2011 (G) View towards the *protocolo* and administration center

2007

2011 (H) Shops and services in the center of Smara

2007

2011 (I) Restaurante Bulautad

2007

2011 (J) Car-repair shops in central Smara

2007

2011 (K) View from the north over camp Smara

2007

2011 (L) Aerial view towards eastern edge of Smara

2007

2011 (M) Aerial view of the eastern periphery of the camp

**Acknowledgments**
This research project was undertaken with the students and staff of ETH Studio Basel during winter and spring 2011. The students, Franziska Biner, Anna Ebneter, Hans Leidescher, Monica Magnone, Jonas Wirth, and Diana Zenklusen did a wonderful job delving into a topic that was previously unknown to them, pulling together a great amount of research material during our stay in the Sahrawi camps near Tindouf. Franziska Biner worked on the topics of planning and living, Anna Ebneter on commerce, Hans Leidescher on health and education, Monica Magnone on moving, Jonas Wirth on recreation and leisure, and Diana Zenklusen on administration and working. I want to thank Jacques Herzog and Pierre de Meuron for giving me the opportunity to conduct this research, my colleagues Charlotte von Moos and Shadi Rahbaran for working with the students, and all of the above for their tremendous and invaluable input and critical support. I also want to thank Eyal Weizman and Michel Agier, who reviewed the work during its development, for their ideas and advice, which helped me tremendously. My wholehearted appreciation and thanks also goes to the ETH Zurich, who generously funded this project, and to the dean of the Department of Architecture, Sacha Menz, and his predecessor, Marc Angelil.

None of this would have been possible without the great support, assistance, and encouragement that we received from the Sahrawi representatives in Geneva and Berlin, especially Elkanti Balla and Jamal Zakari. The most affectionate gratitude goes to all the people we interviewed, met, spoke to, and communicated with during our stay in the camps. Their generosity, friendliness, and openness was compelling, and we felt very welcome. Above all, I want to express my deepest appreciation to Cheikh Mouloud, who showed us all the aspects of the camps, who had the patience to travel with us, to elucidate the hidden aspects of the life in the camps and who, over time, became a good friend.

Manuel Herz

**ETH Studio Basel** was founded in 1999 by the architects Roger Diener, Jacques Herzog, Marcel Meili, and Pierre de Meuron, as part of the Department of Architecture at ETH Zurich, the Swiss Federal Institute of Technology. The institute engages in urban research, teaching, and design work in Switzerland and internationally. Since 2005, ETH Studio Basel has been running a research program focusing on international cities and urbanizing territories. Research subjects have included the Canary Islands, the development of the tri-national region of Basel, the impact of migration flows on the city of Nairobi and the spatial and urban implications of food production and consumption. The institute's publications include: *Switzerland–An Urban Portrait* (2004), *Open–Closed: An Urban Research Study on the Canary Islands* (2007), *MetroBasel–A Model of a European Metropolitan Region* (2009), and *Belgrade: Formal–Informal* (2012).

**Manuel Herz** is an architect, based in Basel. His urban research work focuses on the architecture of humanitarian action with a special emphasis on the planning strategies of refugee camps. His architectural office is involved in building projects in Europe and Asia, and he has undertaken research work in Saharan and sub-Saharan Africa. His recently constructed buildings include the new Synagogue of Mainz. Herz studied at the Architectural Association School of Architecture, London, has taught at the Bartlett School of Architecture, London, and the Harvard Graduate School of Design, and was head of teaching and research at ETH Studio Basel. Currently he is visiting professor for architectural design at ETH Zurich.

All satellite imagery, unless otherwise noted:
Image Source DigitalGlobe supplied by European Space Imaging

Photos:

**AGBU:** 52 (center)
**Albuixech Roselló, Jesús:** 72 (top right)
**Álvarez Muñoz, B:** 87 (top), 355 (bottom)
**ATTSF:** 178 (lower center)
**Biner, Franziska:** 112–113, 115 (except top left and bottom left), 116 (top and bottom right), 117 (top), 118 (top), 123, 124 (top left and bottom), 126 (except top), 127, 130 (top), 131, 132 (center), 135–139, 142 (top), 147 (bottom), 336 (bottom)
**Bourdieu, Pierre:** 57 (center)
**Briggs, Lloyd Cabot:** 256 (upper left), 259
**Castro Mateo, Julio:** 71 (top left)
Ebneter, Anna: 26–27, 147 (top), 170 (center and bottom right), 206, 208, 209 (top), 230, 241 (bottom), 248–251, 257, 270, 271–273, 279 (lower and upper center), 283–287, 289–291, 293, 294 (except bottom), 295, 299 (except upper center left, and lower center right), 300–301, 303, 306–313, 317, 320, 321 (bottom), 490 (bottom right)
**Dominguez, Edelmiro:** 73 (bottom right)
**Feixas Colomer, Joan:** 85 (top), 115 (top left), 255
**Fernández, Julián:** 72 (bottom left)
**Herz, Manuel:** cover, 8, 9 (left), 11 (right), 13–19, 24–25, 30–35, 37, 78–79, 116 (bottom left), 117 (bottom left), 118 (bottom left, bottom right), 119 (top), 121, 124 (top right, bottom right), 125, 141, 142 (bottom), 143–145, 149, 151, 154–155, 157, 169, 171 (middle right, bottom right, bottom left), 173 (top, bottom), 174 (upper middle), 175 (upper and lower middle), 177 (bottom), 184–185, 187, 193, 195, 198 (top left), 209 (bottom), 214, 221–223, 231 (bottom left), 233, 237, 238–240, 241 (top), 242, 243 (right), 244–245, 247 (top), 252–253, 267, 274, 280–281, 294 (bottom), 297–298, 299 (lower middle right), 305, 315, 319, 321 (top), 336 (bottom), 337 (top), 341, 342 (top),
343 (top), 346–347, 349, 357, 367 (bottom left and top), 376–377, 393, 401, 403 (top), 405 (top), 431, 486–489, 490 (bottom left), 491, 493, 496–508
**History of the World** (1897)**:** 70 (top)
**Imagebank WW2 / NIOD:** 53 (center)
**Jesús del Alamo:** 71 (top right), 86 (top)
**Jorge M. H.:** 81, 87 (bottom)
**José Vázquez, Juan:** 354 (top right)
**Leidescher, Hans:** 175 (bottom), 279 (lower center), 299 (upper center left), 350–351, 363, 366 (bottom), 367 (bottom left), 368–371, 373, 378–383, 386–391, 400
**Library of Congress, George Grantham Bain Collection:** 38 (left)
**Lupsedan:** 82-83
**Magnone, Monica:** 188–189, 196–197, 198 (except upper left and right), 203–205, 212–213, 215–219, 224 (except top left), 226, 228–229, 231 (except bottom left), 247 (bottom)
**McDougall, Dan:** 56 (center)
**Municipality of Getafe:** 236
**Pazzanita, Anthony:** 86 (bottom)
**Piqueras Carrasco, Juan:** 355 (top left)
**Ruiz Calcerrada, Santiago:** 73 (bottom left)
**Sahrawi National Archive:** 11 (left), 75 (top), 243 (left), 358, 359
**Sahrawi National Museum:** 74 (center), 162 (left), 353
**Salgado, Sebastio / Amazonas Images / Agentur Focus:** 10 (left)
**Sanchez, Antonio:** 85 (bottom)
**Soller, Charles:** 258
**Sutherland, A:** 50 (center)
**Teniente Ezquerro:** 90 (center)
**U.S. Army Map Service:** 10 (right)
**UNHCR:** 38 (right), 39 (photo: E. Skau), 47, 49 (photo: B. Bannon), 95 (photo: E. Knusli), 111 (photo: E. Knusli), 115 (top left, photo E. Knusli), 235 (photo: S. Hopper), 256 (bottom right, photo: F. Schjander), 263 (photo: F. Schjander), 264 (photo: T. Hubert)
**University of Texas Libraries:** 69
**UNO Flüchtlingshilfe, Dietmar Kappe:** 455 (bottom right)
**Viechange, Michel:** 84
**von Moos, Charlotte:** 93, 126, 129, 130 (middle), 134 (middle), 152–153
**Webster, Alexia:** 9 (right)
**Wirth, Jonas:** 12, 20–23, 28–29, 117 (bottom right), 119 (bottom right), 134 (top), 170 (middle left), 171 (top), 178 (top), 211, 275, 277, 279 (top), 329 (top), 336 (top), 366 (top), 398–399, 403 (bottom), 405 (bottom), 406–407, 409, 411–417, 419–421, 423–425, 427–428, 430, 432–433, 434–438, 440–443, 447–454, 456–459, 461–471, 473, 475–479, 485, 492
**World Humanitarian Marathon Foundation:** 455 (except bottom right)
**Yoly:** 354 (top left)
**Zenklusen, Diana:** 119 (bottom left), 122, 132 (top), 133, 166 (top right and left), 170 (top left and bottom), 171 (center right), 173 (lower and upper center), 174 (except upper center), 175 (top), 177 (except bottom), 178 (except lower center), 179 (except top), 181, 182–183, 198 (bottom left), 234, 325–328, 329 (bottom), 330–335, 338–339, 342 (bottom), 343 (bottom), 344–345

**From Camp to City**
**Refugee Camps of the Western Sahara**

Edited by Manuel Herz

ETH Studio Basel
Jacques Herzog and Pierre de Meuron

Editorial assistance: Jonas Wirth
Research: Manuel Herz with Charlotte von Moos and Franziska Biner, Anna Ebneter, Hans Leidescher, Monica Magnone, Jonas Wirth, Diana Zenklusen
Copyediting: Camilla Cary-Elwes
Proofreading: Elissa Englund
Design: ETH Studio Basel with Integral Lars Müller/ Martina Mullis
Lithography: Ast & Fischer, Wabern, Switzerland
Paper: Hello Fat Matt, 135 g/m²
Printing and binding: Kösel, Altusried-Krugzell, Germany



Lars Müller Publishers
Zürich, Switzerland
www.lars-mueller-publishers.com

ISBN 978-3-03778-291-0

Printed in Germany